READ, WRITE
AND
SPELL IT RIGHT
(THREE VOLUMES IN ONE)

By

Samuel Smith

Gail Kredenser

Harry Shaw

GREENWICH HOUSE
Distributed by Crown Publishers, Inc.
NEW YORK

This 1982 edition is published by Greenwich House,
a division of Arlington House, Inc., distributed by Crown
Publishers, Inc.
Read It Right and Remember What You Read by Samuel Smith
by arrangement with Harper & Row, Publishers, Inc.
Write It Right by Gail Kredenser by arrangement with Sterling
Publishing Co., Inc.
Spell It Right by Harry Shaw by arrangement with Harper &
Row, Publishers, Inc.

Manufactured in the United States of America

ISBN: 0-517-385937
h g f e d c b a

READ IT RIGHT

By
Samuel Smith

Dedicated to

students, teachers, booksellers, and librarians, whose integrity, competent hands, and discerning minds are preserving the values and reshaping the destiny of modern society

CONTENTS

Preface

The purpose of this book is to assist adult readers to become expert readers of newspapers, documents, and books of every description, including poetry, plays, essays, and fiction. Numerous practical suggestions are presented relating to the main aspects of reading: how to test one's speed and comprehension; how to remember what has been read; how to analyze and deal with propaganda and obtain accurate information; how to find and use printed materials most efficiently; how to read contracts and protect one's legal rights; how to read, understand, and enjoy the best works of literature; and how to build a personal home library of worthwhile books, including the classical masterpieces of the past and recent books in literature, philosophy, psychology, religion, science, and the arts. It is my conviction that fair-minded, critical reading is the basis for straight thinking. Furthermore, the quality and extent of critical reading in a community are a sure barometer of its moral and spiritual condition. Critical reading is the pathway to respect for knowledge, for the truth, and for the dignity and worth of the individual.

I am grateful to Miss Frances Caplan, of the Barnes & Noble Editorial Department, for helpful emendations; to the Honorable Harold Roegner, for reviewing the section on the reading of contracts; and especially to Mrs. Peggy Fagin, for reading the manuscript and contributing numerous constructive criticisms and suggestions.

1
How Well
Do You Read?

Printed words are only marks on paper until some thoughtful reader gives them meaning. They are nothing but commonly accepted cues to ideas. To communicate in any language, people must agree on the ideas which their words signify. They could define the moon as a wheel of cheese, but they would have to accept the new meaning in order to understand the statement. Moreover, separate words are not the whole story, for the reader must interpret groups of words, such as phrases and clauses. He must examine word relationships so that the entire word pattern conveys the logical and precise message intended by the writer. This task of interpretation requires skills which can be developed only through years of listening, speaking, writing, and reading. Even a lifetime of reading in a single field, such as literature, will not insure perfection. For example, after three and a half centuries of study, scholars are still trying to find out exactly what Shakespeare meant by many passages in his masterpieces. His work remains a potent influence on our language and ways of thinking, but drastic changes in human experience have dulled or distorted the sharp edges of his felicitous "husbandry."

The efficient reader concentrates on the ideas which he himself must *read into* the words. He recognizes and assigns customary meanings to familiar words in a sentence, and he interprets the words as logically connected groups expressing ideas. He does not stop to explore the implications of every word, but he is alert to the organization of the words and notices how they function as subjects, predicates, objects, prepositions, and conjunctions. He cannot expect merely to look at words and absorb their meanings without thinking; instead he must react sensitively to the words and sentences, since what he gets *out* of them will depend upon the intelligent thought he invests *in* them. He can feel relaxed, enjoying every sentence without tension, yet he must think straight and concentrate on meanings. Clear thinking will reward him with full understanding and appreciation of the writer's message.

On the other hand, superficiality—the quick-and-easy attitude—is a great handicap. For this reason the problem of reading improvement is a moral one; efficient reading requires self-direction, self-discipline, a positive, receptive attitude toward the feelings and ideas of other people. Excessive speed and careless thinking go together. Both must be avoided.

Reading efficiency depends primarily upon the number of ideas per minute that are clearly understood by the reader; or more precisely, it depends upon speed and comprehension.

SPEED

It has become the custom in our society to hurry recklessly from one task to another, often creating new problems instead of really solving the old ones. Without stopping to think, to evaluate our activities, we waste our most precious possession—the time of our lives—on trivia. Less speed and more straight thinking would go far to prevent or remedy many of the world's ills.

Excessive speed in reading, as in driving a car or in performing any other everyday activity, is likely to bring regrettable consequences. Too many of us try to accomplish too much too quickly. In literature and the arts, genuine understanding, enjoyment, and appreciation take time. The reckless driver wrecks his car to save a few worthless seconds. Just as foolish is the man who marches through an art gallery in half an hour, boasting that he has seen scores of paintings any one of which requires careful scrutiny for genuine *seeing*. We need only look about us to witness the consequences of thoughtless haste which produce nothing but confusion and turmoil in our private lives and public business.

What is excessive reading speed? What is the most reasonable and effective rate? Is it 400 or 1,000 or 3,000 words per minute? Whenever the reader fails to understand clearly what the writer has written reading speed is excessive. A rate too fast for one may be slow for other readers better prepared to comprehend the material. Consider, for example, the following sentence:

> *Everything which exists, exists either in itself or in something else.*

The words in this sentence can be read in less than three seconds, yet the sentence is difficult to understand and involves so many implications for the average reader that he could usefully devote an hour of serious thinking to it. The quotation is from *The Ethics* of Spinoza. All the words on any page of that volume could be read in one minute, but for most readers (who are not philosophers) that would be the most inefficient way to read the book. With material requiring close attention, a rate of 300 words per minute might be very fast, even for sentences consisting of short, simple words. Surely it is better to lose a few moments by reading (and thinking) carefully than it is to rush through the page with only a vague or imperfect understanding of the writer's message.

If you usually read a newspaper at the rate of 300 or more words per minute, without hurrying, and if you also understand clearly what you are reading, you need not worry about your reading speed. It will be satisfactory for most purposes. To test yourself, count 300 words in any newspaper column and time your reading. If you finish in less than one minute, your rate is acceptable. But if you require much more time, perhaps 80 seconds or more, to read the material with full understanding, it is possible that some bad habits are slowing you down. Among the most common of these are lip movements, finger pointing, head turning, regressive movements, and word-by-word reading.

Lip Movements. Moving the lips (or subvocalization) is a frequent cause of slow reading. If you consider the differences between oral and silent reading, the significance of this bad habit will become clear. First, since the eyes move faster than the lips, silent reading can be accomplished much faster than oral reading. Pronouncing one or several words as you read will waste time and reduce your rate. Second, subvocalization interrupts your eye movements and thus compels you to read almost as slowly as in oral reading. Lip movements distract your attention from the onward sweep of the eyes and make it difficult for you to grasp the meaning of each sentence as a whole. If you keep your lips still and closed, giving all your attention to one complete group of words, you will be able to go on promptly to the next group, then to the next, and so on. Third, because lip movements force you to emphasize individual words within a sentence, you may not see immediately the connections between one complete sentence and all the other sentences in a paragraph. Finally, since lip movements tend to scatter your attention among the separate words, you may have to reread more often in order to understand each phrase and paragraph as a whole.

Occasional use of lip movements does not, however, require drastic corrective measures. On the contrary, if used sparingly, subvocalization may help you appreciate fully the writer's emphasis and true meaning. Better still is oral reading. Steady, uninterrupted silent reading at a fixed rate can become monotonous, tiresome, and inefficient. At such times, a change to oral reading can be particularly effective. The relative slowness of oral reading gives you time to think carefully while reading aloud and to derive the precise meaning intended by the writer.

Robert Frost, one of America's most gifted poets and minds of the past, wisely advised readers to listen to sentence sounds, the imagined sounds of the words they are silently reading:

> I have known people who could read without hearing the sentence sounds and they are the fastest readers. Eye readers we call them. They can get the meaning by glances. But they are bad readers because they miss the best part of what a good writer puts into his words. You listen for the sentence sounds. If you find some of those not bookish caught fresh from the mouths of people, some of them striking, all of them definite and recognizable, so recognizable that with a little trouble you can place them and even name them, you know you have found a writer. (From Margaret Bartlett Anderson, *Robert Frost and John Bartlett,* published by Holt, Rinehart and Winston.)

However, if lip movements in silent reading are excessive, the real cause may be lack of concentration. If you concentrate on the idea behind a group of words, you will be less apt to stop at every word. Feel free to try oral reading or a minimum of deliberate lip movements to counteract boredom or fatigue—to break the monotony and give yourself a fresh start—but go back to faster silent reading as soon as possible.

Finger Pointing. Do you point a finger at the words you are reading? If so, you are probably reducing your rate and impeding your comprehension. This habit may indicate a failure to concentrate on the material or lack of interest in it; the reader points at the words as if to force himself onward. The remedy is to keep the fingers busy holding the edges of the page and turning the pages. As you read, move your eyes steadily from one group of words to the next. Finger pointing has the same bad effects as excessive lip movements, and the two habits frequently go together. Eliminate them in most of your reading by giving all your attention to eye movements and to the ideas being expressed in each sentence.

Head Turning. Perhaps you have observed someone who as he reads turns his head from side to side, using his head as a pointer to keep track of the words. This is another bad habit easily corrected. Eye movements are faster than head movements, as a rule. Therefore, head turnings can slow a reader down and distract his attention from ideas in the material. If you make these head movements, stop at once and reread the same material, but this time keep your head rigid as your eyes move along the lines and concentrate on the meaning behind each group of words.

Regressive Movements. Another difficulty arises when a reader, usually one who is in too much of a hurry, misses a point which is necessary for correct understanding of the thought in a sentence. He must then go back to reread the entire sentence. Not only does this waste time but, since the eyes traverse the same ground twice, it often interrupts his effort to follow the trend of ideas. The reader has to reject a partial or incorrect meaning and then grasp the corrected meaning. All of this interrupts the flow of his reading and distracts his attention from the writer's message.

Regressive movements tend to increase if the reading material is unfamiliar or poorly organized, or if the reader loses interest in it. The more he has to go back over what he has missed, the more impatient and bored he becomes, thus increasing further the number of regressive movements. Often it is best at this stage to abandon the attempt to read for a brief interval or to try oral reading. If you decide later that the writer's ideas are worth your time, you can resume silent reading and concentrate on his ideas again. Consider, however, whether some of the difficulty might not be of your own making. Perhaps you need to prepare yourself by obtaining a better background of information before reading the material. You may have read too slowly, owing perhaps to excessive worry about possibly missing a minor point here and there, or maybe you have hurried through the important material and thus missed essential points which would cast a different light on the entire work.[1] If you discipline yourself to read carefully but steadily forward and to think about the writer's ideas, you may develop enthusiastic interest. React to what you read, even if only to discuss it with a friend. What we get out of reading depends on what we put into it; needed are serious attention, a sympathetic, receptive attitude, a willingness to think and feel deeply, with liberal use of the imagination. All these things help to increase enthusiasm for reading, and enthusiastic interest impels the reader to progress from one idea to the next without excessive, boring repetition.

Word-by-Word Reading. The reader's eyes should take in a meaningful group of words at a glance, not stopping at each word. Some readers habitually read one word at a time as if they hoped to build up the writer's idea by adding one word to the next. That is a tiresome, inefficient method of reading. The obvious remedy is to look at a group of words at each glance so that the emphasis will be placed on their meaning as an organized set or unit. Readers vary as to their grouping of words within a sentence, but such variations do not matter. Most important is the need for some logical grouping which will bring out the connections among words and make the intended ideas clear.

Variable Speed. In writing music the composer usually includes directions to musicians: for example, *ritardando* is a direction to play more slowly, and *presto* to play rapidly. Since reading materials do not contain such instructions, the reader must adjust his rate of reading to the type of material and to his purpose in reading. He has to bear in mind the degree of understanding he wishes

---

[1] If you are reading a legal contract, an insurance policy, or a similar vital document, be sure to read it as often as necessary before accepting it, because misunderstanding some of the shortest words or missing them could have disastrous consequences. Take plenty of time, ask questions, supplement silent reading with slow oral reading, and get expert advice on any vague or dubious clauses.

to achieve. If he desires only a quick, general idea of what the material is about, he can hurry his reading until he finds out. But if he wants a full understanding, he will devote enough time for careful, thorough reading and thinking. The claim that fast readers also comprehend best what they read may be true, but the reason is their efficient reading habits, not their speed.[2] A slow reader who attempts to increase his rate by hurrying may discover that he has become less efficient, and his comprehension may suffer unless he concentrates on understanding clearly what he reads, regardless of his rate. Comprehension must therefore be the basic consideration for all readers.

COMPREHENSION

In recent decades it has become the fashion to analyze reading comprehension as consisting of four elements: word meaning, sentence meaning, details, and paragraph meaning. This kind of analysis has been widely used by psychologists to measure reading efficiency. Another type of analysis is based on the actual experience of the reader as he reacts to printed material. Such an analysis emphasizes the following elements: preparation for reading; the structure of the reading material; relative difficulty of the material; reactions of the reader to the material. The following discussions will clarify the factors affecting comprehension and help you to evaluate your own efficiency.

Speed and Comprehension. First, however, let us repeat the point that thinking—ideas—should be made the central focus in reading. Reading advisers claim that they can help anyone double his reading rate and at the same time improve his comprehension. They then may attempt to train the reader to move his eyes faster or to hurry through page after page of material. But we should note

---

[2] To measure your normal rate of book reading, take the speed test on page 212.

the practical significance of the first sentence in this chapter: Printed words are only marks on paper until some thoughtful reader gives them meaning. The reader recognizes a group of words as a unit only because he has seen the same symbols repeatedly; as he reads he deliberately concentrates on interpreting them. In other words, seeing is a form of thinking. The entire emphasis must therefore be placed on the idea, the meaning, inherent (or customarily assumed to be inherent) in each group of words. The reader may choose to interpret at a glance a smaller or a larger group of words, but his choice should always be based upon the thoughts (concepts) he forms as he responds to the material. Of course, his thinking and imagination cannot run wild—he cannot really remake the moon into cheese or discover meaningful words in nonsense syllables. Yet the actual limitations on his thinking are self-imposed—the result of repeated experience with the meanings of words during a lifetime of learning. A single letter or word may be significant, although most often it must be seen as joined with other letters and words for efficient interpretation. These relationships take time to be noted and appreciated. The rate of reading should never be so high as to interfere with the degree of understanding desired by the reader.

If fast readers comprehend what they read better than slow readers, should slow readers try to speed up in order to improve their comprehension? Not at all, because the more probable result would be that the slow readers would become more careless if they tried to rush through their reading materials. But if slowness is due to certain bad habits, slow readers can benefit permanently from attempts to achieve a faster rate by eliminating the bad habits. The same good habits which insure acceptable reading speed can also help the reader to achieve better understanding. Thus, if the reader forms the habit of looking for the most significant words in a sentence and grouping them with subordinate words in a meaningful whole, he will quickly grasp the correct ideas and promptly move ahead to the next sentence. Obviously, if he understands the meaning of a clause at once, he can proceed without a stop to the next clause and increase his speed. The development of good reading habits of this kind (in contrast to the bad habits developed by poor readers) explains why many rapid readers are superior to slow readers in comprehension. In any case, understanding, not speed, should be the primary aim.

Second, therefore, let us review briefly the main elements to be considered in achieving adequate comprehension at a reasonable speed.

Word Meaning. How well you read depends in part upon your vocabulary, your storehouse of word meanings. Developing a rich vocabulary can be complicated because many English words have a variety of meanings, depending on their context. The word *get,* for example, has scores of meanings, some of them readily seen in the following sentences:

> Get well. Get me some food. Get along with him. Do you get the idea? Get started. Get her out of trouble. Get over your illness. Get in the house. Get to him by telephone. Get ahead of him. Get down. Get loose. Get together.

Since the meaning of a word is often changed through its relationship to nearby words, the reader must choose the best meaning in each case; and he may misinterpret the sentence if he makes an incorrect choice. Rarely is it sufficient to know only one or two meanings of a word. Instead, the reader should gain real mastery of all the important meanings. An excellent way to do this is to read a variety of books written by competent authors, past and present. Reading the same words in numerous writings will acquaint the reader with their different meanings or shades of meaning.

The greatest difficulty in understanding words comes from excessive speed. If you read too fast, you are likely to interpret some words incorrectly or not quite so clearly as you should. Thus the entire material may seem to you to imply a meaning not intended by the author. To think carefully about the different possible meanings of a word requires time, and this requirement makes excessive speed unwise. Take plenty of time to think of the most likely meanings of a word whenever you have any doubt as to its meaning in a particular sentence. (The test of word discrimination on page 215 will help you to evaluate this phase of your vocabulary. Other phases are discussed in the next chapter.) If you have an extensive vocabulary and read attentively, you will not have to stop too often or reread too many words and sentences.

Sentence Meaning. A single word may be an entire sentence: *Assuredly. Certainly.* Or a sentence may consist of many words organized into logical groups such as phrases and clauses.

> Are you going so early in the morning?
> When I asked what is matter, he replied, "Never mind," but when I asked what is mind, he replied, "No matter."

It is difficult to decide upon the main ideas in these sentences, because the reader has to consider a number of possible ideas and compare one with the others. These ideas depend largely upon key words in each sentence. If, therefore, you notice the meanings of the key words— those which contribute most to a main idea—you will more readily understand the sentence as a whole. Further, most sentences follow or precede others. If you take care to make the connections linking these sentences, you will more easily interpret each of them correctly. Obviously, if you make a mistake in reading a sentence, but remember that the resulting idea would contradict what you have already read in a preceding sentence, you will re-read both sentences carefully to solve the discrepancy. In this way, you use each newly read sentence as a check, a bit of evidence, concerning the probable meanings of the other sentences. Finally, since most of the longer sentences you read will contain one main idea with minor ideas grouped around it, you should note this organization within a sentence and make certain that it is logical.

Details. During their experimental work and testing in the past fifty years, researchers have discovered that readers might grasp the main idea of a sentence or a paragraph, yet might miss or misunderstand minor points of information. Just as there is a tendency for certain slow readers to encounter difficulty with the major ideas and the logical connections among groups of words, so there is a temptation for some faster readers to overlook details. This relationship between main ideas and subordinate information in reading material is, however, still largely unexplored. In some material the details are closely related to the principal idea and may, in fact, lead up to it or clarify its meaning. As a practical matter, the reader should ask himself what he wishes to gain from his reading of the material and should adjust his rate and attention accordingly. If, for example, he wishes to make sure he knows every step in the writer's exposition, he will have to read slowly enough for this purpose, but if he is willing to overlook some minor points on the assumption that omitting them will not affect his interpretation of the main thesis, he can skim them rapidly and go on to the next major idea.

Paragraph Meaning. Most reading materials are organized into paragraphs. Students are told that a typical paragraph contains a single topic discussed in a group of sentences. Writers who are proficient usually organize their works in accordance with this pattern. Nevertheless, readers sometimes have difficulty deciding whether a given paragraph deals with one central idea or with two or more ideas, each of equal or nearly equal significance. The expert grammarian may insist that equivalent ideas should be discussed in separate paragraphs, but the writer may wish to treat them together as a unit in a logically knit group of sentences. Moreover, too many writers display unawareness of grammatical principles in their work. Consequently, the reader must be careful to notice all the main ideas in each paragraph and judge for himself their relationship to sentences within the paragraph and to adjacent paragraphs.

Successive paragraphs, of course, comprise the bulk of reading materials. The skilled reader notes the large topic covered by all these paragraphs in a chapter or section. He looks for a logical or chronological organization as he reads. Bearing in mind what has gone before, he tackles each paragraph while anticipating what he may discover next, and he constantly derives satisfactions either when his expectations are verified by the material or when he is pleasantly surprised by the writer's variations, digressions, and new ideas.[3]

Preparation for Reading. If you were asked to read a novel in a language entirely unfamiliar to you, even the first word would probably mystify you. In all reading, you must have had some experience with both the language and the subject. Yet many readers assume that they can read any material without preparation; for this reason they often form an inaccurate or imperfect impression of the material. As you begin to read, surely you can at least think back to your reading experiences of the past, review information or reawaken memories, and thus enrich or improve your understanding of the new material.

There are two special ways in which the reader's previous reading and experience can help his immediate reading: comparison to note similarities; and contrast to note differences. The reader asks himself, Does what I am reading agree with the things I have read about the same subject? Is the main idea logical and true if judged on the basis of my life experience? What are the strong and the weak points in the material? If the reader has prepared himself well by means of extensive varied reading on the subject and asks these questions as he reads, he will reach a high level of reading efficiency.

The old saying "he who has, gets more" holds good for reading. The person who has read more widely and effi-

---

[3] As we shall see, skill in reading successive paragraphs can be developed. Meanwhile, note that on page 220 there is a test on paragraph meaning which will help you to evaluate your own skill in this central aspect of reading.

ciently and who has enjoyed a rich life experience gets more out of each new reading activity. But it is never too late to make up for neglect of reading, and anyone can easily set aside time, no matter how busy he is, for a regular program of daily reading. The more one reads, the better he is prepared for further reading.

Structure of the Reading Material. Although reading materials are usually organized well enough to give the reader a number of clues or directions to guide his thinking and feeling, they also leave ample scope for use of his imagination and powers of interpretation. Two readers may interpret the same paragraphs quite differently. The meaning of a single sentence or, for that matter, the main point of an entire book may vary widely with different readers. Even expert critics may arrive at opposite conclusions about the writer's purpose and accomplishment. Furthermore, on some important points a few of the foremost authorities may agree with the novice attempting literary criticism. Works of great writers, such as Shakespeare, have been misinterpreted as much by scholars as by unschooled tyros.

Nevertheless, the writer generally organizes his sentences, paragraphs, and chapters sufficiently to provide the reader with considerable guidance in comprehension. There may be a logical or chronological sequence of ideas, or some other systematic arrangement, such as comparison and contrast, development from simple to complex propositions, and organized patterns of introductory, main, subordinate, and concluding sections. With fiction, the reader may note special narrative techniques such as flashbacks, which may require patience and discrimination on his part if he wishes to gain full appreciation of the material.

Difficulty of the Reading Material. It is possible to construct a check list of the things which make reading materials difficult and to rate the materials on a scale of relative difficulty. But what is almost unintelligible to most people might be perfectly simple to readers expert in a special field, such as mathematics or science, music or philosophy, medicine or other professions. The meaning of what is being read today depends upon what has been read, thought, and lived before today. In estimating the difficulty of reading material, one must consider not only the average number of words in sentences, the lengths of the words and sentences, and the complexity of structure, but especially the extent to which the ideas being presented involve or hinge upon the reader's previous reading and experience.

Reactions of the Reader. The best test of understanding is the reaction of the reader to the reading material—what he thinks and does in response to his interpretation. Thus, if he is reading directions, his understanding will be reflected in the way he follows them. If he is reading abstract ideas, his comprehension will be indicated by what he says, thinks, or writes about the ideas. Even when you arrive at incorrect conclusions about what you read, your discussion of the topic will reflect the extent of your understanding; that is, your conclusions will at least be based, rightly or wrongly, on an intelligent grasp of some of the ideas you have read.

2
How To Improve
Your Reading

There is so much to read—books, letters, documents, newspapers, and magazines—that in the limited time available to them many people would like to increase their reading rate in order to absorb more information and ideas. Even the best reader may at times wish to cover more ground if he can do so without misunderstanding what he is reading. Fortunately, psychologists investigating methods of reading which combine high speed and full comprehension have contributed suggestions for reading improvement, some of them temporarily effective, others more lasting and satisfactory. An average reader, so they claim, could double or even triple his reading rate by means of special training and new techniques.

Recently machines have been invented which keep track of the reader's eye movements and help him to eliminate wasteful or careless ways of scanning printed words. Some experts have recommended devices which impel the reader to move his eyes quickly in the proper direction across the page as well as backward and downward from one line to the next. Thus by looking only at the middle part of a group of words, the reader automatically sees the other words, too, and is able to read much more at a glance instead of looking at words in sequence. When psychologists administer tests to readers who have practiced methods such as these, the results often appear to be gratifying. Of course, some readers score high on the tests because they have become adept at taking tests, not necessarily because they have improved their natural reading habits, and in many instances the apparent progress gained through special training disappears when the reader goes back to his old habits or stops trying to read as fast as possible. In fact, concentrating on speed and using devices to increase reading rate may eventually interfere with reading efficiency, which depends upon close attention to the reading material itself.

There are, however, certain effective ways to improve one's natural reading rate and comprehension. Previewing is one of them.

PREVIEWING

It is easy to form the habit of previewing what you intend to read. Previewing is like studying a map before starting on a journey. The map discloses how far you will probably have to travel, where you may stop to rest or to reconsider your route and schedule, where you will have to choose among alternative routes, and speed limits and other conditions of the journey.

Previews of reading material vary in scope from a quick glance at headings and selected sentences to a rather detailed yet rapid skimming of selected parts of the material. You can make good use of previews as preparation for more careful reading of any kind of written or printed text—correspondence, news, feature articles, and fiction or non-fiction books. Previews will help you to adjust your reading speed to the difficulty of the material. On the basis of an adequate preview, you may decide to skip some portions and to concentrate on others, or you may prefer to study every paragraph carefully.

The following group of five sentences illustrates one advantage of previewing.

1. The efficient reader must be logical.
2. The efficient reader must be logical, alert, and attentive.

3. The efficient reader must be logical, alert, and attentive to ideas.
4. The efficient reader must be logical, alert, and attentive to ideas which the writer intended to communicate.
5. The efficient reader must be logical, alert, and attentive to ideas which the writer intended to communicate and must devote adequate time to insure clear understanding.

Notice that each new sentence was made longer through the addition of a few words. If you read the five sentences separately without becoming aware of the pattern, you probably had to read slowly and stop to think about the ideas in each sentence. But if you quickly examined all the sentences and noticed the pattern, you could merely glance at the first part of each sentence and concentrate on reading the added words. In this way a preview of reading material reveals the pattern, the route to be taken on your reading journey. It provides you with a mental map of what lies ahead so that you can adjust your speed of reading to the material and devote your efforts particularly to the most significant passages.

In the sentences listed above, the pattern is one of similarities and differences. There are numerous other patterns to be found in reading materials: for example, some patterns are based on the structure and form of sentences and paragraphs (as in the use of very brief phrases to separate them); others depend upon the author's use of questions, method of alternating short and long clauses or sentences, interpolation of dialogue, logical development of a main thesis, or unexpected changes in point of view. Even an awareness of undesirable patterns, such as monotonous repetition of arguments or adherence to a cut-and-dried, dull organization of data, may help the alert reader to evaluate, comprehend, and recall the reading material.

As a special advantage, previewing provides the reader with an opportunity to estimate what he can get out of the material before devoting a great deal of time to it. When you preview a few pages, ask yourself what information, pleasure, or other benefit you expect to derive from the text. This question will direct your attention to those parts of the material which will contribute most to the results you desire, such as answers to specific questions, explanations of principles, or ideas which should stimulate your thinking, understanding, and appreciation. A preview of anything from a single page to a whole volume, if followed by careful study, can help you to achieve definite goals in reading.

If you are reading an educational book or textbook, preview the structure of each chapter before beginning a detailed study. Note the chapter title, the main and subordinate headings, the amount of space allotted to various topics, the sequence of topics, the questions, references, and citations, and the charts, diagrams, or other illustrations. Then recall what you already know about the topics of the chapter and formulate questions for which you hope to find the answers in the text.

After you have read one section of a book, preview the next section and ask yourself in what ways the two sections are related to each other. Does the new section supplement, reinforce, or counterbalance the old? Does it introduce a new phase or element of the subject? Noting the connections between ideas already read and new passages to come may increase both speed and comprehension. The old material becomes clearer and more meaningful if it is seen to be related to the new. With short stories and novels, try previewing the plot in your own mind—guessing in advance what events are about to be described. As you continue with more careful reading, you will see how the author either met your expectations or shaped his plot quite differently. You may also recapitulate the main events which have already occurred in the story, decide upon several possible outcomes, and later note which ones the author adopted as well as the probable reasons for his choices. A quick preview of the actual plot, followed by detailed reading, will disclose the pattern of the story as a whole and help you to remember essential parts.

If you are reading a short story or suspense novel for enjoyment, you may prefer to read without previewing, because enjoyment of the plot may depend in part upon a surprise element which previewing could spoil. The reader who looks ahead and discovers how the plot is going to end may find the story less interesting or less challenging when he begins to read it more carefully. On the other hand, if the plot is too complicated, previewing will help to make it more intelligible.

Previewing of newspapers and journals can be useful but entails considerable risk of obtaining only a superficial or inaccurate view of the facts. News and feature articles should not be swallowed but digested. Previewing headlines on various pages, or even rapidly skimming a summary of events, should be nothing more than a preliminary step. To understand a news story or a feature article correctly, to avoid error or distortion, preview to select what you want to read and then read the entire story or article. Read every word of it.

Newspaper makeup follows a traditional pattern which helps the reader to select what he is interested in reading. The editor places the most significant news in the extreme right-hand column of the front page, sometimes with related material in adjacent columns. News which is of secondary importance is located in the column at the extreme left of the front page. Some front-page topics may be continued in the inside pages, in which case it is a mistake to read only the part on the front page; you should read the whole story before turning back to the first page for another selection. Often the continuation on the inside pages will change your idea about a topic.

A newspaper story begins with the most significant event and then explains details which preceded the event. It differs therefore from most other types of reading material, which begin with introductory or descriptive information and gradually lead up to the important event or climax. The headlines and lead sentences in a newspaper story are cues designed to attract the attention of readers who may be in a hurry to get the main facts before deciding whether or not to read further. You can use headlines and lead sentences to decide what to read in greater detail, but be sure to read the entire story to determine the facts.

SKIMMING

Skimming is a special form of previewing—a method of exploring reading materials rapidly without stopping to interpret each clause or sentence but with enough attention to obtain a general view of the theme and its development. Skimming can also locate answers to specific questions, points of information, and ideas which interest the reader. Thus, if you wish to ascertain only one or two facts, you do not have to read large portions of a text or reference work. Look up the relevant topic in the index and skim the pages until you come to the data you need. Then read these selected passages carefully.

Do not be misled by the notion that skimming requires only a glance at a few headings or paragraphs now and then without attention to ideas. On the contrary, skimming requires particular alertness to the material being read to avoid the possibility of missing or misinterpreting the writer's message. You must immediately notice any headings and all key statements in complicated passages, quickly grasping what the headings and statements mean, and you must do this without stopping, while continuing to sweep your eyes across and down the page to additional headings and key statements.

Attentive skimming can show you how different parts of reading material fit together to form a logical structure. You can observe relationships among the principal ideas being presented, how one idea or part leads into the next, and which parts will require the most time and effort. By skimming several parts before reading each you can often discover the plan of a book and in this way avoid a common pitfall of the unskilled reader, that of interpreting passages in the wrong sense, only to find, later on, that his views are inconsistent with another portion of the text. Skimming before careful reading will increase your self-confidence, because as you read the author's first ideas you will remember what is coming next and how these ideas are connected with ideas in other sections of the text.

In skimming you must ascertain which sentences on a page contain the main ideas or the important conclusions. These key sentences may be buried within paragraphs or they may be brief statements separating paragraphs. They may be topic sentences, the ones which state the main ideas (or pinpoint the topics) of the paragraphs. A topic sentence is often placed at or near the beginning of a paragraph but sometimes at the end. It may even be in the form of a question which the paragraph answers in considerable detail. The topic sentence summarizes the main point of the paragraph. An experienced skimmer can skim page after page, locating topic sentences from which he obtains the most significant ideas of the book. With continued practice you will develop skill in finding the topic sentences and other key sentences. Bear in mind, however, that you can seldom expect to get enough information from skimming and will usually find it necessary to reread the material carefully from beginning to end. This will be especially beneficial because by repeating the main ideas (noted while skimming), you will be helped in remembering them. Further, you will be reading them in two different arrangements—first, as separate important points, or highlights, of information and, second, as central ideas around which all the other sentences in each paragraph cluster in such a way as to clarify, reinforce, or supplement those ideas.

Occasionally you may be in a hurry to locate and read information, knowing that you will have only a few moments for this purpose instead of an hour or more required for careful reading. At such times, you may use a technique which, at the risk of some inaccuracy, will facilitate high-speed skimming. Close one eye and as you quickly move the other eye down the page, move the index finger of your right hand steadily downward at the right of the printed lines. Your eye movements will become more rapid as you try to make them keep pace with your moving finger in the margin. As you glance at the sentences, look for key words relating to the information you want. By practicing this technique you can greatly increase your reading rate and skim page after page in a fraction of the normal time. However, owing to the danger of superficial or imperfect comprehension of the reading material, this method should be used only in emergency situations. Never mistake skimming for thorough reading of a book; partial information is no substitute for comprehensive knowledge.

READING FOR IDEAS

Although every word in a sentence represents some kind of idea, a great many ideas depend upon groups of logically connected words each of which contributes something to the total message. We communicate our thoughts to other people, not by separating one word from the next, but rather by combining words into phrases, clauses, sentences, and paragraphs, all of which function as cues to the reader, who must then interpret their author's meanings. The meaning of a single word in a group usually varies with its relationship to its neighbors. Thus the word "fall" in "the fall of Rome" means something quite different from the same word in "the fall is a season of the year."

Seeing things in sets, groups, or clusters, not as independent symbols or units, is a universal experience. We see everything around us as groups of things arranged in some sequence or order. Our eyes are lenses in motion through which we examine the shape of the world, and as our eyes move, we see new groups of things which interest us and have meaning for us. When we recognize a friend, we do not look first at his left eye, then at his right eye, nose, mouth, and head. We see him as a composite the parts of which supplement each other and form a pattern or, as some psychologists call it, a gestalt. The same process occurs in reading. We recognize a word as an ordered arrangement of familiar letters. We then recognize several words as an orderly group, interpret its customary meaning, and move on to examine the next group of words. But our eyes stop for an instant just before we move them forward, and it is during this brief pause that we think about the meaning of the group of words we have just read.

The inefficient reader makes too many stops, and each of his pauses is too long. He often reads only one word at a time. The efficient reader, on the contrary, instead of stopping to think about one word, then the next, and so on, sees at once that some words in a sentence belong together, that they are in a definite sequence and are logically connected to each other.

The inefficient way to read is shown in the following example, in which each slant line indicates a pause:

Our/fathers/brought/forth/a/new/nation.

The sentence above should be read in two word groups, with only one quick stop between them, as follows:

Our fathers brought forth / a new nation.

Here we think about two main ideas: the first is suggested to us by four words, the second by three words. This method of reading sets of words, instead of separate words, saves time and makes the meaning of the whole sentence simple and clear.

It may help you to read words in groups if you keep in mind the typical order and organization of words in English sentences. In the sentence above, the words are organized grammatically into the subject (Our fathers), the predicate (brought forth), and the object (a new nation). In a flash you can read the subject and the predicate together (the first four words) and then in another quick glance the object (the last three words), which carries the first idea forward.

The following sentence is more difficult to read:

A square circle must exist, / at least in our minds, / because we can think about it.

A skilled reader will read this sentence quickly, making

only two very brief stops. The two commas help him to see that the sentence consists of three groups of words. A glance at the first group (five words) reveals one main idea; it is a strange idea containing the contradictory notion of a "square circle." The next group (five words) modifies the first meaning by adding another idea (that the thought of a square circle exists). The last group (six words) ends the sentence with an explanation (the reason why), an idea which carries the first two ideas forward and completes the entire proposition. Thus, all three groups of words together form a meaningful sentence which the efficient reader can read and interpret quickly with only two brief pauses.

If you keep looking for meanings as you read, concentrating on the ideas in each sentence, you will soon form the habit of reading for ideas and will seldom, if ever, stop for word-by-word reading.

MAKING SENSE OUT OF WORDS

Some words are so familiar to us that we have no difficulty interpreting their mutual relationships in a sentence, easily noting their correct meanings. But other words seem only vaguely familiar or appear to be altogether unknown. Sometimes, too, we mistake one word for another, perhaps because of similar spelling or appearance. The careful reader must be alert to discriminate among words he is sure about, those he is in doubt about, and those which he is sure he does not know.

There is no such thing as an unimportant word, though some words may be more significant than others in a particular sentence. Consider, for instance, the following two sentences:

Put the money in the desk.
Put the money on the desk.

The tiny words "in" and "on" are extremely important, for they can change the meaning of the whole sentence. How often people sign contracts or other documents without noticing the little words, such as "in," "on," "not," "or," "if," and the like! In most kinds of reading, however, the words you will be especially concerned about are those which seem indefinite or difficult for you to interpret— perhaps because you have not read them often enough to insure thorough understanding of their various meanings.

Many readers have trouble with words which they seldom encounter or use; the less frequently a word is heard, read, or spoken, the more difficult its comprehension is likely to be. Repeated and correct usage of a word in its various meanings will make it so familiar that no longer will you have to stop and think about the best possible meaning when you see it in a sentence; you will know immediately how it fits into and adds to the meaning of the entire sentence. In fact, the best way to enlarge your reading vocabulary is to write down unfamiliar or difficult words when you read them or shortly thereafter and later make use of them when speaking or writing until you feel certain that you will never forget their meanings.

Avoid excessive guessing. Too many readers merely guess at the meaning of a somewhat unfamiliar word instead of consulting a dictionary for several possible meanings from which to select the correct one. Let us suppose you feel uncertain about the meaning of the word *cosmopolite* when you read it in a sentence: "He traveled in many lands, felt at home everywhere, and became a true cosmopolite." We could guess from the context that *cosmopolite* in this sentence refers to a person whose interests and sympathies extend to people far beyond his national attachments. In fact, the dictionary tells us that the word comes from two Greek words: *kosmos,* meaning world, and *politēs,* meaning citizen. The precise meaning is, therefore, "citizen of the world." To remember this meaning of *cosmopolite* permanently, you need only construct many sentences using the word correctly in this sense. For such vocabulary building, you should keep a loose-leaf notebook or an alphabetical card file in which to write all the difficult words you read. You do not always have to interrupt your reading to do this, but try to jot down these words at intervals or during pauses in your reading. Later, preferably once or twice a week, practice using your new words in oral and written sentences. Use each word in several of its principal meanings, not limited to the meaning in the original passage containing it. Consult your dictionary to verify the precise meanings of each new word on your list and, whenever you have time, review some of the old words.

If you notice the origins of a word—its sources as given in the dictionary—you will often be able to apply this information to other words derived wholly or partly from the same origins. Thus, if you look up *cosmopolite* in the dictionary and note the Greek origins (*kosmos* and *politēs*), you will have a pretty good idea of the meanings of such English words as *cosmos, cosmopolitan,* and *cosmopolis,* and you will have a clue to part of the meaning of *cosmology* (from the Greek *kosmos* and *logos,* meaning law) and *cosmography* (from the Greek *kosmos* and *graphein,* meaning to write) when you encounter these words in your reading. There is usually sense in words, including highly technical terms, but often you have to dig in to find the sense. Thus, it may be helpful to notice that *cosmotron* is based on the same Greek word *kosmos* and the suffix *tron* (as in neutron, electron, dynatron, and bevatron); but beware of slight yet significant differences in the origins of similar words—for example, *proton* may seem to resemble *neutron* but is spelled with *ton,* not *tron,* and actually is derived from an altogether different Greek word *prōton,* meaning first, a basic combining form in *protocol, protophloem, protoplasm, prototype,* and *protozylem.*

A linguist can analyze parts of a word and explain what each part contributes to the meaning of the whole word in its setting or context, its function in a sentence. When he looks at the word *unkempt,* for instance, he knows that the prefix *un* means not, that *kempt* comes from the Scottish word for comb, and that therefore *unkempt* must mean "not combed" or disordered, disheveled. You do not have to become a linguist in order to read most kinds of printed matter with satisfactory understanding, but the more you know about some of the common prefixes and suffixes, the easier it will be for you to comprehend unfamiliar words.

Suppose you did not know the meaning of the word *exanimate*. You could probably quickly figure out its meaning in a sentence from the prefix *ex,* which means "out of," and *animate,* which refers to life or a life-giving quality; *exanimate* must therefore mean "out of life" or lifeless. But check your interpretation of such words in a dictionary as soon as convenient, for it is easy to choose the wrong meaning. Thus, *anti* means "against" in *antithesis,* but it means "before" or "bygone" in *antiquarian.*

How does a writer enable the reader to obtain new information from the written material? He does this, first, by selecting words which will be widely accepted as denoting relevant ideas or relationships between ideas; and, next, by arranging these words in the proper order so that the reader's thoughts will begin to flow in the same order. The writer thereby gives the reader a start in the desired direction by means of the arrangement of words which both he and the reader comprehend or agree upon, just as a policeman might use sign language or his index finger to direct a traveler to the right road.

Words change their meanings with the times and with the education and cultural backgrounds of writers and readers. The fine distinctions and implications of a word or even the principal meaning may be so altered that it acquires many meanings instead of one or two. The word *politics* has its origin in the same Greek word *politēs,* which means citizen. Originally it referred only to the art of handling public affairs, but in modern times, including most periods of American history, another meaning has developed—stated in Webster's dictionary as "dishonest management to secure the success of candidates or political parties." Changing conditions change definitions. The word *politics* acquired an evil connotation because political leaders on every level of government too often betrayed their trust for selfish ends. There are, of course, political leaders who possess wisdom and integrity, following the examples of Abraham Lincoln, Theodore Roosevelt, and Woodrow Wilson. Nevertheless, for many people politics has come to mean a dirty game suffused with unprincipled chicanery.

Oddly enough, if you are alert when you read, you can sometimes get much more meaning out of a paragraph than the writer intended to put into it. This is particularly evident when a writer makes a poor choice of words. Have you not received letters from a friend who uses the wrong word to express an idea? You may have said to yourself, "He really meant to write something different," and you will think about a number of ways to improve your friend's writing. In the same way a skilled reader can notice deficiencies in printed matter which stimulate his train of thought, perhaps raising questions which the writer did not even intend to discuss and frequently enriching his understanding of the subject. The printed words are then only the starting point for such a reader's reactions as he embellishes and supplements the writer's work. Sometimes an author may undergo a similar experience when he reads his own work after a lapse of time and thinks differently about what he originally wrote. T. S. Eliot did not like the idea of having one of his works reprinted, because he had changed his mind about many topics and did not wish the public to assume he still held steadfast to his old point of view. The alert reader realizes that there is nothing fixed or unalterable about ideas in print, because ideas, like the words expressing them, inevitably change with changing conditions and audiences. The more you react to your reading material, evaluating, interpreting, protesting, doubting, recasting, approving, the more stimulation and benefit you will derive. You will become a better reader and a more sensitive and cultured person.

REINFORCING YOUR READING

Self-confidence is necessary for efficient reading. The confident reader moves steadily forward from one point to another, avoiding excessive doubts or fears about his progress. Readers who lack confidence keep rereading the same sentences and paragraphs and wondering whether they have misunderstood the author's writing and become confused. Too much self-criticism and rereading can be wasteful and damaging. Nevertheless, even the skilled reader can often benefit by certain techniques for organizing, evaluating, and reinforcing what he has read. The most useful of these techniques are rereading, summarizing, underlining, copying, reviewing, and self-testing.

Rereading. A person without confidence in his reading ability tends to go over every printed line because he thinks he may have missed or misunderstood something important. This assumption is a serious mistake which you should so far as possible avoid. Assume instead that you understood what you have read, go on with your reading, and wait until you finish a passage or section before questioning or testing your comprehension. If you stop to check up after every sentence, fearing that you may have misunderstood it, you will not only waste time but will often fail to grasp clearly enough the main idea of the whole paragraph or discussion. Wait until you finish a passage or two before you consider whether you need to reread the material. If you decide to reread, you can then concentrate on making up for anything you missed by giving it more serious attention. When you reread, note especially the words and ideas which you misinterpreted and compare your second interpretation with the first. This self-evaluation will give you a justifiable feeling of self-confidence, for you will know that you have definitely improved your understanding of the writer's message.

Of course, even the most experienced readers sometimes fall short of perfection—a goal you may not achieve but should always aim at. For that matter, expert writers and publishers also make mistakes. Recently on the front page of a highly respected morning newspaper there were several errors which were annoying and confusing. The word *prospective* had been misused for *perspective*. Another sentence had no predicate whatever and was meaningless. In a third sentence there was an illogical comparison between things which cannot be compared. An efficient reader notices and discounts these errors. He will skip the verb-less sentence without wasting time trying to make sense out of it and may pause a moment to wonder at the careless writing of the third sentence before going on to other passages. Such a reader knows what to do, because he has had rich experience in analyzing words, sentence structure, and the logical organization of complex sentences.

Readers must not expect everything they read to be dedicated to high ideals or to be carefully prepared; they must be ready to deal with imperfect work owing to the haste and lack of pride in performance which have become all too common in our society. Fortunately, there are still some competent authors who observe high standards of creative effort, who make it a habit to write in a clear, candid, interesting style for appreciative readers.

Summarizing. After you have read a few pages in a book or perhaps have finished reading a chapter, you may realize that certain ideas (and related facts) therein vary widely in importance, making it difficult for you to organize and discriminate immediately among them. After all, an author may have toiled earnestly preparing a well organized presentation of a single topic, whereas you depend upon one or two quick readings to gain adequate understanding and appreciation of his work. More often than not, he is an expert on the subject, and you are the learner. Nevertheless, if you get into the habit of summarizing carefully what you read, you can often deepen your insight and sometimes even approximate the author's expertise.

Summarizing reverses the procedure used by many skilled authors. They set down ideas and facts in a well organized outline of the main points and relevant evidence or details, and then they simply elaborate upon the listed statements when they write the full text. The reader, on the contrary, begins with the author's final product. If he reads a section and summarizes it carefully, he should end up with something very much like the author's original plan. His summary will disclose how the various parts were fitted together to provide the central meanings and supporting elements of the discussion.

But summarizing well is no easy task. It requires hard and straight thinking. Whether you summarize mentally, without writing, or take notes in the form of an outline or essay, you must apply yourself with care, patience, logic, and system, and with discrimination and sensitivity to values. First, try to recall all the key ideas in what you have read and consider the order or sequence in which they were presented. Which came at or near the beginning, and how was it introduced? Which came last, and what were the points or concepts leading up to it? Which, if any, important ideas were developed between the first and the last? If you decide to write an outline of the material, set down the main ideas, facts, or principles, leaving space for supporting statements and details.

An acceptable outline of the first part of this chapter is shown in the following example:

Introductory: Caution about Speed and Comprehension

Ways to Improve Reading

  Previewing
    Nature
    Advantages
    Textbooks
    Fiction
    Newspapers and journals
  Skimming
    Nature

       Advantages
       Techniques
         Key sentences
         Finger movements
     Reading for Ideas
       Words and ideas
       Words in a pattern
       Word groups as ideas
   Making Sense out of Words
       Relativity of word meanings
       Importance of small words
       Interpretation of word meanings
   Reinforcing Your Reading
       Rereading
       Summarizing

Each main topic is followed by two or more subtopics. A subdivided main idea has at least two supporting ideas. For each topic the supporting subtopics are equally indented and have the same grammatical structure. This system makes it easy to see the entire framework of a discussion at a glance.

In writing a summary or an outline, you have to decide how many ideas and details of the original material you should include. Summarizing is not a process of merely restating information; it is a distillation of the original material, a result of careful analysis of its ideas and their interrelationships. Putting in too many minor points is just as bad as omitting important ones. If you write complete statements about the main ideas, instead of making a list of topics, your statements should be clear and brief, and the relationship between each important idea and its subordinate ideas should be evident at once.

After completing your summary, go back to the original material, compare the two, and revise your version wherever necessary to insure a full and logical development of the author's ideas. Doing this will often improve your understanding of his work and stimulate your own thinking, and it will certainly help you to remember what you have read.

Underlining. When should the reader underline and what should he underline? Some people refuse to under-

line any book, claiming that such marking is disfiguring
and interferes with another reader's use of the book. To
them books are almost sacred possessions to be preserved,
never to be marred, not even for their greater enlighten-
ment—but why are books written if not for the benefit
of their readers? Others believe that underlining or making notations will increase the value of the book when
they first read it and later when they wish to refer to important parts. Most readers find underlining helpful because it points out statements which are to be specially
noted and remembered and makes a useful distinction
between basic and supplementary information. The
reader must evaluate the material from his own point of
view in order to select key words or sentences to underline. He may underline questionable statements, phrases
not understood, sentences to be referred to later on, or
even entire passages for review. Excessive underlining,
however, tends to destroy the value of this technique by
making no distinction between the most important and
the less important ideas of the text. If you decide to underline selected passages, do so sparingly, with discretion.
You may wish also to write in the margins brief queries
or comments about the underlined passages. If you share
a book with other readers, they will see and perhaps
benefit from your underlining and notations.

Proper underlining can sometimes save time when you
wish to recall ideas or episodes in a book after a long
interval but find it inconvenient or tedious to reread the
entire volume. If you have underlined properly during
your original reading, you will be able to glance through
the underlined sentences, reviewing the main points, and
select immediately those passages you wish to reread
carefully. You can experience once more the same pleasure that you felt during the first reading, even to a greater
degree because you will not have to reread uninteresting
or trivial parts of the book.

Students may use a double line to underline the most
significant points in a textbook and list the double-lined

pages on the inside front cover of their textbook. This technique makes it easy to find the key passages or ideas of an entire book quickly at a future time.

Copying. In view of the current emphasis on speed in reading, it may seem strange to advocate copying as one of the most valuable aids to reading efficiency. In order to copy specific sentences or passages, you must concentrate on the meaning of each sentence or passage and evaluate it before deciding whether or not it is worth copying. Moreover, when you copy anything you are compelled to read slowly and carefully and to think about the author's ideas and their relationship to his preceding ideas. Copying corrects the bad habit of careless skimming over any material which needs to be read slowly and carefully. Try this technique by reading a long letter or document quickly and then setting it aside for an hour or two before copying it. Usually you will notice new information or new implications in the material, things not readily appreciated in a rapid, cursory first reading. You may, for example, read a letter or contract from beginning to end and conclude that everything in it is simple and clear, only to discover that writing a copy reveals omissions, obscurities, or important new points to consider. Therefore, if you wish to make certain that you understand a significant passage thoroughly, take the time to copy it.

Reviewing and Self-Testing. Methods of reviewing and self-testing have frequently been used by students preparing for examinations or advanced study of a subject. Similar procedures are useful for a reader who wishes to remember the information he has read and to derive more benefit from his reading. It is best to review immediately after reading a chapter, article, or book, and thereafter at intervals. If you have written a summary or outline of the material, try at first to recall the details from memory and then compare your mental review with the written résumé. This procedure is especially valuable in preventing you from recalling only a partial or mistaken interpretation of the author's ideas. Too often a reader forgets exceptions or qualifications in the original text and remembers isolated statements out of context as if they were entirely true or adequate. Reviewing with a good outline prevents incorrect assumptions of this kind. It is sometimes better to forget all about an author's ideas than to form a distorted or mistaken view of them. Always check your review carefully against summaries, outlines, or the original work.

Self-testing is an excellent way to review a chapter or section of a book. You may sometimes test yourself by thinking of questions and answers, but it is usually best to write them down. Then consult the original text to check up on any significant points about which you failed to ask questions and to verify your answers. Keep your final list of questions and answers in a notebook so that you will be able to go back to them at intervals to refresh your memory and to insert your new interpretations and reactions.

Another splendid way to review is to explain the author's views to or discuss his main points with other people. Tell them what you think of his ideas and style of writing and ask for their opinions. When you try to teach what you have learned to others, you may sometimes discover that your knowledge is not so nearly perfect as you had assumed it to be, and you will then be able to improve your own understanding of the topic. Above all, hasten to correct your mistakes or prejudiced opinions, because delay may make it difficult or even impossible to correct them.

In short, remember that too many readers postpone careful rereading and then become occupied with other matters, remaining saddled for years to come with distorted or absurd misinterpretations of articles or books they have read. By testing your knowledge about a subject before and after rereading, you can improve your understanding of the subject and discuss it more intelligently with others. But what you do with ideas and information you read will provide the final test of your reading achievements. Experience is the best kind of test.

SELECTING TIME FOR READING

What is the best time for reading? The answer is, Whenever you can put enough time and attention into it to get something worthwhile out of it. You will get much out of your reading if you remember the author's central ideas and most effective passages. Psychologists claim that you will remember these best if you take a complete rest or even sleep after reading a while. The theory is that there will then be very few, if any, conflicting thoughts to interfere with or block out what you have read.

It seems logical to assume that if you read for hours at a time without a stop, hundreds of ideas may so overcrowd your mind that they may prevent concentration upon any of them. If there are too many things to remember, you will tend to forget them all. A rest period will often prevent such overcrowding, clearing the way for later recall of at least a few definite ideas. If you do not rest but continue reading, at least change to another kind of reading material—from rigid or technical matter to popular texts, from serious discussions to humor or light reading, or from history to fiction or poetry. Best of all, after reading an hour or two, take a walk, listen to music, talk with your friends, or follow up some other personal interests. Then go back to your reading with a fresh outlook and renewed vigor. You will enjoy it more and remember it well.

PREPARING TO READ

Most people read to the best advantage in a quiet, well-lighted place, seated in a comfortable but not too comfortable chair, with a dictionary, other reference works, pen, and notepaper handy; others do not mind noise or various distractions and perhaps like to read while listening to music; and some readers like to read leisurely in bed. It is said that Samuel Johnson, during periods of illness, cut holes in his bedsheet so that he could put his hands through them to hold a book which he could read while remaining snug and warm in bed. Abe Lincoln did much of his boyhood reading while stretched out on the floor. Children read all sorts of books in all sorts of places and positions.

There are some well-established practical suggestions about preparing to read. When you expect to read for any extended period, select a firm chair, keep your posture straight without excessive strain, hold the book or magazine in both hands at a distance permitting clear vision with both eyes and with a glare-free light—neither too bright nor too dim—coming either over your left shoulder or from any direction provided that it does not throw a shadow on the page or shine directly into your eyes. Keep your reference works, pen, paper, and clock nearby. If your thoughts stray occasionally while reading, be sure to avoid noise or distractions of any kind and you will find that absolute quiet will help you to concentrate. Some readers like to read with background music, despite the distractions; in most cases they will be disturbed much more by vocal selections than by instrumental (orchestral or chamber) music. In short, plan for the best possible conditions and get into the proper mood for earnest effort if you wish to derive the most benefit from your reading.

Do you often read in bed, either when indisposed or when you retire at night and try to read yourself to sleep? Some poor sleepers read a dull treatise or unexciting story instead of using medication to counteract their insomnia. A good suggestion is to read only a small but complete unit or separable portion of an interesting magazine or book, because you can finish reading that part or at least its main ideas before putting out the light. Make up your mind not to read beyond a certain page or chapter. Set your deadline and hold to it, remembering that tomorrow evening will be another evening for reading.

Some people who ordinarily neglect their reading will occasionally decide to read a large volume or several volumes for hours on end without rest periods. It is far better to plan your reading in accordance with a regular schedule, thus avoiding the danger of eyestrain and damage to health or other personal interests. You will enjoy your reading material more and get more out of it if you divide it into logically separable parts and finish only one or two at a time. In reading, as in most other pursuits, moderation and regularity are usually conducive to the best results.

USING BOOKS MOST EFFECTIVELY

Books contain certain special features, too frequently ignored, which readers can use to good advantage. These include copyright pages, tables of contents, prefaces, and introductions.

Examine the copyright page carefully, noting when the book was first published and whether or not there has been a revised or new edition or a new printing. There can be considerable difference between the copyright and printing dates—it is the copyright date which tells whether the book is a recently created work. Do not be misled by printing dates into assuming that an old book has been brought up to date or that a book with a recent printing date is a new publication. Read the preface without fail, for it may give information about the history of the author's work on the book—why he wrote it, the best way to use it, and what you can expect to get out of it. The table of contents, besides listing the chapter titles and sometimes a good deal more, also shows the arrangement and relationship of the various topics. Finally, if there is an introduction, it is likely to be a significant and useful part of the front matter. An introduction can explain the author's point of view, provide background information about the subject matter, or preview the principal themes of the book. Looking through the front matter of several books may help you to decide which ones to read. For this purpose, one alert reader who prefers light reading at bedtime reads the preface, then leafs through the book quickly to see how much dialogue is included, because complex discussions and descriptions would require serious concentration.

3

How To Remember
What You Read

What is memory? Is it only a shadow of the past? One of the most influential theories, at least two thousand four hundred years old, states that memory depends upon, and consists mainly of, associations among ideas. Plato pointed out in his *Phaedo* that seeing an object may immediately remind us of its owner. It is certainly true that events which go together or occur in close proximity tend to be linked together again in memory. Often when we see two things at the same time we connect them so that we can later think about either of them if the other reappears. The theory of association between ideas has been one of the foundations for modern psychologies of learning. Thus, Pavlov's system of conditioning was based on experiments proving that if an animal repeatedly links two things in sequence, subsequent awareness of one will impel him to recall and react to the other. Freud's system of psychoanalysis is based in part on his discovery that some ideas associated with unpleasant experiences are buried deep in our "unconscious minds" and must be brought to the surface (recalled) in order to cure a neurosis.

As a matter of fact, occasionally we remember things without apparent associations or perhaps with extremely remote associations. Freud's "unconscious," too, does not satisfy us completely as a theory, for we can sometimes submerge or repress painful experiences yet later recall them more vividly than the pleasant ones—all without nervous tension, neurosis, or psychiatric help.

One interesting theory compares memory to the action of electric waves creating pathways or patterns in the nervous system. According to this theory, such waves or currents produce new pathways, some more definite and effective or energetic than others, and new experiences engender additional waves which spread throughout the nervous system until they find and fit into the same pathways as before. An exciting experience is remembered better because its wave currents make deep pathways into which new thoughts fit as memories. The experience of recall not only thus produces an imitation of the original exciting event but also creates energy currents and pathways of its own so that we can later remember that we have remembered the original.

A PRACTICAL VIEW OF MEMORY

The association of ideas has practical value. If you associate a new idea which you have just read with old ones, your subsequent recollection of the old ideas may remind you of the new one. Unfortunately, you may too frequently be unable to recall the old ideas either, making these associations impossible. But this shortcoming of association can to some extent be counteracted by another related factor, namely, repetition. Information that has been repeated often enough with understanding will make a lasting impression and will be recallable later when you need it. But casual repetition of the ideas you read is not sufficient; to remember well, you must also pay attention to the meaning and order (organization) of the words and sentences. Since meaning and order depend upon association of ideas, both repetition and association are usually necessary.

Psychologists today divide memory into three parts: retention (we retain past experience in our mental storehouse for possible recall, never completely forgetting anything); recall (we recollect or think again about some of the stored experiences); and recognition (we recognize things because something about them reminds us of their identity and the fact that we have previously known them). Such an analysis corresponds to our common-sense practical interpretation.

In popular usage, retention refers to all the experiences which we can recall. If we cannot recall something that has happened, we say that we have failed to retain it, that we have forgotten it, and we are surprised if we suddenly remember it at a later time. The original thought or feeling has of course come and gone, but we can think about it again. Thus, memory is spoken of as if it meant the rediscovery of things we had stored away, from which we may eventually select one or more at our will and pleasure.

According to Freud, all ideas and other experiences are still with us, in the storehouse of our minds, including the forgotten ones which are either latent, or repressed in our unconscious (the repressed ones being the unpleasant experiences). He pointed out that thinking and talking about past experiences may help us to recall the repressed ones, recognize them for what they are, and begin to understand why we repressed them, thus relieving nervous tension.

Actually, science knows little that can be proved about the unconscious, the subconscious, or any other fundamental aspect of memory. Many people agree with Freud that the repression of unpleasant childhood experiences can lead to psychological disturbances in adult years. But there is no scientific proof of the existence of an unconscious realm, a subterranean vault in the nervous system; the psychological disturbances of an adult may be due to a feeling of inadequacy—not to repressed memories of his childhood experiences, but simply to a realization that he has been unable to understand or cope with unpleasant conditions (the details of which he has "forgotten")— or to conflicting choices whether to think about or ignore painful incidents. He becomes tense because he does not know how to deal with serious problems, which road to take. A person who keeps thinking about shocking incidents of his early childhood, without feelings of inadequacy or despair, may easily recall the details at a later time and usually without excessive tension or the development of a neurosis. At any rate, for reading improvement, we are here concerned only with practical methods of facilitating recall.

EFFECTIVE WAYS TO RECALL

Among the most effective, practical ways to facilitate recall of reading materials are the following: enthusiastic interest; intention to recall; evaluation; concentration; repetition; application; and organization.

Enthusiastic Interest. If we read a number of passages casually, we may retain them all somewhere in memory but each will be difficult to recall because it will be only one of many comparable units. If we want to recall a particular passage or idea, what will make us think again about that one instead of the others? If we paid special attention to it, the one we later want to remember would have made a stronger impression than the others and would therefore be likely to reappear in our thoughts. But why do we pay special attention to some things instead of others? Usually because they can help us in some way or because they are related to our vital interests and needs. Therefore, one of the best ways to strengthen the impression made by the ideas we want to remember is to connect them with something else that is familiar and important to us.

For example, I had read about a state law affecting property rights but had given it little attention and forgot its provisions. But when I became involved in litigation wherein the same law could seriously affect my property, I reread the law, this time with special interest and attention. Thereafter I could never again forget the provisions of that law. It had become significant reading material worth recalling because I saw its relationship to something about which I was deeply concerned. When you read something you want to remember, try to connect it with as many real interests as possible so that it will long remain near the surface of your memory for instant recall and use. Ask yourself, *How will this infor-*

mation affect me or my associates and why should I try to remember it? The question itself will tend to stimulate your interest and thus greatly increase the likelihood of recall.

Intention to Recall. Much reading material consists of relatively minor points built around or contributing to the main ideas. You will forget such details, but when you come to a significant idea, stop and think of it as something you will want to remember, then reread it slowly and deliberately. You must not only understand and repeat the idea but you must also label it as one worth remembering, that is to say, as one you are determined to recollect at the proper time. (If you have not fully understood the idea, you may remember only the fact that you have failed to understand it, for there will be no clear meaning in your mind to retain. There will be nothing to recall.)

It is sometimes difficult to decide what to reread with intention to recall. Usually the topic sentences or other key sentences are the ones you will select for this purpose. You may also choose key paragraphs to emphasize in the same way. Further, even though the main ideas in the original version are perfectly clear to you when you read them, restate them in your own words, in the habitual vocabulary that you will want to use when you hopefully will recall them. Now they will fit perfectly into the orderly system of those things you are determined to remember. You will be able to concentrate on the ideas themselves as you would express them, without interference from the unfamiliar language of a stranger.

With rare exceptions, it is a mistake to try to read everything with intention to recall. There is a limit to the number of things you can or should commit to memory for recollection, and the effectiveness of the method depends upon discrimination between what is worth the effort and what should be forgotten. Some people read everything too casually, soon forgetting all of it, while others read and reread every sentence too diligently and after the ordeal is over they, too, forget everything. Both types of readers should change their habits and become selective, discriminating, and more alert to the things worth rereading with intention to recall.

Make sure that you correctly interpret what you reread and express it correctly in your own words, for a mistaken interpretation may persist in your memory and may then be extremely difficult to eradicate. Too often people read and reread carelessly and thus fix the errors firmly in their memories so that they recall and repeat the mistakes ad infinitum.

You may wish to test your ability to recall things you have read with intention to recall. For this purpose note the picture on page 47. Examine the picture carefully and as you read the list of forty objects on this page, find in the picture each of the objects listed. Then take a blank sheet of paper and, without looking at the printed list below or at the picture, write down the names of all the objects you can remember. Next compare your written list with the printed one. If you have recalled most of the forty objects listed, you have a superior ability to recall things which you read with intention to recall.

1.	andirons (in fireplace)	21.	knife
2.	ashtray (on mantel)	22.	lamp
3.	ball (in dog's mouth)	23.	log
4.	bottle (on table)	24.	mantel
5.	boy	25.	mirror
6.	chair	26.	picture (shown in mirror)
7.	cord (window shade pull)	27.	pipe (in ashtray)
8.	cup	28.	plate
9.	dog	29.	radiator
10.	doily (on table)	30.	saucer
11.	doll	31.	skate
12.	drape (or curtain)	32.	spoon
13.	electric fixture (on wall)	33.	straw (in bottle)
14.	electric light bulbs	34.	table
15.	electric outlet	35.	teddy bear
16.	electric plug	36.	tray (on table)
17.	fireplace	37.	tricycle
18.	flowers (in vase)	38.	vase
19.	girl	39.	window
20.	gun	40.	window shade (or blind)

Evaluation. I once read a poorly written newspaper column several times, but it left me puzzled and disappointed. I have forgotten the details in that column, but I do remember that the writing was badly organized and ambiguous. Why did I forget the information itself, yet recall easily the poor quality of the writing? Because I had especially noticed and evaluated the inept writing which distracted my attention from the ideas being presented. If I had been able to concentrate on and react to the ideas themselves, they, too, would probably have persisted in my memory. Similarly, in your reading, you will usually remember best the things that impress you sufficiently so that you evaluate or otherwise react to them.

Even in our everyday casual reading, and certainly in our more serious-minded reading, we make distinctions between major and minor ideas. Surely it is impractical to try to recall everything we read, for that, if it could be done, would overload our minds with trivial or useless information. Evaluate carefully what is most meaningful and significant in your reading, and then you will have a good chance to recall these relatively few things when you have need of them. If you read a paragraph and can then say to yourself, *This is an important idea worth remembering,* you will indeed be most likely to remember it well. Such an evaluation involves repetition: first, you think about the meaning of the idea and, second, you think again about the idea when you ascribe great importance to it. But do not make the mistake of exaggerating the significance of so many ideas that the distinction between their values becomes confused. Try to make certain that the main points you select are really the ones that will be most worth recalling.

During the past thirty years or more I have had occasion to read, reread, and edit hundreds of books in various subjects and today remember best those ideas and presentations which I believed to be either unusually good or extremely dubious. I have forgotten most of the detailed information, but can recall those major points which I evaluated. In a sense, all readers should function as book editors to the best of their ability, judging which statements are true or partly true, logical or absurd, clearly set forth or confusing. Sometimes the reading material which is difficult to understand is worth studying until the reader can estimate its truth and importance, because serious study involving a concentrated search for meanings may insure permanent retention and ready recall. You may easily forget what is handed to you ready-made, but you will long remember what you look hard for and find for yourself.

One of the best ways to evaluate reading material, a way often used by experienced book editors, is that of comparison and contrast. An editor compares important ideas and discussions in one book with those in other books, noting in which respects they agree, in which they disagree, and which manner of expression is clearest and best organized. Any reader can make excellent use of this technique. As you read, think back to your past reading of similar topics and compare the present material with it. How do the new ideas differ from the old? Which do you prefer, and which would be most worth keeping in mind for subsequent reference? Are the new ideas true to your life experience? Just as nations can and should (but seldom do) learn from comparisons between present situations and those of the past—from the lessons of history—so you as an individual should learn and well remember present reading by comparing it with your past reading experiences. Sometimes, too, you can compare the same author's ideas with those in other books he has written, noting similarities and differences which you will later easily recall. You may even find inconsistencies in different parts of a single article or book. Note also the manner in which one part supplements or reinforces the others. Analysis of this kind greatly increases the likelihood of recall.

Finally, you should evaluate the reading material as a whole experience. Ask yourself, Did I really enjoy this author's work? If you think about the reasons for your reactions, you will perhaps review some of the highlights of the material and fix them more firmly in your memory. Notice especially any unexpected, disturbing, or unfinished points. If you evaluate the author's work with either favorable or unfavorable criticisms, the special attention you thus bestow upon it will be compensated by more effective retention and recall.

Concentration. Every reader has had the experience of trying to read while distracted by other matters, such as personal problems or annoying interruptions. Efficiency in reading requires concentration upon the author's meaning. If the reader cannot grasp the meaning of what he has read, there will be nothing significant in his mind for him to remember. Concentration means searching for ideas while excluding distractions; it means shutting out irrelevant thoughts in order to follow the trend of the author's words. When your attentive efforts result in understanding, you will tend to remember your achievement—the meanings you have discovered—for most people remember their achievements and forget their failures. Shut out all unrelated thoughts and preoccupations, give your wholehearted attention to the author's main ideas, and you will be likely to understand and remember them.

Often the ability to concentrate depends upon self-interest. If you are reading something which is of no concern to you, which does not affect you, which fails to evoke your sympathy or antipathy, it is quite certain that you will be looking at the words without earnest attention and will quickly forget them. For example, a housewife who is intensely interested in cooking will read recipes with close attention, promptly noticing anything new or particularly useful in them. Someone else, even though skilled in reading, may find the same recipes quite boring, may read them with scant attention, and may impatiently discard and forget them. Thus, to insure serious concentration, you must connect reading material with your favorite interests—your own ideas, experiences, opinions, conversations, associations, and activities.

If you have begun reading without close attention, stop and ask yourself, *Why am I reading this?* If you cannot think of a satisfactory reason, put your reading aside. If you decide that the material is worthwhile, begin again, this time with enough effort to insure close attention and full comprehension. Inattentive reading is careless reading, hasty, superficial, seldom worth the attempt. Anything worth reading at all should be read with attention and concentration.

How much should you try to concentrate on reading at a single sitting? Obviously, if you keep staring at a paragraph and repeating the words, you will soon lose interest and get nowhere. To concentrate, the mind must be active; it must think about one logical point after another or it will go blank. The amount of material you can read efficiently at one sitting will vary with the time available, the difficulty of the text, and your ability to concentrate on it.

Some readers cannot keep their attention steady on a line of thought for five minutes at a time, but wander off, filling their minds with trivial information which crowds out the author's important ideas. Other readers can read on and on for hours without giving more attention to one point than to another. If you wish to improve recall, avoid both extremes. Divide the material into just the right amount of solid intellectual food you can comfortably digest, think about it in a logical way as you read, then pause and let it sink in. When you resume reading, notice the links among the parts and you will have the best chance to remember the whole passage.

The middle parts of a reading selection are usually more difficult to remember than the beginning and end parts. Therefore, before you read each new section, it may be helpful to skim through the preceding sections again, giving special attention to the middle part and linking its ideas to the rest. A novel, for example, can often be subdivided into logical parts based on the plot. Some readers can remember an unfinished story better than a completed one. If you divide a novel into its natural parts and read several with sustained interest, you will be kept in suspense and will remember well the unresolved events. Such unfinished episodes of novels serialized in newspapers and magazines used to attract many readers who could hardly wait to buy the next issue—proving that reading in parts of reasonable length sustains interest and recall.

Repetition. Repetition is a most potent factor in the recall of reading material. It may be partial or complete, direct or indirect, attentive and meaningful or inattentive and casual. Reading materials may be repeated in the same sequence or their order may be modified or even reversed. Moreover, repeated readings can never be exactly the same, because each repetition affects the power of the reader to understand and complete the next rereading, especially since he has now become more alert to what lies ahead of him. Thus, if you read a paragraph once, you may get a general idea of its message; when you read it again, you will find it easier to read quickly and may also notice additional ideas or implications in it. We think with the thoughts we have had in the past.

You do not always have to reread every word. If you are reading a complicated mass of information, try rereading only the main points several times, keeping your mind from being overcrowded or confused by too many details at one time. You may decide to skim over some parts which seem to contribute little to the author's message and to reread the essentials more carefully than before. Often, instead of rereading the original sentences directly from the printed source, you may do better to review them indirectly by rethinking the ideas in your mind. In some cases, you may wish to skip a paragraph here and there, or reverse the sequence, rereading a later part before an earlier one. (But do not lose track of the author's logical arrangement of his ideas.) All these forms of repetition can improve the ability to recall.

Psychological experiments have shown that repetitions

are more effective if they are spread over several periods of time instead of being concentrated into one period. For example, assume that to remember a few selected passages or events you plan to reread them, say, ten times each. You will recall them much better if you read them five times on each of two days than you will if you read them ten times in a single day.

Why does a moderate delay in repetitions help recall? One explanation states that each group of repetitions makes impressions on the mind which grow stronger for a while thereafter; consequently, a waiting period after each set of repetitions allows the impressions to become still more firmly fixed in the memory. But there is doubt as to the validity of this explanation, for impressions usually grow weaker, not stronger, with the passing of time, during which new, interfering experiences crowd into the mind. A more plausible explanation might be that a second set of immediate repetitions are of less value than delayed ones because the reader remembers the first reading well enough, and repetitions add little to his interest or to what he already knows; in fact, he tends to reread hastily or casually. A day later, the reader will still remember part of the material, but he will need another set of attentive repetitions and will concentrate on them because he knows they will help him to recapture the whole story. The things he has forgotten since yesterday are the weak links which the new set of repetitions can emphasize and strengthen. (Athletes, public speakers, and musicians have always been aware of the special value of distributed practice.) Note, however, that if the reader waits too long before rereading, say, several weeks, he will probably have forgotten too much and will have to start all over again.

Early experiments on memory proved that the rate of forgetting is extremely rapid immediately after the first readings. Forgetting continues thereafter, but at a slower rate. For this reason, you should not wait too long before rereading or at least rethinking the materials you may later wish to recall. Unfortunately, many students preparing for examinations repeat a lesson many times in one day and remember enough to pass their examinations the next day, but they will eventually forget nearly everything. Cramming is a useless method of learning even though it enables students to pass examinations.

For practical purposes, when you have read certain ideas which you would like to remember permanently, review them several times in your mind every few days. Do not depend on numerous repetitions within one session only, for you have no immediate need of them, and too many of them can become frustrating and tedious— even though a limited amount of overlearning (unnecessary repetition) is unavoidable and sometimes helpful. On the other hand, do not let too much time elapse before rethinking the same ideas, because additional interfering experiences will blot out the original material. Repetitions must have something to build upon, some partial recall, to fill in gaps or serve as cues to refresh the memory.

Application. One of the best ways to improve recall of reading material is to apply it. Let me cite an example. I purchased an appliance consisting of two machines which had to be put together by means of a hitch. I read the manual of directions carefully, including instructions for assembling and for using the equipment. But when I began putting the two parts together, I could not recall the first steps. Later I could not remember how each step I did recall fitted into the others. So I reread only one sentence at a time and followed its directions meticulously. Now, as I applied what I had read and reread, I understood clearly and remembered easily what each of the directions meant. I soon came to the last sentence, a final step, instructing me to slide the second machine forward on top of the first and then to push a long handle forward. I did these things as directed, but the two parts simply would not remain hitched together. As soon as I pulled one, they separated. Obviously there was something wrong. I lay flat on the ground and, recalling the last sentence in the directions, watched to see what would happen when I pushed the long handle forward. I saw that the two parts to be fastened together did not even touch, so I continued to press forward very hard on the handle until a rod on the first machine pushed a spring down so that the two machines could be moved along until firmly joined together. I have never forgotten these directions because I applied them successfully to solve a real problem. Of course, the manual was at fault because, instead of merely instructing the reader to push the long handle forward, it should have told him to push it forward hard as far as it would go and it should have explained why that was necessary. I supplemented the printed instructions with my own information and the entire solution of the problem remained vividly in my mind thereafter.

Not all applications are so practical as that one. Some of the most useful ones take place in the reader's imagination. Others occur during conversations or other contacts with people. If you wish to strengthen your recall of the significant materials you read, use the ideas in a variety of ways—express them in your own words, discuss them, teach them, write about them, think them over, put them into practice, visualize them, draw pictures or diagrams of them, supplement them with ideas of your own. Such applications improve understanding and facilitate recall. Moreover, do not forget to distribute applications over several periods of time so that both the ideas and their uses will benefit from spaced repetition.

Nearly everything we learn involves the fitting together of old and new information. We apply past learnings to present ones. We think with our past, a reservoir of intellectual tools. There could be no mental experience of any significance without this kind of application. You have learned the meanings of certain words and when you apply the old meanings to new sentences which you are reading, you will usually remember the old ones better than before, and they will serve as foundations for understanding and remembering the new ones. For example, you may recall that *bon* means good in French. When you read the words *bon mot* in an English sentence, you will apply the meaning of *bon* to the word *mot* (meaning word), and thereafter you will recall that the two words together mean "good word," or "clever remark." Thus, application in your imagination, that is, your thinking about the associations between things, is an effective aid to memory. The vigorous interplay of ideas in your own mind can often become the swiftest and most useful pathway to better recall.

Organization. Man is the great systematizer, the organizer par excellence. He puts things together and tears them apart, rearranges them, turns them upside down and inside out, and ties them in neat bundles. Reading, or any kind of logical thinking, depends upon organization of parts within wholes. Not only the individual words or single ideas, but the combinations of them into sentences, paragraphs, and sections are presented as an organized set or system. If you notice and remember the organization as a whole, you will better remember each of its parts.

Reading and rereading a whole set of ideas at one time and rereading each part separately several times will help you to recall all of them. The psychologists call this method the learning of the whole and its parts. If the entire set of passages is not too long or complicated, the first reading provides an adequate framework into which you can fit the various parts. If you wish to remember a discussion, read the whole of it, then read each part several times, and, finally, reread the entire discussion, noting the way in which the parts are linked together.

The surprise element in a sequence or organized pattern of ideas is probably responsible for better recall of reading material. If everything you read were old and familiar to you, you would take it for granted and be inclined to forget it. The same surprise element is often the secret of humor. Consider, for example, the story about Abe Lincoln's journey through a rural community late at night. Abe stopped at the roadside to ask a farmer standing nearby whether he could put him and his horse up for the night. The farmer stared into the sky but made no answer. Finally, Abe rode off and found lodging elsewhere. The next evening he happened to be passing on the same road and there was the farmer, standing in the identical spot and still staring into the sky. As Abe reached him, the farmer nodded his head and gave him his answer, "Yes." The humor in this story depends on the surprise element in the sequence of events—the gap of twenty-four hours between question and answer and the unexpected twist in the idea that the farmer was still thinking about Abe's question. The story is supposed to show how slowly the rural people of his time reacted to emergencies.

When you read, reread, and rethink what you have read, you may omit the less important points, but take special notice of the surprises, difficulties, and unexpected features in the orderly sequence of ideas. Review the pattern of the author's material in your mind. Is it chronological? Are there causes leading to results? Do the main ideas consist of one or several themes or motifs, with supporting evidence or arguments? Does the author supply additional information as the basis for a significant conclusion? Does he approach a problem from several points of view? Does he go back and forth, repeat himself, jump around from one idea to another? If you have grasped the author's plan for a whole section, remembering one part will later remind you of the others. Moreover, since you will usually be able to recall the beginning and the end of the entire material, keeping the author's system in mind will help you to fill in the middle parts.

4
How To Analyze
What You Read

The preceding discussion has reviewed ways to achieve satisfactory speed and comprehension in reading. The most important factors affecting retention and recall of reading materials were also considered. The discussion in this chapter and the next two chapters will deal with methods of reading which distinguish expert readers from merely average readers.

It is their ability in critical reading which characterizes the most alert and efficient readers. In one sense, reading proficiency can be compared with musical accomplishment. Thus, an amateur musician may acquire modest skill in the performance and appreciation of instrumental music, but much more is required of the professional musician. In the same way, readers can go far beyond the mastery of reading habits and methods which result in only average understanding and can become alert consumers of written communications of every kind. By learning and practicing the principles of critical reading to be discussed, you can develop some of the advanced skills of the truly expert readers, delving more deeply and carefully into each author's work. Furthermore, you will be less apt to become a victim of careless or unscrupulous writers interested chiefly in money-making or one-sided propaganda instead of intellectual service to mankind and the diffusion of knowledge through communication of the truth.

The writer's work reflects to some extent his own character and experience. (Rare indeed are the universal geniuses, such as Shakespeare, whose masterpieces fail to reveal much about the personal backgrounds of their authors.) At the same time, however, the meaning and power of the words presented by the writer depend upon the ability of the reader to interpret them. He gets out of them only what he himself puts into them. Obviously, to get the most out of his reading, he must devote adequate attention and thought to the material being read. Too many people derive little benefit from their reading because they fail to make sufficient preparation for it. They do not even resolve to be careful and critical, but simply plunge ahead from one paragraph to the next, often overwhelmed by what appear to be convincing facts or arguments. They interpret everything on the basis of previous untested opinions and assumptions, thus confirming their own prejudices and reinforcing their own mistakes. The expert reader, on the other hand, is well-versed in the logic of reading—in the rational principles of communication and the skills necessary for comprehension in depth.

THE LOGIC OF READING

The most useful principles of the logic of reading can be applied easily by any reader who will discipline himself to remember and make regular use of them. The basic principles are those of inclusiveness, reality, proportion, momentum, analogy, emphasis, and implication. Observation of these principles in practice will deepen and enrich the reading of newspapers, periodicals, and books.

Inclusiveness. In any kind of printed matter, serious omissions of relevant ideas or information, whether purposive or inadvertent, need to be detected and counteracted by the reader, because such omissions can greatly affect his understanding of the work. They impair the validity and quality of expression in fiction or nonfiction, news, prose, drama, or poetry. Consider, for example, the following paragraphs entitled *Flag-Waving, Flag-Burning,* and *Flag-Saving.*

Flag-Waving

This country enjoys the highest standard of living in the world. It has nearly half the world's telephones. It has four times as many automobiles as any other nation and 58 per cent of the total, produces more than twice as much electricity as any other country, nine times as many miles of airlines, three times as much aluminum, twice as much rubber, has the largest merchant fleet, leads the world in cement production, petroleum, lead, coal, copper, steel, zinc, cheese production, cotton, oats, and meat. With only 6 per cent of the world's population, we own about 50 per cent of its wealth. We lead the world, too, in education, literacy, life insurance, science and invention, home ownership, railroad mileage, radio and television sets. We enjoy free enterprise, free speech, free education, and the best health aids and medical facilities of any people in history. Moreover, we have sent to foreign countries 100 billion dollars to assist them in meeting their economic and social problems. We have never lost a war. We lead the world in space exploration. All these achievements have been made by our free people in a competitive, profit-making society which has proved itself to be superior to any other, past or present. It is no wonder that millions of people have come to us from all parts of the earth to escape enslavement, lack of opportunity, and oppression.

Everything in the preceding paragraph is consistent with the facts. If the reader merely accepts these statements without critical analysis, he will inevitably conclude that all is for the best in this best of all possible worlds—and he will be doing inestimable damage both to his own conscience and to the well-being of his country. The prospect of social progress becomes extremely dubious if citizens assume that perfection or near-perfection has already been attained. Any reader sincerely concerned about the welfare of his own community and nation should read such information in the light of life experience and the conflicting evidence offered by writers presenting a different view of the same subject. The following paragraph, *Flag-Burning*, contrasts sharply with the one above, and yet its information, too, is quite true and consistent with the facts.

Flag-Burning

This nation is afflicted by one of the highest crime rates in the world, with nearly three million major crimes reported in a single year and more than four million arrests. In many cities violence occurs so often that it has been unsafe to walk in the streets. Presidents and other leading citizens have been assassinated. Large-scale organizations of gangsters operate in all parts of the country, frequently with the connivance of official-dom. Family life is at a low level, with one in every four marriages ending in divorce. The strain and stress of our society are reflected by the fact that half a million patients are being treated in mental hospitals at any one time, and they are only a small part of the millions in need of therapy. We own more automobiles than any other country and drive them farther, but at a price of 55,000 deaths each year in automobile accidents—one death every eleven minutes day and night—and millions of accidents, partly due to chronic alcoholism among drivers, disregard of others, and unsafe cars distributed by corporations which must earn profits for stockholders by manufacturing, advertising, and marketing over-sized, superficially pleasing but flimsy and dangerous over-powered and frequently defective vehicles. We are the world's largest producers and consumers of tobacco, which has caused millions to die prematurely and pain-fully from heart disease, lung cancer, and other ailments. Yet, those who manufacture or advertise such deadly products as tobacco earn handsome profits and become respected pillars of the community. They persuade people to use more of their toxic products and then they boast that they are merely giving them what they want. Six million of our people are confirmed alcoholics. The very air, waters, and forests of our land are constantly being polluted for the temporary benefit of the money-makers. We send our youth off to wars resulting in millions of casualties in order to protect financial interests and national power and prestige throughout the world. Everywhere we find instances of deception, chicanery, rationalization, flag-waving, schemes to acquire wealth, and deceitful advertising, business monopoly, labor racketeering, corruption even in the arts and professions. The social climate remains muddied by racial and religious hatred and bigotry and class antagonisms.

Obviously, this second paragraph is just as one-sided as the first, and just as dangerous. Both comments suffer from omissions, from disregard of the principle of inclusiveness. The alert reader will find each of them unconvincing. The next paragraph, entitled *Flag-Saving,* suggests the method whereby readers can fill in the omissions of ideas in reading material to achieve accurate and balanced understanding of a subject.

Flag-Saving

Our country, though beset with serious problems and difficulties, has numerous achievements to its credit. We have made mistakes, tragic ones, yet it has been better to face our problems boldly than to do nothing about them, for inaction is the greatest mistake of all. Standards of living are comparatively high, but we must admit that the price being paid by the people is also high. If we lead in transportation, we also lead in accidents; if we enjoy a high level of education, too much of the effort is superficial, wasteful, and ineffective. We should balance the good in our society against the evil—blinding ourselves to either will only conceal the truth necessary for the enlargement of our freedoms and the improvement of our condition. We have indeed failed to prevent disastrous trends in domestic affairs and have become embroiled in violence abroad, yet we have been prime movers in efforts to prevent further catastrophes and to build a world of peace, justice, and order.

Disregard of the principle of inclusiveness affects all forms of reading material. The skilled novelist or playwright develops his characters to make them seem really true to life and therefore genuine, interesting personalities. The unskilled novelist or playwright portrays wooden people or distorted characters with an ineptness that ruins his work. Perhaps the most serious defect in modern news-reporting and advertising is this lack of adequate information. Readers should discover this defect and reject such materials as a rational basis for reactions and decisions.

If you demand inclusiveness, you will eventually get it.

I recall that when I was a businessman in Boston, one of my customers was a famous old retail store, Raymond's "Where U Bot the Hat," a prosperous enterprise which owed much of its success to absolute honesty in its advertising and dealings with suppliers and patrons. If there was anything not quite perfect about its merchandise, Raymond's considered it a duty to so inform the public. People liked to trade in that store because it could be trusted never to conceal the truth. There are laws prohibiting fraudulent claims by merchants, but often appeal to the law is more costly than the damage caused to the individual—and there are few laws against silence. It has become common practice to tell people only what is good about a product or service, yet is this not just as deceitful as an outright falsehood? Indeed, far worse, for readers can sometimes investigate and reject a false statement but they are seldom expert enough to fill in the information which has been deliberately omitted. A small step has been taken to protect the public through laws regulating the purchase of insurance, stocks and bonds, and a few other products. But the best means of protection are twofold: an honorable business community, and truly alert consumers of information determined to deal only with those merchants and community leaders who can be trusted to "tell the truth, the whole truth."

Reality. The principle of reality, as applied to reading materials, refers to the degree of agreement between an author's works and the experience of the reader. When reading novels, even those featuring mythical, miraculous, or imaginary situations and events of the strangest kind, the expert reader measures the presentation against the yardstick of his life experience. The good and evil characters in literature are illumined through the recollection of events, dreams, and visions of living human beings. Even God is envisioned by pious men as all-wise, all-knowing, all-merciful, and the like—the familiar human qualities known to us all but now extrapolated to the highest level. The expert reader analyzes an author's

work to ascertain in what ways it is true to life itself—
how it is either similar to life experience or contrasted
with life experience.

A modern reader generally does not believe in witches.
Yet, when witches are encountered in masterpieces of
literature, the reader forgets his cynicism and skepticism,
allowing his imagination to roam freely in the author's
fantastic world and seeking out the special qualities,
powers, and activities of mythical beings *as if* he believed
in them—*as if* they were true to life, and indeed they
must be so in some way in order to be understood.

Thus, note the following passage from *Hamlet,* spoken
by Hamlet as he takes the skull of the former King's
jester Yorick from the grave. Hamlet muses that his
wicked mother, the Queen, will, like the dead jester, some
day die and turn into dust—so what good will her evil
deeds do her then?

> Alas, poor Yorick! I knew him, Horatio: a fellow of
> infinite jest, of most excellent fancy: he hath borne me
> on his back a thousand times; and now, how abhorred
> in my imagination it is! my gorge rises at it. Here hung
> those lips that I have kissed I know not how oft. Where
> be your gibes now? your gambols? your songs? your
> flashes of merriment, that were wont to set the table
> on a roar? * Not one now, to mock your own grinning?
> Quite chap-fallen? ** Now get you to my lady's cham-
> ber, and tell her, let her paint an inch thick, to this
> favour she must come; make her laugh at that. . . .
> (*Hamlet,* Act V, Scene 1)

The alert reader of this magnificent passage must recall
the jolly people who made merry in his childhood years,
now dead and gone—the jolly people who, like Yorick,
were so clever, gifted, playful—who have now, as all men,
become lifeless bones, skulls that cannot grin or jest or

---

* The jesters told their jokes to the guests at the dinner table
and they would roar with laughter.

** A word such as "chap-fallen" puzzles the modern reader or
playgoer (it meant loss of the lower jaw as in the skull) but even
here the sense is lifelike and carries the implication of coming to
a bad end.

frolic again; so, too, will the clever Queen, the vain creature who paints her cheeks thickly, be unable to avoid the same fate; and if she realizes this, perhaps she will not be quite so lighthearted about her dishonor. Notice especially the repetition of reality in the repeated reminders that the dead jester had done so many happy things, yet now is but a horrible, detestable thing of dust —a fate shared by all mankind.

This passage was written by Shakespeare more than 350 years ago, but the reader can understand its universal meanings as he compares them with his own life experiences. As the noted Shakespearean scholar George Lyman Kittredge often reminded his students, Hamlet was not an artificially created type or formula but an individual caught up in the tragedy of his group, the royal house. Hamlet was a man of utmost sensitivity, like people we have all known, and we understand his words as the natural self-expression of such an individual in his life situation. True, not all readers will interpret his character precisely alike, but if they think critically as they read, they will see him as he would be in reality.

The principle of reality permeates social literature in writings and ideas of idealists such as Thomas Paine, Abraham Lincoln, and Ralph Waldo Emerson, in the works of novelists such as Theodore Dreiser, and of reformers such as Henry George. The reader must compare their sentiments with his own background of experience before he can fully appreciate the significance of the truths in their writings. Consider, for example, a few of the statements of these men:

Thomas Paine—"The contrast between affluence and wretchedness is like dead and living bodies chained together." (Works, III, 337)

Abraham Lincoln—"We don't propose any war on capital, we do wish to allow the humblest man an equal chance to get rich with anybody else . . ." (New Haven speech)

Ralph Waldo Emerson—"The highest end of government is the culture of men, not the protection of property rights." (*Essay on Politics*)

> Theodore Dreiser, expressing the philosophy of a character in *The Financier*—"It is a grim, bitter world we are all born into . . . who was to straighten out the matter of unjust equipment with which most people began?"
>
> Henry George—advocating "a rearrangement of the industrial and social system on a higher ethical basis."

When you read and interpret ideas such as these, measure their validity against your own life experience with the people and institutions of your community. We expect authors of fiction to intermingle the real with the fantastic, what exists with the things they dream about, attempting to dress the mixture of fact, illusion, and fantasy with language most appropriate in mood and tone. But even the most imaginative of them put living people into their works—and the most gifted of them have sometimes been sued for portraying persons so realistically as to make them recognizable. On the other hand, too many works of literature are weakened by inclusion of lifeless or unrealistic character portraits. A humorous anecdote circulating in publishers' offices tells about a prospective author who attached a note to his manuscript stating that "the characters in my novel are not real persons and bear no resemblance to any persons living or dead." The publisher's rejection slip contained the brief comment: "That is precisely what is wrong with this manuscript." It is the principle of reality that gives strength and meaning to an author's works, and the expert reader goes back to life itself as a basis for understanding them in depth.

Proportion. Closely related to the principle of reality is that of proportion, which refers to the twofold process of exaggeration and understatement. These qualities in reading material are like magnifying and reducing mirrors held up to the realities of life. The reader must cope with exaggeration and understatement if he wishes to understand the true significance of many ideas.

Exaggeration magnifies reality and attracts the reader's attention to a stated or implied truth. Thus, Cervantes, the author of the powerful novel of the seventeenth century, *Don Quixote,* was enabled to exaggerate reality by making his hero a man driven insane from reading the chivalric tales then universally popular. Those tales relating the exploits of noble knights performing brave deeds are duplicated by Don Quixote as he converts his bony nag into an imaginary handsome charger, the flat-nosed, plain farm girl into a beautiful princess, and a paunchy farmer into his aristocratic squire. All sorts of exaggerated, impossible deeds are thereafter described in a most effective, humorous style by contrasting the theoretical ideals of chivalric literature with the totally contradictory, crushing, sordid realities of the times. The moral implications of this novel paved the way for a new attitude in literature and society—believe what you can see and feel, the world as it is, not the fanciful, never-existing world of your dreams.

Exaggeration is highly effective in stimulating or sharpening the impact of an author's ideas. I recall reading Heinrich Heine's observations about the town of Göttingen when he was leaving the university there after some bitter experiences. He commented that he had admired the beautiful limbs of the Göttingen ladies and had even thought that he might draw pictures of their legs— if he could find paper large enough for that purpose. Exaggeration is more often not quite so direct and pointed, but more indirect and subtle.

The principle of proportion suggests that you should evaluate the extent of exaggeration in reading materials and balance it with its opposite, understatement. The truth will usually lie somewhere between the two extremes. If all horses are noble champions and Don Quixote's nag Rocinante is a horse, then Rocinante is a noble champion despite her old age and bare bones— until you believe the evidence of your own eyes and hands when you see and touch her. You can admire the stubborn hero as he breaks his own ribs in fantastic adventures, and then appreciate fully the disillusionment he suffers when he comes to his senses and realizes the contrast between his visionary world of miracles and the world of evils, follies, injustice, the world as it is. Always, then, the exaggeration in great literature can be traced to the world of reality which it exaggerates. The reader must himself put the author's words and ideas into perspective, into correct proportions, and thus enrich his own understanding of the reading material.

Exaggeration and understatement are legitimate tools and techniques of the news reporter, novelist, essayist, playwright, and poet There is no news in the millions of normal, everyday activities of people; there is news in murder, conflict, fire, catastrophe, the serious problems and difficulties of individual or community. The author selects one aspect of life to portray in his work and necessarily magnifies it while understating competing aspects. If he describes the condition of the poor, he must usually minimize the charities of the rich, for the reader's attention must not be too greatly distributed but must be concentrated upon the main theme. If, on the other hand, he selects aristocrats of a society for his central characters, he cannot portray fully all the customs and problems of the masses. It is your responsibility as an alert reader to put the contents of news reports, novels, plays, poems, into proper balance and proportion. In portraying the evils of slavery, Harriet Beecher Stowe was quite justified in selecting illustrations of cruelty and injustice; in depicting the evils of child labor and the economic system of his time, Charles Dickens did well to emphasize the despicable conditions of the poor and the grasping motives of the wealthy; in describing the evils of tyranny, war, and corruption, creative writers such as Ibsen, Tolstoy, and Upton Sinclair made those aspects of life the principal themes of their works. Few readers read enough to gain a balanced view of life and society from news or literature alone—they must sympathize, understand, but take into account exaggeration and understatement, the principle of proportion.

Momentum. Just as water in a stream flows on and on, so ideas in a novel or discussion seem to possess a forward impulse or momentum of their own. An unscrupulous or careless author gives his readers some facts in sequence, together with partial truths which they tend to accept and which precede untrue ideas tacked on at the end. Truth can easily carry falsehood along with it in the reader's mind. Conversely ideas which seem quite dubious may be rejected by a reader who later cannot accept the truth because he has lost confidence in the author's judgment. The main momentum comes from the accumulation of small ideas which induce the reader to accept larger conclusions or a point of view. Plausible opinions become the foundation of doubtful generalizations. Sometimes the conclusions may be correct and appropriate, but the reader should not assume this to be so. He should weigh and consider, never merely accepting submissively or uncritically the intellectual menu of subtle, one-sided, or superficial reading materials.

Beware of accepting so much of what you read that you begin to worship the printed word, the authority, in essays, newswriting, and fiction. Do not be misled by the momentum of dialogue, plot, or discussion. Pause in your reading to inquire, To what extent is this idea still true and cogent? Has there been a change in premises, events, circumstances? Am I in danger of being brainwashed into acceptance of new ideas because they have been joined with old ones? Why has the writer abandoned some considerations for others, or why has he continued to reiterate a theme or thesis from one stage of the work to another?

The political agitator and the representative of special interests in a society make effective use of the principle of momentum. A candidate or protégé, for example, may be portrayed at his best through a truthful but out-dated account of worthy deeds and self-sacrifice—and then, when the great issue at stake is about to be considered, the reader is inclined to follow in the footsteps of so kindly and self-sacrificing a person, who may be a genuine rascal. The propagandist becomes skilled in relating an abundance of minor facts or details, building the confidence of his readers, who become his victims as they unthinkingly accept his deceit. The reader must protect himself from the momentum of such a stream of ideas by testing them against experience, organizing them into commonsense categories of truths, half-truths, partial falsehoods, complete falsehoods, and questionable statements. The expert reader of literature, too, keeps a sharp eye on characters who behave "in character" and compares them with people in real life situations. Thus, he shows himself to be not only an experienced reader but also a true critic, for the two functions of reading and criticism accompany and complement each other.

In many works of fiction and drama, and in some poetry as well, the accumulation of unresolved dilemmas and complex events and information has the special effect of building psychological tension in the reader. Situations, characters, and unsolved problems multiply, taxing the memory, perhaps threatening to confuse the intellect and overburden the emotions. For this reason the skillful author interrupts the onward sweep of his plot by introducing light dialogue or humor or some diversionary episodes before carrying the central theme forward. If you can read an exciting mystery story or a play with enjoyment in a receptive, unruffled frame of mind despite repeated suspense and climaxes, you should thank the author whose creative artistry has made provision for the relief of mounting tension. Inferior works do not arouse intense feelings as do those masterpieces which require a breathing spell to interrupt the momentum of events. The author who creates a literary masterpiece sustains your interest by keeping you in suspense, absorbed in what is about to happen, just as a composer creates a melody that produces almost unbearable tension so long as it remains unfinished, the tension being relieved when the listener hears a satisfactory ending. Such an author understands and provides for the effects of momentum and the psychological reactions of his readers. His is the work you are likely to appreciate and enjoy.

Analogy. Most works of literature portray characters and situations which remind us of similar characters and situations we have encountered either in life or in our other reading. It has been said that there is nothing new under the sun and that the only new truths are the old ones. Nevertheless, there are also individuality and uniqueness in the creations of competent novelists, playwrights, and poets. As you read a literary work, analyze it to note any resemblance to other works, any similarities and differences between the characters and the people you have known or read about, and those qualities of theme or style which seem to you to be uniquely characteristic of the author.

Thus, in reading the Utopian works of Plato, Sir Thomas More, Francis Bacon, and Edward Bellamy, note the ways in which their ideal societies resemble and differ from one another: for example, the ideal community in Plato's *Republic* was a society of three rigid classes; in More's *Utopia* it meant a communistic life without any classes; in Bacon's vision it was a scientists' paradise; and in Bellamy's goal it was a socialistic commonwealth controlled by the state. Comparisons and contrasts of this kind sharpen critical analyses and deepen the understanding of literature.

Writers often utilize analogy in describing characters or in advocating ideas and points of view. Examine their analogies carefully to decide whether or not they are logically correct and reasonable and whether you should agree, disagree, or reserve judgment. Perhaps the comparison drawn between two people or between a person and some object in nature is actually distorted or unreasonable. Analogies to prove an argument may also be overdrawn or illogical. The writer may compare parental authority with autocratic rule, for instance, and he may ignore or minimize an important difference between the two while advocating that children should not be disciplined by their parents, the implication being that such display of authority would be as reprehensible as arbitrary dictatorship over a people. But an alert reader will notice crucial differences vitiating such analogies; for example, parental authority may be motivated by love of children instead of a desire to dominate over them. Critical readers should analyze analogies, detect special pleading based on faulty comparisons, and put the author's conclusions or implications to the severest test of logic and experience.

Emphasis. A skilled writer gives much more space to the important ideas and events in his work than he does to lesser ones, and the careful reader is expected to appreciate the reasons for these differences in emphasis. Of course, such a quantitative measurement is only a rough approximation and there are exceptions. A brief episode or even a significant brisk remark can sometimes change the entire trend of a plot or theme, especially if it comes at the climax to preceding sections. Nevertheless, unless he tries to evaluate variations in emphasis, the reader may underestimate the key points in a literary work or, for that matter, in any kind of written material. This principle is also applicable to news reports, essays, fiction, poetry, and drama.

In conversation, emphasis becomes apparent when the speaker raises his voice, repeats an idea, or makes use of gestures. (The humorous reference to a gossip who could be kept quiet only by tying her hands has an element of truth in it.) In reading, the author may include these same indications of emphasis indirectly by describing or referring to them, but more commonly the absence of direct clues as to the relative importance of any part compels the reader to search for and evaluate the significant elements. Reading the views of book reviewers and critics or discussion with other readers can often help to illuminate the relative importance of different ideas, characters, and events in a work of literature, but the reader should arrive at his own independent judgment based upon his analysis of the work itself. In some instances, he may feel that the author has overemphasized by excessive, tiresome repetition or superfluous discussion. You should appreciate the author's intent and read his work sympathetically, yet after so doing, feel free to criticize and consider whether a change in emphasis might not have made the work more interesting and true to life. Always the question to ask is: Why did this or that character, episode, idea, or argument receive so much or so little attention and emphasis?

Implication. The experienced author knows how to suggest ideas forcefully to readers without stating them directly. What he writes may carry a significant implication with it, a hint of additional meanings or of possible future events. The reader is expected to read between the lines, accepting impressions and views based upon subtle cues instead of specific information and evidence. Implication can take on a dramatic, evasive form, as in the biblical story of Cain and Abel, in which Cain, having slain Abel his brother, replied to God's query about the whereabouts of Abel, "I know not; am I my brother's keeper?" implying he did not know *because* it was not his duty to watch over his brother. The reply implies much more about Cain's character than a simple direct statement, "I know not," would have revealed. Very often the subtleties in great poetry imply also a wide range of possible interpretations, some of them intricate and almost inexpressible in words. The sensitive poet's choice of words, rhythm, imagery, alliteration, and sequence of ideas, and his use of repetition, contrast, and allusion all contribute to the total effect of his implied moods and meanings.

By striving to explore the implications of an author's words, the reader adds the power of his own imagination and in effect participates in bringing the work to a satisfying conclusion or state of effectiveness. An example of a simple conclusion implied by the ideas of a fictional character is the following paragraph from *Huckleberry Finn*, which implies that prayer is only a gesture in futility—a point of view which Mark Twain himself shared:

> I says to myself, if a body can get anything they pray for, why don't Deacon Winn get back the money he lost on pork? Why can't the widow get back her silver snuffbox that was stole? Why can't Miss Watson fat up? No, says I to myself, there ain't nothing in it. I went and told the widow about it, and she said the thing a body could

get by praying for it was "spiritual gifts." This was too many for me, but she told me what she meant—I must help other people, and look out for them all the time, and never think about myself. This was including Miss Watson, as I took it. I went out in the woods and turned it over in my mind a long time, but I couldn't see no advantage about it—except for other people; so at last I reckoned I wouldn't worry about it any more, but just let it go.

Mark Twain stated the same conclusion explicitly in his own notebook, as follows:

I do not believe in special providences. I believe that the universe is governed by strict and immutable laws. If one man's family is swept away by a pestilence and another man's is spared it is only the law working: God is not interfering in that small matter, either against the one man or in favor of the other. . . . If I break . . . moral laws I cannot see how I injure God by it, for He is beyond the reach of injury by me—I could as easily injure a planet by throwing mud at it. (A. B. Paine, *Mark Twain: A Biography*)

The words of Huck Finn which imply the author's disbelief in prayer are more persuasive than Twain's own statement. What an author implies in the words of his characters can be more convincing than what he directly states.

ANALYSIS OF PROPAGANDA

Propaganda is the use of language to influence the minds of men. Its most gullible victims are those readers who have developed excessive confidence in the printed word. The expert reader recognizes propaganda in many kinds of reading materials and knows how to deal with it. He reads critically in self-defense and depends upon his own earnest analysis and judgment before accepting ideas or conclusions.

Propagandists may be well-intentioned. But even gifted, sincere writers can misinterpret our world, sometimes more than those of us who read their eloquent words with admiration. I recall writing to the eminent playwright

George Bernard Shaw for his interpretation of Nazi totalitarianism and for suggestions to prevent its spread, and he replied (June 2, 1934) that he sympathized with Mr. Hitler "on nearly every point except the quaint notions of ethnology and biology which he seems to have picked up at an impressionable age from Houston Chamberlain's fascinating and suggestive but fundamentally imaginative and unhistorical work called The Foundations of the Nineteenth Century." True, Hitler was undoubtedly misled by his reading of the Chamberlain propaganda, but if a keen student of the human condition like Shaw could also be so tragically deceived by Hitler's own propaganda into misinterpreting political and social realities, obviously we, being less experienced interpreters, must take special care not to be similarly misled into making grave errors of judgment. It is far better to doubt all works and ideas than it would be to accept them blindly, better to analyze than to swallow uncritically, better to dissect than to embrace without prudent investigation and critical evaluation.

During the 1930s and 1940s, pioneering studies in the analysis of propaganda were contributed by Professor Clyde R. Miller of Columbia University, who had inaugurated courses in this field at the university and had later served as a founder and secretary of the Institute for Propaganda Analysis. Dr. Miller summarized seven basic propaganda devices in his *The Process of Persuasion* as card-stacking, name-calling, glittering generality, transfer, testimonial, plain folks, and bandwagon—devices which have been widely accepted as the most common techniques of the propagandist.

Dr. Miller's list of devices may be explained as follows: *cardstacking*, arranging plausible assertions in a sequence to trap the reader into accepting them and rejecting contrary statements; *name-calling*, attaching a contemptuous label to a proposition, thereby inducing the reader to reject it; *glittering generality*, making a flat assertion or broad assumption repeated as often as necessary to impel acceptance without critical analysis; *transfer*, associating the reputation of a respected person, tradition, or institution with propaganda so that readers will be inclined to accept it; *testimonial,* citing the approval of authorities to induce acceptance of propaganda; *plain folks,* making an appeal based on the desire of readers to follow the traditional practices and ideas of their group and thus avoid eccentric or exceptional behavior; *bandwagon,* making an appeal to join the winning team or crowd in their acceptance of propaganda.

There are several ways to analyze propaganda. We may consider the subject from the points of view of the sociologist, the psychologist, and the linguist, respectively. The sociologist investigates the use of propaganda as a means of controlling social institutions and public opinion and policy. The psychologist seeks to track down the effects of propaganda upon the thinking and behavior of individuals. The linguist studies the language of propaganda as a method of persuasion. Readers will be better prepared to cope with propagandist writings if they become familiar with all three points of view towards propaganda.

The Sociology of Propaganda. Language is essential to human association and survival. The members of any society must exchange information and share ideas by oral or written communication. Such exchange and sharing are part of the normal process of satisfying elementary human wants. Propaganda surpasses commonplace types of communication and applies forceful, convincing language to influence people and control their reactions. To accomplish these purposes, the propagandist attracts the serious attention of his audience, sustains their favorable interest in his message, which he must make as clear, simple, and emphatic as possible, and presents assertions and evidence which will appeal to the recipients and be accepted by them as means of attaining their own goals.

Sources of Propaganda. In assessing the impact of propaganda upon ourselves, we need to know the sources from which such materials emanate. We are in danger of becoming innocent victims unless we investigate these sources and their output. The first question to ask, then, is, from the sociologist's point of view: Who are the propagandists?

Propaganda is constantly being poured into newspapers, periodicals, pamphlets, and books by all sorts of groups, including business associations, unions, political parties, government agencies, civic associations, international organizations, and the professions. Fortunately, publishers have been on the alert to prevent censorship and to maintain a free press as a marketplace of competing information and ideas. The reporting of every conceivable type of news and opinion makes it possible for readers to evaluate all points of view in printed materials without restriction—if they take the time and trouble to do so. On the other hand, publishers must attract their audiences and at the same time retain the goodwill of merchants and advertisers. As a consumer of the printed word, therefore, it is up to the reader to strike a balance between no-truths, half-truths, and whole truths, without swallowing extremist doctrines which may have a superficial appeal because of their dogmatic simplicity. Readers of newspapers cannot expect them to disclose that a particular advertisement is concealing facts or that a news handout by the government is self-serving, incomplete, or inaccurate. They need the built-in protection of their own reading attitudes and skills. They need to understand, evaluate, and counteract the principal techniques of the propagandist, yet they must be just and fair to his point of view.

Consider, for example, the propaganda for and against the legal and medical professions, whose honorable traditions and service to mankind go back to antiquity. Today, attorneys and physicians are sensitive to criticism, for they prefer to handle mischievous procedures quietly, "within the club." Consequently, the public has too often formed a low opinion of these professions, generally unaware that the medical societies and bar associations have been working very diligently to eradicate shortcomings and bring everyday practices into conformity with the highest ethical standards. The public does not hear about these constructive efforts, but only about cases in which a successful plaintiff obtained little compensation for his serious injury or losses and expenses while his lawyer received an excellent return without substantial service of any kind. The public knows little about the heavy overhead costs of attorneys, the wasted time because of court congestion, delays by ingenious opposing counsel, and the lack of dependable employees, and sees only that the system of law and justice has become inefficient, expensive, and sometimes even corrupt, that the wealthy man willing to pay an experienced, clever attorney has an advantage over the less affluent citizen. Justice is at best dubious under these circumstances.

It may be true that the majority of persons defeated or convicted in court proceedings deserve their fate, but this defense of inefficiency does not satisfy the critical reader, who knows that persons with limited means cannot employ numerous investigators and attorneys to represent them, that such persons, in civil cases, compete with powerful adversaries, that innocent persons, in criminal cases, are often convicted owing to insufficient funds for investigators and skilled counsel or actual neglect and negligence by disinterested counsel, that if convicted such persons frequently are unable to appeal or to prove extenuating circumstances and good character, and therefore often receive severe penalties (imprisonment for minor offenses is not unknown) while wealthy defendants delay or even defy justice with impunity. Leaders in the profession are among the first to point out that the judicial system should not be turned into a one-sided affair in which justice (ideally depicted as blind to artificial conditions) depends upon the individual's power, influence, class, or race—wealth or status—in society.

The propaganda of physicians, who are also reluctant to publicize the evils afflicting their profession, is likely to be as one-sided as the propaganda directed against their profession. Medical education has been costly, and physicians resent interference by the public which might endanger their opportunity to recoup substantial investments in medical education and might impede their efforts to serve their patients expertly while enjoying that high standard of material comfort which they deserve. Concerning an admitted shortage of skilled physicians, they point out correctly that reduced fees and lower earnings would merely discourage talented young people from entering the profession. Well-trained doctors possess considerable technical knowledge and useful means of diagnosis and therapy, and many of them attempt to practice the ethical standards of their calling, to put service to patients ahead of their own gain and convenience. Nevertheless, the medical professions are plagued with conditions of scarcity of qualified personnel, excessive costs and fees, overwork, and poor rapport with patients, who, in turn, tend to regard the physician as a businessman waiting to be paid handsomely by insured clients or by government agencies. Even those increasing numbers of dedicated doctors who employ adequate skills and medicines carefully and effectively are extremely busy and often fail to inform patients about the details of the medicines being prescribed under brand names or the accomplishments and problems of the profession. Some physicians depend on a mysterious air of busy authority to impress their patients, who eventually grow suspicious and resentful. Millions of people resort to self-treatment or to quackery. Other millions are simply careless, irresponsible victims, including six million alcoholics and multitudes of drug addicts, ignoring or rejecting medical advice, apparently willing to risk chronic illness from obesity, smoking, drinking, or other selfabuses. The reader should consider these sad realities when reading propaganda against physicians as well as the defensive propaganda of the profession.

MOTIVES FOR PROPAGANDA. Readers need to consider not only who are the propagandists but also what are their motives for the dissemination of propaganda. In the case of business organizations the motive is one of profit-making, and that can be a quite worthy one if based on honorable standards of conduct. It is most regrettable and dangerous, however, when propaganda is devised to protect the power and increase the profits of unethical enterprises.

Thus, the American public has long been disturbed by the high incidence of automobile accident fatalities— a total of 56,000 annually. Many causes have been cited for this appalling situation, such as drunken driving, improperly constructed roads, incompetent or careless or discourteous drivers, and defective automobiles or tires. When the writer Ralph Nader investigated the situation and attributed many of the accidents to unsafe vehicles, a leading automobile manufacturer attempted to silence him. Detectives were employed to observe Mr. Nader and report any behavior which might be used to discredit his reputation or compel him to cease his criticisms of the industry. When this effort at censorship was exposed, the American reader became fully aware of Mr. Nader's sincerity and the real motives behind the manufacturer's activities—the willingness to go to any lengths to protect profits even at the cost of thousands of lives sacrificed because of defective vehicles. Eventually the federal government required automobile manufacturers to make public periodic reports concerning hundreds of thousands of defective cars recalled for repair. Alert readers will henceforth have no confidence in the pronouncements of automobile manufacturers, and this consequence will be most unfortunate, for certainly the industry as a whole does not wish to deceive its millions of customers. Like most other business enterprises, that industry can remain prosperous and still tell the truth, the whole truth, while earning handsome profits for shareholders, paying satisfactory wages to employees, and saving thousands of lives annually by admitting deficiencies and taking appropriate remedial action, such as manufacturing much sturdier, safer vehicles, going far beyond the very few standards set by slow-moving government agencies.

Readers can, if they will, detect the motives and nullify the efforts of propagandists. Thus they know that the leaders of political parties aim to control appointments and to obtain lucrative contracts or other favors from elected candidates; that the managers of large corporations and their advertising agencies are interested in increasing sales and profits; that labor organizations attempt to win public support for higher wages and to increase their membership; that universities issue rosy reports about their services and plans in order to extract funds from alumni; that the directors of health associations publish half-truths about accomplishments or potentialities in the hope that additional money, prestige, and public support will enable them to expand their enterprises. Readers cannot expect such propagandists to disclose their wasteful practices, shortcomings, or mistakes. Many worthy causes suffer because skeptical readers have become resistant to all propaganda. More and more readers are becoming immune to the tons of propaganda, good, partly good, or evil, to which they are constantly being subjected. Increasingly, they demand, and should demand, an answer to the question, *What have you, the propagandist, really accomplished for the betterment of conditions?*

The Psychology of Propaganda. Masterpieces of literature influence the reader through appeals to his emotions as well as to his reason. They awaken in him sympathy, admiration, or pity for the characters being portrayed, and often feelings of wonder, pleasure, or gratification from reading about places and events in such works. But there is no attempt to mislead the reader with half-truths, concealment of facts, or deliberate falsehoods. On the contrary, the creative writer exposes his fictitious characters to the light of day and invites the reader to explore the truth, the whole truth, about people, places, and events. Quite different are the motives and techniques of the propagandist, who deliberately attempts to arouse in the reader emotions of fear or excessive pride, feelings of inferiority or superiority, anger, envy, hatred, uncertainty, and frustration, thus easily beguiling him to accept fallacies or irrational views.

THE APPEAL TO AUTHORITY. A reader burdened with a feeling of inferiority is likely, for example, to be susceptible to propaganda based on authority. Approval by an authority makes him more confident about his own ideas. When I was a young student, I was often guilty of accepting some idea merely because an "eminent" person had approved it. But one eminent philosopher, Ralph Barton Perry, of Harvard University, cured me of that habit by asking for my authority and then asking who would be the authority for that authority. He pointed out that such an appeal would carry us back to an endless list of authorities and would leave no time for examination of the idea itself. It is true, of course, that ideas developed by people highly experienced in a relevant field of knowledge are worthy of the reader's attention, but never are they worthy of acceptance without criticism, investigation, and independent judgment. On most subjects there are conflicting authorities, none of whom is always right about everything. The expert in one field is often sadly mistaken in another. Beware, too, of the propagandist who cites common knowledge in support of his idea, beginning with "As everyone knows, such and such is the case." He is appealing to your natural desire to behave like all other intelligent people by accepting his statements, which may actually consist of half-truths or false assertions rejected by most people.

Authorities such as physicians and other professionals seem to be particularly susceptible to the propaganda of their own authorities. An amusing consequence of the blind acceptance of medical authority is related in Molière's comedy, *Love Is a Doctor*, in which it is reported that a sick coachman has suddenly died. But the physician in attendance refused to believe that his patient had died and had been buried, for the patient had been ill for only six days and, according to the great authority Hippocrates, such an illness could not end during the first thirteen days. "Well, well," was the commonsense reply, "Hippocrates or no Hippocrates, the coachman is dead."

FLATTERY. Flattery is another common technique of the clever propagandist. This appeal is effective among readers with a feeling of superiority. They like to be flattered because flattery reinforces their claim to superior intelligence. Hitler's propaganda was based on this appeal addressed to the German people, who felt that they were superior human beings constituting a "master race." In such propaganda the readers are reminded of their "special" virtues, power, and knowledge and praised for their ability to understand and appreciate the propagandist's ideas. The propagandist implies that only a select group will really be able to comprehend the full significance of his views, but that you, the superior reader, will of course understand everything without difficulty, even though you are only one among many thousands of his readers, all of whom are being reminded that they are superior to others and particularly to all "outsiders," or foreigners, or opponents. Flattery works too often because you the reader may at the time be perhaps weary of problems, susceptible to being patted on the shoulder by someone whose words will pacify you, provide some carefree illusion, and strengthen your self-assurance. The alert reader should detect flattery promptly and resist such an ingenious attempt to stifle his power of independent judgment.

GULLIBILITY. There are many other psychological appeals used by propagandists. For example, the newspaper columnist may try to form an intellectual partnership with readers, taking them into his confidence by revealing "secret" information shared only with millions of other readers; the politician may appeal to the readers' feelings of generosity and sympathy, confessing that his proposal is not perfect but the best he has been able to do so far; the advertising genius may inform readers that for years some lady endured illness and pain until suddenly a neighbor introduced her to the remarkable headache powder being advertised—so, you readers, too, can be cured with the same patent medicine. The propagandist who wants to shake the confidence of the reader in some idea may humbly confess that he used to think that way, too, but changed his mind as a result of hard experience. Contradictory arguments may be presented to confuse the reader until he is ready to accept a one-sided, plausible conclusion. The reader's best protection against all these psychological appeals of the propagandist is the intellectual armor of complete skepticism, perhaps best expressed in the challenging retort, *I'm from Missouri; show me!*

Of course, writers often make legitimate, constructive use of psychological appeals. Thus, I have myself frankly confessed youthful adherence to erroneous notions since abandoned, and there is no harm in so informing sympathetic readers and encouraging emulation. At one time I was even gullible enough to accept the absurd claim of a prominent advertising-oriented psychologist that his then unique attempts to associate a product being advertised with the subconscious longings and psychological susceptibilities of consumers were morally justifiable. I was gullible enough to edit and publish his book explaining the techniques he used. In later years I realized that it is ethically wrong to advertise a soap by appealing to the reader's nobility of soul, his faith in chastity and purity as exemplified by the whiteness of the soap, for I knew that the competing soaps were quite as good though not so pure in color. Confessing my mistake, I trusted that confession is good for the soul and good for the dissemination of the truth.

PROPAGANDA FOR PROPAGANDA. One defense offered for the use of ingenious, misleading psychological appeals in propaganda and advertising is the assertion that the public is getting only what it wants or is willing to accept. The question arises, If readers display poor taste in books, for instance, is that because trashy materials have popularized low standards, or are the trashy materials being made available because many readers have already developed low standards otherwise and now demand them? Both views are probably partly true. But I am reminded of those automobile manufacturers who produce costly oversized unsafe cars which they advertise through psychological appeals to the consumer based on his feeling of superiority over his neighbors, thus reinforcing his reprehensible attitude (often a form of compensation for repressed feelings of insecurity and inferiority). Then the same manufacturers have the effrontery to claim that they are merely giving the consumer what he wants and demands from them! If the reader of offensive advertisements of this kind can be made to realize what the advertisers are trying to do— beguile him by taking advantage of his psychological weaknesses—and if he can become sufficiently skeptical and fact-minded, a critical reader, he will perhaps turn away from the advertisements and also reject the misrepresented products advertised. He will then get what he really wants and needs, namely, honest, full information in advertisements and genuinely superior products at reasonable prices.

Not all advertising is deceptive; nevertheless, the reader should always be skeptical enough to detect abuses. In this respect the book industry has an exceptionally good record. Publishers have generally observed high standards in the publication and promotion of literature. In response to the expectations and discriminating tastes of experienced readers, they continually strive to improve their product as well as their advertising appeals. There are many conscientious writers and ethical advertisers and distributors of books. A great deal of the writing in newspapers, journals, and books is well-intentioned, constructive, and well-balanced, even when it includes emphatic appeals to the reader's pride and sympathies. As for the hucksters, in the last analysis if enough readers become aware of what the propagandists are attempting to accomplish and analyze their appeals severely, there will soon be an end to the flood of one-sided, deceptive, "mismotivated" forms of propaganda and advertising.

The Language of Propaganda. The propagandist influences readers by means of language skills applied in accordance with a definite strategy. He takes into account the sad immoral conditions of the time, knowing that many people have become so accustomed to deceiving others and to being deceived by others that a truly honest appeal would come as a shock, something almost unbelievable. He can always count on enough psychologically weak or gullible victims to bring him considerable success.

FAMILIAR DEVICES. Among the age-old language devices still in wide use are those of repetition of statements without evidence; exaggeration; understatement of opposing views; diversion of critical thought through humor or sarcasm; and omission of facts. When the skilled propagandist repeats an idea, he varies the words to avoid monotony and to convince more readers, for he knows that some words will appeal to one reader while others will convince another. Exaggeration and understatement are not overdone, but are applied gradually and subtly; so, too, are humor and sarcasm, which might otherwise distract the reader's attention from the propaganda message. Omission of unfavorable information must often be accompanied by extensive discussion of the propagandist's own proposition in order to obscure or conceal the omissions.

OTHER LINGUISTIC TRICKS. Misquoting is another old device, especially effective when statements are taken out of context to change the original meaning of the quote. Ambiguous or vague statements often help to deceive readers—for example, statements about merchandise being "guaranteed or your money back," when there is no elucidation of what the guarantee covers. Dubious, unproved assertions are used as the basis for unjustifiable conclusions, as, for instance, in the statements: "The tax rate in our town is unfair. If the new schools are built, the unbearable taxes will never be reduced." (Note that *unfair* in the first sentence becomes *unbearable* in the second.) In such ambiguities, two of the most common misused words are *because* and *average*. The fact that night follows day does not mean that night causes day, but the propagandist often mixes up cause and mere sequence. An average is misleading unless fully explained: thus, if one man earns $10 while another earns $50, the average is $30, but the statement that the average earnings are $30 is misleading, since neither man earns anything like that amount. Readers need to be always alert to counteract these linguistic tricks of the propagandist.

The Miseducation of Propagandists. The propagandist's deceitful habits are learned chiefly in the home and community. Schools and colleges do what they can to raise standards of language usage, but in general they have been more successful in teaching future propagandists to master the linguistic tools of their trade than they have been in teaching them the ethical use of such tools.

Of course, the strategy of modern propagandists and hucksters is nothing new. It is the same as the very ancient strategy of all scoundrels throughout history, as expressed and advocated by Machiavelli in *The Prince* (1532) when he advised rulers to be cunning like a fox, never honest or compassionate, or faithful, humane, or sincere, but always to seem so, for that is the way to convince people that their leader is a good person who means them well. To become a successful leader, you must be a hypocrite and dissembler, said Machiavelli, for that is the only way to control the minds of the people, who are simple-minded souls unable to see beyond their noses. He assumed, moreover, that the common people are themselves greedy and corrupt and that they would betray their leaders and one another, too, if they could get away with it. He said that the ruler should therefore never hesitate to mislead them into believing him to be a saint, for very few would be clever enough to discover his true character, and the masses would richly deserve their fate. Today the propagandist is merely implementing Machiavelli's advice in a sophisticated way, taking advantage of troubled minds and misusing the ideas of psychologists such as Pavlov, Adler, and Freud. Indeed, the deceitful strategy of the propagandist has become universal throughout the occupations and human relationships of our society. It is the primary cause of man's persistent problems of war, poverty, and crime, and the true cause of the revolt of idealistic youth against the institutions, standards, and customs of the older generation.

5

How To Discover
The Truth

Reading is a primary road to learning, to the discovery of the truth. The spoken word is useful, but it is fleeting, quickly heard and gone, replaced by other words. But printed words remain at the reader's disposal, waiting to be understood, and are subject to repeated examination and interpretation. Many spoken words are impromptu, often thoughtless or unfounded, whereas printed words reflect the author's experience and technical skill. Therefore careful reading of newspapers, journals, and books can mold the minds and enrich the personalities of old and new generations alike.

The cause of reading has its foes and friends, its roadblocks and gateways to learning the truth. Among the roadblocks are censorship, misinformation, and habits of uncritical reading. Among the friends who hold open the gateways to learning are the libraries and bookstores, the governmental, social, and scientific organizations, and the schools and universities. These friends of reading are the promoters of light and knowledge pitted against the forces of darkness and ignorance.

CENSORSHIP

Censorship represents the authoritarian view that certain individuals should decide what is best for other people to read and, therefore, to think and believe.

Censorship is based on the notion that self-appointed or selected authorities should prescribe limits on the freedom to write and to read, deciding what is good and pure and wholesome for all. They are to be the maîtres d'hôtel who present us with an intellectual menu from which we as humble diners are to make a choice under their watchful supervision.

What would happen if censors could eventually discover what is truly good and pure and what is evil and impure in the realm of ideas and could then compel us to accept their decisions? If all our books thereafter contained only good and pure ideas and information, would corruption, greed, and falsehood be eliminated? If not, then our purified books would deprive us of any means of learning about such evils as they exist in our world and thus any hope of evaluating and rejecting loathsome ideas and practices. Since these purified books would give us a distorted view of the world, quite contrary to life as it exists in our society, they would only teach us untruths, misleading us, and there would be no value in reading them.

From the earliest years of childhood, the minds of men are molded by models in their homes and communities. The feignedly pious, self-deceiving parent who would suppress the thoughts of children, as of adults, is the very person who sets an example of autocracy, unreasonableness, deceit, and hypocrisy. It is he who needs to be re-educated so that he will think critically as he reads and will teach his children to develop critical judgment and self-direction. Guidance and good example are essential, but any form of censorship is a confession of the failure of society to produce a generation of honest, critical readers qualified to discriminate between wholesome and corrupt literature.

Some well-intentioned people, believing that "evil" writings may increase a reader's tendency to commit immoral or criminal acts advocate censorship by government agencies. These well-meaning persons mistakenly assume that prohibition will improve character or prevent the deterioration of character. On the contrary, repression destroys every possibility of character development. Guidance toward discovery, and acceptance, of the truth builds character. Books must not be distortions; they must reveal all the good and evil in society if readers are to learn anything from them and if there is to be any hope of social improvement.

If large numbers of the population prefer slipshod, salacious, or dishonest newspapers, journals, films, and books, this is a danger signal indeed, a warning not that repressive laws must be passed but that the real causes of deceit and depravity must be revealed and counteracted, causes such as commercial greed, excessive competition for profits, injustice, parental and educational neglect, poverty, and, above all, hypocrisy—that observable contrast between national ideals and collective behavior, the same hypocrisy that argues for the censorship of books. Let the censors therefore seal their own lips and censor themselves instead of attempting to control the minds of their equals or betters in our society—the creative minds of writers and the critical minds of alert readers.

If there is censorship anywhere, there can be no faith in literature, no opportunity for the reader to evaluate literature and decide for himself the genuine worth of printed materials. Under censorship there can be no critical, intelligent reading and therefore no honest, intelligent citizenship. The existence of censorship in any community is a barometer of its lack of culture, a shameful proclamation that its adult citizens cannot be trusted to discriminate intelligently, to think straight, to display good taste, to live decently, and to grow in the power of critical reading.

In the books of the Holy Bible, the ancient prophets of Israel presented the facts of evil together with the good, including obscenity, venality, treachery, violence, treason, human sacrifice, idolatry, murder, adultery, and almost every conceivable crime. These were to be taken to heart by youth and adults alike. The founders of the United States of America realized that all men must have freedom to seek the truth and to know and reject evil, and that meant absolute freedom to write and to read anything in the realm of ideas. They inserted a guarantee in the Constitution, forbidding any law "abridging the freedom of speech, or of the press," for they had studied history and had also had experience with oppressive authorities threatening to control their minds and institutions. The language of the United States Constitution is simple, unqualified, precise, unmistakable in meaning and intent. It does not say, as can be pointed out to fearful lawmakers and jurists, that freedom of the press can be abridged if the writing is accompanied by salacious advertising or base appeals to depraved tastes. It says in plain language anyone can understand that there shall be no abridgment whatever, that is to say, no political control over the communication of ideas, so that even speech or writing widely considered harmful to the state must be tolerated. To forbid a single word of an individual means to abridge the freedom of speech or press of all citizens. The Constitution does not forbid some reasonable regulation of the time or place for public speeches, but it does forbid all regulations which prevent anyone from expressing his ideas to anyone else willing to listen or read. (Legally, freedom of the press carries with it the freedom to read, for there would be no writing at all without readers. Communication of ideas is meaningless unless the audience has freedom to hear or to read them.)

The proper alternative to repressive censorship is to encourage by purchase and merited acclaim the publication of more and more good books which people will insist on reading and evaluating for themselves. The heavy hand of censorship smothers the minds of men, deprives them of the intellectual air which they must have for mental development, and stifles their independent thinking. Even the young need abundant opportunity to detect evil and replace it with wholesome experience, to develop taste and appreciation by critically evaluating, within the limits of their growing capacity, and for valid reasons rejecting falsehood, partial truths, depravity, greed, and bigotry. Only those men who read and analyze ideas without restrictions can be trusted to despise evil and to develop high standards of judgment and morality. When men have too often been deprived of the right and opportunity to evaluate ideas, they behave stupidly or irrationally and accept like sheep such despicable evils as censors and censorship. Freedom to write and to read as we please is the cornerstone of our democratic way of life.

Certain legal experts have sometimes defended a limited censorship of speech and press by asserting irrelevant arguments, such as, "No one has the right to shout 'Fire!' in a crowded theater," or "No one has a right to print a libel or endanger the safety of the nation." All such arguments are deliberate evasions of the issue and bear no pertinence whatever to our constitutional guarantees of free speech and a free press, which protect the right of all the people to hear and read any ideas about their institutions and mode of society, without limitation, and to judge for themselves which ideas are worth considering or accepting as the basis for public policy, taste, and preference. Freedom of speech and freedom of the press have nothing to do with using a printed page to set fire (directly or indirectly) to a theater, with defaming the character or invading the privacy of a citizen. They are basic rights which must not be restricted, and those who would in any degree abridge them—whether lowly demagogues or high jurists—show little faith in the judgments of the people and truly endanger the cause of freedom and the nation itself.

MISINFORMATION

Incorrect information is often partly true. Propagandists, for example, spice false assertions with a little truth, sweeten the bitter with a bit of honey. But misinformation can be spread innocently, carelessly, by other writers as well. Certain types of evasion and deception have become fashionable and so common that readers need to be always on guard to counteract them, even in such ordinary material as weather reports. Direct predictions of rain or sunshine, of warm and sunny weather, or of cold and wet weather, are a thing of the past. Today the weather reports indicate that there is a 10 percent chance of rain, or that it will be partly cloudy, or partly sunny. Such predictions can scarcely be wrong. If it rains, the 10 percent chance of rain has happened; if it does not rain, the 90 percent chance of fair weather has come to pass. The weather reporter should give us the old-type honest prediction, "It will rain tomorrow," and if it does not rain, frankly admit his error.

Not only weather reports and routine news announcements but more important official government statements can be quite misleading. I recall preparing a research study about the educational system of a foreign country, depending heavily upon information supplied by its government. Later I discovered that the data could not possibly be correct, for no combination of the statistics added up to the required totals. I wrote to the foreign consulate about the discrepancies as well as various contradictions between the alleged facts and broad conclusions in the government literature, and was eventually informed that all the errors and deficiencies were due entirely to clerical mistakes! In most countries, there is a lack of information about innumerable matters and guesswork is unavoidable, but it should be labelled as estimates, not as verifiable truths.

It is unfortunate that most readers do not have an opportunity to consult original sources. Information is apt to be secondhand, borrowed by careless writers from reliable scientific and professional journals, but taken out of context and distorted in newspapers or magazines, much to the dismay of the original investigators. Scientific publications report thousands of preliminary researches or experiments in the fields of health and medicine, psychology, and physical sciences. Then reporters and feature writers eager to attract more readers select those reports which can be converted into spectacular news. It is no wonder that readers are becoming disillusioned about all such information, for they read about highly-promising, sensational new developments and discoveries, yet never hear about them again. Critical-minded readers no longer believe such reports, not even those with little exaggeration, for they have been too often misled. Readers have grown more and more skeptical; before accepting stories about significant contributions to human well-being, they demand evidence, particularly the scientist's own statements about his work, which always contain cautious qualifications and reservations. Alert readers analyze all news accounts carefully and in most instances are compelled to conclude that there is little of value in sensational reports.

UNCRITICAL READING

It may seem odd to assert that a great deal of misinformation is manufactured by the reader himself while he is reading. Ask several people to read a news report about some controversial subject, and after reading it they will give you a variety of interpretations. Each will omit what is of little interest to him, emphasize what he likes, and slight or perhaps ignore the important points he dislikes or disbelieves. To read critically, you must look within yourself, become aware of your own bias or assumptions, and interpret the material, not as a means of reinforcing your past prejudices and conclusions, but as a method of discovering what the writer really intended you to learn from his words.

Uncritical reading results in misconceptions, misinterpretations, of the author's ideas. Not only is the ordinary reader too often guilty of hasty conclusions because he fails to study the author's work, but even the best-known literary critics and book reviewers have sometimes been rightly accused of failure to read thoroughly and carefully. Not all reviewers have the necessary time and patience to give books the comprehensive analysis they deserve; some betray their trust, reading only a few pages to obtain a partial or incorrect view of a book, and on this basis recommend or disparage it. The best reviewers, however, insist upon reading and rereading a book before evaluating it. They feel an obligation to guide their audience wisely and strive to provide a well-balanced appraisal. Every reader should follow the example of such reviewers by asking himself what is new, old, unusual, good, bad, most provocative and interesting in their reading material. Fortunate is the reader who finds sufficient reason in his reading to modify his own ideas, for that is evidence of value received, the most that any author can do for his readers.

LIBRARIES AND BOOKSTORES

The most useful things in the world are free, such as loyal friends, peace of mind, agreeable conversation, appreciation of music and art, and the opportunity to read fine books in public libraries. Next to the books you own and treasure, those in the public library can be the greatest source of pleasure and fulfillment. The library is the foremost gateway to freedom and truth. Do you make full use of your library?

Library Resources. Currently the number of libraries in the United States exceeds 28,000, of which nearly 12,000 are free public libraries of local communities. There are thousands of school, college, and university libraries, as well as more than 5,000 special libraries, including medical, technical, industrial, business, and miscellaneous private libraries. The largest library is the Library of Congress, with its 13½ million books and pamphlets; next to the largest is the New York Public Library, with its 7½ million books. These two libraries alone possess more books than most nations have at their disposal. Very few countries have free public library systems comparable to those in the United States on the basis of population, although substantial library facilities are readily accessible to readers at little or no cost in the British and Scandinavian countries. The Soviet Union is reported to have as many as 400,000 libraries, among which are the Lenin State Library with 15 million books and pamphlets, the Leningrad Public Library with 10 million books, and the library of the Academy of Sciences with 8 million volumes. The Soviet libraries are, of course, state institutions which must provide many millions of copies of books for the dissemination of state political doctrines; nevertheless, the current reported total of nearly 2 billion volumes represents a remarkable achievement.

Readers who use typical American public libraries are provided with stimulating ideas and information, quiet relaxation, and communion with gifted authors, past and present, representing all conceivable points of view. Library materials include all sorts of periodicals and pamphlets, historical documents, government publications, and educational, recreational, and reference books. The library usually has comfortable accommodations for reading, convenient procedures to borrow books, and competent guidance and advice for readers. Books are classified into groups corresponding to ten subject areas covering all fields of knowledge so that any reader can easily find information in philosophy, psychology, religion, all the social sciences, philology, science, the useful arts, the fine arts, literature, and history, as well as miscellaneous sources, such as encyclopedias. Many libraries participate in a regional system, so that books not available in one library can easily be obtained for the reader from some other library in the system. Most readers can find the materials they need either in or through their nearby library, but if they cannot do so on occasion, they can always inquire where the desired information may be obtained. Thus, if you wish reports of researches in a special field, such as health or medicine, the librarian can usually give you the names and addresses of specialized journals or associations to which you can write for such reports.

Periodical indexes in the library—for example, the *Reader's Guide to Periodical Literature* (for 100 American and Canadian journals) and the *International Index* (for over 250 American and foreign scholarly journals)—index articles in magazines. There are various subject indexes, such as the *Education Index* (for teachers). There are indexes to all the news reported in the *New York Times*. Valuable information about books can be found in the *Book Review Digest*, which reprints excerpts from reviewers' comments about current books. Encyclopedias, such as the *Britannica, Americana, Colliers, Columbia, Grolier Universal,* and *World Book,* are filled with useful information, as are certain widely used reference books, namely, *Statistical Abstracts* (for data about United States institutions, business, etc.), the *Statesmen's Yearbook* (for data about foreign countries), the *World Almanac,* the *New York Times Encyclopedic Almanac,* and the *Information Please Almanac,* and numerous gazetteers, atlases, dictionaries, travel guidebooks, and reference books about reference books (such as the excellent volume, *Basic Reference Books,* by Louis Shores). *Webster's Geographical Dictionary, Webster's Biographical Dictionary,* Edward C. Smith and Arnold J. Zurcher's *Dictionary of American Politics,* and Harold S. Sloan and Arnold J. Zurcher's *Dictionary of Economics* are particularly useful sources of accurate data. There can be no reason for American readers to complain about the accessibility of information and ideas in the public libraries.

Librarians have been in the forefront in the continuous battle for the right of citizens to read whatever they please. Bookstores, too, defend this basic American principle, but sometimes booksellers are plagued with narrowminded, prejudiced individuals who have so little faith in the American way of freedom that they object to the sale of books with which they disagree. Occasionally booksellers may withdraw such books because they must earn a profit to remain in business and they fear the loss of trade—though most booksellers refuse to yield to this form of intellectual blackmail. Rare indeed is the librarian who will bow to such un-American pressures. The librarians welcome books expressing many different points of view and will generally be pleased to order controversial books requested by readers if sufficient funds are made available for this purpose.

Libraries, together with bookstores and schools, are an accurate reflection of the moral and intellectual health of a community. All these cultural institutions indicate a respect for knowledge, for the truth, for the dignity and worth of the individual—respect of the people for each other and for humanity as a whole. We must beware of any community, and hold its people in contempt of the good opinion of mankind, if it deprives libraries of necessary resources while supporting fully the profit-making activities of questionable enterprises. The hand which bars the library door to knowledge is the hand which stifles the soul of the community.

Bookstores. Bookstore owners are booklovers and friends of all booklovers, dedicated to the interests of readers, young and old. They invest their time and savings in a business from which they hope to derive more of pleasure and fulfillment than of riches. The problems of retail bookselling are complex; the tasks involved require technical training and skill, experience, up-to-date knowledge of books, the ability to get along well with people, and a reasonable amount of business acumen. The bookseller must order his stock of books carefully (usually a few thousand titles selected from lists of perhaps two hundred thousand or more) and arrange them to the best advantage, for he has limited space and must use it for those books which will be especially interesting and helpful to readers. But, of course, he is always willing to order a book not kept in stock if so requested by a serious-minded customer. Patronize your local or nearby bookstores, for they are among the most reliable of the sources of information and centers of culture in American society.

The number of books sold in this country has constantly increased at a faster rate than the population. Annual retail sales of new books amount to nearly 3 billion dollars. In addition, there is a brisk business in the sale of used books and in book collecting. More than 22,000 new titles were published last year (by more than 800 American publishers), besides 8,000 new editions of old books. The new publications covered a wide variety of subjects, arranged according to the number of titles published as follows: economics and sociology (with the largest number of titles); juveniles; science; fiction; religion; literature; technology; medicine; history; education; biography; art; travel; poetry and drama; philosophy and psychology; business; languages; sports and recreation; general reference works; law; home economics; agriculture; and miscellaneous subjects. Including old and new books, more than 80,000 titles (printed in hundreds of millions of copies) are available in low-priced paperbound editions.

There are thousands of regular bookstores (including over 2,000 college bookstores) and, in addition, more than 100,000 stores and stands which display books along with newspapers, magazines, and other merchandise. It is true that millions of people still do not live near a library or bookstore and fail to read books regularly. Nearly everyone reads newspapers and magazines. Daily newspaper circulation is in excess of 61 million copies, while the total annual circulation of magazines is estimated in billions (the circulation of general magazines exceeds 238 million copies per issue). Of course, a single copy of a magazine or a book may be read by dozens of readers. Obviously, the American reader enjoys access to an enormous quantity and range of printed information, much of which is readily available in local or regional libraries, bookstores, and other retail stores.

GOVERNMENTAL, SOCIAL, AND SCIENTIFIC ORGANIZATIONS

Readers can obtain a wide variety of information and useful advice from United States government publications (for a monthly list you can write to the Superintendent of

Documents, Government Printing Office, Washington, D.C. 20402). Research reports, pamphlets, periodicals, and books in all sorts of subject fields are published with a total annual output of more than 60 million copies.

American government publications are respected for their accuracy and objectivity. They are instruments of scholarship useful to all readers, not propaganda tools of any political or ideological group.[1] Many of the publications are printed in large quantities and supplied at little cost to readers. The numerous executive departments of government issue reports on their work, as do the various committees of Congress. Readers can subscribe to the *Congressional Record,* which records in daily issues the proceedings of the House of Representatives and the Senate and includes all votes, speeches, and debates, as well as inserts of political materials. Current lists of new government publications are available in public libraries, and readers can also ask to be placed on the mailing list and deposit funds with the Superintendent of Documents for periodic purchase of pamphlets. Books and pamphlets on child care, home improvements, consumers' problems, gardening, health, science, technology, business, labor, commerce, agriculture, and the arts have been distributed in the millions of copies. Not only do the Department of Defense and the several departments of the armed forces have book libraries containing many millions of copies (for men in the services), but they issue reports and instructional texts printed by the Government Printing Office. Similarly, the Department of Health, Education, and Welfare issues numerous publications, including reports on the researches of the National Institutes of Health and the popular, valuable reports of the United States Office of Education.

Among the innumerable publications of social and scientific organizations most worthy of mention are those

---

[1] An excellent guide to selected government publications, arranged by subject fields, is W. P. Leidy's *A Popular Guide to Government Publications* (Columbia University Press, New York, 1968).

of the American Medical Association, the American Historical Association, the American Sociological Association, the Foreign Policy Association, the National Education Association, the League of Women Voters of the United States, the American Management Association, the Chamber of Commerce of the United States, the National Association of Manufacturers, the American Federation of Labor and the Congress of Industrial Organizations, the Public Affairs Committee, the American Association for the Advancement of Science, the American Library Association, the American Psychological Association, the National Safety Council, the American Standards Association, and the various agencies of the United Nations. Almost every conceivable subject of interest to citizens is represented by some organization and its publications.

SOURCES OF INFORMATION

For most readers, the best single source of information about all book publications in the United States is *Books in Print* (vol. 1, authors; vol. 2, titles), a comprehensive annual guide to all books still in print in the English language. *Books in Print* (published annually by R. W. Bowker Co., New York, N.Y.) is available for consultation in libraries and bookstores. Also available are R. W. Bowker Co.'s *Publishers' Weekly* and *Library Journal,* indispensable journals of book information and news for booksellers and librarians. For readers interested in the names and addresses of publishers of various types of books and magazines, there is a particularly helpful guidebook, a veritable "bible" of the book industry, namely, the *Literary Market Place,* an annual business directory providing information about American and Canadian publishing enterprises.

In the not too distant future, the reader will probably have at his disposal extraordinary new electronic devices which will bring him copies of publications instantaneously. It will then be possible for him to request a book or a portion of any publication by telephone and to be provided with printed copies in his own home at once. Within a few years hence the home library will perhaps contain a million books in microscopic form for immediate selection and magnification. Meanwhile, however, such facilities not being available, readers should certainly make much more frequent and efficient use of those which are on hand, namely, the libraries and bookstores.

SCHOOLS AND UNIVERSITIES

More than 60 million Americans attend some type of school or college and thus constitute a vast audience for the publications discussed above. Books are still the mainstay of instruction in educational institutions on all levels. In thousands upon thousands of day and evening schools and colleges, courses are provided in many hundreds of subjects, cultural, vocational, and social or recreational. With the rise of junior and community colleges, which now exceed 950 in number and enroll about 2 million students, most readers have access to instruction of some kind in fields of interest to them. Highly trained instructors devote special attention to the selection of textbooks and other publications in their subjects and are always pleased to enroll adult students in special groups or at least to provide information about worthwhile books to read. (In addition, about 6 million students are enrolled in home study courses which include many subjects not always available in local schools or colleges.)

Colleges and universities have been experiencing difficult problems owing to their close relationship to contemporary affairs and the revolt of youth against the low standards of activity among leaders of community institutions. The best solution to the problem of higher education is to provide genuine higher education through the serious study of books representing all points of view on controversial matters. Critical, efficient reading is the proper main function of education, and the gap between new and old generations will be closed when both begin to realize that this is indeed the principal business of our schools and colleges. Reading and reasoning are the keys to modern culture and social progress.

READING AND REASONING

Reading requires the reader to understand the logic in an author's ideas and arguments. The reader can usually detect shortcomings and fallacies in printed material if he takes the time to study it carefully. But reading an author's ideas is often only the first proper step in a continuous process of reflection and reaction. What happens after reading—how the reader thinks and feels and what he says and does—determines whether or not the author's work was worth creating and publishing. An author does not write symbols for the purpose of decorating paper; his work is of little value unless it awakens a spark of intellectual life in his readers.

The reader, in effect, begins where the author left off. He digests and absorbs, molds the ideas into the fiber of his own mind. He must be careful to do this correctly, in accordance with the laws of straight thinking. Otherwise, he will only distort the author's material into illogical, confusing, or incorrect conclusions and applications. Efficient reading depends therefore upon straight thinking both during and after the reading experience. The following are a few simple rules of straight thinking.

Rule 1. For straight thinking, the elimination of all prejudice, and I mean *all* prejudice, is absolutely necessary. I recall a brilliant historian who had somehow, as a result of unfortunate experiences, developed a prejudice against Irish Catholics. I could never understand his attitude, for I had myself been happy to associate with Irish Catholics during my childhood and school years and in business, professional, and social enterprises, and had always admired their warmth, sympathy, eloquence, loyalty, and other fine qualities. But he could not read an article or book by anyone named O'Flaherty or O'Brien without at once finding fault. Nearly everything he read by such an author he characterized as part of a plot contrived by the Pope to control the world. How blind are those who will not see the truth! In vain I pointed out that all religious leaders believe their own religion to be the true one, the best, and others to be on the wrong road. Prejudiced readers are totally unable to appreciate the element of truth in social, political, economic, literary, and philosophical views with which they disagree. Thus, unfortunately, the prejudiced reader mistakes his own imperfect vision of the truth for perfection and misses the opportunity to learn from ideas and principles different from his own.

So the first rule of straight thinking is simply to think straight instead of being diverted by prejudice, or more specifically, to follow the author's ideas wherever they lead and to judge them on the basis of his facts and evidence.

Rule 2. Another rule of straight thinking is to assume a position of neutrality when an author's view differs from the popular opinion on any subject. Give him the benefit of the doubt until you consider his facts and evidence. Some readers reject an author's idea immediately because they know or believe that most people do not accept it. This habit is a great mistake. Every reader should consider each idea or proposition on its merits. Sometimes, truth can be popular, but frequently it is very unpopular; in certain historical instances, it has been known to only one man or to only a few men.

Rule 3. The reader should also put aside his emotions when he reads unusual, disturbing ideas or arguments. A person who feels angry or fearful, for example, is not in a good condition to judge another person's ideas justly or correctly. If you are emotionally upset when you read a passage in a newspaper or book, be patient, wait a few days, and reread the same material when you are in a calmer frame of mind. You will then be in a better position to evaluate its message accurately—and discover the truth.

Rule 4. Still another rule of straight thinking tells us that we cannot always depend upon our so-called common sense or even sense perception to find the truth. Things are not universally what they seem to be, for our senses are imperfect and our reasoning powers are limited. So readers should be open-minded about strange ideas presented by any author. How many people fifty years ago would have believed that splitting the atom, which no one could even see, would release vast amounts of energy?

Rule 5. When thinking about an author's ideas, you may obtain fresh insight by turning them inside out or upside down, and then inquiring into the consequences. I have frequently used this technique to good advantage. When I first read about the successful method of nuclear fission, the splitting of atoms, I imagined at once what the opposite process would be, namely, instead of splitting atoms, combining them—the process of fusion. It is probable that many readers thought in the same way. Scientists soon applied high temperatures to create the fusion process of the hydrogen bomb. This reversal of an idea can often lead into new, promising concepts and more useful, and hopefully in the future, morally praiseworthy results.

Rule 6. Finally, the reader should not hesitate to strike out boldly into new paths of imagination during and after his reading. I have had the experience of plunging ahead with new ideas, as in my inventions of instructional materials, testing different arrangements of such materials until I found some that worked effectively. This procedure is not merely trial-and-error thinking, but rather an attempt to organize ideas into a pattern based on a specific goal—for example, to simplify a machine or device or to save time.

6

How To Read
Business Contracts And
Protect Your Legal Rights

People today often find it necessary to read a variety of legal documents, including contracts to purchase merchandise or real estate, leases, insurance policies, and warranties. These contracts are prepared by specialists who have mastered a technical terminology and language structure protecting their own interests or those of their business clients. But the nonspecialist reader has had little opportunity to become expert in the fine points of such reading materials. Hence he must either employ a specialist to advise him or risk serious misinterpretation and consequent damage to his interests.

Nevertheless, you can learn to read legal documents expertly and derive special advantages from such knowledge and ability. You will then notice at a glance whether or not a particular document is complicated enough to require professional advice. If you employ a specialist, you will better understand the value of his services and will also be in a position to raise questions in case of omissions or forgetfulness on his part. Even attorneys can make mistakes, which an alert reader can sometimes pinpoint. Furthermore, you will be able to remind your adviser about special personal circumstances which might affect the terms or interpretation of a contract or similar legal document. You should not, of course, attempt to be your own lawyer, insurance agent, or product-testing laboratory, but should be prepared to read documents with care and understanding before signing them.

WHAT YOU SHOULD KNOW ABOUT CONTRACTS

Usually some kind of oral or written discussion or negotiation precedes the signing of a contract. The parties may exchange considerable correspondence about the terms and the purpose they have in mind. There might even be a preliminary written agreement to perform certain tasks prior to the signing of a final contract. Any such materials (including memorandums of conversations, with dates and contents threof) should be kept on hand permanently or at least during the life of the contract, for they may have a decisive bearing on the interpretation of some of the terms should controversy come about among the parties.

For example, a troublesome dispute once arose when a business firm sent its contract with a letter stating that the instrument would put into technical form the terms agreed upon in conversations and correspondence with the firm's representative. This statement in the covering letter was incorrect and opened the door to a dispute concerning the meaning and intent of several clauses in the contract. The customer later claimed, and produced letters in support of his claim, that he had never agreed upon what appeared to be specific terms in the signed contract, including especially a clause calling for advance payments for partial performance. A costly lawsuit might well have been avoided if the covering letter had not in effect pointed to the possibility of error or lack of good faith, owing to discrepancies between the contract terms and preceding correspondence.

Legal Advice. If you have had correspondence about the terms of a contract, or if you prepare letters of this kind, show them to your attorney and ask his advice again before signing the contract. What you write in letters may or may not affect the contract, but it could lead to unnecessary disputes. The terms should be spelled out so clearly in the contract itself as not to require further comment or elucidation on your part. Remember, too, that you must not depend on oral modifications or explanations as a means of assuring yourself that the clauses in a contract are accurate and satisfactory.

Sometimes evidence of conversations between the parties can throw light on certain clauses in a faulty contract or can be used to show that the contract is illegal, or that it was signed in error, or that it should be voided as contrary to the laws of a particular state. Notes of these conversations might shed light on the relationships contemplated by the parties, the failure to fulfill conditions on which the enforcement of the contract depends, or subsequent agreements to modify the terms. But courts are reluctant to allow the use of such verbal testimony merely to prove that one of the parties did not mean what the written contract actually states. You should therefore read each clause thoroughly, decide whether it is absolutely correct, consult your attorney, and insist upon the insertion of any necessary change before signing. Minor changes made thereafter will have to be mutually agreed upon and initialled in the margins by the parties, while major changes may make it necessary to supplement or substitute for the original document—in accordance with procedures that will be familiar to your attorney.

Preliminaries. The first statements in a contract identify the parties to the agreement and specify its purpose. This part may be a simple matter, but it is not always so simple as it seems. All parties must be correctly named and identified, their legal addresses should be given, and the date should be filled in as of the day on which the final signature (that of the issuing party) is appended. These details may become important if questions should arise about the terms and performance under the contract.

Parties to a contract should notify each other about changes in their addresses.

Not only the full legal names and addresses, but also the facts of citizenship of the parties should be stated in the contract. Complications may develop if one party is not a citizen. Further, the citizen of one state can sue citizens or firms located in another state either in the state courts or in federal courts as he chooses. Your attorney should make the decisions called for by circumstances of this kind, but it will do no harm to bring them to his attention.

Legal Validity. For a contract to be valid and enforceable, certain conditions must obtain, as follows: (1) there must be a meeting of the minds of the parties to the contract, as to the intent and terms thereof; (2) the agreement must be in writing if the laws of the particular state (in which the contract is made) so provide, but other types of contracts may be oral, although in most cases a detailed written contract is best; (3) the consent of each party must be genuine and voluntary—not induced by mistake, fraud, misrepresentation, undue influence, or compulsion; (4) there must be consideration —that is, something which a party to a contract agrees to do or to refrain from doing in return for the promises, acts, or forbearance by the other party; (5) the parties must be legally competent to enter into the contract (for example, adults can be held to their contract with an infant, but the latter can rescind the contract if he so desires and regain his property); and (6) the agreement must be legal as to its purpose and its performance.

Bear in mind that you will be bound by any contract you sign unless you can prove mistake, fraud, trickery, compulsion, or illegality. Even if you have signed a legal contract without reading it, you will be held responsible for performance in accordance with its terms. An experienced attorney once failed to read his own contract before signing it. I had arranged for a payment to be made to him upon his delivery of one-half of an acceptable manuscript, but he failed to make delivery on time because he had not read the contract. Later he sent more than half of his manuscript and requested payment, which had to be refused because his material was neither acceptable nor delivered on the date specified in the signed contract. This attorney's attorney advised him correctly that he could not make a claim that would be upheld in court. Surely attorneys should know better than to sign contracts without reading them.

If a contract states no date for performance of obligations, each party must perform them within a reasonable time. If, however, the time is specified and is stated to be the essence (the indispensable condition) of the contract, failure of one party to perform on time frees the other party from contractual obligations. If the time element is not of critical importance, failure to perform on time will still be a breach of the contract (subject to suit by the injured party for damage sustained by him as a consequence), but usually it will not give the injured party the right to abandon the entire contract. Unintentional failure to live up to the terms of a contract is no excuse. Each party is held responsible for full performance of his responsibilities at the time and in the manner specified and described in the agreement.

Contracts contain statements of facts and conditions which induce the parties to sign them, and the parties must be able to depend upon the accuracy of these statements. Look for the factual statements, make a list of them, be sure they are accurate, and decide whether any should be changed, deleted, or supplemented. If one party misrepresents or conceals an important fact, the other party may cause the contract to be declared fraudulent and void, and he may sue for damages resulting from the fraud. If both parties make an honest but important mistake on the same matter, either one, if he feels injured by the error, can usually void the contract. If only one party makes an honest mistake, however, he can still be held to the terms of the contract unless the error was obviously known to the other party at the time of his acceptance of the offer.

WHAT TO DO BEFORE SIGNING A CONTRACT

Before signing any contract, read every word and make sure you understand every sentence. Reread every paragraph, noting all facts and obligations. Finally, reread the entire contract and find the answers to the following questions:

1. What statements of fact are included? Which clauses contain these statements?

2. What can either party do if there is a breach of the various terms of the contract by the other party? Which clauses refer to possible failure to perform and the consequences or remedies?

3. Is there a stated time or times for performance? Is time stated to be the essence of the contract? Which clauses specify the time or times for performance?

4. What is the period of the agreement, and how can the contract be terminated?

5. What is said about waivers and changes in the terms of the contract?

6. What is said about the effect of the contract upon heirs, administrators, and executors of any of the parties? About successors and assigns?

Enforcement of Contracts. Consult your attorney immediately if there is doubt as to the correct answers to any of these questions. Do not sign the agreement until you are entirely satisfied with all the statements of facts, conditions, and obligations. Once you have entered into a legal contract, you must expect to live up to all of its terms. Even a state government cannot interfere with enforcement of private contracts. Such interference would deprive citizens of their property illegally under the Fourteenth Amendment to the United States Constitution. Moreover, the Constitution explicitly protects private contracts from violations by the states. Section 10 of

Article 1 provides that no state shall pass any law "impairing the obligations of contracts," and even in an emergency a state can only delay execution of contracts for the public welfare a reasonable time while conserving fully the interests of all parties thereto.

Complexity of Contracts. Obviously, contract law is highly complex. It is usually necessary to consult an attorney because contracts today are not based on a single, simple idea, such as the idea that men should always keep their promises, or the idea that they should be compelled to live up to a bargain once made, or the idea that they should not give up something they own without receiving equal value in return. Simple ideas of this kind just do not work well in modern business. Talk is cheap, for instance, and many promises do not have to be kept so far as the law is concerned. Bargains made can be illegal or ambiguous. Anyone should be free to give up his property without an equal return if he so chooses. Our contract laws are a complicated mixture based partly on these ideas, but also upon state and federal laws, established business customs, and numerous court decisions. On many points the legal experts themselves disagree. So there is no way out of the dilemma. You must read your contracts carefully, consult a conscientious, reputable attorney, and try to transact your business with people whom you can trust.

It is easy to read a contract quickly and assume that everything is quite satisfactory and in order, but that can be a dangerous assumption. The following examples indicate only a few of the problems which can arise in this complicated business. Even if these particular examples may not apply to your immediate situation, they will remind you of important points to consider whenever you contemplate signing a contract of any kind.

1. Apartment leases are contracts which usually provide for some means of terminating the lease. In leases extending for a definite period of time, the last day of tenancy is always stated, but thereafter the tenant can continue as a month-to-month tenant with the consent of

the landlord. For a lease of one year or longer, the landlord can in many cases choose between extending the lease another full year or dispossessing the tenant holdover. In some leases, a renewal clause provides that the tenant must notify the landlord (within a stipulated period) of his intention to vacate the premises, and often there is a clause stating that the lease will be automatically renewed unless the tenant so notifies the landlord. (Of course, you can agree with your landlord either orally or in writing to terminate the lease at any time before the final date.)

Most of the standard printed leases tend to protect the interests of the landlord. They specify, for example, that he can evict the tenant for non-payment of rent or of certain expenses for upkeep if these are stated in the lease. As a tenant, however, you should know that you, too, have rights under the law of *constructive eviction.* Thus, you can move out and sue for damages if the landlord fails to furnish services agreed upon, such as heat, conceals a dangerous condition, or allows the premises to be infested with pests or to become uninhabitable in part or in whole. So read your lease from beginning to end and ask your attorney's advice before signing it.

2. Sometimes a contract may be so worded as to grant you rights and privileges of which you may not be fully aware. Be sure to inquire about such possibilities when you consult your attorney. For example, contracts between authors and publishers usually stipulate that "without the written consent of the Publisher . . . the author shall not write, edit, print or publish . . . any other literary work of so similar a character that it would be liable to compete or interfere with or injure the sale" of the author's book.

How often authors have assumed that such a clause prevents them from writing another book for a different publisher on the same subject! In most instances they are perfectly free to write additional books on the same subject, provided that the new books are larger works priced so much higher than their first book that there would be no competition between them. Certainly journal articles would ordinarily not compete with their book, but rather would help the sale. The key words in the contract are "liable to compete or interfere with or injure the sale," as applied to the original book. Obviously, it would not be fair to expect the publisher to invest heavily in an author's work and then allow the author to publish a directly competing work with another publisher.

3. You can sometimes arrange for modification of your contract by mutual agreement. Contracts generally include a clause stating that "no waiver of any breach of any term or condition of this Agreement shall be binding unless the same is in writing and signed by the party waiving such breach . . . No provision of this Agreement may be changed except by an instrument in writing signed by the parties." According to this clause, if one party fails to fulfill a specified obligation under the contract, it is still possible for the other party to eliminate the obligation by signing a written statement to this effect. That statement actually changes one of the terms of the contract and should therefore be signed by both parties. Such a change will not then injure or destroy the contract or modify it in any other respect.

4. An automobile liability insurance contract protects you against claims by other people for injury to them or damage to their property. Read your contract carefully and consult your agent immediately in case of accident. To collect damages from your insurance company, a claimant must theoretically prove that you were negligent and that he did not contribute to the accident through his own negligence. It has become the custom with most insurance companies, however, to pay moderate claims instead of going to the expense of a lawsuit. They seem to be quite willing to pay claims against you in accordance with the contract, but remember that they will probably raise your annual premium and the increase will continue for several years. It will therefore be a costly experience. Many automobile owners have preferred to pay small claims themselves, even when they

are not at fault. They keep their accident policy in force as a means of protection in the less likely event of serious or fatal accidents. The injustice of the present system, with its bickering, confusion, long delays in litigation, costly expenses for lawyers' services, and opportunity for chicanery, has become so apparent that the public is demanding a new system of liability insurance (comparable to the best types of fire insurance) which would ignore the question of negligence or blame and compensate the victim for his actual injury or property damage.

Troubles with contracts occur because the average person has neither the time nor the resources to compete with business organizations which can afford to employ batteries of attorneys throughout the year to construct, interpret, and enforce their complicated contracts. If you sign a homeowners' insurance policy, for example, the total cost of the insurance might be only a few hundred dollars over a period of several years. You would not employ an expert attorney for a period of six months to study your contract or to protect your interests. Your attorney may give you a half-hour for consultation, but he starts at a disadvantage. A large insurance firm has prepared the same contract for thousands, possibly hundreds of thousands, of individual policyholders. It can afford to hire the best talent in the legal profession for careful preparation and interpretation of the contract so as to protect the company against high risks and bring in the maximum profit.

Among the most objectionable of the complex contracts are some in the field of installment purchases. These contracts may include clauses whereby the debtor gives up his right to question the justice of the debt even if he later discovers that he has been victimized; or clauses which allow the lender (seller) to sell the credit contract to a finance company which can then collect payments from the customer even if the seller has defrauded him by delivering defective merchandise. Several organizations, including the Consumer Federation of America and the American Federation of Labor and Congress of Industrial

Organizations, have been active in condemning such unjust contracts. But why have not the business associations of this country taken appropriate action to protect consumers? One can only conclude that higher and higher profits take precedence over the ideals of fair play and public welfare, a shortsighted policy of neglect which can only severely damage the long-term interests of business. You must therefore study any such contract carefully and obtain competent legal advice before signing it. Very few of the states have enacted adequate legislation to protect the consumer from abuses perpetrated by means of these ingenious contracts. Unfortunately, there seems to be no substitute for stringent federal laws to protect the average citizen, together with full publicity about conditions by organizations representing the consumer, and certainly no substitute for the rule that every citizen should become an alert, critical reader of contracts.

On the other hand, there are many business managers of high integrity who strive to be fair and honest in their contractual relationships. In the publishing industry, reputable firms have developed satisfactory contracts, based upon decades of experience, which protect fully the interests of the author as well as those of the publisher. But I have seen contracts of certain publishers which were ingeniously drawn in such a way as to make it highly improbable that justice could ever be done to their authors. In some contracts, ambiguous terms are included, as well as obligations of the author to pay costs which he could not possibly anticipate or verify. I have seen a contract which actually ties the authors down to the publisher in such a manner as to prevent them from ever escaping his clutches. In the publishing industry there is an authors' association which has begun to advise authors about these troublesome contracts. In most business transactions, however, the millions of American consumers have no organization to analyze and protect their individual contractual interests. Consequently, it will become increasingly necessary in these vital matters for elected representatives in the state and federal governments to intervene and represent the people who elected them. In addition, a consumers' legal research association is urgently needed, an organization which would do nothing else but study and publicize contract practices from the point of view of the virtually defenseless individual citizen.

THE LANGUAGE IN CONTRACTS

Most of the words in printed contracts are familiar to readers and give them little difficulty, but there are a few words with special meanings and these can be so confusing or disturbing to a reader that he is tempted to sign the contract without fully understanding all the clauses. Be sure to ask your attorney to explain the meaning of any terms in your contract which you do not understand.

The following terms are used frequently in many types of contracts. The explanations may be quite helpful during your negotiations and reading of a contract. By learning the precise meanings of these terms you will not have to waste your attorney's time on them.

acquittal, or acquittance. A release or discharge of a party from a contract obligation.

affidavit. A written, sworn statement.

affidavit of title. In the sale of real estate, a written statement made by the seller under oath, attesting to the identity of the owner of record, his lack of knowledge concerning unrecorded encumbrances or ownership claims by others, his marital status if he and his wife execute the deed, and his assurance that there are no unrecorded judgments against him.

arbitration. In disputes as to the terms of a contract, a method of settlement by submitting the matter to mutually agreed upon persons for their decision or award.

assignment. The transfer of contract rights and obligations by one person (the assignor) to another (the assignee) who becomes a new party to the original contract.

chattel mortgage. A mortgage on articles of personal property, movable or immovable, as distinguished from real estate or things which are considered to be part and parcel of real estate.

closing of title. The transfer of title to property through the delivery of a deed by the seller to the buyer.

consideration. Something given up by one party to a contract, or something he agrees to do or to refrain from doing, in return for the promises, acts, or forbearances of the other party.

contract under seal. A contract which contains a signatory's symbol in the form of a seal, such as a wax impression, scroll, or other symbol.

conveyance of title. An instrument (such as a deed) or method for transferring one's title to and interest in real estate or one's property rights to another person.

covenant. A legally valid, enforceable agreement, undertaking, or promise. In a covenant deed, the grantor affirms stated facts and conditions and agrees that, in case of dispute, he will uphold the grantee's title and his right to use the transferred property.

coverage. The total amount of risk assumed by an insurance company, including all its liabilities for payments to the insured in case of eventualities stated in an insurance contract.

deductible. An amount, specified in an insurance contract, which the insurance company deducts from the total payment that would otherwise be due to the insured under the terms of his contract.

deed. A written instrument under seal conveying title to and rights to the use of real estate from a seller (or grantor) to a buyer (or grantee).

default. Failure to fulfill or obey the terms of a contract. Failure to appear in court proceedings on time may cause a party to lose his case by default.

demised premises. Premises entrusted to a person for his use in accordance with the terms of a lease, implying his right to quiet enjoyment of the premises.

easement. The right of a person, either as set forth in

a written contract or as otherwise acquired or allowed by law, to use the land of another person for stated purposes.

encumbrance. A lien or claim against the property of one person by another.

fee simple. Lifelong, inheritable, unrestricted ownership of real estate property, including the right to keep, use, and dispose of it, subject only to regulations imposed by law.

fiduciary. A person acting in the capacity of trustee, i.e., holding property in trust for another person and obligated to conserve his interest therein.

full covenant and warranty deed. A deed for the conveyance of real estate property whereby the grantor guarantees the accuracy of facts and conditions stated therein—including his ownership and right to transfer it, and the absence of any encumbrances—and agrees to provide any evidences needed to perfect the title or to guarantee the title in perpetuity.

indenture. An official or formal document, such as a deed or a written contract, which sets forth the facts, conditions, promises, acts, and terms agreed upon by the parties.

infringement. Any breach or violation of the terms of an agreement, or any trespass by one person against the rights or privileges of another person.

larceny. In insurance contracts, the unlawful removal of personal goods without the consent of the rightful owner and with the intent either to deprive the owner of their use or to use them for the thief's own purposes.

lien. A claim, charge, or encumbrance against property, real or personal, based upon the owner's debt or obligation to the person holding or legally entitled to the lien.

limit of liability. In insurance contracts, the maximum amount which the insurance company is obligated to pay as compensation to or in behalf of the insured.

merger. In real estate law, when one person has two rights, one broader or more important than the other, the narrow right is destroyed by being merged, or absorbed, into the broad one. Thus, if a tenant has a lease but later becomes owner of the same property, his rights as a tenant disappear because they have been merged into his broader rights as the owner.

obligee. In business contracts, a person who is entitled to payments or other benefits to be derived from the other party's performance of a specified obligation.

obligor. In business contracts, a person who has agreed to perform (or to refrain from performing) a stated act or to make specified payments.

pilferage. In insurance contracts, the illegal appropriation of small amounts of money or articles of little value without the owner's consent.

quitclaim deed. A deed whereby the grantor surrenders any of his own interest in or ownership claims to property described therein, but without giving the grantee any guarantee or warranty of title.

robbery. In insurance contracts, the unlawful taking and removing of personal property from an owner usually by violence or threat of injury.

stipulations. Specific conditions and terms stated in a contract. In court cases, facts or evidence mutually agreed upon by opposing attorneys.

successor in title. The person who takes over the title to real estate property from a previous owner.

summary dispossess proceedings. In real estate contracts, a procedure whereby a landlord petitions a court to order a tenant to vacate the owner's premises for non-payment of rent or other stated reasons, the tenant either appears to oppose the petition or fails to appear, and the court makes the decision to issue or not to issue a warrant of dispossess. If the warrant is issued, it may be delayed for a reasonable time by the court, after which the tenant can be forcibly removed by a marshal.

survival clause. In real estate transactions, a special clause in the contract of sale which keeps a stated provision or obligation in force after the delivery of the deed;

in the absence of such a clause, the contract of sale
is destroyed by being merged into the deed.

theft. Identical with larceny, except that theft is sometimes defined to include not only unlawful appropriation or swindling, but also the act of obtaining possession of another's personal goods legally and then
later misusing them for the thief's own purposes. Insurance policies use both terms (theft and larceny)
to make certain that all such acts are included.

trustee. A person who holds property in trust for the
benefit of another person and has legal title thereto
until the purposes of the trust have been carried out.

waiver. A contract clause or a written instrument whereby
a person agrees to surrender stated legal rights. Sometimes the acts of a person may indicate that he intends
to waive (abandon) certain contractual or legal rights.

warrant. This term means to guarantee that specified facts
and conditions are true.

7

How To Appreciate
Literature And
Enjoy Your Reading

The enjoyment of literature begins with attentive, thoughtful interpretation of the author's purpose, design, and message. The reader cannot derive true understanding and enjoyment through superficial or careless reading, which is, in fact, the principal obstacle to the appreciation of literature. He must keep his eyes and mind open and alert to the author's language, pausing now and then to think and rethink what has been read and to ask, "What was particularly pleasing, unusual, effective, or significant in such passages?"

Thoughtful Review. You should review and recall the material you have read in any magazine or book and thus take pleasure again, perhaps more deeply than before, in its ideas and presentation. The experience of rethinking what you read is comparable to the pleasant recollection of tasty food you have eaten with relish, a source of repeated satisfaction and delight.

Elimination of Irrelevancies. Do your best to ignore jarring or unpleasant aspects of reading material. On occasion, rough expressions and horrifying incidents are natural or even essential ingredients of literature, depicting realities and truths. However, smut inserted gratuitously and artificially creates an obnoxious obstacle to reading enjoyment, revealing lack of taste on the part of the author or perhaps excessive zeal to attract and enlarge his reading audience. The sensitive reader's enjoyment is blunted and sometimes ruined by these annoying irrelevancies, just as the enjoyment of a fine dinner can be disturbed by unclean silver or a soiled tablecloth. There is no excuse for intruding bodily functions unnecessarily or excessively into literary work which should appeal to the deepest understanding and highest aspirations and loftiest sentiments—the great concerns and interests—of mankind. For the maximum enjoyment of reading, concentrate upon the effective, convincing, natural, significant, outstanding elements, applying to each passage and work as a whole a sense of alert discrimination and appreciation.

Critical Evaluation. Search out, recognize, and admire the special skills of the author, his choice of apt, vivid language, variety of style, lively rhythm, striking characterization, and his use of suspense, implication, exaggeration, understatement, irony, and other techniques. As you read, take note of these special qualities which lend power and eloquence to the language, and as you recall what you have read, anticipate more of the same enjoyment from what you are about to read.

Sharing of Experience. We understand, appreciate, and enjoy most of all the experiences which we share with others. Readers should pause frequently in their reading to express their innermost thoughts and feelings about the author's work. Often it is helpful to predict events, ideas, or moods in sections you are about to read, just as you anticipate events in real life, even though things may not always turn out precisely as expected. There is satisfaction when one's expectations are realized, but also when one is pleasantly surprised by unanticipated events.

ASPECTS OF LITERARY APPRECIATION

There are five main aspects or qualities of literature, which may be described as architectural, pictorial, musical, philosophical, and psychological, owing to the resemblance of the literary art to these other forms of creative expression or experience.

The Architectural Aspect. The architectural aspect of literature refers to the overall design of a literary work, to the elements of balance and harmony prevailing among its parts, and to the unification of these elements so that the work as a whole appeals to the reading audience as a significant experience. When we view with wonder and awe masterpieces of our architectural heritage—such as the Gothic cathedrals of Europe, with their soaring arches, delicate vaults, and spires reaching to the sky, their grotesque statues and decorations, and their brilliant stained glass windows—we see unification through design, color, and ornament. Literature, too, must possess a unified structure, a joining of harmonious parts. Although the reader need not attempt detailed analysis during his reading, he should observe the overall plan, because an awareness of the work as a whole will illuminate each of its parts. Often a preview of the author's plan, by rapid skimming, will clarify separate passages and link them in a meaningful, symmetrical structure. Thus the reader fits each part at once into the skeleton on which the author has built linguistic flesh and blood.

The structural framework of a literary work links the main and subordinate themes. The reader naturally is eager to know what the author had in mind, what his principal message or idea consists of, how the first section introduces the next, how the early parts lead to the main points or climaxes, and how the flow of words and ideas, whether continuous or reminiscent, is brought to a fitting, satisfying close. For most readers, it is enough to note the design and arrangement employed by the author and to bear them in mind as they concentrate on each part in turn. In this way they will more clearly grasp the significance of the author's ideas, language, themes, moods, and implications. Reading separate parts without a view of the whole is comparable to visiting a once inspiring or beautiful edifice now bereft of walls and roof—no longer a thing of beauty but a ruin until repaired and skillfully restored.

Pictorial Aspect. The pictorial aspect of literature corresponds to an artist's work which fills in and gives body to his overall design—the sensitive, graceful lines and forms, delicate or sparkling colors, shadows, and contrasts, backgrounds, orderly arrangements, and picturesque effects which are to be found in art. In literature, comparable details fill in the design and impart distinctive qualities to a poem, story, play, or essay—a fresh or unusual setting, unique characters, significant expressions and central motifs, the flesh and bones that fit into the author's framework and give substance to his work. The reader needs to ask again and again as he reads, *What is distinctive about this part, unusual or striking, natural or surprising, particularly convincing and effective?* Such questions, by helping him enlarge the scope of his attention and notice what might otherwise be lost to him, effectively broaden and deepen his appreciation and enjoyment of literature.

Pictorial effects in poetry and prose may be either specific or merely implied. The author uses familiar words in new ways and arrangements to produce these effects. In art, a painting such as the Mona Lisa will possess striking natural, lifelike form and coloring, and, at the same time, that imaginative quality of vague suggestibility represented by the variant tones and graceful smiling lips of the mysterious lady as depicted by Leonardo da Vinci. Picasso, like an author using familiar words, starts with commonplace objects but adds his own vision as he creates, to form significant, powerfully suggestive works, combining classical with modern, that are subject to widely different interpretations. In literature, too, interpretations of meaning will differ widely with readers; painter and author both intermingle clear and simple ideas with impressions.

If literature is abstracted, digested, abridged, or compressed excessively by editors, the original work may be seriously mutilated, and the reader of such versions will receive a distorted impression, just as if masses of color were detached from a painting. With links and joints gone, the body of the work becomes merely a trunk without head or limbs. Authors, like painters, should never permit mutilation of their work. Readers should notice and appreciate the significance of the large, central themes, but see them as parts of the whole, not as if detached from the author's overall plan.

Similarly, if the flow of literature is interrupted with too many explanations or discussions, as in certain educational methods which dissect unnecessarily, the author's art may be destroyed, thus stimulating distaste instead of enthusiasm for creative masterpieces. Therefore, when you read, give your attention wholeheartedly to the author's design and postpone serious analysis and investigation, excepting a minimum of information or allusions required for understanding the main themes of the work.

Musical Aspect. Literature has musical qualities that are created by sound, rhythm, repetition and rhyme, phrasing, length and variety of words, pauses, and the flow of, and linkage between, main and subordinate themes. The author selects words to express a mood or a motif; his message may be stated directly or by implication. Just as the abrupt, descending, glissando notes of music may remind one of a waterfall, so do the author's choice of words and their arrangement reflect the meaning of his theme. Thus, Iago's drinking song, sung to the clinking of wineglasses, in Shakespeare's *Othello,* applies sound, rhyme, repetition, and emphasis:

> And let me the canakin clink, clink!
> And let me the canakin clink!
> A soldier's a man;
> A life's but a span:
> Why, then, let a soldier drink.
> (Act II, Scene iii)

The words almost make their own music, as the reader imagines the voice and glasses producing these sounds. Alert readers enjoy such musical qualities as they journey along the heights and valleys of the author's landscape, a creative adventure reflecting his plan, vision, and skill.

Philosophical Aspect. The philosophical aspect of literature offers the discerning reader models of clear thinking, logical ideas, and rational meanings. He asks, *What do these passages signify as to truth, reality, insight into nature and the nature of man? How do the author and his characters interpret the values of life?* The thoughtful reader will agree, disagree or suspend judgment.

An author's philosophy of life can be expressed directly in a few lines, as in Walt Whitman's notes:

> After you have exhausted what there is in business, politics, conviviality, love, and so on—have found that none of these finally satisfy, or permanently wear— what remains? Nature remains; to bring out from their torpid recesses, the affinities of a man or woman with the open air, the trees, fields, the changes of seasons— the sun by day and the stars of heaven by night.

Or the ideas of a particular society, historical period, or individual may be developed gradually in the plot, the dialogue, or the commentaries. Often the author's personal views are unknown, for he may present characters adhering to diverse philosophies of life without taking sides. The reader must ponder and appreciate explicit or implied values, moral or spiritual standards and insights, encountered in his reading.

Psychological Aspects. Finally, and most importantly, the author and his readers participate in a joint psychological enterprise. Even though his own philosophy of life may not be revealed, something of the author's personality and spirit shows itself in his language, characters, and themes. Only a sensitive, imaginative person can create a literary masterpiece. Further, the characters in a play or novel speak and act in ways which grow out of their inner thoughts or feelings. They may expand or deteriorate psychologically, display emotions and motives or conceal them, behave in or out of character, and it is a task and challenge for the reader to appreciate all such characteristics. It is indeed the reader's task to speak with the speakers, think with the thinkers, feel with the characters—in other words, at least for the time being, identify himself psychologically with the ideas, purposes, emotions, and spirit infusing the work. For the fullest appreciation and enjoyment of literature, the reader must momentarily feel as the villain feels, as the hero feels, as the author feels, despite reservations or revulsion which may afterward impel him to reject any and all.

ENJOYMENT OF POETRY

If you noticed the sadness of a lonely friend, perhaps you would wonder in commonplace language, "What is wrong? My friend is out of sorts today." The following stanza of a poem by the sixteenth-century poet Thomas Wyatt expresses his reactions to the sadness of a friend:

> Her pains tormented me so sore
>   That comfort had I none,
> But cursed my fortune more and more
>   To see her sob and groan:
>   Alas the while!

Wyatt's lines provide a clue to the chief differences between poetry and prose. *First,* the word order in his poem differs from the usual order in prose, thus lending greater force and power. *Second,* the words are arranged in a rhythmic pattern (and include rhyme) with stress on the same words, use of alternately short and long syllables, and corresponding breath control, as in oral reading or speech. Wyatt's poem should be read aloud. *Third,* the language is extremely intense, compressed, and highly emotional, expressing deep feelings through the intimate union of sound and meaning, that is to say, through the use of words which, when spoken, will impart emphasis and power to the author's intended mood and idea. (The short emphatic words and repetition of the consonant *s* in Wyatt's stanza illustrate this effect.)

·Finally, the overall theme and effect are much more dramatic than is customary in prose—comparable, in fact, to the dramatic themes and effects of words and music in grand opera. The best of prose writings may bear some resemblance to the rhythms and other imagination-stirring characteristics of poetry, but poems exhibit in greater measure the qualities of word power, rhythm, emphasis, emotion, and dramatic implication. They possess a unique depth and beauty of expression, inspiring and fascinating the sensitive reader. Their essence flows from these unique qualities in which the details of information, explicit ideas, and events, so important in prose, are subordinated. The dominance of rhythmic sound (sometimes including rhyme), unusual order and emphases, and dramatic or ultra-sensitive moods reflecting the poet's attitude make poetry the most musical and emotionally stirring of literary forms.

Rhythm and Rhyme. The rhythm and rhyme of poetry are powerful aids to memory. We can long remember words of a poem because they are arranged in regular groupings connected by means of the same or similar repeated sounds. Poetry may have originated in ancient times as ballads sung to report events people wanted to remember. The rhymes of the ballads made recall much easier. Moreover, the earliest peoples depended upon speech and song for their information. Most of them could neither write nor read, but all could speak and sing.

As a child I lived in a poorly constructed wooden house with an upstairs neighbor partial to liquor who resented what he regarded as excessive rents. He was a sturdy fellow and one day, under the influence, doubled up his fists and smashed them through the flimsy boards of the hallway. Ordinarily I would have forgotten the incident, for drunkenness and violence were as common then as they are today. But I composed a ditty about the event and to this day, sixty years afterward, both the circumstances and the silly doggerel verse remain vivid in my memory:

The landlord said to the tenant,
"I've come for the rent."
The tenant said,
"I will not pay the rent."
The landlord went away,
And the tenant said,
"In the hall I'll make a dent."
So he made a hole
In the wall of the hall.

The landlord came and asked,
"When will you pay the rent?"
The tenant answered, "Never.
Look at the dent.
Look at the hole
In the wall of the hall."
The landlord hit the tenant
And the tenant hit the landlord.
Each hit the other gent.

Moral for landlords:
Never ask for the rent.

Indeed, the reader can best remember and enjoy poems by noting their regular pattern and sounds and by relating them to his own experience.

The words in a line of poetry possess much more rhythm and more regular patterns than those in a prose sentence. Noting the rhythmic patterns used in a poem can often make it easier to read, understand, remember, and enjoy. Sometimes, unless you recognize the pattern, you can misread the poet's meaning and intention.

The most common pattern is the iambic, in which there is stress on the second of each pair of syllables. The following example is from Coleridge's *The Rime of the Ancient Mariner:*

He wént like óne that háth been stúnned,
And ís of sénse forlórn:
A sádder and a wíser man
He róse the mórrow mórn.

In prose, the same ideas would be expressed in sentences lacking such regular meter and rhyme, as, for example:

"He walked around like someone in a state of shock, deprived of his senses, but when he got up the next morning, he was a sadder and wiser man." Poetry depends upon a more or less regular rhythmic arrangement of words for its special images and moods, but the lines must not become too monotonous. A certain amount of irregularity must therefore be introduced:

> Sweetly, sweetly blew the breeze—
> On me alone it blew.

Here Coleridge has avoided monotony by using trochaic meter in the first line (stressing the first of two syllables) and iambic meter in the second line. (A stressed syllable tends to be held a little longer than an unstressed one.) The mixture of rhythmic forms can be so irregular that there is little uniformity of rhythm, no rigid pattern of meter, from one line to the next, as in free verse:

I think I could turn and live with animals, they are so placid
    and self-contained;
I stand and look at them long and long.
They do not stand and whine about their condition;
They do not lie awake in the dark and weep for their sins; . . .

Here the free verse of Walt Whitman in *The Beasts* comes close to the rhythm of speech, yet retains a certain repetitive sameness among some of the phrases and lines to make them more convincing and emphatic than ordinary conversation.

Among the most common metric patterns are the following:

He práyeth wéll, who lóveth wéll Both mán and bírd and beást.	(iambus) (iambic tetrameter)
Swíftly, swiftly fléw the shíp	(trochee) (trochaic tetrameter)
Yet shé sailed sóftly tóo:	(iambus) (iambic trimeter)
We can líve without boóks, We can't líve without coóks.	(anapest) (anapestic dimeter)

When I pláy on my fíddle   (anapest) (anapestic trimeter)
  in Doôney,
Folk danće like a wave of
  the séa;

Oń to the boúnd of the   (dactyl) (dactylic trimeter)
  waśte,
Oń, to the Cíty of Gód.

Lísten to mé and obéy: (dactyl) (dactylic trimeter)
Ońe, twó, thŕee, fóur,   (spondee) (spondaic tetrameter)
Knóck at the doôr.   (dactyl) (dactylic dimeter)
Twó, foúr, síx, eíght;   (spondee) (spondaic tetrameter)
Wáit at the gáte.   (dactyl) (dactylic dimeter)

I spráng to the stírrup, and (amphibrach, tetrameter)
  Jóris, and hé;
I gálloped, Dirćk gálloped,
  we gálloped all thŕee;

Just as doctors and lawyers use a technical language
(derived in part from Latin) which oǹly confuses their
clients, so the critics and teachers of literature use technical words which annoy readers interested in learning
more about poetry. A line of poetry is divided into feet,
each consisting of stressed (or strong) and unstressed
(or weak) syllables. If a line has five feet, each made
up of one weak syllable followed by one strong syllable,
why not call it a weak-strong five-foot line, instead of
using the technical term, *iambic pentameter?* Technical
language can be saved for the advanced students or
specialists, although many of them, too, might join the
majority of readers who prefer ordinary English. Thus,
iambic trimeter could be known as weak-strong three-foot
lines; *anapestic dimeter*, as weak-weak-strong two-foot
lines; and *dactyllic hexameter*, as strong-weak-weak six-
foot lines.

Some contemporary poets intermingle various rhythmic patterns, using pauses, swift changes of pace,
alliteration, analogy, metaphors, figures of speech, and
omissions of expected words to express vivid emotions
and images. They create lyric poetry, short, personal,
intensely emotional poems, the most musical of literary
forms, particularly effective when read aloud with em-

phasis and intonation pattern attuned to the poet's mood
or message. Few poets attempt to create narrative poems
built around the story element as a central core, or to
emulate the long, heroic narratives or the classical epics,
the historical accounts dramatized by means of steady
metrical patterns and powerful rhythms of majestic,
dignified language. Modern poetry depends upon its
capacity to suggest moods and meanings, impressions,
inexpressible truths.

Repetition of a single poem can be overdone, just as
in prose excessive use of an expression makes it stale,
a cliché. Similarly, in music, we can enjoy a melody
repeated a few times, but cannot endure excessive repetition. It is best to read a wide variety of poems,
although we may never weary of memorable works
recited at reasonably frequent intervals if we can divine
new, fresh meanings in them.

Translations. Poetry has been recited or written abun-
dantly in hundreds of languages. All emotions are ex-
pressible in any language, even though a particular language may seem to have a structure more effective in
expressing one kind of feeling than another. (In my own
subjective experience with poetry in languages other
than my native, superbly eloquent English, I have felt
poetry in Hebrew to be uniquely dignified and dramatic,
that in Latin to be most heroic and emphatic, that in Russian to be strongly measured, deeply moving, and intense,
that in German to be extremely sensitive and affecting,
that in French to be most thoughtful and inspiring, that in
Italian to be the most musical and emotional.) There is
no adequate substitute for reading the original poem in
the author's native language. True, an approximate notion
of theme, action, or mood can often be duplicated by a
skilled translator, yet even the best will come short of
the original, sometimes distorting it, failing to reproduce
its true meaning. Indeed, as the gifted poet and discerning interpreter of poetry, Stanley Burnshaw, has pointed
out in his significant book, *The Poem Itself,* "Regardless

of its brilliance, an English translation is always a different thing; it is always an *English poem* . . ." and each individual word in a poem is "a unique totality—unique in sound, denotation, connotation, and doubtless much more." [1]

To appreciate every aspect of a poem—architectural, pictorial, musical, philosophical, and psychological—you must become familiar with its original language, and also with its related people and culture, the native speakers and writers, to capture all its nuances, moods, emphases, rhythms, and implications. A translation may be all you have for the moment, yet it is only a pointer to the original, just as a sensitive painter's rough, preliminary sketch gives only a hint of his final masterpiece. Most often in fact, it is better to learn enough of another language to read its poetry and catch the spirit of the poet and his people than it would be to read only the translations. Examine two or three translations of a classic; they may differ so widely that you will wonder whether they are translations of the same original. To appreciate and enjoy poetry created in a foreign language, it is necessary to learn the basic essentials of the language and then to read the original together with the best available translations and commentaries.

ENJOYMENT OF PLAYS

Some readers avoid plays, even the works of Shakespeare, often because an uninspired teacher in the past has dissected the plots and language into tidbits or absurdities which distorted the architectural grandeur,

---

[1] Stanley Burnshaw, *The Poem Itself* (New York: Holt, Rinehart & Winston, 1960; paperbound edition, Schocken Books, Inc., 1967), p. xii. See also Stanley Burnshaw's illuminating discussion of this point in his *The Seamless Web* (New York: George Braziller, Inc., 1970), pp. 209–212; and his comments (using Thomas Mann's *Tonio Kröger* as an example) on translation of prose writings in his *Varieties of Literary Expression* (New York: New York University Press, 1962).

language, and emotional impact of each work. Reading
a play should be almost the same as observing the identical things being said and done in life situations by
real people corresponding precisely in every respect—
costume, appearance, speech, motives, capacities, virtues,
and failings—to the characters in the play. The reader
should read a play, not through the eyes of a teacher
or a critic, but through his own eyes and ears, reading
aloud, as if he were a spectator of the events, or at least
part of a theater audience. In this way the playwright's
true design and intent, his aggregation of things done,
said, and seen, will inspire a sympathetic understanding
and response in the reader's mind and heart. Later, but
only later, he may enrich and deepen his insight, preferably after attending a performance of the play itself.
Then, not before, is the time for guidebooks, lectures,
and readings of commentaries or dramatic histories.

The Play Itself. So, I say, "To the works themselves!"
Read and reread them, just as you look again and again
at a beautiful painting by Raphael or listen again and
again to a Beethoven symphony—and there will be time
thereafter for discussion, dissection, and interpretation.
Do not ruin the immediate experience by suffering
interruptions with bits of humdrum remarks, but give
your attention to each work as a whole in its master's
dress.

Beware of truncated versions of plays. Abridgment of a
play to fit it into an hour's time instead of three can
distort the work. The overemphasis on one or more of
its parts, the lack of unified appreciation, the separation
of meanings which should be joined like inseparable
twins—these are the means used by overspecialized
critics to spoil the best of dramatic literature by bringing
it down to the level of commonplace, amateurish con-
ceptions. It is no wonder that many readers learn mainly
distaste for the best of drama, as well as poetry and
prose. So I say, again, "To the works themselves!"

Use of the Imagination. What do we in our imagination
see, hear, and feel when we read a play such as Shake-

speare's tragedy, *Macbeth?* Consider the opening scene of Act I.

We see before us a desolate bare plot of land swept by a violent thunderstorm. Suddenly the dim, grotesque figures of three old witches appear out of nowhere. We picture them as bent-over hags in black, with pointed noses and long, sharp nails. We hear their harsh voices croaking:

> When shall we three meet again in stormy weather?
> Before the sun sets.
> Where?
> Upon the heath.
> To meet Macbeth.

As we watch and listen tensely, we sense that something is wrong, out of joint, and we feel trouble coming as the three old hags screech together their chant that their world is an evil one, upside down—that what is good for people is foul to witches:

> Fair is foul, and foul is fair.
> Hover through the fog and filthy air.

And they melt away into the windstorm. Now we know that we must expect trouble ahead and that Macbeth, a general in the king's army, will be in it.

Let us go on to the second scene of Act I and imagine ourselves at the military headquarters of Duncan, King of Scotland. We see the King and his two sons strolling on the camp grounds with the Scot nobleman Lennox and a few servants when there is shouting nearby and a sergeant stumbles before them bleeding from his battle wounds. We hear the King ask, "Who is this bleeding soldier? Perhaps he can tell us what has happened in the battle of the rebels against my authority."

> What bloody man is that? He can report,
> As seemeth by his plight, of the revolt
> The newest state.

The King's son recognizes the wounded sergeant as a brave soldier who had helped to rescue him in battle, and urges him to speak up:

> This is the sergeant
> Who like a good and hardy soldier fought
> 'Gainst my captivity. Hail, brave friend!
> Say to the king the knowledge of the broil
> As thou didst leave it.

We hear the sergeant explain that the rebels had been winning in the desperate battle until Macbeth rushed forward recklessly, swinging his hot sword of steel, killed many of the enemy, and finally ripped their leader in two from his navel to the jaw and strung him up on a wall. We notice the wounded soldier's sincere admiration for Macbeth's courage:

> For brave Macbeth—well he deserves that name—
> Disdaining fortune, with his brandish'd steel,
> Which smoked with bloody execution,
> Like valour's minion carved out his passage
> Till he faced the slave;
> Which ne'er shook hands nor bade farewell to him,
> Till he unseam'd him from the nave to the chaps,
> And fix'd his head upon our battlements.

If we continue to imagine, think with, and share the feelings of the characters, reading the play will be a most enlightening and enjoyable experience and an excellent preparation for watching an actual performance. As we read about and envision the events before and during the murder of the King by Macbeth, and what follows, we shall appreciate the exquisite language expressing the outstanding qualities of each character. We shall understand Macbeth's gentleness toward his wife, who considers him to be "full o' th' milk of human kindness"; his feelings of guilt and despair as he, the murderer of his King, exclaims, "Will all great Neptune's ocean wash this blood/Clean from my hand?"; and his wife's tigerish courage as she demands, after the murder, "Give me the dagger . . . My hands are of your colour; but I shame/ To wear a heart so white."

Thus we can follow the structure, plots, and human beings throughout the five acts of the play until, in the last, climactic scene on the battlefield, the loyal nobleman,

Macduff, kills Macbeth and brings the murderer's head to Malcolm (son of the murdered King) who graciously invites all the assembled nobles and soldiers to his coronation: "So, thanks to all at once and to each one,/ Whom we invite to see us crown'd at Scone."

A playwright seldom gives us direct information about the events and characters in his play, but lets the settings, conversation, and actions tell us what is most important. Actors, playgoers, and readers must fill in omitted details by using their imagination. One actor will speak the same lines more sharply than another, the interpretations by the audience will vary, and readers, too, will differ in their reactions. Is it not so with events in life also? We cannot expect everyone to think or respond in the same way to any significant problem or situation. As you read, however, you will appreciate and enjoy the play more and more if you attempt to sympathize with the characters and understand why they speak and act as they do.

Reading and Rereading. A first quick reading of a play should provide some familiarity with its main features. Its architectural aspect can be readily understood by noting the various settings, characters, dialogue, climaxes, and conclusion, the highlights which disclose the entire framework. At the same time, the first reading will also reveal changing moods, themes, and plot development—the large blocks of speech and action constituting the colorful, pictorial aspects. The attentive reader will surely enjoy some of the musical aspects, reflected in the outstanding speeches, eloquent expressions, and flow of language. The philosophical aspects, the ideas or messages, may challenge or reinforce his cherished assumptions or stimulate new thoughts. Finally, from the psychological point of view, the reader will react, at least tentatively, to the motives and actions of the principal characters and share their sentiments.

A second reading will deepen and enrich the reader's understanding and interpretation of the play as he views the plot, subplots, dialogue, and events step-by-step, sympathetically acting out the role of each character.

Now he will consider a few points of evaluation: How convincingly are the various problems and situations of the play introduced? What are the most impressive features, such as surprise developments, crises, climaxes, outstanding moods, and memorable remarks? What makes the characters seem real and true to life, or unreal and artificial? As the reader evaluates the play in ways such as these, he will rightly feel himself to be contributing something of his own to it, almost as if he were an actor, a playgoer, or even an assistant to the playwright himself. As he reads aloud, he imagines or impersonates each actor as one who will "suit the action to the word, the word to the action," without overstepping "the modesty of nature" by excessive exaggeration or under-emphasis, for the purpose of a play (to quote Shakespeare further) is "to hold as 'twere, the mirror up to nature; to show virtue her own feature, scorn her own image, and the very age and body of the time his form and pressure," making all things real and true to life.

ENJOYMENT OF NOVELS

The novelist usually has much greater opportunity than the poet and dramatist to paint backgrounds or settings, to explore characters and ideas in detail, and to introduce all sorts of illuminating information and comments that will help the reader to understand events, emotions, and human relationships essential to the story. He can describe the personality or motives of characters as if he were able to detect their innermost thoughts. He can devote many pages of description to the locale of the story. He can discuss historical events or social conditions which influence the characters in his novel. He can go back and forth in time and space, make fantastic assumptions about people, institutions, inventions, intermingle realities and truths with dreams and myths. For the sake of the story, readers will accept all such devices insofar as they shed light upon the pattern of events which propel the narrative steadily forward from its beginnings through its climaxes to its end. They expect truth, but not necessarily true details; rather, they look for universal truth about man and nature, truth about what could happen in some kind of world—in the world depicted by the author—be it a world of dreams or a world of reality or both.

Empathy. A novel has at its core a unified story, usually developed by presenting the thoughts, spoken words, and actions of the characters; the plot is supplemented by comments and information which may often tell us much about the backgrounds and traits of the characters. The reader must not only notice what the people in the novel say and do, but he must also interpret the reasons for their behavior, the true reasons or the mere rationalizations, the motives which impel them to act, and the connections between parts of the story. He must imagine himself to be each of the persons being portrayed, putting himself in his place, as if he had the same knowledge and personality and faced the same problem or situation. If there is a single sequence of events as there is in many novels, the reader will find it easy to understand the plot; but if there are numerous disconnected fragments or episodes, or if the story goes backward as well as forward in time, the task of following all the relationships among the parts may become complicated or confusing. In the latter case, the alert reader may reread some of the episodes to refresh his memory so that he can see the entire panorama of the novel as it unfolds—as if it were a unified, growing organism but with some portions growing at different times and more quickly than others.

Like the playreader and playgoer, too, the reader of a novel must evaluate the personality of each character as an individual who speaks to others, and behaves toward them, in the precise manner stated or implied by the story. Often the author will provide direct information about each person's background of experience, attitudes, purposes, and ideas. Such information will help the reader to understand the characters, just as he would after long association with them in real life situations.

The characters may be logical, impulsive, inconsistent, now admirable, later despicable, or even two-faced, and the reader cannot always pigeonhole each person in some narrow moral compartment. As in life, people in a story do not always behave as they normally should. Surprising, inconsistent behavior is a significant fact to be appreciated.

Suspense and Novelty. The plot of a novel is customarily developed from an introductory stage to an intermediate stage of mounting tension which keeps the reader in suspense until a climax is reached. Suspense and novelty are the two most distinctive and enjoyable qualities found in many masterpieces of fiction. There may be numerous suspenseful situations and surprises, lending spice to an appetizing menu. In most novels, the air is cleared at the end, with complexities resolved and the remaining characters either rewarded or punished or passing through new thresholds of experience with this stage of their lives brought to a fitting conclusion.

Consider a novel such as Hawthorne's *Scarlet Letter*, with which many readers will doubtless be familiar. In the introduction, Hawthorne tells us that he based the story upon some old papers and a scarlet cloth, shaped like a letter A, which he had found in the custom-house at Salem, Massachusetts, where in 1846–49 he was employed as a surveyor. Immediately, we are intrigued by this strange symbol "A," and begin to feel suspense.

> My eyes fastened themselves upon the old scarlet letter, and would not be turned aside. Certainly there was some deep meaning in it. . . . I happened to place it on my breast. It seemed to me, then, that I experienced a sensation not altogether physical, yet almost so, as of burning heat; and as if the letter were not of red cloth, but red-hot iron. I shuddered, and involuntarily let it fall upon the floor.

Who could read such passages without becoming most eager, impatient, to read on and on until this mystery of the symbol could be explained?

As we read on, everything bears out the mysterious,

somber atmosphere implied by the author's comment in his introduction. Hawthorne himself explained, in his notes--written, strange as it may seem, in 1844, long before he worked at the custom-house—that he wrote the introduction to "relieve the shadows of the gloomy story." All the characters speak and act in this serious, depressing, tense tone; the story is filled with sadness— tragedy in the events, desperation in its personalities, "unrelieved gloom" even in the descriptions of the locale.

The story begins at a scaffold in the courtyard of a prison in seventeenth-century Puritan Boston, as the convicted adulteress, Hester Prynne, is sentenced to wear the letter "A," the mark of shame, forever on her bosom. The popular minister, Dimmesdale, Hester's lover, calls upon her to name the guilty man (that is, himself), but she refuses. Disputing the justice of man-made laws and penalties, she shields her lover from them and cares devotedly for their daughter, Pearl. Thus we are launched upon a suspenseful adventure, and we cannot pause in our reading but must continue as Hester's aging husband vows revenge upon the unknown guilty man. The somber tone of the novel—the Puritanical obsession with sin, punishment, and death—thus prevails and persists throughout to the end.

Reality and Truth. The reader will note how each main episode is described in the same dramatic terms and tone, reflected alike in the language of the dour, severe characters and the moralistic comments of the author. Thus, when Hester rents a small cottage near the town and works as a seamstress, she defiantly wears her symbol of shame and bears firmly the insults of the Puritan rabble while earning a livelihood with needlework and also sewing "coarse garments" free for the poor. Hawthorne comments: "Lonely as was Hester's situation, and without a friend on earth who dared to show himself, she, however, . . . possessed . . . the art—then, as now, almost the only one within a woman's grasp—of needlework. The child had a native grace . . . So magnificent was the small figure . . . that there was an absolute circle of radiance around her, on the darksome cottage-floor. . . ." Later, in the same mood of sad dignity, the minister, Hester's secret lover, appeals to the authorities to leave the child with Hester: "She recognizes, believe me, the solemn miracle which God hath wrought, in the existence of that child. . . . For Hester Prynne's sake, then, and no less for the poor child's sake, let us leave them as Providence hath seen fit to place them!"

Hawthorne's novel consists of dramatic episodes which fit into the plot as a whole but give the impression of separate events, or separated parts of a chain of events, and the reader must depend upon his own imagination for connecting links between them. We must admire this novelist's fluent language, his ability to develop themes of immense dignity, to create a steady, uniform atmosphere, and to set forth numerous details of speech and action which strongly impress the reader. Perhaps the sustained somber tone of the story reflected Hawthorne's personal experience of tragedy, tension, and poverty in his family, contrasted with the successes of his distinguished ancestors. He felt keenly, as he wrote to Sophia Peabody, "the entangling depths of my obscurity." But he accepted the Puritan concept that sin must be punished. In *The Scarlet Letter* the guilty couple are doomed irrevocably to pay dearly for their sin. Hawthorne understood but condemned the romantic sentiments of his time, the rebellious spirit represented by Hester, yet he also objected to the excessively harsh judgments of society. This attitude may explain why the novel dramatizes the difference between Hester, who sinned on impulse, and her husband, Chillingworth, who deliberately plotted evil and revenge. At the end the author praises Hester for her self-reliance and charity, though he cannot side wholeheartedly with her against the rigid moral standards of Puritanism. Although he pictured Hester as one who believed in her own right to live and love as she chose, Hawthorne attributed her choice to moral weakness, and he attempted to show that "human frailty" would inevitably bring sorrow in its train. Yet, after all, he finally portrayed Hester as a noble woman endowed with patience, courage, and hope for a new morality, a more just and free society.

Thus we see that genuine understanding and enjoyment of a well-written novel require close attention to its pervading principle, to its central truths about human beings, but, more than this, they require of the reader that he identify himself wholeheartedly and sympathetically with the characters, that he make their personal, intimate feelings, problems, moods, and thoughts part of himself, for the characters must through their words and deeds impart reality and truth to the author's work.

8
How To Choose What To Read

The selection of reading materials can be a task so complex and troublesome that some prospective readers may be tempted to give up in despair and take refuge in time-wasting competitive attractions or aimless activities devoid of intellectual, moral, cultural, material, or physical benefits. With more than 250,000 books in print in the United States alone, as well as hundreds of older (out-of-print) books still available to American readers, it is no wonder that many people do not know where to begin the process of selection. How easy it is to turn on the radio or television set and just sit while whatever happens to be presented, good or bad, captures one's attention and too often consumes with trivia a person's most precious asset—the time of his life! On the other hand, the person who prefers to devote his time to worthwhile reading must think for himself, make some intelligent effort, some logical decisions, and some deliberate choices, inquiring into his own needs and interests as he builds a personal library of worthwhile journals and books.

Nevertheless, nothing invested, nothing gained. More and more people, young and old, are reading more—and more intelligently—because they realize that life is short, that it should be lived to the full, that it should be significant, enjoyable, earnest, meaningful, stimulating, creative, educative, and uplifting in the finest sense; and they know that, in modern times, these values can best be achieved through discriminating selection and attentive reading of periodicals, pamphlets, and books, encompassing news, feature articles, poetry, drama, short stories, novels, essays, and works of philosophy, psychology, religion, science, art, music, history, biography, folklore, humor, and other fascinating and useful subjects communicated by means of the printed word.

I do not mean to condemn other media of communication. In fact, there are worthwhile programs on television, including excellent discussions of books, but even the best of its plays, concerts, exhibits, demonstrations, and discussions are often ruined by offensive advertisements for inferior products, prepared by hucksters oblivious to the sensibilities and intellectual sensitivities or interests of the audience. I wonder what would happen if publishers insisted on inserting moronic advertisements for a piece of soap between the stanzas of a great poem, between the scenes of an absorbing drama, or between the paragraphs of a suspenseful novel! Yet commercial television networks utilize the public channels of communication to sell soap and other profitable commodities, not to provide the cultural experiences and wholesome enjoyments for which the airways belonging to the people should be used. How fortunate are those millions of readers who can choose their own entertainment because they have built personal libraries at home and can quickly choose among hundreds or thousands of literary masterpieces and other printed sources of ideas and information, wisely devoting their precious time to them!

SELECTION OF BOOKS

Readers building their personal library of the "best" books will naturally differ in their approach to this formidable task. Some may wish to become familiar with the significant writings in each period of history, beginning perhaps with *The Book of the Dead,* which nearly six thousand years ago set forth ideas (about justice, law, morality, and immortality) still part of our heritage, then reading the literature of each civilization, ancient, medieval, and modern. Other readers may prefer to devote most of their reading time to specific types of literature, in English or in translation, such as poetry, drama, fiction, myths, histories, biographies, essays, or religious, scientific, and philosophical works. Still others may be attracted especially to the writings of some of the most renowned or influential geniuses—a long line of masters of the written word from Vergil to Shakespeare, Goethe, and Shaw, whose works can be read in English and in many other languages. Finally, there are readers who have no set plan or program but simply obtain books through recommendation, reports by critics, displays or advertisements, browsing in stores or libraries, or participation in some class, discussion group, or club.

There is nothing wrong with any of these approaches to the selection of books. Nevertheless, in view of the hundreds of thousands of books available, most readers could benefit from a systematic planning of their selections. I should like, therefore, to suggest a program of book selection which would fit the needs and interests of different types of readers. This program is divided into (1) a core list of books everyone should own and (2) a special list of significant books in literature, philosophy, psychology, religion, science, and the arts. The core list of foundation books will be discussed in the remainder of this chapter. The list of books in special fields will be presented in the next chapter.

A CORE LIST OF BOOKS

The following core list represents an indispensable collection of works of writers and thinkers who have shaped the minds and enriched the lives of all humanity. For this foundation set of books, I have selected the works of thirty authors which have not only been accepted universally as literary masterpieces, or superb examples of a literary form, but have also had an enduring, pervasive influence upon mankind in their own and succeeding ages. The authors, arranged chronologically by date of birth, are: Homer, Aeschylus, Sophocles, Euripides, Aristophanes, Vergil, Plutarch, St. Augustine, Dante, Chaucer, Erasmus, Montaigne, Cervantes, Spenser, Shakespeare, Milton, Molière, Defoe, Swift, Voltaire, Samuel Johnson, Rousseau, Emerson, Dickens, Stowe, Thoreau, Melville, Ibsen, Shaw, and Whitman. Their works include plays, novels, poetry, satire, essays, criticism, and biography. Their writings span a period of 2,800 years, from the birth of Homer ca. 850 B.C. to the death of Shaw in 1950.

Any home which does not possess in its library representative works of all or nearly all of these great authors and thinkers is indeed culturally deprived. There are, of course, hundreds and thousands of other gifted writers whose works and ideas have endured to our time, but surely those named here are indispensable.

Great Dramatists. Our core list contains the names of eight famous playwrights: Aeschylus, Sophocles, Euripides, Aristophanes, Shakespeare, Molière, Ibsen, and Shaw.

AESCHYLUS (525–456 B.C.), author of ninety-two plays, was one of the foremost dramatists of ancient times. He wrote the classical trilogy *Oresteia,* consisting of three interrelated Greek plays depicting the sacrificial murder of his daughter Iphigenia by King Agamemnon to appease the goddess Artemis, a deed which causes so much pain to his wife Clytemnestra the Queen (the "pain that never sleeps") that in revenge, with the aid of her lover, she murders the victorious King on his return from the conquest of Troy; the murder of the Queen and her lover by her own son Orestes and daughter Electra to avenge their father follows; and, finally, divine forgiveness is granted the conscience-stricken son for his crime of matricide. The drama teaches that horrible, unnatural sins must be punished, but that there is hope of forgiveness for the criminal who has acted from a sense of duty and has suffered torment of conscience and sought atonement for his sin.

(There are various editions and translations of the trilogy, including *Oresteia,* translated by Richmond Lattimore, edited by David Grene and Richmond Lattimore, paperbound, published by the University of Chicago Press; also, 3 volumes, paperbound, translated by Gilbert Murray, published by Oxford University Press. Be sure to read, too, another classical drama by Aeschylus: *Prometheus Bound,* translated by Gilbert Murray, paperbound, published by Oxford University Press.)

SOPHOCLES (ca. 496–406 B.C.), Athenian genius, wrote the masterpieces *Oedipus the King* (or *Oedipus Tyrannus*), *Oedipus at Colonus, Antigone,* and other superbly constructed dramas. The background of *Oedipus the King* is that the King and Queen of Thebes are warned by an oracle that their son Oedipus, soon to be born, will murder the King and have incestuous relations with his mother, the Queen, so they order the newborn infant to be tied up and exposed to die. Their order is not obeyed, and Oedipus grows up to carry out the predicted crimes, though without knowing the identities of his victims. In the play, a plague strikes the city and, it is believed, will not pass until the old King's murderer is punished. When the truth is revealed, the Queen hangs herself and Oedipus inflicts upon himself the terrible punishment (blinding) which he had decreed for the then unknown murderer.

(Read *Sophocles I, Three Tragedies,* and *Sophocles II, Four Tragedies,* two paperbound volumes edited by David Grene and Richmond Lattimore, published by the University of Chicago Press.)

EURIPIDES (ca. 480–402 B.C.) was a revolutionary Greek dramatist, realistic, and more modern than many modern playwrights. In his plays he explored the psychological conflicts within the soul of man as he struggles heroically against human and natural evils, against war, cruelty, and injustice, and against man's inhumanity to man—burdens from which he must free himself without help from the gods or fickle fortune. Euripides' *Medea* is one of the most moving, vivid, and "modern" plays ever written, a play about Jason (of Golden Fleece fame), a royal mismarriage, an unfaithful husband, and the terrible revenge taken by his jealous, betrayed wife. *The Trojan Women* is the most eloquent peace propaganda ever written, depicting the pitiful fate of the women of Troy carried off as slaves by the Greek conquerors of their native land: "piteously . . . weeping, with fear striking our hearts, for we are slaves."

(Read *Medea, The Trojan Women,* and eight other plays in *Ten Plays by Euripides,* a compact paperbound volume of translations by Moses Hadas and John Harvey McLean, published by Bantam Books.)

ARISTOPHANES (ca. 448–380 B.C.), Greek master of plays containing beautifully musical poetry and powerful propaganda, bitterly opposed Euripides' ideal of individual self-direction and wrote hilarious comedies (such as *The Frogs* and *The Clouds*) which ridiculed the literary, political, and intellectual leaders of Athens, exposed and condemned the corruption, mobocracy, immorality, and hypocrisy of his time, attacked the new ideas of Socrates (who wanted everyone to think for himself about truth, beauty, and morality), and pleaded, as some conservative writers might today, for a return to old traditions and simple ideals in government, literature, and education. Of eleven comedies extant (out of more than forty he wrote), *Lysistrata* is a most wonderful, fun-filled farce of special interest to modern readers because it tells how the women of Athens and Sparta used every conceivable means of stopping the senseless war between the two nations and even refused to live with their husbands unless the men made peace. Their strategy was successful in restoring tranquility and harmony.

(Read *Lysistrata, The Frogs, The Clouds,* and two other plays by Aristophanes in the paperbound volume, *Five Comedies of Aristophanes,* translated by Benjamin B. Rogers, edited by Andrew Chiappe, published by Doubleday & Co., Inc.)

SHAKESPEARE, WILLIAM (1564–1616) was the greatest of dramatists and the greatest of poets; his art continues to remake the minds of men, inspiring them through its architectural perfection, masterly portrayal of human nature and universal truths, depth of meaning, exquisite eloquence, and wisdom. Of Shakespeare the man we know so little that controversies rage about his identity. The best answer to the question, "Who was Shakespeare?" is a quotation from one of his own works: "That which we call a rose by any other name would smell as sweet." His colleague, Ben Jonson, tells us, in a brief but significant appraisal of Shakespeare's character, that "he was indeed honest and of an open and free nature." That comment helps to explain why everything this greatest of all masters wrote was more nearly real and true to life and nature, and more nearly perfect, than the works of any other writer before or since. There has been but one Shakespeare, however he be named, and mankind may rightly boast of genuine cultural progress in some future age if another such as he is born.

I recommended a few years ago that leading Shakespearean scholars be invited to prepare a series of explanatory guidebooks to accompany the bard's original works, and the distinguished editor selected for the task of editing the series completed a national survey to determine which of Shakespeare's thirty-seven plays are being most widely read. The most popular plays were found to be the six tragedies of *Macbeth, Julius Caesar, Hamlet, Romeo and Juliet, Othello,* and *King Lear,* and two comedies, *The Merchant of Venice* and *A Midsummer Night's Dream.* (The number of young readers in their teens ranged from 130,000 for *A Midsummer Night's Dream* to 1,260,000 for *Macbeth.*)

All these magnificent plays are available in numerous low-priced paperbound editions, as well as in handsome hardbound editions, and all should become treasured volumes in every home. In addition, there are several excellent paperbound editions of Shakespeare's *Sonnets,* the most nearly perfect poetry ever written. Bookstores and libraries stock attractive one-volume editions of Shakespeare's complete works in a durable cloth binding, as well as numerous special collections of plays—volumes of four plays, of five plays, of eight plays, of comedies, of tragedies, and of histories, many in paperbound editions.

In *Hamlet*, the most famous and influential of all plays, Hamlet is the enigmatic, hesitant, melancholy, tragic prince of Denmark who, despite his native sensitivity and romantic idealism, faces a terrible moral dilemma and inner conflict as he is impelled to revenge the murder of the King, his father, by the "incestuous, murderous, damned Dane," the murdered King's brother. Yet Hamlet must make certain, first, that his uncle actually committed the murder, and second, that if his uncle should prove to be guilty, Hamlet can bring him to justice and at the same time win public approval for ridding the nation of a fratricidal villain. By mistake, Hamlet impulsively kills the King's Lord Chamberlain, Polonius, a "wretched, rash, intruding fool," instead of the guilty King. Hamlet's sweetheart, Ophelia, daughter of Polonius, is driven mad by the Prince's weird behavior and commits suicide. The furious plots and counterplots of the two main antagonists—Hamlet and his uncle, the usurper —end in the final duel scene of the last act with the violent deaths of the three royal characters: the Queen, the King, and Hamlet himself. (This play is available in sixteen paperbound editions.)

Macbeth, too, is a powerful tragedy centering in regicide and the usurpation of a throne, that of Scotland. As in *Hamlet*, so in *Macbeth* an overambitious pair contrives to assassinate their King. Here the royal victim is Duncan, "gracious ruler," whose generosity and "virtues will plead like angels against the deep damnation of his taking-off; . . ." As in *Hamlet*, the plot in *Macbeth* ends with the violent deaths of the usurper and his accomplice. I include excerpts from *Macbeth* on page 137. (There are seventeen paperbound editions of this play available.)

Julius Caesar depicts the assassination of the greatest military genius, "mighty Caesar," who ruled the Roman world "like a Colossus," but whose vanity and ambition brought about his downfall. His traitorous friend Brutus, patriotic, gullible leader of the assassins, called him "the noblest Roman of them all." The play traces the fate of the assassins from the aftermath of the conspiracy and murder to the final battle scene where both of their commanders (Brutus and the shrewd, cynical Cassius with the "lean and hungry look") are defeated by the loyal Mark Anthony, "well beloved" friend of Caesar, and Octavius, Caesar's grandnephew and heir, and commit suicide. This greatest of political plays is lifelike and powerful in every scene and action as it relates the events which decided not only the fates of individual characters but also the destiny of the Roman republic and turned into a new direction the entire course of world history. (There are thirteen paperbound editions of *Julius Caesar* in print.)

In *Romeo and Juliet,* Romeo, heir of the wealthy Montague family of Verona, who is at first an infatuated sensualist, is transformed by his trysts with Juliet (whose beauty "doth teach the torches to burn bright") into "gentle Romeo," a sincere, honorable, sensitive, impetuous lover. Juliet, a girl of fourteen, daughter of the Capulet family (bitter enemies of the Montagues) fears that disaster impends but dreams of her true love, defies parents and convention, breaking a promise to accept her mother's choice of a husband for her, and seizes the happiness of devoted, mutual love with Romeo which, however, she insists must be genuine, reciprocal, and thoroughly honest on both sides:

"O swear not by the moon, the inconstant moon . . .
Lest that thy love prove likewise variable."

The feud between the lovers' families divides the entire city into warring factions and sharpens the significance of the young couple's secret marriage in defiance of parental authority. Their elopement, however, is doomed by tragic accidents and mistakes of judgment, ending in the suicide of both unhappy lovers. Only then are the two families reconciled, too late to prevent tragedy, yet at last uniting the divided city. (Twelve paperbound editions of *Romeo and Juliet* are available.)

Othello, the Moor of Venice, tells the story of Othello, the proud Moorish nobleman and general who, being "great of heart" and "of a free and open nature," believes that only his accounts of dangerous exploits had won for him the love and loyalty of the gracious beauty Desdemona, daughter of the Venetian nobleman and senator, Brabantio. Their elopement (compare it with the similar elopement of Romeo and Juliet) met with the bitter opposition of her father, who turned against them, especially since he had favored a more attractive suitor for his daughter's hand. Othello is driven insanely jealous by the hints of his villainous ensign, Iago, that Desdemona has betrayed him for the sake of a handsome lieutenant, Cassio. Enraged by Iago's planted evidence (including Cassio's possession of a handkerchief—Othello's first gift to Desdemona), the Moor strangles his wife in bed as she desperately pleads innocence; then, learning the truth about the trusted villain's perfidy, he kills Iago, stabs himself, and kissing the lifeless lips of his innocent Desdemona, exclaims in his dying moments:

> "I kiss'd thee ere I kill'd thee . . . no way but this,
> Killing myself, to die upon a kiss."

(Ten paperbound editions of *Othello* are available.)

King Lear is a doubly tragic story about two old men and their children, whose characters they misjudge with disastrous consequences. King Lear is the headstrong, foolhardy, stern, and proud ruler of Britain who demands of his three daughters that they proclaim their complete devotion and loyalty to him above and beyond any other obligations, proving themselves worthy of being heirs to his kingdom. Two deceitful daughters ("gilded serpents," "tigers, not daughters") make a pretense of their love for him, but the third and youngest, his favorite Cordelia (whose voice "was ever soft, gentle, and low"), tells him the truth—that she cares for him as a daughter should, yet reserves her deepest affection for some future husband. In a sudden, topsy-turvy misunderstanding of his daughters' real motives, Lear disowns the honest, loyal

Cordelia and hands over his realm to the two cruel, greedy daughters who later mistreat him horribly and cast him out to madness in the countryside. Similarly, the second rash, gullible, old man, the Earl of Gloucester, a faithful supporter of Lear's, makes a crucial mistake about his own two sons, punishing the loyal, legitimate son, Edgar, and rewarding the evil, traitorous, "rough and lecherous" bastard son, Edmund. Gloucester is tortured and blinded by Lear's wicked daughter Regan and her husband, but the latter and the two evil daughters, the "she-foxes," meet a violent death, one daughter poisoning the other and then stabbing herself to death. Meanwhile, Gloucester's bastard son Edmund, then commander of the British army, has seized Lear and hanged the gentle Cordelia. In the last scene of the play, the pitiful Lear dies with her dead body in his arms. (There are ten paperbound editions of *King Lear* available.)

In the *Merchant of Venice,* the merchant is the generous, loyal Antonio who pledges his own body as security when his friend Bassanio borrows from the vengeful moneylender, Shylock (a Jew who hates the Christians for their insults and is enraged further when his daughter steals his money and elopes with a Christian), money needed for his expenses in paying court to the beautiful, virtuous, gracious Portia, fair lady whose "sunny locks" hang upon "her temples like a golden fleece." Bassanio wins the fair lady by choosing the correct casket while blindfolded in a contest against other suitors. When misfortune prevents Antonio from repaying the loan, Shylock demands his "pound of flesh," rejecting Portia's plea for mercy:

> "The quality of mercy is not strain'd,
> It droppeth as the gentle rain from heaven
> upon the place beneath. . . ."

Portia, disguised as a noted lawyer, has been invited to serve as judge in the case. She renders judgment strictly —ruling that, in accordance with the contract for the loan, the moneylender must not shed a drop of blood nor take even an ounce more or less than one pound of Antonio's flesh, thus circumventing the terms of the contract—and then imposes on Shylock a severe penalty for illegally plotting against the life of Antonio, a Venetian citizen. The play ends with justice done, friendship and love rewarded, as Portia discloses her disguise to Bassanio. (This play is available in fifteen paperbound editions.)

A Midsummer Night's Dream is a delightful comedy reflecting the two themes that "the course of true love never did run smooth" and that the enchantment of moonstruck lovers, whether produced by their "seething brains" "that apprehend more than cool reason ever comprehends" or by love potions prepared by fairies, impels them to act like madmen, for "the lunatic, the lover and the poet" are alike, and "Lord, what fools these mortals be!" This play is a magical, fantastic one with a happy ending for three pairs of lovers—after merry entanglements and woodland adventures—as the fairies bless "with sweet peace" the sleeping lovers in their chambers and also their future children so that they will be born perfect with never a "mole, harelip, nor scar, nor mark prodigious, such as are despised in nativity. . . ." (There are nine paperbound editions of this play available.)

MOLIÈRE, JEAN BAPTISTE POQUELIN (1622–1673) was the greatest of French playwrights and comparable to Shakespeare in the creation of lifelike comedies exposing people as they are in themselves—weak, selfish, capricious, cunning, deceitful—not sincere, charitable, wise, and pious, as they appear to be on the surface. Each comedy strikes at a central weakness of human nature, and many of the comedies reveal the truth about unscrupulous scoundrels and their gullible victims.

Molière's *Tartuffe* was at first the most hated of comedies because church leaders interpreted the play as an attack upon them. One called Molière a "demon clad in human flesh" and suggested that burning him in eternal fires of hell would not be too harsh a punishment. Actually, the play (which Molière rewrote again and again) condemned religious impostors, not religion. Tartuffe, the

pious hypocrite, poses as a grateful, self-sacrificing fol-
lower of the church, induces the wealthy Orgon to hand
over all his property to him, encourages plans for marriage with Orgon's daughter, and then is caught making
love to Orgon's wife. All ends well for everybody except
the scoundrel Tartuffe.

In *Don Juan*, Molière pays his respects to those unscrupulous aristocratic libertines who excuse their vices
on the specious ground that "everybody is doing it," when,
of course, it is mostly they themselves who are "doing it."
The plot is based on Tirso de Molina's play about the
Spanish legend of Don Juan (in which the villain betrays
Don Gonzalo's daughter, kills the father in a duel, and is
strangled by a statue of Gonzalo). In Molière's version,
Don Juan abducts and marries a convent girl, then deserts
her, rationalizing that it had been a sin anyway to have
taken her from God's service for sake of marriage to a
man like him, a free-and-easy lover of all women. He
cunningly promises to repent and reform but knows he
never will, for he has no real faith in heaven or hell but
only in his own pleasures.

Other comedies portray similar human frailties, greed,
and deceit. *The Miser* is about rich Harpagon, who cares
for nothing but money and uses his son and daughter to
get more of it. But all his schemes are in the end frustrated. *The Misanthrope* is based on the theme that stupid,
stubborn people must expect disaster such as afflicted the
hero Alceste, unhappy lover of the fickle flirt Célimène.
The Doctor in Spite of Himself tells about a medical impostor whose deceits fool most people but eventually
boomerang; however, the faker is saved from hanging,
and all turns out well.

(Read *The Misanthrope and Other Plays*, five plays
translated by John Wood, including *Tartuffe* and *The
Doctor in Spite of Himself*; and *The Miser and Other
Plays*, five plays translated by John Wood, including *Don
Juan*.)

IBSEN, HENRIK (1828–1906), creative gift of Norway
to the literature, the culture, and the social progress of

Europe and Western civilization, found himself ostracized in his native land because his plays attacked established institutions and illuminated the sore thumbs of society. His plays call a spade a spade, telling the facts of life about the game of life and all the players in it. He had no final answers to social problems but exposed the double standard—the gap between what people want others to do and what they themselves do, between high ideals and evil practices, between the rare, honest, unselfish person and the multitudes of cowards, hypocrites, and stubborn self-seekers who fear and resist reforms which might upset their genuine ambitions.

A Doll's House exposes the false morality which kept unhappy wives tied by convention to their husbands who used them to bolster their own pride, treated them like innocent dolls and often like slaves, and thus deprived them of their identities as human beings, their minds and souls as individuals. The condition of women has improved in Western countries since Ibsen's time—read Ashley M. F. Montagu's *The Natural Superiority of Women*, reflecting a new attitude of respect for the female sex. In Ibsen's view, the abuse of women by their male masters was only one aspect of the despicable social order, with its injustice, cruelty, disillusionment, and obstinate blindness to the truth. The wife, Nora, changes from a traditional doll-like, contriving, submissive creature into a passionate rebel against unjust laws and customs, a rebel who abandons husband and children in order to become a whole human being in her own right, an individual.

Other representative plays by this master dramatist are *Brand*, in which an honest preacher is utterly destroyed by his congregation when he expects them to practice the religious ideas to which they give lip service; *The Pillars of Society*, which shows how the most respected leaders of the community conceal skeletons in dark closets—in this drama truth is discovered and genuine repentance follows; *Ghosts*, which depicts the immoral blindness of church and society to scientific facts, such as the spread of venereal disease; *An Enemy of the People,* which shows what happens when the so-called "good people" of a community face the challenge of someone who insists on telling the truth about their germ-polluted water supply (how modern this story about pollution seems today!); *Hedda Gabler,* which portrays an evil, domineering woman who brings pain and destruction to everyone, including herself; and *The Master Builder,* which tells how the fondest, hidden dreams of gifted creative persons may remain buried in the depths of their inner being, resulting in a lack of perfect fulfillment which can drive them on and on to desperation and catastrophe.

(Read *Six Plays,* a book in the Modern Library with an introduction by Eva Le Gallienne and including *A Doll's House, Ghosts, An Enemy of the People, Rosmersholm, Hedda Gabler,* and *The Master Builder; Brand,* translated by Michael Meyer; *Peer Gynt,* translated by Michael Meyer; and *The Wild Duck,* translated and edited by Kai Jurgenson and Robert F. Schenkkan.)

SHAW, GEORGE BERNARD (1856–1950), who admired and defended Ibsen as "a man of genius," wrote with the same sympathy for the oppressed and unfortunate (for example, the patient neglected by doctors who treat people as things, not as people), condemning cruelty of all kinds, including the torture of animals for profit (he was a vegetarian because he respected and valued all living creatures). No one knew better than Shaw what he intended to do in his plays, and no one expressed his intentions more pointedly and convincingly than he did in the prefaces to his first two books of plays (*Plays: Pleasant and Unpleasant*) published in 1898, in which he wrote in behalf of the "general onslaught on idealism . . . implicit in *Arms and the Man* and the realistic plays of the modern school." He was no longer "satisfied with fictitious morals and fictitious good conduct, shedding fictitious glory on overcrowding, disease, crime, drink, war, cruelty, infant mortality, and all the other commonplaces of civilization which drive men to the theatre to make foolish pretenses that these things are progress, science, morals, religion, patriotism, imperial supremacy, national greatness and all other names the newspapers call them." We find this attitude of respect for truth and reality in Shaw's great predecessors Shakespeare, Molière, and Ibsen, but Shaw wrote in a sophisticated, brilliant style about paradoxical situations and ideas which delighted his audiences of well-to-do theatergoers, each of whom felt clearsighted enough to appreciate the facts of life as revealed in the plays in contrast with the foolish dreams and misconceptions afflicting "less clearsighted people."

Shaw fought for Ibsen because he shared the latter's devotion to the cause of individual freedom and social reform. There is no question about Shaw's sincerity, reflected in his influential leadership of the Fabian Socialists in England as well as in his exposure of social hypocrisy and inhumanity by means of his masterly plays. In addition to the plays, be sure to read Shaw's essays, "The Economic Basis of Socialism" and "The Transition to Social Democracy," in *Fabian Essays in Socialism,* and other essays in the paperbound volume, *Selected Non-Dramatic Writings of George Bernard Shaw,* edited by Dan H. Laurence. Read also *Shaw on Music,* brilliant selections compiled by Eric Bentley, now available in paperbound format.

Among the early Shaw plays were *The Widower's Houses* and *Mrs. Warren's Profession,* both contrasting the standards people profess to believe in with the things they actually believe and do.

The Widower's Houses has as its central theme the commonplace truth that young men with high theoretical ideals are easily corrupted by evil institutions, the establishment, of their community. Dr. Trench refuses to marry the daughter of a slum landlord because she will bring him tainted money which he discovers to have been earned through illegal neglect of houses for poor tenants. But then he is shocked to learn that his own small income has for years been derived from illegal and immoral profits from the same properties, on which he held mortgages. When his accustomed income is endangered, he decides to live with the evils he had always condemned as shameful—a familiar story today as we see young people meekly take their comfortable places as obedient robots in the worst of our contemporary enterprises. Shaw would admire the young men and women who dare to defy immoral institutions and customs.

Mrs. Warren's profession of prostitution, in *Mrs. Warren's Profession*, complicates her sheltered daughter's romance with a young man who turns out to be the son of one of her former lovers (a clergyman) and therefore her daughter's half-brother. Mrs. Warren's business partner and financier, the aristocrat Sir George Crofts, offers marriage to her daughter Vivie, but Vivie is horrified to learn from him the true source of her income (compare this with the similar discovery by Dr. Trench in *The Widower's Houses*). At the end, Vivie says good-bye forever to her half-brother and to her mother, resolved to earn her own living in a decent way: "If I had been you, Mother," she says, "I might have done as you did; but I should not have lived one life and believed in another. You are a conventional woman at heart. That is why I am bidding you good-bye now."

Important plays by Shaw include *Arms and the Man*, which ridicules silly notions of military glory; *Candida*, which contrasts poetic love and practical common sense; *Man and Superman*, in which the revolutionary philosopher John Tanner, a disciple of Nietzsche, succumbs to the life force of a superwoman, Ann; *The Man of Destiny*, about Napoleon, who admits there is "only one universal passion: fear . . . It is fear that makes men fight . . . Pooh! there's no such thing as a real hero"; *Major Barbara*, about Barbara, major in the Salvation Army and daughter of a munitions maker whose cause wins out in the end when the daughter and her lover, a professor of Greek, rejoin the world of practicality and realism; *Saint Joan*, about a clever, humane, brave Joan of Arc, who is eventually vindicated and canonized; *Pyg-*

malion, ironic portrayal of high society which anyone willing to work hard enough can be trained by linguistic experts to fit into quite comfortably. Read also *Back to Methuselah, Caesar and Cleopatra, Heartbreak House, The Devil's Disciple, The Doctor's Dilemma*—all of them important plays now available in paperbound editions.)

Great Novelists. There are hundreds, even thousands, of famous novelists whose works deserve an honored place in the home library. For the indispensable list of core books, I have chosen the following five novelists whose writings are loved and admired throughout the Western world: Cervantes, Defoe, Dickens, Stowe, and Melville.

CERVANTES SAAVEDRA, MIGUEL DE (1547–1616), a contemporary of Shakespeare, write numerous stories, poems, and plays, yet none but the novel *Don Quixote* could be called a masterpiece, and none brought him more than the barest sustenance. He died in the same year as Shakespeare, a poor man, renowned, however, for his one great work which had a profound influence upon the society of his time and stimulated the minds of men in succeeding ages up to the present. *Don Quixote* (begun while the author was in prison for debt) portrays hundreds of characters, from the poorest to the richest, as they go about their selfish, illogical business of everyday living in the midst of illusion and self-deception, yet ready to beat down the idealistic dreamer and reformer, who is compelled at last to acknowledge that the world is a world of rogues and schemers who have no use for the chivalrous knights and virtuous ladies idealized in the literature of that materialistic age. Cervantes might have asked himself what would happen if someone really believed the fantastic stories about noble knights and fair ladies and went forth into the world with his head full of such dreams. *Don Quixote* was the answer, for Don Quixote soon discovers how quickly the foolish hypocrites and schemers will resent and resist the right-minded reformers, the simpleminded dreamers like Don Quixote, who mistake what is for what should be, fight windmills they mistake for giants, and eventually die in despair.

(There are several excellent translations of *Don Quixote* available in paperbound editions, including an unabridged edition translated by Walter Starkie. There is also a paperbound volume, *The Portable Cervantes*, containing most of *Don Quixote* and two of his short novels, translated and edited by Samuel Putnam.)

DEFOE, DANIEL (1659?–1731) was about sixty years old when he turned to the writing of fiction after a checkered career as a journalist and secret government agent. He wrote *Robinson Crusoe*, a fascinating story in autobiographical form about a self-reliant British hero, based on the real experiences of a sailor who had lived five years on a deserted island; *Moll Flanders*, about a frail, passionate woman of loose morals (Twelve Years a Whore, Twelve Years a Thief, and so on) but later reformed and retired in wealth; *A Journal of the Plague Year*, an extraordinarily vivid description of what might have been and probably were the horrible events of the great plague of 1665 in London; *Roxana, the Fortunate Mistress*, a story about a greedy, repulsive sex-pot who ended her mad career in tragic wretchedness; and numerous minor works reflecting his personal dogmatic religion-based morality, painstaking attention to details and logic, but utter lack of any appreciation of love and sentiment, for he painted everything either black or white, and nothing in between could be tolerated.

Robinson Crusoe is Defoe's universally admired masterpiece, ingenious, and highly convincing because of the author's meticulous attention to the tiniest details affecting the shipwrecked sailor's struggle to survive alone, as he did for twenty-five years, on the deserted island. The story reads like a detective thriller, each problem being handled with perfect logic and practicality, whether it be building a shelter, making a chair, planting corn, or trapping wild goats—a perfect tribute to the ability of an independent, resourceful Englishman, stripped bare of most of the resources of civilization, but able to overcome nature and win the battle for survival with his two hands and the consoling help of the Good Book, his constant guide and companion.

(Read, in addition to *Robinson Crusoe*—available now in a half-dozen paperbound editions as well as in attractive hardbounds—*Captain Singleton* [about adventures in Africa], *Moll Flanders, A Journal of the Plague Year,* and *Roxana, the Fortunate Mistress.*)

DICKENS, CHARLES (1812–1870) was one of the most gifted and prolific creators of literary masterpieces in modern times. He was a genius of very little schooling who worked as a child in a blacking factory and later as a reporter, turning to his true occupation as a novelist at twenty-four years of age. His first two novels were *The Pickwick Papers* (published initially in serial form), in which he touched the spirits of all readers by infusing the story with lively, happy characters and incidents, and *Oliver Twist,* in which he touched the hearts of all readers by portraying the tragic, sorrowful, cruel, and bitter sides of places and persons.

In *The Pickwick Papers*, Mr. Pickwick is misunderstood by his landlady, Mrs. Bardell, who mistakes his remarks for a proposal of marriage and then sues him for breach of promise. He is convicted and ordered to pay damages but prefers to go to the horrible, grim debtors' prison instead. Mrs. Bardell, too, is sent to prison because she cannot pay the costs of the case. Everything is straightened out when Mr. Pickwick pays the costs for her, she withdraws her complaint, and both are released from prison. Many exciting, humorous incidents fill the pages of *The Pickwick Papers*, a most enjoyable example of Dickens's imaginative and inimitable style.

In *Oliver Twist*, Oliver is born in a poorhouse (shortly before his mother dies) and lives nine years in the almshouse, from which he is expelled to work as an apprentice for an undertaker. He falls into the hands of the master teacher of pickpockets, Fagin, who takes him along to watch his pickpockets pick pockets. Being innocent, Oliver stands his ground, is captured by the police and taken to court, but is befriended by the pickpockets' intended victim, Mr. Branlow. He is then kidnapped by Nancy, a girl in Fagin's gang, and forced to watch a burglary. Nancy, who has discovered Oliver's true identity as the heir to a fortune, discloses the truth even though she is then beaten to death by her lover, Sikes of the Fagin gang. The facts of poverty, crime, deceit, and the tribulations of well-meaning people are vividly portrayed so that they become real to us, just as real as the same deplorable facts in our own society today.

In *David Copperfield,* another sad story about poverty and despair, one of the world's prime masterpieces, based in part on Dickens' own life, David's father dies when David is only six months old, and his mother marries again, this time a cruel, tyrannous man who sends David off to a harsh life in school. Later David makes his honest way in the world, experiencing various crises familiar in the lives of the poor, losing loved ones and best friends, but, always with a kindly thought for others, finally settling down with a loving wife, Agnes Wickford, who has ever been his sympathetic inspiration.

A Tale of Two Cities is a stirring novel about the French Revolution and the Reign of Terror, a story filled with emotion, bravery, passion, self-sacrifice, violence—characters like the cold, bloodthirsty Madame Defarge, knitting while she counts the number of heads being chopped off by the guillotine, and Sidney Carton, the English lawyer who calmly gives his life to save the life of the man loved by the woman he himself loves. This superb masterwork captures the hearts and minds of all its readers, young and old, and sustains attention from its first page to the last through unforgettable, dramatic events and personalities.

(Read also *Great Expectations,* about Pip, the boy who, when his expectation of an inheritance is disappointed, becomes a blacksmith but learns to distinguish the real and the good from the false and the evil in life; *Hard Times,* about hard times in a dirty, sooty town dominated by the villainous rich man, Bounderby, and about his unfortunate mill workers who dared to expect education for their children but were themselves misled by a greedy demagogue; the famous story, *A Christmas Carol,* about the transformation of an old miser into a kindly man of charity; *Bleak House, Dombey and Son,* and *Our Mutual Friend,* all exposés of the slum conditions of London in Dickens' time, conditions quite familiar to us in our own land today. Read these masterpieces available in numerous paperbound editions as well as hardbound editions.)

STOWE, HARRIET ELIZABETH BEECHER (1811–1896) wrote several fine works (*The Minister's Wooing, Sam Lawson's Old Town, Old Town Folks, The Pearl of Orr's Island, Palmetto Leaves*) but of course her imperishable work of social literature was *Uncle Tom's Cabin,* now available in numerous paperbound and clothbound editions.

Uncle Tom's Cabin, Lincoln is reported to have said, was written by the little lady who caused the tragic Civil War, but he was mistaken. The Civil War was caused, not by this masterpiece of social literature which aroused the sympathy of decent people in the North and abroad, but mainly by the clash of crass materialistic interests of North and South. Mrs. Stowe's book became a propaganda weapon in the battle between economic rivals, and it failed to remedy the disease of racism which eventually spread throughout the land. The black people in her novel were rightly portrayed as patiently suffering, brave, idealistic, and far superior in many ways to the southern aristocracy whose inhumanity brought the nation to the brink of ruin. The proofs of universal racism accumulated during the century after the end of that war until at last the fact became undeniable that the majority of whites and their leaders, North and South alike, have always been unjust, cruel, and stupid in their human relationships.

It is with special satisfaction that I point to my own writing in the volume *Education and Society* in which, several decades before a Presidential commission (The

Kerner Commission of the Johnson regime) arrived at the same conclusion, I deplored the rank mistreatment of American minorities in their own country and demanded an end to that injustice and a beginning of the effort to make amends for the past. My message was read by a few thousand teachers of whom perhaps a half-dozen paid serious attention. Americans have needed more than one *Uncle Tom's Cabin* in a century to remind them of their passivity in the face of injustice; they need to read great books of this kind every year in every decade if they are to achieve a sane and just society. The majority and their leaders are rightly concerned today, but chiefly for the wrong reason—namely for the reason that violence, riots, and even the danger of revolution are at last threatening their peace of mind and comfort, as the desperate black, Spanish, Mexican, and Indian minorities, comprising thirty million people (whose cause is supported by millions of decent persons in the majority), are ready to fight and die for their basic human rights. In another civil war or guerrilla war, the property and lives of many people would be destroyed. Instead of violence and another civil war, then, let us read *Uncle Tom's Cabin*.

Uncle Tom's Cabin told a little of the truth about that huge concentration camp, the entire region of the South, in 1852, but where are the great novelists who have told the truth about the concentration camp of the entire society, imprisoning the souls of minorities, North and South, East and West, throughout the intervening century? So I write another warning: Be sure to read again *Uncle Tom's Cabin* and be sure that every child reads it again and again, if you wish to see a lasting, decent social order in the nation. I repeat my message of the year 1942: "Is it not hypocritical to preach democracy while denying any minority the chance to live free, useful, happy lives? . . . Our best facilities and educational opportunities ought to be given to the victims of discrimination, to our oppressed minorities." Do read *Uncle Tom's Cabin* again and ask yourself, *Am I my brother's keeper?* The days of noble, patient, kindly, suffering Uncle Toms are gone forever, and this nation must choose either to divide itself again in hatred, bloodshed, and inevitable ruin, or unite justice with brotherhood and mutual respect.

MELVILLE, HERMAN (1819–1891), although locally known for his published stories, was otherwise an unrecognized, unacknowledged genius during his lifetime, who worked as a ship's cabin boy, whaler, farmer, and sailor in the United States Navy. In 1851 he wrote America's great epic, *Moby Dick,* which is now appreciated as an enduring masterpiece of world literature.

Moby Dick is the huge, whiteheaded whale whose sharp, snapping jaws had cut off Captain Ahab's leg like a flash of lightning when the captain attempted to kill him to get tons of precious oil and his teeth and jawbone. Ahab's pious mind and ungodly heart are filled with hate as he vows to find Moby Dick and take revenge. Only Starbuck, the first mate, and Ishmael the sailor (Melville) who lived to tell the tale, understand that the whale had, like all God's creatures, done nothing but defend itself, that man is a mad and evil brute when he seeks vengeance on a dumb animal which is driven to attack his attackers in order to survive in a hostile universe. But Captain Ahab hates the whale for its power and strength; he must have vengeance against even the sun if it should seem to insult him. To him Moby Dick is the symbol of all the insuperable obstacles which evil men face and fear during their short and tragic careers. More sensible is the British captain Boomer, whose arm was snapped off by Moby Dick's teeth, for he feels no malice and keeps out of the monster's way. Other boats and crews are lost in the mad chase to harpoon the whale until at last Ahab in his boat sights him—but Moby Dick rises under the boat and snaps it in two; sighted again next morning, Moby Dick entangles himself and a mauled sailor in the ropes, smashes two more boats to pieces, and hurls Ahab and his boat high into the air.

The next day, the whale is attacked again, and now he

smashes the ship itself. Ahab's harpoon strikes hard, yet only infuriates the whale, whose mad rush forward fouls the rope and thus hurls Ahab to his death. Ishmael, clinging to a canoe, is picked up by a passing ship— Ishmael the wanderer, sole survivor of a man's mad defiance of nature, sole survivor of the wicked attempt of evil-hearted vengeful man to hunt and kill and prove himself to be the evil thing he knows himself to be, a creature who follows vengeance and hate instead of God and love.

(Read this intensely passionate adventure tale of man in a brief, wild encounter with nature—read it in any of thirteen excellent paperbound editions or in an attractive clothbound edition published for your permanent home library.)

Melville's captain in *Billy Budd* is the perfect model of stupid, stubborn (do not these qualities go together?), hidebound, rigid military officers throughout history, oblivious to the true distinction between the spirit and the letter of the law—destroying in their vicious self-pride the minds and hearts of men while pretending to defend the people—the perfect model of the most arrogant, deceitful gang of cowards convinced of their duty and posing as heroic leaders of their gullible fellows. Only on their own deathbeds, if then and when it is too late, can they, like the captain in *Billy Budd,* catch a fleeting glimpse of the truth about life and death, the true consequences of what they have done against the souls of men and nations.

Innocent Billy Budd, impressed into the British Navy, is falsely accused of conspiring to mutiny, and he strikes out at his accuser, the mad ship's officer Claggart. When Claggart dies, Billy is sentenced to death by Captain Vere, who could love Billy almost as a son but is obsessively devoted to strict discipline and the law which prescribes the death penalty for killing an officer. Later the captain is himself killed in battle, dying griefstricken, knowing as a God-fearing man that he has killed an innocent human being, but still convinced that he has done his military duty, though now it is too late for him to be rewarded on earth as a good captain should. The British Navy reporters (propagandists like all other military reporters of yesterday and today because they think it is their duty to lie as well as to kill for their country) then publish the news that the depraved mutineer Budd, who had stabbed and murdered a respected officer of the man-of-war, the H. M. S. *Indomitable*, has been convicted and executed for his dastardly crime, so that peace and harmony have been restored to His Majesty's indomitable *Indomitable*.

(Read *Billy Budd* in any of a dozen paperbound editions, or, with other shorter works in the paperbound volume, *The Shorter Novels of Herman Melville* [*Benito Cereno; The Encantadas, or Enchanted Isles; Bartleby the Scrivener;* and *Billy Budd, Foretopman*], with Introduction by Raymond Weaver, published by Fawcett Publications, Greenwich, Conn. Read also Melville's *Typee,* with Introduction by Clifton Fadiman; *The Confidence-Man: His Masquerade,* edited by Hennig Cohen; and *Israel Potter: Fifty Years of Exile.*)

Great Poets. The poets chosen for our core list of masterpieces are Homer, Vergil, Dante, Chaucer, Spenser, again the peerless Shakespeare, Milton, and Whitman. Their imperishable masterpieces, reflecting the spirit as well as the life and customs of the past, are known, loved, and admired in all lands. There are no substitutes for these fundamental works in every reader's personal library.

HOMER (ca. 800 or 900 B.C.), the world's first great storyteller, is assumed to have been the blind author of *The Iliad* and *The Odyssey,* the two Greek epics each of which presented in a single set of books the oral tales popular in the Western world three thousand years ago. The modern reader, like the ancients, is enchanted by the swift narrative, simple yet dignified language, and nobility and grandeur of Homer's works. These epic poems prove how little human beings have changed, how very little for the better, during the past three millennia. We see in them as we read the same confused mixture of hate and love, greed and nobility, violence and remorse, arrogance and humility, crime and punishment, truth and falsehood, stupidity and wisdom, evil and good universally familiar in all regions of the world today.

The Iliad tells about the most critical event in the Trojan War, about 1200 B.C. Paris, Prince of Troy, and guest of King Menelaus of Sparta, has run off with Helen, wife of the King, to Troy, and the Greeks in a thousand ships, led by King Agamemnon of Mycenae, brother of Menelaus, have sailed to bring Helen back. For more than nine years they have besieged Troy in vain. The story begins with a quarrel about women captives between Achilles, Greek hero and champion, and King Agamemnon. Proud Achilles shocks the Greeks by retiring to his tent and refusing to fight, but changes his mind when his dearest friend is slain by the Trojan prince Hector, and vows revenge. Homer describes the ferocious duel between Achilles and Hector, in which the Greek warrior finally hurls his spear straight into Hector's neck and then taunts the dying hero who begs to be sent home for a religious death ceremony: "Dog, you need not beg at my knees. Never will the mother who gave you life lay you out in death and mourn over you, but the dogs and birds, they will feast their fill on you." And after Hector dies, Achilles ties the body to his chariot and drags it in the dust before the Trojan multitude, as Hector's mother mourns and tears her hair at the sight, and his father groans pitifully, while Hector's noble widow Andromache, who had begged him not to fight, and the people of Troy weep bitterly at the loss of their mighty champion. At last, Achilles relents and surrenders the slain hero to his father, King Priam of Troy, for a ransom, and Hector is at last accorded the burial rites due to an honored hero.

(Read the translation by Richmond Lattimore in the paperbound volume, *The Iliad of Homer*, published by the University of Chicago Press, Chicago, Illinois. Other good translations are those by W. H. D. Rouse; by Andrew Lang, Walter Leaf, and Ernest Myers; by E. V. Rieu; and by Samuel Butler.)

The Odyssey, the world's most famous adventure story, tells about the exploits of the Greek warrior Odysseus during his years of wandering after the ten-year siege and conquest of Troy. An additional ten years were to pass before he could rejoin his son Telemachus and his faithful wife Penelope on their native island of Ithaca— ten years of battling against odds, against gods, storms and seas, cannibals and monsters, including the one-eyed Cyclops, Scyilla the sea-devil, Charybdis the sea-sucker, and other fearsome creatures, while a hundred insolent suitors pester Penelope at home, telling her that Odysseus will never return and urging her to choose one of them for a husband. The traitors even plot to murder Telemachus. In the end the noble Odysseus, disguised as a beggar, joins his son in Ithaca, and they trap and kill the suitors, restoring peace to their household and their strife-torn land.

(There are a dozen fine translations of *The Odyssey* available in paperbound editions.)

VERGIL, PUBLIUS VERGILIUS MARO (70 B.C.–19 B.C.), next to Homer the most gifted poet of the ancient world, was inspired not only by Homer's work but by his own patriotic love of the Roman Empire, and the Emperor Augustus encouraged and befriended him. After composing two exquisite books of poetry extolling the peaceful country life of his age in Italy (in one, the ten charming, sensitive, separate poems of the *Eclogues,* which prophesied that a Saviour would come to purify the world, and in the other, the beautiful, rhythmic paean to farming and virtuous, glorious living in Italy, the fascinating *Georgics*—both fortunately combined and available now in excellent paperbound editions), Vergil devoted to his masterwork, the national epic *The Aeneid,* the last ten years of his lifetime.

The Aeneid, combining heroic adventures and romantic stories with patriotic and religious glorification

of Rome, of Italy, and of the emperor Augustus, with
its beautiful sound and rhythm and its alliteration, became a model poem for poets of succeeding ages, especially for Milton and Tennyson. After the conquest of
Troy by the Greeks, the Trojan hero Aeneas escapes from
the burning city with his men in twenty ships, reaching
the palace of Queen Dido of Carthage who falls in love
with the wandering hero. Aeneas tells Queen Dido how
the Greeks had built a giant wooden horse, left it filled
with soldiers in front of Troy, then sailed away, tricking
the Trojans into opening the city gates and bringing the
Trojan horse and soldiers into the city, where they were
joined by the returning fleet and together slaughtered
the Trojans. Thus fell the city of Troy at last. Aeneas
continues the story of his escape from the burning city
and his wanderings, ending with the death of his father
Anchises.

Queen Dido begs Aeneas to remain in Carthage, not
to desert her, but he feels that Fate, to him personified
by the gods, compels him to leave for Italy. When he
departs without showing her any tenderness or concern,
the angry, brokenhearted, desperate Queen kills herself
with her sword. Aeneas goes to Sicily where funeral
games are held in his father's memory. He then sails to
Latium in Italy, where King Latinus offers him his
daughter Lavinia in marriage. But the queen Amata and
Turnus, Lavinia's betrothed, condemn the proposed marriage, and civil war results, in which Aeneas kills Turnus
in a duel. Thus it is the destiny of Dido to die despite her
love for Aeneas, it is the destiny of Turnus to die despite
his love for Lavinia, and it is the destiny of Aeneas and
his descendants to lay the foundations of the Roman
Empire.

(Read *The Aeneid,* packed with adventures, history,
prophecies, deeds of evil and of justice, magical incidents,
omens, strategies, romances, acts of duty and patriotism,
journeys to Hades and to the Elysian Fields, triumphs
and tragedies, wars and death, and, in the midst of war,
a constant thirst for enduring peace, the Roman peace

of the glorious Empire founded by Romulus and ruled by the great Augustus—read this ancient masterpiece which mirrors the world of humanity of yesterday and today, in any of a dozen excellent translations from the Latin, in paperbound editions, among which are translations by C. Day Lewis, W. J. Jackson Knight, Rolfe Humphries, Patric Dickinson, Kevin Guinagh, and James H. Mantinband.)

DANTE, ALIGHIERI (1265–1321), Florentine soldier, statesman, poet, artist, philosopher, inspired by his love of Beatrice to attain a higher, immortal, spiritual love, wrote in the musical, rhythmical Italian language *The New Life*, the story of his love for her, and then, after her death, devoted his lifetime to creating the most famous and influential masterpiece of the Middle Ages, *The Divine Comedy*.

The Divine Comedy (Dante called it simply *Commedia*, not *Commedia divina*) describes the destiny of human souls after death, in Hell, Purgatory, and Paradise; and the punishment of men for their evil deeds, or their rewards for good ones. The poem is in *terza rima*, a form of triple rhythm, in stanzas of three lines each, the second line of one stanza rhyming with the first and third lines of the next stanza. There are a hundred cantos in three parts: the *Inferno*, with thirty-four cantos; the *Purgatorio*, with thirty-three cantos, and the *Paradiso*, with thirty-three cantos. The rhythmic poetry reflects the ideas of Vergil and other Latin poets as well as those of the Hebrew prophets of the Old Testament.

The story tells how the thirty-five-year-old Dante is guided by Vergil's spirit (sent by the spirit of Dante's beloved lady Beatrice) out of the corrupt world of lustful, avaricious mankind into the Lord's "mountain of delight." They defy the power of obstructing beasts (leopard, lion, and she-wolf). They journey from the bleak plain of Anti-Hell (where the neutral souls, neither good nor evil, rush after a false banner throughout eternity) into Hell itself, populated by malicious, beastly, gluttonous, sinful souls. And so on, into the world of Limbo (with

its virtuous heathens and unbaptized children); Upper
Hell (with carnal, naked sinners who are whirled end-
lessly around and around in the darkness, the storms, the
black mire, and mutual torture); into the city of eternal
fire and intolerable stench; to the rivers of boiling blood
where murderers, suicides, blasphemers, and the rich
noblemen of Padua and Florence, the usurers and not the
Jews, are cruelly tortured; and on and on through hellish
depths, up, up to the world of Purgatory, inhabited by
repentant and hopeful souls, to the place where Dante's
beloved Beatrice (whose perfect ideals he had never
attained) awaits, into the nine heavens of Paradise itself,
where Beatrice leads Dante higher and higher into the
realm of the angels with its divine light, beauty, peace,
liberty, justice, piety, fortitude, truth, knowledge, eternal
life, and supreme love which "moves the sun and the
other stars" ("L'amor che move il sole e l'altre stelle.").

(A new three-volume bilingual prose edition of the
Temple Classics edition of *The Divine Comedy* in English
and Italian by J. H. Carlyle and others is available [E. P.
Dutton, 1933, clothbound; Modern Library, 1950, paper-
bound; Random House Vintage Books, paperbound].
Another bilingual edition with the English translation
in prose is that of J. D. Sinclair in three economical
paperbound volumes, published by Oxford University
Press. A translation of the first two parts [Inferno and
Purgatorio] in verse by J. Ciardi is highly recommended.)

CHAUCER, GEOFFREY (ca. 1340–1400). Compassionate, humorous, cynical yet romantic poet, soldier, dip-
lomat, and government official, Chaucer was the true
father of English poetry. His works of genius picture for
us the men and women, ideas, superstitions, and customs
of all classes in his time—the lovers, knights, faithful
and faithless women, sentimental warriors, physicians,
parsons, monks, priests, and nuns, clerks, stewards,
merchants, carpenters, millers, royal aristocrats, loud
and coarse characters, adulterers, lawyers, country gentlemen and other gentle men, misers, fools and liars,
serfs, kings, dreamers, astrologers, heroes, fakers, and

rogues—every conceivable kind of character familiar in his age and ever since. Chaucer was himself a London townsman, endowed with common sense and a sense of humor, who loved country life as well and also journeyed to foreign lands, especially to Italy where he was influenced by and borrowed from the writings of Dante and those of the great contemporary authors Petrarch and Boccaccio. He painted people as they were, tolerant of the failings of men and women but telling the precise truth about them, making them seem so real and lifelike that we feel as if we have met each of them and know them well.

Chaucer's *Canterbury Tales*, by far his greatest work, is poetry created in an imaginative, ironic, sophisticated style, consisting of twenty-four fascinating stories, most of which are related in rhythmic, rhyming verse, by pilgrims to their companions on a pilgrimage from London to the shrine of Saint Thomas à Becket at Canterbury. The first two stories, *The Knight's Tale* and *The Miller's Tale*, illustrate the style and mood of all the rest.

The Knight's Tale is a tale of two Theban knights, lifelong friends, who, while in prison at Athens, see at a distance and fall in love with a beautiful, virtuous maiden, Emelye. One of the knights, Arcite, is released from prison on condition that he leave the region and never return. Thus, both knights are brokenhearted, for neither will be able to see their beloved Emelye again. But, after several years, Arcite, whose appearance has changed so much that he cannot be recognized, returns, and the other knight, Palamon, escapes from prison. The two knights are caught fighting a duel over their beautiful beloved, chaste Emelye, and the King of Athens orders them to be executed. The Queen and other ladies intercede to save the knights because, after all, they had made fools of themselves only through being in love. The tale ends with the accidental death of Arcite, who dies urging Emelye to love his worthy, gentle friend Palamon, saying that he, Arcite, would be "now in his colde grave alone, without any compaigne. Fare well, my sweete foo, myn

Emelye!" Thus, Palamon is left to marry the beautiful
lady and cherish her forevermore in "parfit joye." So the
fates, the gods, decree, for so the world is made, and
we must all accept it as it is.

The Miller's Tale, told by the drunken miller, is about
a wealthy old carpenter, married to Alisoun, a girl of
eighteen ("Her mouth was sweete as bragot or the meeth,"
that is, sweet as honey and ale or mead) but they have
a lustful boarder, the poor scholar Nicholas, who secretly
loves Alisoun and tricks the stupid carpenter into sleeping
on the roof in a tub because another Noah's flood is
coming. As the two young lovers meet, another, the
churchman Absalon, who also yearns to make love to
Alisoun, stands at her window and begs for a kiss which
she gives him on her extended buttocks, until he hears
Nicholas laughing heartily inside the darkened room.
Absalon, enraged, gets his revenge by placing a hot plowshare against Nicholas's bottom (also extended at the
window to repeat Alisoun's trick), and amid the noise
and confusion the carpenter and all the neighbors are
awakened. So it comes about that the jealous old husband
is twice deceived and the two lecherous young men are
suitably punished, but Alisoun escapes the hot plowshare
meant for her. (For young ladies like her, and for more
virtuous ones, I recommend a book of musical poems,
rhythmic, rhyming ditties, by Robert Warren, offering
them wise counsel about the values of true love: *Facts
of Wife,* published by Rodney Publishing Company, New
York.)

(Read all the stories in the *Canterbury Tales,* for they
are inimitable sources of pleasure. There are easy-to-read
bilingual editions in paperbound format, as well as several
interlinear and modern English versions. Read also
Chaucer's *Troilus and Criseyde* in modern English verse
by George Philip Krapp.)

SPENSER, EDMUND (1552?–1599), worthy successor
to Chaucer and contemporary of Shakespeare, wrote exquisite, classical poetry admired as inspiring models by
poets such as Milton, Keats, Burns, and Tennyson—

smoothly flowing, meditative poems in praise of friendship, love, beauty, joy, and truth, formal and dignified in tone, establishing what became known as the Spenserian stanza of nine lines, consisting of eight lines in iambic pentameter (weak-strong five-foot lines) and a ninth line in iambic hexameter (weak-strong six-foot line), created specially for use in his *Faerie Queen.*

The Faerie Queen, Spenser's best-known work, in six books (and a seventh unfinished) praises six of the twelve virtues advocated by Aristotle, all six combined in the great idealistic hero, Prince Arthur, that magnanimous gentleman, that "noble person in vertuous and gentle discipline," soon to become the renowned King Arthur.

Thus the first book is about *Holiness* and tells the story of the slaying of the devilish Dragon Errour (the "damned feend") by Georgos, the Redcrosse Knight (Saint George in later times) to liberate the castle of princess Una's father in the Kingdom of Eden. In Book II, Guyon, the knight of *Temperance,* captures Acrasia, the seductive, evil enchantress and is himself rescued from enemies by Prince Arthur. In Book III, a tribute to true love and *Chastity,* the heroine Britomart, guardian of purity in love, releases the virgin bride-to-be Amoret from the clutches of the evil magician Busyrane. Book IV, with its numerous suspenseful adventures, eulogizes loving *Friendship* and tells how quarrels among friends are settled by true friendship and peaceful affection, as in a good marriage. Book V tells of *Justice* being meted out by the fairy knight Artegall who judges like King Solomon in a murder case and saves the queen Irena from a wicked giant. Book VI praises *Courtesy* and the gentle tongue while telling the story of how the knight Calidore captures the slanderous monster, the Blatant Beast. Book VII, unfinished, has two cantos, praising stability and peace which will come (despite unhappy changes) to the land of glorious Queen Elizabeth, the "faerie queen."

(Read at least the paperbound volume, Edmund Spenser's *Faerie Queen; Books I and II, The Mutability Cantos,* and *Representative Minor Poems,* edited by Robert L. Kellogg and Oliver L. Steele, published by The Odyssey Press, Inc., New York.)

SHAKESPEARE, WILLIAM (1564–1616), in addition to the exquisite poetry of his peerless plays (see p. 151), wrote the most nearly perfect poems ever written, the *Sonnets,* in iambic pentameter (weak-strong five-foot lines), expressing deeply philosophical and sensitive, emotional, yet highly intellectual ideas, sentiments, and ideals, exploring his inner soul and relationships to his beloved dark lady, human destiny, hopes and fears, the wonders of man and nature.

But who can speak for Shakespeare better than Shakespeare? The following is a *Sonnet* (the Seventy-First) to his beloved:

> No longer mourn for me when I am dead
> Than you shall hear the surly sullen bell
> Give warning to the world that I am fled
> From this vile world, with vilest worms to dwell:
> Nay, if you read this line, remember not
> The hand that writ it; for I love you so
> That I in your sweet thoughts would be forgot
> If thinking on them then should make you woe.
> O, if I say, you look upon this verse
> When I perhaps compounded am with clay,
> Do not so much as my poor name rehearse,
> But let your love even with my life decay,
>   Lest the wise world should look into your moan
>   And mock you with me after I am gone.

(Read William Shakespeare, *Sonnets,* edited by Douglas Bush and Alfred Harbage, a paperbound volume published by Penguin Books, Inc., New York; or *The Sonnets, Songs, and Poems of William Shakespeare,* a paperbound volume edited by Oscar J. Campbell, published by Bantam Books, Inc., New York.)

MILTON, JOHN (1608–1674), author of heroic, religious, formal, musical, philosophical poems in blank verse (unrhymed verse), was a man of great ideals passionately devoted to human liberty and moral integrity. It was he who wrote the famous essay, *Areopagitica,* in defense of a free press more than three hundred years ago. He wrote those magnificent masterpieces of poetry, *Paradise Lost* and *Paradise Regained*, in his later years, when he was totally blind. His poetry, including the superb poetic drama *Samson Agonistes* (in a form based upon ancient Greek tragedies), pleaded eloquently for the cause of human freedom, humility, dignity, "virtue and public civility," condemning all forms of corruption, whether they be in politics or even in the church itself, and appealing at all times to the highest spiritual aims of man.

Paradise Lost tells in a grand style the grandest story of the contest between good and evil, Satan and the fall of man in the Garden of Eden, and the terrible punishment which inevitably results from wickedness and sin—the story

> Of Man's first Disobedience, and the Fruit
> Of that Forbidden Tree, whose mortal taste
> Brought Death into the World, and all our woe,
> With loss of Eden, till one greater Man
> Restore us, and regain the blissful Seat,
> Sing, heavenly muse, that on the secret top
> Of Oreb, or of Sinai, didst inspire
> That shepherd, who first taught the chosen seed,
> In the beginning, how the heavens and earth
> Rose out of chaos: . . .
> And justify the ways of God to men. (Book I, Invocation)

(Read *John Milton: Poems and Selected Prose*, a paperbound volume by Marjorie Nicholson, published by Bantam Books, Inc., New York; or *The Portable Milton: Paradise Lost, Paradise Regained, Samson Agonistes,* and *Comus,* edited by Douglas Bush, published in paperbound form by Viking Press, Inc., New York); or any of a number of other popular collections available in paperbound or clothbound editions.)

WHITMAN, WALT (1819–1892), pioneering creator of spontaneous, musical but irregular free verse, was a poetic seer, our foremost poet of democracy, who wrote the message of democracy, human brotherhood and mutual respect, which today gives us hope of a new

society, for he taught us that society makes men what
they are and men make society what it is.

> You felons on trial in courts,
> You convicts in prison-cells, you sentenced assassins
> Chained and hand-cuffed with iron,
> Who am I too that I am not on trial or in prison?
> Me, ruthless and devilish as any, that my wrists
>   are not chained with iron, or my ankles with iron?

In his masterwork, *Leaves of Grass,* Whitman inspired
all men with his vision of a new freedom, a true democratic spirit, for no single nation, not the best or might-
iest, can tell the whole story of the individual soul or
shape the destiny of the race. So Whitman insisted upon
telling the whole truth about American life—its virtues
and its corruption, its dreams and its despair, but always
ending with hope for the future of the Earth which
"grows such sweet things out of such corruption, . . . It
gives such divine materials to men, and accepts such
leavings from them at last."

(Read Whitman's *Leaves of Grass* in any of a half-
dozen paperbound editions, or in collections such as
The Portable Walt Whitman, a paperbound volume edited
by Mark Van Doren, published by Viking Press, Inc.,
New York. Among contemporary poets searching for a
fresh approach to our own times, as Whitman did in his
time, is Elie Siegel. Be sure to read his *Hail American
Development*—containing 178 poems, including thirty-
two translations from Catullus, Verlaine, Basho, Endre
Ady, Martin Luther, La Fontaine, and Baudelaire—published in a revised paperbound edition, as well as a
handsome clothbound edition by Definition Press, New
York, in 1968.)

Great Satirists, Essayists, Critics, and Biographers. Every
home library should contain representative works of the
famous prose writers who influenced the minds of men
and the shape of the modern world. The following indispensable works are available in paperbound editions.

PLUTARCH (46?–120 A.D.), Greek biographer, wrote
Parallel Lives (about the lives of famous men), which

was translated by Sir Thomas North in 1579–1603. The following paragraph is quoted from North's translation of *The Life of Julius Caesar* (from Walter W. Skeat, *Shakespeare's Plutarch*, London, 1875):

> Now Caesar immediately won many men's good will at Rome through his eloquence in pleading of their causes, and the people loved him marvelously also, because of the courteous manner he had to speak to every man, and to use them gently, being more ceremonious therein than was looked for in one of his years. Furthermore, he ever kept a good board, and fared well at his table, and was very liberal besides: the which indeed did advance him forward, and brought him in estimation with the people.

(Read the paperbound volume, *Plutarch's Lives of Nine Illustrious Greeks and Romans*, translated by John Dryden and Arthur H. Clough, edited by Wendell Clausen, published by Washington Square Press, Inc., New York.)

AUGUSTINE, SAINT (354–430 A.D.), great church philosopher, wrote *The City of God* and the autobiographical *Confessions*. *The City of God* blamed the destruction of Rome by the Goths (in 410 A.D.) upon the unwise faith of men in many gods and upon sinful living on earth, and envisioned the rise of another city in which all men could live in peace, with allegiance only to God— the City of God. The *Confessions* explains that the author had studied many philosophies and religions before choosing the path of Christian virtue, rejecting evil pleasures and disorderly systems of ideas.

(Read the *Confessions of Saint Augustine*, translated by John K. Ryan, and *The City of God* [abr.], edited by Vernon J. Bourke, both volumes published in paperbound editions by Doubleday & Co., New York.)

ERASMUS, DESIDERIUS (1466?–1536), native of Rotterdam, was a noted theologian and scholar, who attempted to reconcile his friend Luther's doctrines with those of the Catholic Church. He wrote his satire, *The Praise of Folly*, to expose the foolishness of the customs, beliefs, behavior, and institutions of mankind. We should praise, and be thankful for, universal folly, he said, because it succeeds so well in producing what exists today, namely, lazy people, drunks, warring nations, bigheaded (or pigheaded) persons, and stupid, arrogant men, and even perpetuates the race, for if men were wise, they would never think of marrying, of having children, or of keeping our mad world from collapsing. Give thanks to folly, for it is folly that fools foolish people into being the fools they are and doing the foolish things they do.

(Read *Essential Works of Erasmus,* edited by W. T. H. Jackson, a paperbound volume published by Bantam Books, Inc., New York.)

MONTAIGNE, MICHEL DE (1533–1592), French skeptic, wrote the *Essays,* consisting of ninety-four brilliant, frank, lucid, lively essays about human nature, its good and bad sides, being careful not to praise nor to condemn either himself or others, balancing virtues with vices and finding them all within himself: bravery and cowardice, egotism and humility, cruelty and remorse, the entire gamut of human contradictions and extremes of character.

(Read *The Complete Essays of Montaigne,* translated by Donald M. France, Jr., a paperbound volume published by Stanford University Press, Stanford, California; or *Selected Essays of Montaigne,* translated by John Florio, edited by Walter Kaiser, a paperbound volume published by Houghton Mifflin Co., Boston, Mass.)

SWIFT, JONATHAN (1667–1745), Irish-born writer of satire, wrote the masterpiece *Gulliver's Travels,* a fantastic tale, to dramatize the follies of society and the defects of human nature. The ship's surgeon, Lemuel Gulliver, tells the story of four amazing, imaginary adventures on journeys to four foreign lands. He bitterly attacks established institutions, including the Church, and even portrays men as lower and more fiendish than beasts. In one of his fantastic tales, despicable men become slaves to an intelligent community of horses, and the horses are so far superior to human beings that Gulliver can scarcely endure the sight of people when he returns to their evil civilization and compares them to the noble race of horses.

(Read *Gulliver's Travels* in any of fifteen good paperbound editions, which include *The Portable Swift*, edited by Carl Van Doren, published by Viking Press, New York.)

VOLTAIRE (FRANÇOIS MARIE AROUET) (1694–1778), the great French freethinker, wrote more than seventy volumes which disregarded conventional ideas and demanded with a very sharp, cynical, witty pen that men use their reason and the right of free speech to investigate and tell the truth about social institutions, literature, and religion. In *Candide,* which he wrote at the age of sixty-five years, he shows how accidents and calamities can upset human ambitions and he satirizes with savage irony the easy optimism of philosophers about this world as the best of all possible worlds. In his *Philosophical Letters,* he attacks contemporary institutions, including the futile French Academy, praises the influence of the British shopkeepers but condemns the literature of England for its disorder and lack of good taste. In his alphabetical *Philosophical Dictionary,* he expresses liberal, rational views on government, religion, and innumerable other topics in every field of human interest. He insists on complete separation between church and state, with the state in full control over social institutions and policies.

(Read *Candide* in any of numerous translations in paperbound volumes, including the bilingual edition translated by Lowell Bair, published by Bantam Books, Inc., New York; and *Philosophical Letters,* translated by Ernest N. Dilworth, published by Bobbs-Merrill Co., Inc., Indianapolis, Ind.)

JOHNSON, SAMUEL (1709–1784), author of the first great English dictionary (in two volumes, the model for all later dictionaries), the romantic, moralistic tale *Rasselas,* the remarkable work of masterly criticism, *Lives of the English Poets,* and numerous essays, poems, and plays, became the subject of the famous *Life of Samuel*

Johnson by James Boswell, one of the most entertaining, vivid, and admired biographies ever written. Johnson was by far the leading literary personality of his time, a master of words, the foremost and most influential conversationalist, a versatile literary giant unequaled to this day. Many definitions in his dictionary still remain valid two centuries later. The romantic novel *Rasselas* is a moralistic discussion of man's vanity and his vain search for happiness. *The Lives of the English Poets* contains penetrating critical opinions about the works of fifty-two poets, especially Milton, Swift, and Pope, delightful, spirited, inspiring biographical masterpieces. Boswell's *Life of Samuel Johnson* records Dr. Johnson's eloquent conversations (particularly those with associates in The Literary Club), anecdotes, and letters.

(Available in paperbound editions are: Johnson's *Rasselas, Poems and Selected Prose*, edited by Bertrand H. Bronson, published by Holt, Rinehart & Winston, Inc., New York; *Lives of the English Poets—Selections*, edited by Warren Fleischauer, published by Henry Regnery Co., Chicago, Ill.; and several editions of Boswell's *Life of Samuel Johnson*, including the original work edited by R. W. Chapman, published by Oxford University Press, New York.)

ROUSSEAU, JEAN JACQUES (1712–1778) was the philosophical giant of early modern philosophy of the state and pioneer in the history of education, intellectual godfather of the American Revolution, the French Revolution, and other revolutions, past and future, based on the ideas of human rights, democracy, and liberty. His radical, impassioned small book, *The Social Contract*, denounced monarchy and aristocracy of any kind and demanded their destruction by the only means then possible—revolution—and advocated a new political and social order controlled by and for the common people, the key to which is rule by majority vote, by enlightened, free majorities. Rousseau was Jefferson's teacher by proxy of *The Social Contract* and therefore the true spiritual founder of American democracy, to whom too little credit or appreciation has been shown by Americans. His masterpiece *Émile* is probably the most influential, inspiring, and sound book on education ever written, the foundation for every decent trend in modern education, pleading for the study of nature, learning by doing, thinking, and living co-operatively with one's fellow human beings, with respect for the individual's abilities, desires, and psychological needs. His pioneering book *Confessions* laid bare his own emotional life, including his affairs with women, and set a precedent for all future investigations and writings about the psychology of sex and human relationships.

(Read these indispensable books by Rousseau in paperbound editions: *The Social Contract*, edited by Charles Frankel, published by Hafner Publishing Co., New York; *The Émile of Jean Jacques Rousseau*, translated by William Byrd, published by Teachers College Press, Columbia University, New York; and Rousseau, Jean-Jacques, *The Confessions*, translated by J. M. Cohen, published by Penguin Books, Inc., New York.)

EMERSON, RALPH WALDO (1803–1882), New England's visionary poet, essayist, radical in religion, and critic, wrote in behalf of fundamental American ideals of his time—self-realization, self-reliance, independence of spirit, hope in the future of each human being, subordination of the state to the individual citizen (the less government we have, the better, he said), toleration of differences in opinion and religion, social change to achieve noble ideals—and he expressed these ideas in all his poems, essays, and lectures.

(Read any of a dozen collections of Emerson's writings available in paperbound form, including such collections as: *The Portable Emerson*, edited by Mark Van Doren, published by The Viking Press, Inc. New York); or Ralph Waldo Emerson, *Selected Prose and Poetry*, edited by Reginald L. Cook, published by Holt, Rinehart & Winston, New York.)

THOREAU, HENRY DAVID (1817–1862), another New England visionary poet and essayist, carried Emerson's individualism into practical affairs by refusing for six years to pay his taxes, and accepting a night's imprisonment as penalty in protest against slavery and the Fugitive Slave Law. In his revolutionary essay, *Civil Disobedience*, Thoreau explained that the citizen has a duty to resist any government which accepts or helps preserve immoral institutions such as slavery. His principles had great influence on Mahatma Gandhi and thus eventually resulted in the liberation of India from British rule. Thoreau lived as a hermit in a hut for months at Walden Pond, in Massachusetts, where he planned his famous book, *Walden*, extolling the simple life (and man's search for his own fulfillment as part of nature) in preference to the trappings, restraints, and artificiality of society.

(Thoreau wrote many poems, reflecting his personal experiences and independence of mind, as well as travel books, including: *A Week on the Concord and Merrimack Rivers*, edited by Walter Harding, paperbound, published by Holt, Rinehart & Winston, New York; *Cape Cod* and *The Maine Woods*, both paperbound volumes published by Apollo Editions, Inc., New York. Numerous editions of his classic *Walden* are available in paperbound form; a good sourcebook is *Thoreau: Walden and Other Writings*, edited by Joseph Wood Krutch, published by Bantam Books, Inc., New York.)

9

Special Books in Literature, Philosophy, Psychology, Religion, Science, and The Arts

In the spiritual house of learning, there are millions of living voices, books created in the past three thousand years representing the thoughts and feelings of countless generations of human beings who labored to fashion these treasures, ever growing sources of inspiration and knowledge for our and future generations. Indispensable foundation books have been named in the preceding pages. The books listed below comprise significant additional contributions by creative minds to several branches of the glorious tree of knowledge: literature, philosophy, psychology, religion, science, and the arts.

Most highly recommended for everyone's home library are the works of those authors whose names are printed in **bold type**. For the first time in history, nearly all of these books are available in economical, paperbound editions so that millions of readers can obtain them. Many of them are also published in attractive clothbound editions. For information about the publishers and prices, consult *Books in Print* and *Paperbound Books in Print,* both published by R. R. Bowker Company, 1180 Avenue of the Americas, New York, N.Y. 10036. These guidebooks can be found readily in most bookstores and libraries.

Aesop (6th century B.C.). *Fables*, translated by S. A. Handford.

Addison, Joseph (1672–1719) and Steele, Sir Richard (1672–1729). *Selections from the Tatler and the Spectator*, edited by R. J. Allen.

Aiken, Conrad (1889–   ). *Selected Poems. Collected Short Stories.*

Albee, Edward (1928–   ). *Who's Afraid of Virginia Woolf? Ballad of the Sad Café.*

Alcott, Louisa May (1832–1880). *Little Women.*

Aleichem, Sholom (Solomon Rabinovitz) (1859–1916). *The Tevye Stories and Others. Adventures of Mottel the Cantor's Son. Great Fair: Scenes from My Childhood.*

Andersen, Hans Christian (1805–1875). *The Snow Queen. The Owl and the Pussy Cat.*

Anderson, Maxwell (1880–   ). *Four Verse Plays (Elizabeth the Queen, High Tor, Winterset, and Mary of Scotland).*

Anderson, Sherwood (1876–1941). *Winesburg, Ohio. Short Stories.*

Anouilh, Jean (1910–   ). *Becket. Five Plays.*

Apollinaire, Guillaume (1880–1918). *Alcools: Poems 1889?–1913. The Cubist Painters.*

Apollonius of Rhodes (late 3rd century B.C.). *The Voyage of Argo.*

Apuleius (2nd century A.D.). *The Golden Ass.*

Aquinas, Saint Thomas (1225?–1274). *On the Truth of the Catholic Faith*, 4 vols. *Philosophical Texts.*

Arabian Nights, The (ca. 900–1500). Anonymous. Translated by Richard F. Burton.

Archimedes (287–212 B.C.). *Works*, edited by T. L. Heath.

Ariosto, Lodovico (1474–1533). *Orlando Furioso*, translated by Sir John Harrington.

Aristotle (384–322 B.C.). *Ethics. Metaphysics. Poetics. Politics. The Rhetoric of Aristotle.*

Arnold, Matthew (1822–1888). *The Portable Matthew Arnold. Culture and Anarchy.*

Auden, Wystan Hugh (1907–   ). *Poems. For the Time Being. The Age of Anxiety.*

Aurelius, Marcus (121–180). *Meditations.*

Austen, Jane (1775–1817). *Emma. Pride and Prejudice. Mansfield Park. Sense and Sensibility. Persuasion.*

Babbitt, Irving (1865–1933). *Rousseau and Romanticism.*

Bacon, Francis (1561–1626). *New Organon. The Advancement of Learning. The New Atlantis.*

Balzac, Honoré de (1799–1850). *Père Goriot,* translated by M. A. Crawford. *Cousin Bette,* translated by M. A. Crawford. *Eugénie Grandet,* translated by Henry Reed.

Barrie, Sir James (1860–1937). *Peter Pan.*

Baudelaire, Charles Pierre (1821–1867). *Flowers of Evil,* translated by George Dillon and Edna St. Vincent Millay.

Beaumarchais, Pierre-Augustin Caron de (1732–1799). *The Marriage of Figaro* and *The Barber of Seville,* both translated by John Wood, Jr.

Becket, Samuel (1906–   ). *Waiting for Godot. Poems in English.*

Bellamy, Edward (1850–1898). *Looking Backward.*

Bellow, Saul (1915–   ). *The Adventures of Augie March. Herzog. Henderson the Rain King. Seize the Day.*

Benét, Stephen Vincent (1898–1942). *Selected Poetry and Prose.*

Bentham, Jeremy (1748–1832). *An Introduction to the Principles of Morals and Legislation.*

Beowulf (ca. 8th century A.D.). Anonymous. Translated by David Wright.

Bergson, Henri (1859–1941). *Creative Evolution.*

Berkeley, George (1685–1753). *Berkeley's Philosophical Writings.*

Bible, The Holy. Old Testament. New Testament.

Blake, William (1757–1827). *Songs of Innocence. Songs of Experience.*

Boccaccio, Giovanni (1313–1375). *Decameron. Fates of Illustrious Men.*

Boethius, Anicius Manlius Serverinus (480?–?524). *Consolation of Philosophy.*

Boileau (Despreaux), Nicolas (1636–1711). *Selected Criticism.*

Bolt, Robert (1924–   ). *A Man for All Seasons.*

Boole, George (1815–1864). *Laws of Thought.*

Boswell, James (1740–1795). *The Life of Samuel Johnson.*

Brecht, Bertolt (1898–1956). *Mother Courage. Galileo. Jungle of Cities and Other Plays.*

Brontë, Charlotte (1816–1855). *Jane Eyre.*

Brontë, Emily (1818–1848). *Wuthering Heights.*

Brooks, Van Wyck (1886–   ). *Flowering of New England. Ordeal of Mark Twain.*

Browning, Elizabeth Barrett (1806–1861). *Sonnets from the Portuguese.*

Browning, Robert (1812–1899). *The Ring and the Book.*

Bryant, William Cullen (1794–1878). *Selections,* edited by Samuel Sillen.

Bunyan, John (1628–1688). *Pilgrim's Progress.*

Burke, Edmund (1729–1797). *Reflections on the Revolution in France.*

Burns, Robert (1759–1796). *Selected Prose and Poetry of Robert Burns,* edited by Robert E. Thornton.

Butler, Samuel (1835–1902). *The Way of All Flesh.*

Byron, George Gordon (Lord) (1788–1824). *Don Juan. Selected Poetry and Prose of George Gordon Byron,* edited by W. H. Auden.

Caesar, Gaius Julius (100 B.C.–44 B.C.). *The Gallic Wars and Other Writings,* translated by Moses Hadas.

Calderon de la Barca, Pedro (1600–1681). *Four Plays,* translated by Edwin Honig.

Calvin, John (1509–1564). *On the Christian Faith (Selections from the Institutes, Commentaries, and Tracts).*

Camus, Albert (1913–1960). *The Plague. Stranger.*

Čapek, Karel (1890–1938). *R. U. R.*

Carlyle, Thomas (1795–1881). *Past and Present.*

Carroll, Lewis (Dodgson, Charles L., 1832–1898). *Alice in Wonderland. Nonsense Verse.*

Cary, Joyce (1888–1957). *The Horse's Mouth. Charley Is My Darling.*

Castiglione, Baldassar (1478–1529). *Book of the Courtier.*

Cather, Willa (1875–1947). *My Antonia.*

Catullus, Gaius Valerius (ca. 84–54 B.C.). *Poems of Catullus,* translated by Peter Wigham.

Cellini, Benvenuto (1500–1571). *Autobiography of Benvenuto Cellini,* translated by J. A. Symonds.

Chateaubriand, François René de (1768–1848). *Atala,* translated by Walter J. Cobb.

Chekhov, Anton (1860–1904). *Six Plays of Chekhov,* translated by R. W. Corrigan.

Chesterton, Gilbert Keith (1874–1906). *The Man Who Was Thursday.*

Cicero, Marcus Tullius (106–43 B.C.). *On the Commonwealth,* translated by G. H. Sabine and S. B. Smith. *On Old Age,* and *On Friendship,* both essays translated by H. G. Edinger.

Clausewitz, Karl von (1780–1831). *War, Politics, and Power.*

Cocteau, Jean (1891–1963). *The Infernal Machine and Other Plays.*

Coleridge, Samuel Taylor (1772–1834). *Coleridge: Poetry and Prose,* edited by Carlos Baker.

Collins, William Wilkie (1824–1889). *The Women in White. The Moonstone.*

Confucius (ca. 551–479 B.C.). *Analects of Confucius.*

Congreve, William (1670–1729). *The Way of the World.*

Conrad, Joseph (1857–1924). *Lord Jim. Nostromo. The Nigger of the Narcissus.*

Cooper, James Fenimore (1789–1851). *The Last of the Mohicans. The Pathfinder. The Deerslayer.*

Corneille, Pierre (1606–1684). *The Cid,* translated by R. Feltenstein.

Cozzens, James Gould (1903–   ). *Last Adam. The Just and the Unjust.*

Crane, Hart (1899–1932). *The Complete Poems and Selected Letters and Prose of Hart Crane,* edited by Brom Weber.

Crane, Stephen (1871–1900). *The Red Badge of Courage. Stories and Tales.*

Dalton, John (1766–1844). *New System of Chemical Philosophy.*

Descartes, René (1596–1650). *Meditations. Discourse on Method.*

De Quincey, Thomas (1785–1859). *Confessions of an English Opium-Eater.*

Dewey, John (1859–1952). *Democracy and Education. Experience and Nature.*

Dickinson, Emily Elizabeth (1839–1886). *Selected Poems and Letters.*

Diderot, Denis (1713–1784). *Rameau's Nephew. Encyclopedia Selections.*

Donne, John (1573–1631). *Selected Poems,* edited by John Hayward.

Dos Passos, John Roderigo (1896–   ). *U. S. A. The 42nd Parallel. Manhattan Transfer.*

Dostoievski, Fedor Mikhailovich (1821–1881). *The Brothers Karamazov. Crime and Punishment. The Idiot.*

Doyle, Arthur Conan (1859–1930). *The Adventures of Sherlock Holmes.*

Dreiser, Theodore (1871–1945). *An American Tragedy. Sister Carrie. The Financier.*

Dumas, Alexandre (1802–1870). *The Count of Monte Cristo.*

Durrell, Lawrence (1912–   ). *Balthazar. Justine. Poetry of Lawrence Durell.*

Einstein, Albert (1879–1955). *Relativity, the Special and General Theory. The Meaning of Relativity.*

Eliot, George (Mary Ann Evans) (1819–1880). *Adam Bede. Middlemarch. Silas Marner. The Mill on the Floss.*

Eliot, Thomas Stearns (1888–1965). *The Sacred Wood.*

The Waste Land and Other Poems. Murder in the Cathedral.

Ellis, Havelock (1859–1939). *The Psychology of Sex.*

Epictetus (First century A.D.). *Moral Discourses,* translated by Carter-Higginson, edited by Thomas Gould.

Euclid (ca. 330–275 B.C.). *Elements.*

Farrell, James T. (1904–   ). *Studs Lonigan.*

Faulkner, William (1897–1962). *The Portable Faulkner,* edited by Malcolm Cowley.

Fielding, Henry (1707–1754). *Tom Jones. Joseph Andrews. Amelia.*

Fitzgerald, F. Scott (1896–1940). *The Fitzgerald Reader. The Great Gatsby. Tender Is the Night.*

Flaubert, Gustave. *Madame Bovary. Sentimental Education. Three Tales.*

Forster, Edward Morgan (1879–   ). *Passage to India. The Longest Journey. Room with a View.*

Francis of Assisi, Saint (1181–1226). *Little Flowers of Saint Francis,* translated by Leo Sherley-Price.

Franklin, Benjamin (1706–1790). *Autobiography. Benjamin Franklin Papers.*

Frazer, Sir James G. *The New Golden Bough,* abridged, edited by Theodor Gaster.

Freud, Sigmund (1856–1931). *The Psychopathology of Everyday Life. On Dreams. An Outline of Psychoanalysis. On Creativity and the Unconscious.*

Frost, Robert (1876–1963). *Robert Frost's Poems.*

Fuentes, Carlos (1929–   ). *The Death of Artemio Cruz,* translated by S. Hileman.

Galilei, Galileo (1564–1642). *Dialogues Concerning The Two Chief World Systems. Dialogues Concerning Two New Sciences.*

Galsworthy, John (1867–1933). *Man of Property. The Apple Tree and Other Tales.*

Genêt, Jean (1910–   ). *The Blacks,* translated by Bernard Frechtman.

George, Henry (1837–1897). *Progress and Poverty.*

Gibbon, Edward (1737–1794). *The Portable Gibbon: The Decline and Fall of the Roman Empire,* edited by Dero A. Saunders.

Gide, André (1869–1951). *Journals, Vols. I and II. Strait is the Gate. Lafcadio's Adventures. Dostoevsky,* with Introduction by Albert Guerard. *Montaigne. Marshlands* and *Prometheus Misbound,* translated by George D. Painter.

Giraudoux, Jean (1882–1944). *Three Plays,* translated by Phyllis La Farge and Peter Judd.

Glasgow, Ellen (Ellen Anderson Gholson) (1874–1945). *Barren Ground. The Collected Stories of Ellen Glasgow,* edited by Richard K. Meeker. *Vein of Iron.*

Goethe, Johann Wolfgang von (1749–1832). *Faust,* bilingual edition translated by Walter Kaufmann. *Hermann and Dorothea,* translated by Daniel Coogan. *Götz von Berlichingen,* translated by Charles E. Passage. *The Sorrows of Young Werther,* bilingual edition, edited by Harry Steinhauer. *Torquato Tasso,* translated by Charles E. Passage. *Wilhelm Meister's Apprenticeship,* translated by Thomas Carlyle.

Gogol, Nicolai (1809–1852). *Dead Souls. Evenings Near the Village of Dikanka. The Inspector General. Overcoat and Other Tales of Good and Evil.*

Golding, William (1911–   ). *Lord of the Flies. The Inheritors. Pincher Martin. Free Fall. The Spire.*

Goldsmith, Oliver (1728–1774). *Four Plays,* edited by George Pierce Baker. *The Vicar of Wakefield. The Citizen of the World.*

Gorky, Maxim (1868–1936). *The Lower Depths and Other Plays,* translated by Alexander Bakshy and Paul S. Nathan. *Reminiscences* of *Tolstoy, Chekhov, and Andreyev,* Introduction by Mark van Doren.

Graves, Robert (1895–   ). *Collected Poems. Good-bye to All That. I, Claudius.*

Greene, Graham (1904–   ). *Brighton Rock. The Power and the Glory. The Heart of the Matter. A Burnt-Out Case. The Quiet American. Loser Takes All. Twenty-One Stories.*

Grimmelshausen, Hans Jakob Christoffel von (1620?–1676). *The Adventures of a Simpleton.*

Grotius, Hugo (1583–1645). *Prolegomena to the Law of War and Peace,* translated by Francis W. Kelsey.

Hamsun, Knut (1859–1952). *Pan.*

Hardy, Thomas (1840–1928). *Far from the Madding Crowd. Jude the Obscure. The Mayor of Casterbridge. The Return of the Native. Tess of the D'Urbervilles.*

Harte, Bret (1836–1902). *The Luck of Roaring Camp and Other Sketches.*

Harvey, William (1578–1657). *On the Motion of the Heart and Blood.*

Hauptmann, Gerhart (1862–1946). *Five Plays by Gerhaupt Hauptmann,* translated by Theodore Lustig, Introduction by John Gassner.

Hawthorne, Nathaniel (1804–1864). *The Scarlet Letter. The House of Seven Gables. The Blithedale Romance. The Marble Faun. Twice-Told Tales.*

Hegel, Georg Wilhelm Friedrich (1770–1831). *Lectures on the Philosophy of History,* translated by J. Silbree.

Heine, Heinrich (1797–1856). *Religion and Philosophy in Germany,* translated by John Snodgrass. *Buch der Lieder.*

Hellman, Lillian (1905–   ). *Six Plays,* in Modern Library.

Hemingway, Ernest (1898–1961). *A Farewell to Arms. For Whom The Bell Tolls. To Have and Have Not. The Old Man and the Sea. The Snows of Kilimanjaro and Other Stories.*

Herder, Johann Gottfried (1774–1803). *God, Some Conversations,* translated by Frederick H. Burkhardt.

Herodotus (ca. 484–425 B.C.). *History of the Greek and Persian War,* translated by George Rawlinson.

Hersey, John (1914–   ). *A Bell for Adano. Here To Stay,* including *Hiroshima. The Wall.*

Hobbes, Thomas (1588–1679). *Leviathan. Selections,* edited by Frederick E. Woodbridge.

Hochhuth, Rolf (1931–   ). *The Deputy*, translated by C. and R. Winston.

Hölderlin, Friedrich (1770–1843). *Hyperion. Selected Verse*, edited by Michael Hamburger.

Hopkins, Gerard Manley (1884–1889). *A Hopkins Reader*, edited by John Pick.

Horace (Quintus Horatius Flaccus) (65–8 B.C.). *Odes and Epodes of Horace*, translated by Joseph P. Clancy. *Satires and Epistles of Horace*, translated by Smith Palmer Bovie.

Housman, Alfred Edward (A. E.) (1859–1936). *A Shropshire Lad. Selected Prose*, edited by John Carter.

Howells, William Dean (1837–1920). *A Modern Instance. The Rise of Silas Lapham. The Hazard of New Fortunes.*

Hugo, Victor (1802–1885). *The Hunchback of Notre Dame. Les Miserables. Three Plays by Victor Hugo*, edited by Helen A. Gaubert.

Hume, David (1711–1776). *Essential Works of David Hume*, edited by Ralph Cohen.

Huxley, Aldous (1894–1963). *Brave New World. Collected Essays of Aldous Huxley. Grey Eminence. Antic Hay and The Gioconda Smile*, Introduction by Martin Green.

Ionesco, Eugene (1912–   ). *The Bald Soprano* in *Four Plays*, translated by Donald Mallen. *Notes and Counter-Notes*, translated by Donald Watson.

Irving, Washington (1783–1859). *The Sketch Book. A History of New York. The Legend of Sleepy Hollow. Selected Prose*, edited by S. T. Williams.

Isherwood, Christopher (1904–   ). *The Berlin Stories. Vedanta for the Western World. Down There on a Visit.*

James, Henry (1843–1916). *The Ambassadors. The Portrait of a Lady. The Great Short Stories of Henry James*, edited by Philip Rahv. *Washington Square. Selected Literary Criticism*, edited by Morris Shapera.

James, William (1842–1912). *Will to Believe and Human*

Immortality. Pragmatism and Other Essays, Introduction by Joseph L. Blau. *Psychology: The Briefer Course,* Introduction by Gordon Allport.

Jonson, Ben (1573–1637). *Three Plays, Vol. I; Three Plays, Vol. II;* both edited by Brinsley Nicholson and C. H. Herford.

Josephus, Flavius (37?–100). *The Jewish War and Other Selections from Flavius Josephus,* translated by H. St. J. Thackeray and Ralph Marcus.

Joyce, James (1882–1941). *Finnegan's Wake. The Portable James Joyce,* edited by Harry Levin.

Juvenal (Decimus Junius Juvenalis) (60?–?140 A.D.). *The Satires of Juvenal,* translated by Rolfe Humphries.

Kafka, Franz (1883–1926). *Amerika,* translated by Edwin Muir. *Parables and Paradoxes. The Penal Colony.*

Kant, Immanuel (1724–1804). *Critique of Pure Reason. Selections,* edited by Theodore M. Greene. *Groundwork of the Metaphysic of Morals* translated by H. J. Paton.

Keats, John (1795–1821). *Complete Poetry and Selected Prose,* edited by Harold E. Briggs.

Keynes, John Maynard (1883–1946). *The General Theory of Employment, Interest, and Money. A Treatise on Probability. Essays on Persuasion.*

Kipling, Rudyard (1865–1936). *Captains Courageous. The Jungle Books. Kim. Just So Stories. A Choice of Kipling's Verse,* edited by T. S. Eliot.

Kleist, Heinrich von (1777–1811). *The Broken Jug,* translated by John T. Krumpelmann. *The Prince of Homburg,* translated by Charles E. Passage. *Amphitryon,* translated by Marion Sonnenfeld.

La Fontaine, Jean de (1621–1695). *The Fables of La Fontaine,* translated by Marianne Moore.

Lagerlöf, Selma (1858–1940). *The Story of Gösta Berling.*

Lamb, Charles (1775–1834). *The Portable Charles Lamb,* edited by John Mason Brown.

La Rochefoucauld, François (1747–1827). *The Maxims.*

Lawrence, D.H. (1885–1930). *The Complete Short Stories*

of *D. H. Lawrence*, 3 vols. *Four Short Novels. Lady Chatterley's Lover. Women in Love. Selected Literary Criticism*, edited by Anthony Beal. *The Rainbow*, Introduction by Richard Aldington.

Leibniz, Gottfried Wilhelm (1646–1716). *Selections*, edited by Philip P. Weiner. *Discourse on Metaphysics*, translated by George Montgomery.

Lenin, Nikolai (Vladimir Ilich Ulyanov) (1870–1924). *Essential Works of Lenin*, edited by Henry Christman. *What Is To Be Done? Teachings of Karl Marx.*

Lessing, Gotthold Ephraim (1729–1781). *Emilia Galotti*, translated by Edward Dvoretsky. *Laocoön*, translated by E. A. McCormick. *Nathan the Wise*, translated by Bayard Quincy Morgan.

Lewis, C. S. (1898–1963). *That Hideous Strength. Out of the Silent Planet. Perelandra. The Great Divorce.*

Lewis, Sinclair (1885–1951). *Arrowsmith. Dodsworth. Main Street. Elmer Gantry. Babbitt. Cass Timberlane. Kingsblood Royal.*

Lewis, Wyndham (1882–1957). *The Apes of God. Self Condemned.*

Lincoln, Abraham (1809–1865). *Selected Speeches, Messages, and Letters*, edited by T. Harry Williams.

Livy (Titus Livius) (59 B.C.–17 A.D.). *The Early History of Rome*, translated by Aubrey de Selincourt. *The War with Hannibal.*

Locke, John (1632–1704). *Locke's Essay Concerning Human Understanding*, 2 vols., edited by Alexander Campbell Fraser. *Treatise of Civil Government* and *A Letter Concerning Toleration*, edited by Charles L. Sherman. *John Locke on Education*, edited by Peter Gay.

London, Jack (1876–1916). *The Sea Wolf. Great Short Works of Jack London*, edited by Earl Labor. *Martin Eden.*

Longfellow, Henry Wadsworth (1807–1882). *The Essential Longfellow*, edited by Lewis Leary.

Lope de Vega (1562–1635). *Five Plays*, translated by Jill Booty.

Lorca, Federico Garcia (1899–1936). *Three Tragedies,* translated by Richard O'Connell and James Graham Lujan.

Lowell, Robert (1917–   ). *Imitations. The Old Glory* (including Benito Cereno, etc.).

Lucian (2nd century B.C.). *Selected Satires,* translated by B. F. Reardon.

Lucretius (Titus Lucretius Carus) (96?–55 B.C.). *On Nature,* translated by Russel M. Geer.

Luther, Martin (1483–1546). *Martin Luther: Selections from His Writings,* edited by John Dillenberger.

Macaulay, Rose (1881–1958). *The Towers of Trebizond.*

Macaulay, Thomas Babington. *Critical and Historical Essays,* edited by H. R. Trevor-Roper.

Machiavelli, Niccolò (1469–1527). *The Prince and Other Works,* translated by Luigi Ricci, Introduction by Max Lerner.

MacLeish, Archibald (1892–   ). *The Collected Poems of Archibald MacLeish.*

Maeterlinck, Maurice (1862–1949). *The Intruder,* in *Five Modern Plays* (*The Dreamy Kid* by Eugene O'Neill; *The Farewell Supper* by Arthur Schnitzler; *The Lost Silk Hat* by Lord Dunsany; *The Sisters' Tragedy* by Richard Hughes; and *The Intruder* by Maurice Maeterlinck, edited by Edmund R. Brown.) *The Blue Bird.*

Mailer, Norman (1923–   ). *The Naked and the Dead. Barbary Shore. The Deer Park.*

Maimonides (Rabbi Moses Ben Maimon, or RaM-BaM) (1135–1204). *Guide for the Perplexed,* translated by M. Friedlander. *Preservation of Youth.*

Malamud, Bernard (1914–   ). *The Assistant. Idiots First. The Magic Barrel. The Natural. A New Life.*

Mallarmé, Stephanie. *Selected Poems* (bilingual edition), translated by C. F. MacIntyre.

Malory, Sir Thomas (ca. 1470). *Le Morte d'Arthur: King Arthur and the Knights of the Round Table,* by Keith Baines, Introduction by Robert Graves.

Malraux, André (1901–   ). *The Conquerors. Man's Fate. The Royal Way.*

Malthus, Thomas Robert (1766–1834). *Population: the First Essay.*

Mann, Thomas (1875–1955). *Buddenbrooks. Death in Venice and Seven Other Stories. The Transposed Heads.*

Manzoni, Alessandro (1785–1873). *Betrothed (I Promessi Sposi)*, translated by Archibald Colquhoun.

Maritain, Jacques (1882–   ). *Art and Scholasticism and The Frontiers of Poetry. A Preface to Metaphysics. The Range of Reason. Saint Thomas Aquinas.*

Marlowe, Christopher (1564–1593). *Complete Plays of Christopher Marlowe*, edited by Irving Ribner.

Marquand, John P. (1893–   ). *The Late George Apley. Wickford Point. Point of No Return. Repent in Haste. The Last of Mr. Moto.*

Martial (ca. 40–104). *Martial: Selected Epigrams*, translated by Rolfe Humphries.

Marx, Karl (1818–1883). *Das Kapital* (abr.). *Early Writings*, translated and edited by T. B. Bottomore. *Selected Writings in Sociology and Social Philosophy.* Marx and Engels, *Basic Writings on Politics and Philosophy*, edited by Lewis S. Feuer.

Maugham, W. Somerset (1847–1966). *Cakes and Ale. Moon and Sixpence. Of Human Bondage. The Razor's Edge.*

Maupassant, Guy de (1850–1893). *Portable Maupassant*, edited by Lewis Galantiere.

Mauriac, François (1885–   ). *The Lamb. Woman of the Pharisees*, translated by Gerard Hopkins. *Thérèse (Thérèse Desqueyroux).*

Maurois, André (Émile Salomon Wilhelm Herzog) (1885–   ). *Ariel: The Life of Shelley. Atmosphere of Love*, translated by Joseph Collins. *Byron.*

Mencken, Henry Louis (1880–1956). *Prejudice: A Selection*, edited by James T. Farrell. *Treatise on the Gods. Vintage Mencken*, edited by Alistair Cooke.

Meredith, George (1829–1909). *The Egoist. The Ordeal of Richard Feverel.*

Middleton, Thomas (1570?–1627). *A Mad World, My Masters. Michaelmas Term. The Changeling* (with William Rowley).

Mill, John Stuart (1806–1873). *Autobiography. Essential Works of John Stuart Mill,* edited by Max Lerner.

Millay, Edna St. Vincent (1892–1950). *Collected Sonnets of Edna St. Vincent Millay. Collected Lyrics of Edna St. Vincent Millay. The Letters of Edna St. Vincent Millay,* edited by Allan Ross MacDougall.

Miller, Arthur (1915–   ). *The Crucible. Death of a Salesman. Focus. Incident at Vichy. A View from the Bridge.*

Montesquieu, Charles de (1689–1755). *The Persian Letters. The Spirit of the Laws.*

Moore, Brian (1921–   ). *The Emperor of Ice-Cream.*

Moore, George (1852–1933). *Confessions of a Young Man. Esther Waters,* edited by Lionel Stevenson. *Mummer's Wife.*

Moore, George E. (1873–   ). *Philosophical Studies. Principia Ethica.*

Moore, Marianne Craig (1887–   ). *The Marianne Moore Reader.*

More, Sir Thomas (1478–1535). *Utopia,* translated by Peter K. Marshall.

Murdoch, Iris (1919–   ). *Under the Net. The Bell. The Flight from the Enchanter. A Severed Head. The Unicorn.*

Musset, Alfred de (1810–1857). *Seven Plays,* translated by Peter Meyers.

Nerudo, Pablo (1904–   ). *Selected Poems* (bilingual), translated by Luis Monguio.

Newton, Sir Isaac (1642–1727). *Newton's Philosophy of Nature,* edited by H. S. Thayer. *Principia, Vols. I and II. Optics.*

Nietzsche, Friedrich (1844–1900). *The Portable Nietzsche,* edited by Walter Kaufmann. *Thus Spake Zarathustra,* translated by R. J. Hollingdale. *Unpublished Letters. Use and Abuse of History,* translated by Adrian Collins.

O'Casey, Sean (1884–1964). *Drums under the Window. Five One-Act Plays. Three Plays. Three More Plays. I Knock at the Door.*

Odets, Clifford (1906–1963). *Six Plays. Golden Boy* (with William Gibson).

O'Neill, Eugene (1888–1953). *Nine Plays. The Iceman Cometh. The Emperor Jones.*

Orwell, George (Eric Blair, 1903– 1950). *Burmese Days. Animal Farm. Nineteen Eighty–Four,* edited by Irving Howe. *The Orwell Reader.*

Ovid (Publius Ovidius Naso) (ca. 43 B.C.–17 A.D.). *Metamorphoses,* translated by Rolfe Humphries. *Art of Love. Love Poems of Ovid,* translated by Horace Gregory.

Pascal, Blaise (1623–1662). *Pascal's Pensées,* translated by W. F. Trotter, Introduction by T. S. Eliot.

Pasternak, Boris Leonidovich (1890–1960). *Dr. Zhivago. Safe Conduct. I Remember,* translated by David Magarshack.

Paton, Alan (1903–   ). *Cry, the Beloved Country. Tales from a Troubled Land. Too Late the Phalarope.*

Pavlov, Ivan Petrovich (1849–1936). *Conditioned Reflexes. Essential Works of Pavlov,* edited by Michael Kaplan. *Essays in Psychology and Psychiatry.*

Peirce, Charles Sanders (1839–1914). *Selected Writings,* edited by Philip P. Wiener.

Petrarch, Francesco (1304–1374). *Selected Sonnets, Odes and Letters,* edited by Thomas Goddard Bergin.

Pindar (522?–444 B.C.). *The Odes of Pindar,* translated by Richard Lattimore.

Pinter, Harold (1930–   ). *The Collection. The Caretaker. The Homecoming.*

Pirandello, Luigi (1867–1936). *Naked Masks: Five Plays,* translated by Eric Bentley.

Plato (Aristocles) (427?–347 B.C.). *The Portable Plato,* edited by Scott Buchanan; or *The Works of Plato,* translated by Benjamin Jowett, edited by Irwin Edman.

Plautus, Titus Maccius (254?–184 B.C.). *The Haunted House. Six Plays of Plautus,* translated by Lionel Casson.

Pliny the Elder (23–79). *Pliny's Natural History,* edited by Lloyd Haberly.

Poe, Edgar Allan (1809–1849). *Selected Prose and Poetry,* edited by W. H. Auden. *The Narrative of Arthur Gordon Pym.*

Pope, Alexander (1688–1744). *An Essay on Man. Poems of Alexander Pope,* edited by John Butt. *Eloisa to Abelard.*

Pound, Ezra Loomis (1885–   ). *Selected Poems. ABC of Reading. Translations,* Introduction by Hugh Kenner.

Priestley, John Boynton (1894–   ). *The English Comic Characters. The Good Companions. The Doomsday Men.*

Proust, Marcel (1871–1922). *Swann's Way,* translated by C. K. Scott Moncrieff. *Aphorisms and Epigrams from Remembrance of Things Past,* translated and edited by Justin O'Brien.

Pushkin, Alexander (1799–1837). *Eugene Onegin. The Queen of Spades and Other Stories,* translated by Rosemary Edmonds. *Selected Verse,* edited by L. I. Fennell.

Rabelais, François (1495–1553). *The Portable Rabelais,* translated by Samuel Putnam.

Racine, Jean (1639–1699). *Five Plays,* edited by Kenneth Muir.

Renan, Ernest (1823–1892). *The Life of Jesus* (Modern Library).

Renault, Mary (1905–   ). *Bull from the Sea. Charioteer. The King Must Die. Mask of Apollo. Promise of Love.*

Rice, Elmer (1892–1967). *Three Plays.*

Richardson, Samuel (1689–1761). *Clarissa. Pamela.*

Richter, Conrad (1890–   ). *The Fields. The Town. The Trees. The Sea of Grass. The Light in the Forest.*

Roberts, Elizabeth Madox (1886–1941). *Time of Man,*

Introduction by Robert Penn Warren. *Great Meadow,* Afterword by Willard Thorp.

Robinson, Edwin Arlington (1869–1935). *Selected Poems of Edwin Arlington Robinson,* edited by Morton D. Zabel.

Rostand, Edmond (1868–1918). *Cyrano de Bergerac,* translated by Brian Hooker.

Russell, Bertrand Arthur William, Earl (1872–1970). *Principles of Mathematics. Mysticism and Logic. Basic Writings of Bertrand Russell,* edited by R. E. Egner and L. E. Dennon.

Salinger, Jerome David (1919–   ). *Catcher in the Rye. Franny and Zooey. Nine Stories. Raise High the Roof Beam, Carpenter;* and *Seymour an Introduction.*

Sandburg, Carl (1878–1967). *Abraham Lincoln,* 3 vols. *Harvest Poems: Nineteen Ten to Nineteen Sixty. Honey and Salt. Wind Song.*

Santayana, George (1863–1952). *The Last Puritan. Interpretations of Poetry and Religion. Persons and Places. The Sense of Beauty. Skepticism and Animal Faith.*

Sappho (ca. 650 B.C.). *Poems of Sappho,* translated by S. Q. Groden. *Love Songs of Sappho,* translated by P. Roche.

Saroyan, William (1908–   ). *The Time of Your Life and Other Plays.*

Sartre, Jean-Paul (1905–   ). *No Exit and Three Other Plays. The Devil and the Good Lord and Two Other Plays. Essays on Existentialism. The Age of Reason. Nausea. What Is Literature? Saint Genet. The Words.*

Schiller, Friedrich von (1759–1805). *Mary Stuart. William Tell. Love and Intrigue. On the Aesthetic Education of Man. Don Carlos. Wallenstein.*

Schnitzler, Arthur (1862–1931). *Dance of Love,* edited by Eric Bentley.

Schopenhauer, Arthur (1788–1860). *Works of Schopenhauer,* edited by Will Durant, Introduction by Thomas Mann. *World as Will and Representation,* 2 vols., translated by E. F. Payne.

Scott, Sir Walter (1771–1832). *The Fortunes of Nigel. Heart of Mid-Lothian. Ivanhoe. Quentin Durward. Waverley. Lady of the Lake and Other Poems. Life of John Dryden. Rob Roy.*

Seneca, Lucius Annaeus (ca. 4 B.C.–65 A.D.). *Four Tragedies and Octavia. Medea,* translated by Moses Hadas.

Shelley, Percy Bysshe (1792–1822). *Poetical Works,* edited by T. Hutchinson, *Shelley's Critical Prose,* edited by B. R. McElderry, Jr.

Sheridan, Richard Brinsley (1751–1816). *Rivals. School for Scandal.*

Sidney, Sir Philip (1554–1586). *Astrophil and Stella,* edited by M. Putzel. *Selections from Arcadia and Other Poetry and Prose,* edited by T. W. Craik.

Siegel, Eli (1902–). *James and the Children. Hot Afternoons Have Been in Montana: Poems. Hail, American Development. Aesthetic Method in Self-Conflict.*

Sinclair, Upton Beal (1878–1968). *Jungle. Oil. Dragon's Teeth. Cup of Fury.*

Smith, Adam (1723–1790). *Enquiry into the Nature and Causes of the Wealth of Nations,* 2 vols.

Snow, Sir Charles Percy (1905–). *The Search. Strangers and Brothers. The Masters. The New Men. The Light and the Dark. Time of Hope. Corridors of Power. Two Cultures and a Second Look.*

Spinoza, Baruch or **Benedict** (1632–1677). *Ethics: The Road to Inner Freedom. Selections,* edited by J. Wild. *Book of God.*

Staël, Madame de (Anne Louise Germaine Necker) (1766–1817). *Unpublished Correspondence of M. de Staël and the Duke of Wellington,* edited by Victor De Pange, translated by H. Kurtz.

Stein, Gertrude (1874–1946). *Autobiography of Alice B. Toklas. Making of Americans. Picasso. Three Lives.*

Steinbeck, John (1902–). *The Portable Steinbeck. Tortilla Flat. Grapes of Wrath. Cannery Row. Pearl. Travels with Charley. Wayward Bus. East of Eden.*

Stendhal (Marie Henri Beyle) (1783–1842). *Charter-*

house of Parma. Lucien Leuwen, 2 vols. *Private Diaries of Stendhal. The Red and the Black. On Love. A Roman Journal.*

Sterne, Laurence (1713–1768). *Tristram Shandy. A Sentimental Journey through France and Italy and the Journal and Letters to Eliza.*

Stevens, Wallace (1879–1955). *Poems*, edited by Samuel French Morse. *The Necessary Angel.*

Stevenson, Robert Louis (1850–1894). *Treasure Island. Dr. Jekyll and Mr. Hyde. Kidnapped. The Master of Ballantrae. Black Arrow. Child's Garden of Verse. Great Short Stories of Robert Louis Stevenson.*

Strindberg, August (1849–1912). *Eight Expressionist Plays. Miss Julie. Vasa Trilogy.*

Sumner, William Graham (1840–1910). *Folkways. Conquest of the United States by Spain. Social Darwinism: Selected Essays of William Graham Sumner.*

Swedenborg, Emanuel (1688–1772). *Divine Love and Wisdom. Divine Providence. Heaven and Its Wonders and Hell.*

Synge, John Millington (1871–1909). *Complete Plays of John M. Synge. Aran Islands and Other Writings of John M. Synge.*

Talmud of Jerusalem, edited by D. D. Runes.

Tasso, Torquato (1544–1595). *Jerusalem Delivered.*

Tennyson, Lord Alfred (1809–1892). *Idylls of the King. Poems of Tennyson*, edited by J. H. Buckley.

Terence (Publius Terentius Afer) (185–159 B.C.). *Comedies of Terence*, translated by F. O. Copley.

Thackeray, William Makepeace (1811–1863). *Henry Esmond. Rose and the Ring. Vanity Fair.*

Thomas, Dylan (1914–1953). *Under the Milk Wood. Adventures in the Skin Trade. Beach of Falesa. Quite Early One Morning.*

Thucydides (ca. 455–399 B.C.). *Peloponnesian Wars*, translated by Benjamin Jowett.

Tolstoi, Leo (1828–1910). *Anna Karenina. Childhood, Boyhood, and Youth. Last Diaries. Great Short Works of Leo Tolstoy,* edited by J. Bayley. *Kreutzer Sonata. Resurrection. War and Peace. What Is Art?*

Trilling, Lionel (1905–). *Matthew Arnold. E. M. Forster. Experience of Literature. Beyond Culture. Liberal Imagination.*

Trollope, Anthony (1815–1882). *Barchester Towers. Doctor Thorne. Last Chronicle of Barset.*

Trotsky, Leon (1877–1940). *Basic Writings of Trotsky,* edited by I. Deutscher. *Literature and Revolution. Russian Revolution. Terrorism and Communism. Trotsky's Diary in Exile.*

Turgenev, Ivan (1818–1883). *The Vintage Turgenev,* 2 vols. *Three Famous Plays.*

Twain, Mark (Samuel L. Clemens) (1835–1910). *Connecticut Yankee in King Arthur's Court. Innocents Abroad. Prince and the Pauper. Pudd'nhead Wilson. Roughing It. Tom Sawyer Abroad.*

Unamuno, Y Jugo, Miguel de (1864–1936). *Three Exemplary Novels,* translated by Angel Flores. *Abel Sanchez and Other Stories. The Agony of Christianity,* translated by Kurt F. Reinhardt. *Tragic Sense of Life.*

Veblen, Thorstein Bunde (1857–1929). *The Theory of the Leisure Class. The Theory of Business Enterprise. The Instinct of Workmanship. Higher Learning in America. The Engineers and the Price System.*

Vega Carpio, Lope Felix de (1562–1635). *Five Plays.*

Verlaine, Paul (1844–1896). *Selected Poems* (bilingual edition), translated by C. F. MacIntyre. *The Sky Above the Roof,* translated by Brian Hill.

Villon, François (b. 1431). *Complete Works of François Villon* (bilingual edition), translated by Anthony Bonner, Introduction by William Carlos Williams.

Vitruvius, Marcus (Marcus Vitruvius Pollio) (First century B.C.). *The Ten Books on Architecture.*

Warren, Robert Penn (1905–). *All The King's Men. Night Rider. Segregation. Wilderness. Band of Angels.*

Waugh, Evelyn (1903–   ). *Bridehead Revisited. Decline and Fall. Handful of Dust. Vile Bodies. Men at Arms* and *Officers and Gentlemen. Helena.*

Weiss, Peter (1916–   ). *The Persecution and Assassination of Jean-Paul Marat as Performed by the Inmates of the Asylum of Charenton under the direction of the Marquis of Sade,* translated by Adrian Mitchell and Geoffrey Skelton. *The Investigation,* translated by J. Swan and U. Grosbard.

Wells, Herbert George (1866–1946). *The Island of Dr. Moreau. The Invisible Man. The War of the Worlds. The First Men in the Moon. The War in the Air* and *In the Days of the Comet* and *The Food of the Gods. The History of Mr. Polly. Tono-Bunguay. Mr. Britling Sees It Through. Joan and Peter. Three Prophetic Novels (When the Sleeper Wakes; Story of Days to Come; The Time Machine).*

Werfel, Franz (1890–1945). *The Forty Days of Musa Dagh. Jacobowsky and the Colonel. The Song of Bernadette.*

West, Rebecca (1892–   ). *The Thinking Reed. The New Meaning of Treason.*

Wharton, Edith (1862–1937). *The Age of Innocence. The House of Mirth. Ethan Frome. Hudson River Bracketed. Roman Fever and Other Stories.*

White, Elwyn Brooks (1899–   ). *E. B. White Reader. One Man's Meat. Second Tree from the Corner.*

Whitehead, Alfred North (1861–1947). *Science and the Modern World. Modes of Thought. Process and Reality. Alfred North Whitehead, An Anthology. Science and Philosophy. Aims of Education and Other Essays. Principia Mathematica* (with Bertrand Russell).

Wilde, Oscar (1854–1900). *Selected Plays. De Profundis. Picture of Dorian Gray. The Selfish Giant.*

Wilder, Thornton (1897–   ). *Three Plays.*

Williams, Tennessee (1911–   ). *The Glass Menagerie. A Streetcar Named Desire.*

Williams, William Carlos (1883–1963). *The Farmers' Daughters: The Collected Stories of William Carlos*

Williams, Introduction by Van Wyck Brooks. *Many Loves: Collected Plays (Many Loves; A Dream of Love; Tituba's Children; The First President). Selected Poems,* Introduction by Randall Jarrell.

Wilson, Edmund (1895–   ). *Apologies to the Iroquois. Axel's Castle. Galahad* and *I Thought of Daisy. Memoirs of Hecate County. Shades of Light. To the Finland Station.*

Wodehouse, Pelham Grenville (1881–   ). *Heart of a Goof. Hot Water. Return of Jeeves. How Right You Are* and *Jeeves.*

Wolfe, Thomas Clayton (1900–1938). *The Hills Beyond. From Death to Morning. Look Homeward, Angel. The Lost Boy. Of Time and the River. The Web and the Rock. You Can't Go Home Again.*

Woolf, Virginia (1882–1941). *Common Reader: First Series. A Haunted House and Other Short Stories. Jacob's Room* and *The Waves. Mrs. Dalloway. Orlando. A Room of One's Own. Three Guineas. To the Lighthouse.*

Wordsworth, William (1770–1850). *Poetical Works,* edited by T. Hutchinson. Or *The Prelude, Selected Poems and Sonnets,* edited by Carlos Baker.

Wright, Richard (1908–   ). *Black Boy. Native Son. Outsider. Uncle Tom's Children. Savage Holiday.*

Yeats, William Butler (1865–1939). *Eleven Plays by William Butler Yeats. Selected Poems of William Butler Yeats. Autobiography of William Butler Yeats.*

Zola, Émile (1840–1902). *L'Assommoir,* translated by A. H. Townsend. *Germinal,* translated by L. W. Tancock. *Nana,* translated by L. Bair.

Appendix A

READING SPEED TEST—PART I
(204 WORDS)

Directions: Read the paragraph below at your usual speed. Be sure that you understand each sentence. Use a watch with a second hand to time yourself. Note the exact position of the second hand when you start reading. As soon as you finish the paragraph, look at your watch. Your score is the number of seconds from start to finish.

Start here: The best readers find that there are some things which they should read slowly. In this way they make sure that they really understand everything they are reading. On certain occasions they do have to read quickly—for example, when they must get information at once, or when they must read a great deal in just a short time. They know that it is a great mistake to try to read everything at the same speed. In reading simple material such as this, they move their eyes along steadily from one group of words to the next. But in reading difficult material, they have to slow down a bit, stop more often to think things over, and take care that they understand everything important. Sometimes their reading rate may be four hundred or more words per minute, at other times less than two hundred words per minute. They know that the greatest mistake of all is to rush through every page so that they miss the main points or misunderstand the author's meaning. These skilled readers prefer to read fifty pages at average speed but with full understanding instead of one hundred pages at high speed but with imperfect or incorrect understanding.

END OF TEST—PART I. Look at your watch. What was your score for Part I?

READING SPEED TEST—PART II
(343 WORDS)

Directions: Read all six paragraphs below at your usual speed. Be sure that you understand each sentence. Use a watch with a second hand to time yourself. Note the exact position of the second hand when you start reading. As soon as you finish all six paragraphs, look at your watch. Your score is the number of seconds from start to finish.

Start here: Over two thousand years ago, a group of men known as the Essenes lived in Palestine. These men did not allow women to join the group, but they did take in children from nearby places. The people owned all property in common, and for this reason there were no rich or poor among them. They believed in God, in Moses his prophet, in the moral law, and in love and justice for all.

The Essenes built a temple to God. Although they did not marry, they allowed their adopted children to do so. Anyone who applied for membership had to give up all his possessions, usually selling them and giving the money to needy members. He had to prove himself to be a man of high character. Every candidate had to wait during a trial period of two years before being accepted as a regular member.

Shortly after the Romans destroyed the city of Jerusalem, the historian Josephus wrote a book *(Wars of the Jews)* in which he described the Essenes as a people who loved everything good and true, hated evil, and lived in close brotherhood. According to Josephus, they were skilled craftsmen and diligent workers. Everyone obeyed the customs of the community, yet the individual enjoyed a great deal of personal freedom.

Among the Essenes the most severe punishment for sins was expulsion, but some of the exiles were eventually forgiven and re-admitted.

Josephus tells us that some of the Essenes permitted members to marry because that was the only way to insure continuance of the community. But the Alexandrian historian Philo insists that they were all forbidden to marry or to beget children, the reason being the desire to avoid any division of loyalty between the family and the entire group.

In recent years archeologists have found and translated the famous Dead Sea Scrolls believed to date back to the time of the Essenes. Certain ideas in these scrolls are like those of the Essenes, and for this reason some scholars believe that they wrote a number of the scrolls.

END OF TEST—PART II. Look at your watch. What was your score for Part II?

Add your scores for Parts I and II. Then compare your total time in seconds with the scores below.

TOTAL SCORES (Parts I and II)	WHAT THE SCORES MEAN
55 or less	Very fast
56–85	Fast
86–115	Average
116–145	Slow
146 or more	Very slow

Appendix B

TEST OF WORD DISCRIMINATION

Directions: Below there are twenty-eight unfinished sentences, each of which ends with a blank space. Each sentence is followed by four words. For each sentence, select the *best one* of the four words to finish the sentence. Write down the twenty-eight words you select.

1. He speaks English very_____.

   plain   neat
   close   well

2. When James was in trouble, he came to us for _____.

   help   thanks
   pain   rewards

3. I could not hear her words because she spoke too _____.

   slowly   wisely
   nicely   quietly

4. Fred voted in the election because he considered voting to be a_____.

   mistake   duty
   desire   skill

5. The widow's large gifts to the poor proved her to be rich and_____.

   careless   ungrateful
   generous   reliable

215

6. The journey took much longer than any of us _____.

regretted	realized
doubted	deserved

7. Joan spoke about her friend's stupid actions in words of utter_____.

gratitude	praise
courtesy	contempt

8. I warned our driver that in winter the roads would be extremely_____.

complicated	distant
disturbing	dangerous

9. A patient who refuses to take his medicine will have to suffer the_____.

costs	disappointment
consequences	rewards

10. Everyone present voted for the bill except Philip, who voted in_____.

opposition	support
favor	agreement

11. The weeping mother of the wounded child wrung her hands in_____.

despair	vigilance
safety	joy

12. With hundreds of spies in our midst, we must realize that the price of our liberty is constant_____.

prosperity	vigilance
agreement	disaster

13. Paying no attention to William, Jane treated him with complete_____.

attention	indifference
devotion	recognition

14. Among all the people I met in my travels, he was
    the strangest person I ever_____.

    reconsidered   miscalculated
    ignored   encountered

15. For the defense a new attorney presented the
    _____.

    arraignment   conviction
    evidence   verdict

16. Since he and I agreed on everything, his comments
    on what I said were naturally_____.

    positive   critical
    negative   contradictory

17. These unexpected events annoyed me so much that
    I became quite_____.

    exasperated   important
    ridiculous   reassured

18. Since we were humble and loyal citizens, we greeted
    our king's representative with_____.

    scorn   deference
    violence   humiliation

19. The young lady became so confused that her peculiar
    statements no longer seemed_____.

    unreasonable   absurd
    rational   baffling

20. Fred lost his grip and fell from the ladder_____.

    mercifully   continuously
    brazenly   precipitately

21. I trust, sir, that your gross error will not have serious
    _____.

    reversals   repercussions
    modifications   advantages

22. Although the inventor worked very well alone, eventually he agreed to accept_____.

    detractors   opportunists
    collaborators   honoraria

23. The author's manuscript had to be rejected because of its numerous_____.

    qualifications   qualities
    attributes   infelicities

24. Our attorney fortunately discovered a fraudulent clause whereby the contract was_____.

    validated   modified
    vitiated   misconstrued

25. In my statistical tables some important figures were missing and had to be_____.

    interposed   interpolated
    restricted   retroverted

26. Reflecting her impatience and anger, Mary's retort was_____.

    considerate   judicious
    verbose   vitriolic

27. William was a man of parts, expert in many pursuits, therefore a man of_____.

    versatility   credibility
    impenetrability   specialization

28. The serious charges of the plaintiff against the defendant have yet to be_____.

    differentiated   substantiated
    pre-empted   disentangled

END OF TEST. Compare your answers with the printed answers on page 223. Your score is the number right. Compare your score with the scores below.

SCORES	WHAT THE SCORES MEAN
24–28	Excellent
19–23	Very good
14–18	Good
9–13	Fair
0–8	Poor

Appendix C

TEST OF PARAGRAPH MEANING

Directions: Below there are five paragraphs, each of which is followed by two questions. Read each paragraph only once but carefully. For each question, select and write down the best answer. Your answer should be based on the paragraph.

PARAGRAPH I

A story which is untrue but well written will keep us interested while we are reading it. We forget the untrue parts and follow the plot with eager enthusiasm if the events and characters are lifelike.

1. Paragraph I is about
   a. philosophy
   b. fiction
   c. science

2. Paragraph I tells us that a skillful author can
   a. write clearly and concisely
   b. make dead things come alive
   c. make imaginary events seem real

PARAGRAPH II

Our community is confronted with serious difficulties. There are economic hardships, which include unemployment and inflation. There is a high incidence of mental illness. The most urgent difficulties, however, are those of racial antagonism and conflict.

3. Paragraph II is about
   a. a corrupt society
   b. social problems
   c. the medical profession

4. Paragraph II tells us that in our community there are serious
   a. economic, psychological, and moral shortcomings
   b. programs to alleviate unemployment and illness
   c. failures in science and education

PARAGRAPH III

Newspapers, magazines, and books often contain maps which help the reader to understand the information being presented. Too many readers are unfamilar with the sizes and locations of continents, countries, cities, rivers, and other physical features involved in historical events. Maps supplement and illuminate the reading material so that the reader can easily see how geography affects history.

5. Paragraph III is about
   a. mapmaking as a science
   b. the purpose of maps
   c. the reason why geography is difficult for most readers

6. Paragraph III tells us that maps are useful because the information in them
   a. helps readers to understand events
   b. is usually accurate
   c. cannot be found in books

PARAGRAPH IV

The skin consists of two main portions. These are the epidermis or upper portion and the corium or deeper portion. There are four layers of cells but no blood vessels in the epidermis. The corium (also called the dermis) has an upper layer of cells extending into the epidermis and a lower layer of cells made up of white fibers and elastic tissue.

7. Paragraph IV is about
   a. functions of the skin
   b. the nature of cells
   c. the structure of skin

8. Paragraph IV tells us that
   a. the deeper part of the skin has two layers of cells
   b. the upper part of the skin is made of elastic tissue
   c. there are no blood vessels in the dermis

PARAGRAPH V

Scientific experiments in psychology and other sciences depend upon certain well-established steps or techniques.

These include accurate observation, the collection and organization of pertinent facts, the development of hypotheses and tentative theories, and the verification of theories by application of them under controlled conditions. The experimenter compares the behavior of a control group with that of his experimental group. In this way he attempts to discover the factor which causes the differences in the behavior of the two groups.

9. Paragraph V is about
   a. the prejudices of scientists
   b. methods of scientific investigation
   c. socially desirable control of group behavior

10. Paragraph V tells us
   a. the limitations of science as a set of theories
   b. why it is necessary to conduct experiments in psychology
   c. scientific research methods which disclose laws of behavior

END OF TEST. Compare your answers with the printed answers on page 223. Your score is the number right. Compare your score with the scores below.

SCORES	WHAT THE SCORES MEAN
10	Excellent
8 or 9	Very good
6 or 7	Good
4 or 5	Fair
3 or less	Poor

Answers For Tests

APPENDIX B	APPENDIX C
TEST OF WORD DISCRIMI-NATION	TEST OF PARAGRAPH MEANING

1. well	1. b
2. help	2. c
3. quietly	3. b
4. duty	4. a
5. generous	5. b
6. realized	6. a
7. contempt	7. c
8. dangerous	8. a
9. consequences	9. b
10. opposition	10. c
11. despair	
12. vigilance	
13. indifference	
14. encountered	
15. evidence	
16. positive	
17. exasperated	
18. deference	
19. rational	
20. precipitately	
21. repercussions	
22. collaborators	
23. infelicities	
24. vitiated	
25. interpolated	
26. vitriolic	
27. versatility	
28. substantiated	

INDEX

(For authors of special books in literature, philosophy, psychology, religion, science, and the arts, see alphabetical lists on pages 190–211.)

WRITE IT RIGHT

By
Gail Kredenser

Contents

1. The Art of Word Watching

If you juggle words like hot potatoes on paper, if your sentences are always running out of control, if your paragraphs seem to tangle like a snarled skein of wool—then perhaps word watching is the hobby for you. You won't need binoculars for this sport—just a few simple rules to help you express yourself better in writing. This book will show you some tools that will be useful no matter what kind of writing you do, be it letters to friends or family, themes for college, résumés or other formal letters.

Who Is a Word Watcher?

A word watcher is as dedicated a fellow as a bird watcher. As the latter is fascinated by the bright hues, songs and habits of his feathered friends, so a word watcher is fascinated by the meanings of words, by their origins, by the way in which people use them. A word watcher knows that language is a living, growing thing. He is intrigued by the symbols we choose to express our thoughts and by the way language changes. For words are never static. Justice Oliver Wendell Holmes put it nicely: "A word," he said, "is not a crystal, transparent and unchanging. It is the skin of a living thought and may vary greatly in color and context according to the circumstances and time in which it is used." A word watcher is aware of the power of words and the value of effective writing.

What Is Good Writing?

Some standards apply no matter what type of writing we talk about. Effective writing is clear. It is easily understood by the reader; it is not open to misunderstanding. Effective writing is well organized, so that the reader need not struggle through an underbrush of verbiage to get to the point. Good writing has simplicity, conciseness, strength. Good writing is also grammatical.

Why Write Well?

A letter is an extension of your personality. A lively, well-written letter tells the reader something about you; so does a wordy, dull, badly constructed letter. A poorly written essay in an exam may obscure the fact that you really know your material. A badly organized résumé could lose you a job; a garbled business letter could cause misunderstanding, antagonism, costly errors. Thus it becomes important for many reasons to be able to organize your ideas, to express yourself simply and forcefully in writing.

Who's on the Other End?

When you sit down to write, it is important to have a clear idea of the reader. Many letters turn out to be stilted partly because the writer forgets that there is a human being at the receiving end who will be reading what he writes. A letter to a friend is just another way of talking to him. Would you really say: "Dear John . . . How are you? I am fine," every time you see him in

person? And when you write a formal letter—of complaint, perhaps, or to order merchandise—do you get wound up in institutionalese:

Dear Sir:

In regard to your advertisement which appeared in the "Daily Herald" of January 27, 1968, I am wondering if it is still possible for you to send me two sets of ———, one red and one blue, as advertised. If these colors happen to be out of stock, you may then send them in the colors of yellow and green.

Or, visualizing the man behind the counter, do you say:

Dear Sir:

Please send me one red and one blue set of ———, as advertised in the January 27 "Daily Herald." If these colors are not available, please send yellow and green instead.

245

And, when you write a job résumé, do you think of the person who will read it? You must state what the most important facts are—the facts he should know first.

Analyze, Analyze!

Be aware of good writing. One way to become conscious of good style is to keep a notebook filled with samples of good writing. Top-notch newspaper and magazine columnists are really writing short essays. Some may be serious discussions of current affairs; others may be humorous and satirical. Keep samples of good newspaper reporting, as well as good passages from short stories and other types of writing. Be critical—try to analyze just what makes these samples so good. Perhaps it's the author's taut organization and the way he builds a logical argument; perhaps it is a terse, yet precise use of vivid adjectives and action verbs; perhaps it is the way an author uses the rhythm of his sentences to build excitement. You cannot learn to be creative—creativity is a natural talent. But you can learn from others how to discipline your writing and make it do what you want it to do. By reading critically, you can attain a sense of style that will help you to develop your own.

Diagnosing Sentences

Some people tend to write by ear—that is, they will use a construction, put in a comma, change a tense because they "feel" that a sentence *sounds* correct if they do it that way. But what would you think if a doctor prescribed medication for you because he "felt" it was the right medication; if he diagnosed your ailment according to the way he "felt" about it? Doctors do not diagnose and prescribe on the basis of a vague sense that something is wrong, but according to a set of clearly defined scientific rules. And a word watcher does not base his writing on a vague sense that a sentence *sounds* right or wrong—he uses a solid set of grammatical rules.

You may turn up your nose at grammar; but a skyscraper can't go up without internal steel beams to support it, and your pure flights of fancy words will surely collapse in a heap if they are unsupported by sound grammar and good writing principles. Effective writing depends upon a knowledge of these principles. Grammar is based on common sense. The rules of grammar developed from many sources, and some rules may seem archaic in terms of today's usage. Many grammar rules are arbitrary—but so are traffic lights. Red could just as easily mean *go*; but drivers are expected to go on green. Like traffic signals, grammar rules also provide a set of standards recognized by everyone so that we can all use our language with the assurance that we all follow the same set of rules.

In this book we will be talking about several important writing principles:

1. Show clearly the relationship between ideas.
2. Punctuate for meaning.
3. Make words do your bidding.

Once you understand these and other principles, you will be able to improve your writing—and you will qualify as an expert word watcher.

2. Semantic Antics

Part of the fascination of words is in the qualities they possess. Basically, a word is nothing more than a symbol for a concrete thing. The word *table*, for example, could have been chosen to represent an animal—perhaps a cow. But it was chosen to represent a particular piece of furniture—a concrete object. Words can be symbols for abstract ideas, as well: *truth*, for instance, or *beauty*. Words themselves are abstractions of reality. One word may possess many meanings; the writer must make sure that his reader understands the precise meaning that he, the writer, intends. Down through the centuries, some meanings have changed beyond recognition. King James, for example, once described a cathedral as "amusing, awful and artificial." At that time, "amusing" meant *amazing*, "awful" meant *awe-inspiring* and "artificial" meant *artistic!*

The Slang Syndrome

When can you use slang? It may be permissible in personal correspondence (provided the person to whom you are writing understands it, too): "Like, man, the show was a gas, but my date was a real grundge." But you wouldn't use slang in a letter to a prospective employer, in a business letter or in an application to graduate school. On the other hand, not using slang doesn't mean that your letters must be stilted, full of archaic language and, as a result, deadly dull. You can use *current* language to say what you mean clearly and concisely. By current language, we mean not fad words that come and go like jetliners at an airport, but modern expressions that have replaced their antique counterparts. You need not say, "Please advise . . ." when you can say, "Please inform . . ."

Drawing Word Pictures

Words have color and texture, just as paintings do, and, to obtain the effect you want, you must choose your words as carefully as an artist chooses the colors on his palette. Perhaps the first rule to remember is to choose the *concrete* word in preference to the *abstract*. Don't say "building" if you can say "store" or "house."

Even these two words can be made more concrete: "department store," or "grocery," and "mansion," or "tenement." Part of the art in short-story writing lies in the writer's ability to convey a sharp picture quickly in a limited number of words.

The Subject's the Thing

Often, especially in "official" correspondence of one sort or another, writers have a tendency to emphasize impersonal abstractions as the subjects of their sentences and relegate *people* to second place.

> Dear Sir:
>
> Please be advised that the protection afforded our workers is not complete. However, efforts are being made by union officials to have benefits extended by the company . . .

Turn this around, and you have a livelier, more concise communication that makes the reader feel that perhaps humans are involved after all!

> Dear Sir:
>
> Industrial workers are not completely protected. However, union officials are trying to persuade the company to extend the benefits . . .

As you may have noticed, the road to abstraction is paved with passive verbs. When you want to be concrete and lively, try to use as many active verbs as possible. Remember: people like to read about *people*. Often, too, a writer will pick the wrong subject word, thus emphasizing the wrong thing and producing a dull sentence.

> The function of the new department is the co-ordination of traffic and transportation . . .

A "function" doesn't make particularly exciting reading. Why not say:

> The new department will co-ordinate traffic and transportation . . .

How Not to Win Friends

Most of the time it's easier to be diplomatic verbally than it is in writing, for when you are speaking to someone, you have a host of inflections and facial expressions at your command. In writing, you should be aware that many words and expressions are "loaded"—they carry overtones that can antagonize your reader. For instance, no one likes to be told he's made a mistake, but that's the impression you'll create if you use expressions like these:

BAD: *You misunderstood* my instructions . . .

BETTER: There has been a misunderstanding . . .

BAD: *You failed* to enclose the check . . .

BETTER: We did not find a check enclosed . . .

BAD: *Your error* has resulted in . . .

BETTER: An error has occurred which unfortunately resulted in . . .

Try to use the passive voice when pointing out an error.

These expressions do not accomplish what you want as they tend to doubt the reader:

BAD: We have not received the check you *claim* to have mailed . . .

BETTER: The check you mailed has not yet reached us . . .

BAD: The books you *allegedly* sent on the first have not arrived . . .

BETTER: We have not yet received the books you mailed . . .

Some expressions will make it seem as if you were talking down to your reader:

BAD: You realize, *obviously*, that what he said couldn't possibly be true.

BETTER: It doesn't seem possible that he has described the situation accurately.

BAD: You have heard, *undoubtedly*, of the . . .

BETTER: Perhaps you have heard of the . . .

BAD: It is well known, *of course*, that he . . .

BETTER: It has been said that he . . .

Using expressions such as "it stands to reason," "I would like to point out," or "I am sure you can see" will very likely ruffle some feathers, whoever your reader is. It is better to use gentler but firm words. Remember, too, that some words have a positive connotation, others a negative one. People tend to like words such as *love* or *victory*; they dislike words such as *death* and *defeat*. Using positive words and avoiding negative ones can pay off in better personal public relations.

ability	fair	please
achieve	guarantee	reasonable
advantage	helpful	reliable
benefit	liberal	service
comprehensive	industrious	useful
determined	judgment	you

SOME NEGATIVE WORDS

alibi	exaggerate	prejudiced
allege	hardship	ruin
blame	impossible	standstill
complaint	insolvent	unfair
deadlock	liable	waste
discredit	oversight	wrong

The Milquetoast Manner

WORDS THAT WEAKEN

apparently	ordinarily	as a rule
it appears	usually	in most cases
seemingly	as a usual case	in many instances
it seems	generally	seems to indicate
normally	in general	commonly

If you want to sound as if you know what you're talking about, try not to use words that will weaken your sentences. Sometimes you will find it necessary to qualify a statement; then words such as "apparently," "usually," and "seemingly" will have their place. But used habitual-

253

NOW WE ARE MORE OR LESS ENGAGED IN A RATHER GREAT CIVIL WAR. SORT OF TESTING WHETHER WHAT I WOULD CALL THAT NATION...

ly in your sentences, these words will impart a hedging tone to your writing and imply that you aren't quite sure about your facts. Suppose President Lincoln had written his Gettysburg Address this way:

> *Approximately* four score and seven years ago, our forefathers *seemingly* brought forth upon this continent *what would appear to be* a new nation *apparently* conceived in liberty and *ordinarily* dedicated to the proposition that all men are *usually* created equal . . .

The Precise Word

Just how do you make sure that your reader understands your meaning? Following the rules of grammar, knowing how to write a clear sentence, being able to organize a paragraph—all these are certainly important. However, unless you develop a certain mastery over words themselves, you are liable to leave your reader pondering over fuzzy meanings. This mastery over language is what enables the writer to choose words that convey his meaning accurately. Here's a rather fuzzy paragraph:

Representatives to the conference said the discussion related to the major issues involved in the decision. They indicated that they had found no further information that would cause them to change their opinions. One delegate noted that it would be necessary for them to operate only in certain areas for a length of time.

Notice all the general words in this paragraph: *related to, involved, indicated, operate.* These words—and others like them—have so many meanings that, used carelessly, they only obscure the thought behind them. (Perhaps that is what the writer intended.) Words like "related to," "in relation to," "in connection with," "with respect to," are vague. They show only that some relationship exists between two ideas. For a clear understanding, the reader should know *exactly* what relationship this is. For example:

GENERAL: His speech *covered* current fiscal policy.

SPECIFIC: His speech *approved* current fiscal policy.
His speech *attacked* current fiscal policy.
His speech *criticized* current fiscal policy.
His speech *challenged* current fiscal policy.

Nuances of meaning are often subtle, and choosing

just the right words is not always easy. Lyndon B. Johnson, in a speech in Chicago on April 1, 1967, to the National Association of Broadcasters, expressed it this way:

"How does a public leader find just the right word or the right way to say no more or no less than he means to say, bearing in mind that anything he says may topple governments and may involve the lives of innocent men?

"How does that leader speak the right phrase in the right way under the right conditions to suit the accuracies and contingencies of the moment when he's discussing questions of policy so that he does not stir a thousand misinterpretations and leave the wrong connotation or impression?"

Your writing may never shake nations, but you should be as meticulous about choosing meanings as any President.

A New Look at Old Friends

Those of us who grew up speaking English tend to take our language for granted. Our heritage is an infinitely rich vocabulary, although most of us use only a small percentage of these words in our everyday speech and correspondence. Many of us use the most common words without really knowing their exact meaning. Can you define the difference, for example, between *mistake* and *error*? Between *correct, accurate, exact* and *precise*? Between *inept* and *clumsy*? Or *apt, likely* and *liable*? Or between *evidence* and *proof*? Between *resist* and *oppose*? *Verify* and *confirm*? *Modify* and *qualify*? *Practical* and *practicable*? *Transparent* and *translucent*? If you want

256

your writing to be precise you will need to be aware of the subtle differences between words that are similar.

How can you gain mastery over words? The best way to learn about words is to read. Read the masters to see how they use words. Study the meanings of the words in context, and compare each learned meaning with your own understanding of the word. You will sharpen your understanding in the process. In addition, you will find words that are not part of your working vocabulary, but which turn up as acquaintances here and there. To increase your vocabulary, keep a list of such "acquaintances" and their meanings, and find ways to introduce them into your own speaking and writing until they become not just acquaintances, but friends.

A writer's best friend is his dictionary. It is a treasure chest that holds many valuables. Use it to check meanings as well as spellings. Good dictionaries often provide groups of synonyms. Mastery over words which are similar but different will bring words into sharper focus.

For example, how many words can you find to take the place of *said*? Here are a few:

maintained	assumed	declared
implied	guessed	roared
insisted	shouted	supposed
stated	claimed	believed
asserted	whispered	suggested

Newspapers prefer *said* because it is short and simple and because it is objective—it is really the weakest in leaving an impression of the manner in which a statement is delivered. Notice what different impressions are conveyed by the other words listed above.

A thesaurus will also provide fascinating lists of synonyms that will help you find the precise shade of meaning you are searching for. Learning to differentiate meanings and continually building your vocabulary will allow you to sample the richness of expression that is available in English. In mastering our language, you will be rewarded with writing that sparkles with life, clarity and accuracy.

3. A Question of Style

We said at the beginning of this book that your letters reveal something about you. The image that your letters present is conveyed by your *style*. Style is a hard word to define. Let's say it is your *way* of writing; it leaves its personal stamp as clearly as your fingerprints do. Style is inherent in your writing from the beginning; but you can work to improve it. Professional writers each have a style, and, just as a painter's style may change and develop over a long period, a writer's style, too, may evolve into something quite different from the one he began with.

Going Formal

Just as you would dress one way for a football game and another way for a dinner dance, you must consider in what language you wish to dress your letters according to their purpose and destination. What style is appropriate? If it is a business letter, a technical or academic paper, a letter accompanying a job résumé (or the résumé itself) or any other document, you will want to use a *formal* style. Among the characteristics of the formal style are:

Wording: Words are chosen from a large vocabulary and tend to be more precise and complex than ones we would ordinarily use in spoken English. Contractions and abbreviations are seldom used. Technical terms need not be avoided nor oversimplified, although they may require explanation according to the purpose of the letter or paper.

Sentence structure: Sentences tend to be long and complex; however, they should not be tangled or garbled. They should be carefully planned and constructed, using the devices covered in this book to promote clarity.

Grammar: Formality demands good grammar; rules should be obeyed and constructions permissible in informal writing should be avoided here. Formality means proper usage.

Remember: A formal letter can be dignified and elaborate; this does not mean that it cannot at the same time be clear, interesting and human.

The Informal Touch

Informality is the keynote for letters to friends and family, short business notes and other communications which do not require the formal style. Unless the correspondence is personal, slang should be avoided. Informality in this sense is basically well-spoken language transferred to paper.

Wording: The vocabulary for informal language is chiefly that of everyday speech. The words may be shorter, more direct and perhaps less exact than those of formal English. Lively idioms and contractions are part of the informal style.

Sentence structure: Sentences tend to be shorter and more direct. Loose sentences may be used, with less complex construction.

Grammar: Popular usage tends to be the rule here, as opposed to the strict grammar of formal English. Punctuation, too, is less formal.

Remember: Informal English can be lively, fluent and spontaneous. However, the writer should guard against overdoing it; sentences should not ramble, nor should the letter have a tone of false sincerity or artificiality.

Salt and Pepper

Style means learning to vary your sentence types in order to avoid monotony. A string of short sentences will put a reader to sleep as quickly as a string of long ones.

MONOTONOUS:

```
Dear Mom and Dad,
We arrived safely under lowering skies.
A few minutes later it began to rain.
We got soaked to the skin.  The hotel is
nicer than we expected.  The food here
isn't as good as in Paris.  Tomorrow we
start our sight-seeing.
```

BETTER:

```
Dear Mom and Dad,
We arrived safely under lowering skies
that threatened to open up at any
moment.  A few minutes later they did.
We were drenched!  The hotel is nicer
than we expected, although the food
isn't as good as it was in Paris.
Tomorrow, on with the sight-seeing!
```

Style also means learning to place the emphasis just where you want it. Remember that the beginning and

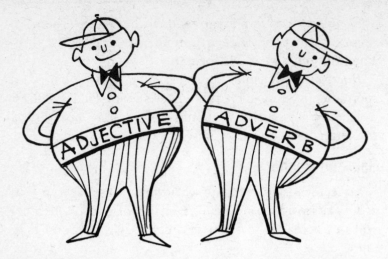

the end of a sentence carry emphasis, just as the beginning and end of a paragraph do. You can also use
sentence structure as a tool to provide emphasis—for
example, a short, simple sentence packs a big punch
when used after a long one, or a series of long ones.
Try it.

Watch the number of adverbs and adjectives in your
sentences. Overusage can make writing sound gushy,
insincere and biased. Adverbs and adjectives are
"loaded" words—they carry opinions. Use them sparingly when you want to be objective.

Note: Sometimes it helps a great deal to read what you
have written aloud. Listen to yourself. Does what you
are saying sound clear, forceful, lively? Does it make
sense logically? Do you sound sure of yourself, or are you
hedging? Is the tone and style appropriate? Is this the
image of yourself you wish to convey? Does it say what
you want to say the way you want to say it? If it does,
you've got style.

Style as Form

Style can also mean the distinctive form in which a document is written. Newspaper stories have a certain style; that is, the stories follow a certain pattern. Academic papers such as term papers and master's and doctoral theses also have a distinctive style—they must conform to certain rules concerning footnotes, organization, bibliography, etc. Style also means a set of rules governing the manner in which certain elements are written. In newspapers, for example, style usually requires that numbers below ten be written out (one, two, three, etc.) and numbers starting with ten be written as numerals (10, 11, 12)—except when they begin a sentence. An individual newspaper's style may require reporters to use an upper case A.M.—or, a lower case a.m. There are available guides for "style"— punctuation, spelling, capitalization, abbreviation. Bookstores usually carry manuals on the form and style for term papers and theses.

4. Think First, Write Later

Whether you are writing home to your family or trying to describe Aristotle's definition of tragedy in 20 minutes, your biggest help will be the time you take to organize your thoughts. If you are working on a long paper, a written outline will be indispensable. If you are working under the pressure of time during an examination, don't be afraid to spend the first few moments thinking about what points you want to make. You will gain time when you put your pen to paper, and your writing will be clearer. You needn't ramble on paper; if you organize your thoughts, your points will follow a logical order. Your sentences and paragraphs will be more effective because you'll know what you want to say before you write it. Suppose the founders of America hadn't stopped to think about the preamble to the Constitution? It might have turned out like this:

> In Order to form a more perfect Union, and to secure the Blessings of Liberty to ourselves and our Posterity, We the People of the United States, in Order also to establish Justice, do ordain and establish this Constitution for the United States of America. The aforesaid Constitution is established also to promote the general Welfare and insure domestic Tranquility.

Somehow, it doesn't have quite the same effect.

Organizing Letters

What makes a letter effective? Consider the types of letters you may want to write: letters to family and friends; letters to newspapers or magazines; business letters; letters of complaint. In business, you may write letters to ask for information, evidence or action; to make or answer inquiries; to report; to acknowledge comments, suggestions and opinions; to transact ordinary business; to amend or adjust.

Standards of conciseness, good grammar and clear sentences apply in all types of letters. Here is an example of an informal "asking" letter written by President Lincoln to his Secretary of War:

> "It is a question whether we shall accept the troops under the call of Governor Curtin for 9-months men and 12-months men. I understand you say it rests with me under the law. Perhaps it does; but I do not wish to decide it without your concurrence. What say you? If we do not take them after what has happened, we shall fail perhaps to get any on other terms from Pennsylvania."

"Asking" letters have a twofold duty: (1) to state what is wanted, and (2) unless the reason is obvious, to tell why. When the reason is impelling, the reader is prepared and perhaps more receptive if the reason is stated first. Sometimes, as in the following letter signed by President Franklin D. Roosevelt, the request is suggested at the beginning, but is actually drawn as a conclusion:

265

"Following the submission of the Baruch rubber report to me in September, I asked that mileage rationing be extended throughout the nation. Certain printing and transportation problems made it necessary to delay the program until December first."

Why:

"With every day that passes, our need for this rubber conservation grows more acute. It is the Army's need and the Navy's need. They must have rubber. We, as civilians, must conserve our tires."

The Conclusion:

"We must do everything in our power to see that the program starts December first because victory must not be delayed through failure to support our fighting forces."

It is the logical sequence of ideas that makes this letter so forceful. Note also the use of active rather than passive verbs, and the simplicity of the language, which lends this "request" so much strength.

In order to achieve the effect you want, you must decide how to arrange the topics to be covered in your writing.

Building the Framework

One of the most important aids to a writer is his preliminary outline. The "Harvard Outline" form provides a solid framework, permitting the writer to list major and minor points in the order in which they are to be covered. The more complete and detailed the outline, the easier it will be for the writer to compose the finished product. The form looks like this:

I.
    A.
        1.
            a.
            b.

Had Aristotle used the Harvard Outline when he began to write his *Politics*, the outline might have looked something like this:

I.   Theory of the Household.
    A.   The Political Association and Its Relation to Other Associations.
        1. All associations have ends; the political association has the highest; but the principle of association expresses itself in different forms, and through different modes of government.
        2. To distinguish the different forms of association we must use an analytic or genetic method, tracing successively the association of the
            a.   household
            b.   village
            c.   polis (city)
    B.   The Association of the Household and Its Different Functions.
        1. The constituent elements of the household.
            a.   The relations of master and slave.

        b.   The relations of husband and wife.

        c.   The relations of parent and child.

        d.   The element of "acquisition."

  2.   Slavery.

        a.   The instruments of the household form—its stock of property.

        b.   They are animate and inanimate.

        c.   The slave is an animate instrument, intended (like all the instruments of the household) for action, and not for production . . .

II. Review of Ideal States

  A. Ideal States in Theory

    1. Plato's Republic

        a.   Political association is a sharing.

        b.   How much should be shared?

        c.   Plato's scheme of communism.

    2. Plato's Laws . . .

Put It in Writing

Another indispensable tool is the index card system used to record research. When you are writing a lengthy paper involving extensive research, you may want to use this system. The $5'' \times 8''$ size card is handy because it holds a great deal of information, will be less likely to get lost and, as many a scholar will tell

you, will fit nicely into a shoe box. Index cards (3″ ×
5″) are good for several reasons: putting each point on
a separate card will help you organize your paper more
effectively; listing quotations and other information on
cards with their sources and page numbers will help in
the writing of footnotes and bibliographies.

To be most efficient, an index card should carry at
least the following information: A key word to tell you
what the information is about; the information, be it
quotation, statistics or other notes; the title of the source
from which the information was taken; the number of
the page on which the information appears; the author
and publisher of the source and the date and place of
publication. Here is a sample index card:

```
education
     "Education is not confined to children:
in fact liberal education is mostly adult
education, and goes on all through life in
people who have active minds instead of
secondhand mental habits.  But adult educa-
tion takes care of itself: all that the
State can do is to take care that the
materials for it, the libraries and art
galleries and orchestras and open spaces are
at hand for it."
                    George Bernard Shaw
          Everybody's Political What's What?
The Wit and Wisdom of Bernard Shaw p. 181.
Ed. by Stephen Winsten  Collier Books  New
York 1962  paperback $1
```

For less formal work, for certain aspects of creative
writing, for interviews and other purposes, you may find

a notebook more practical than index cards. Carrying a small notebook or steno book will allow you to jot down ideas wherever you are, to record notes if you are acting as a reporter, and generally will prove of great value as a portable record.

The Essence of the Essay

If the thought of having to write an essay makes your fingers tremble upon the typewriter keys, cheer up. Tools do exist to help you. The first is your index card file or notebook containing the fruits of your research (or, if an essay for an examination, your study); your second is your outline, which should be as complete as possible. The third is the knowledge that there is a form and sequence that will help you to put your ideas in logical order and help you to express yourself effectively. The form, in its simplest version, has three parts: exposition, development and conclusion. In the exposition, the writer puts forth his main idea, stating the main topic of the essay. In the development which follows, he elaborates on this idea, perhaps explaining it in detail, perhaps stating arguments for a point of view, perhaps expanding on the idea. The conclusion often restates the writer's main point in a forceful way, or sums up his ideas in a final statement.

There can be many variations of this form, which is extremely flexible. An "essay" may be anything from a humorous piece of satire to an article of dramatic or literary criticism; from a newspaper editorial to an individual's letter stating his political views on some subject. It can be a learned article in any field.

270

The Terrifying Term Paper

Writing a term paper often seems to students to be a monumental task, especially at the beginning, when the assignment is given. And if you are a person who has difficulty putting words on paper, the task is likely to loom even larger. But term papers, like essays, generally follow the exposition-development-conclusion format. Again, if you have done the preliminary work well, using your index cards to record your research accurately, if you have prepared a detailed outline, the writing will be easier and, in fact, can be the most satisfying part of the work. In addition, most term papers, because of the necessity to document the research, require a certain form to include footnotes listing reference sources. If your teachers do not indicate exactly how they wish the paper prepared (and if you're not sure, it doesn't hurt to ask), many bookstores sell manuals which describe the form in detail. Generally speaking, term papers require: a title page including the

271

title of the paper, your name, the name of the course and the date; an outline; a table of contents; and a bibliography listing all publications and articles used in your research.

The Art of the Résumé

Just as a letter reflects your personality, the résumé of information that you send to prospective employers also reflects the type of person you are. The personnel director of a national organization has said: "A résumé is definitely indicative of the person who wrote it." The image the résumé presents may affect that employer's opinion of you even before he meets you.

What counts in writing a résumé? These things all count: *neatness, organization, wording, spelling.* You may have an impressive education and background, the best experience and top qualifications; but the way in which you present this information and, thereby, yourself, is highly important to the person who must decide whether to hire you.

You must marshal all the facts and present them clearly and in a logical order, with the most important facts first. The clearest way is probably an outline format. The résumé should be written concisely—the employer doesn't want flowery phrases, just the facts. They are usually presented in the following order:

Vital information (top left corner of the page): Name, address, telephone number.

Job objective: What position are you seeking? What do you hope to accomplish in this position? What salary range are you looking for?

272

Most recent experience: Position, name of employer, dates job was held, your duties and responsibilities.

Previous experience: Other jobs, dates held, responsibilities. These jobs should be listed in order, dating from the most recent.

Educational background: List schools attended, education relating to the job you are seeking, degrees received, etc.

Awards and honors: If you are a student, these entries would most likely relate to extracurricular activities or academic achievements; anyone who has been working for a few years would list more recent awards and honors, achieved during the course of his career and his civic and community activities. (If you have no awards to list, expand on your personal qualifications—see below.)

Affiliations: Students would list school and community organizations of which they are members; others would list professional organizations and civic and service organizations.

Personal information: Age, marital status. Hobbies and interests. Other information, such as languages spoken, books or papers published, and any other data that may be valuable in terms of the job you are seeking, such as specialized books you have read.

Limit your résumé to one page if possible, to make it easier to file and so that there will be less chance of pages being separated and lost. If there are more pages, be sure your name and address is on each. If you plan to send out many résumés, it may be a good idea to invest a few dollars and have them printed or photocopies made; the results will pay off in neatness and a professional look.

Here is a fictitious résumé to give you an idea of how to organize your own:

```
John H. Smith
233 North Ridge Rd.
Los Angeles, Calif.            213 -345- 1093
```

Objective:

Magazine editor. Wish to have responsibility for editorial decisions (in consultation with publisher, of course), as well as responsibility for art and design. Am seeking a creative challenge that will allow me to develop stories, plan layouts and story treatment, select art, work with writers and artists.
Salary range: $15,000 minimum.

Previous Experience:

1965-1968: Editor, Handy Home Journal, Lawton-Rose Publishing Co. Responsibilities included development of story ideas, layouts, much of the writing. Also did occasional photography.
Monthly magazine of do-it-yourself carpentry, home crafts and building.
1963-1965: Editor, real estate section, Green Banks Weekly News (circulation 60,000). Reported on and edited real estate news. Dummied pages for composing room, planned and wrote special weekend features. Also wrote a weekly column on home crafts.

	1960-1963: Reporter, Cranfield (Wash.) Press. Covered general assignment news; doubled as photographer on many stories.
Education:	Graduate of Seattle, Wash., public schools; B.S. in Journalism, Lackawanna University, Ohio; one year graduate study in economics, University of London.
Awards:	1966: Best magazine feature, Home Craft Writers Association annual contest; 1963: Best series, Cranfield Press Association annual contest (for exposé of slum clearance scandal).
Affiliations:	Member, California Press Association; member, Magazine Writers' Council (President, 1966-67); Guest Lecturer, Lackawanna University School of Journalism; Member, Sigma Delta Chi, Journalism fraternity.
Personal:	Age: 35; married; two children. Speak French; hobbies include photography, sailing, swimming and reading. Have basement workshop where I have tried out projects later written up in the magazine. Have completed Reserve duty with the Army; have discharge papers.

Writing for Publication

Many good books on creative writing—writing short stories, novels and dramas—are available in libraries and bookstores, and courses in creative writing are

275

taught in schools and colleges. In this book we will talk about some general rules which any writer interested in publication may find helpful.

The basics of good writing which we have discussed apply to all types of writing. Creative writers who have mastered proper grammar and conventional style may go on in their fiction writing to abide by or break those rules for a desired effect. However, when we talk about magazine writing, journalism and other *non*-fiction, we consider those rules to be part of the requirements. Each of these fields has its own particular requirements, as well.

Know Your Market

A writer who wishes to submit an article to a publication should know the type of material which that publication is apt to prefer. A magazine in which stories are bright, breezy and informal will most likely turn down a story that is heavy and serious. A magazine that publishes political commentary will probably reject a story which has no relationship to this field. A scholarly journal will have its own requirements for publication. You should also have some idea of the average length of articles appearing in the publication in which you are interested. In certain cases it may be wise to submit an outline for a story first. In any case, make it a point to study the publication you are aiming at.

Use a Display Window

In magazine and newspaper writing, the single most important sentence in an article is the opening one. In newspaper language it is called a "lead," and it is this sentence which must catch your reader's interest and draw him into the story. So it is important that your lead be interesting and lively, for, before you catch the reader's attention, you will have to catch an editor's attention and make him want to continue the story—and buy it. There are many types of leads—questions, quotations, short, punchy declaratives, and "combination" leads that unite several facts in one or two sentences. All these should have a common denominator: the ability to spark the reader's interest.

You should decide which aspect of your story is most important—what fact or facts, what style of lead will provoke the most interest. A lead for an informative article may be handled quite differently from a "feature story" lead. A news story lead, concerned with getting the information as fast and as briefly as possible to the reader, may begin:

> "Three men were injured seriously last night when the car in which they were riding struck an embankment and overturned on Route 3 in Ridgewood."

A feature story lead can be handled differently. The light approach was appropriately used for a story about a woman who won a Mississippi riverboat, paddlewheel and all, on a TV quiz show. The woman had to park the boat in her driveway for weeks while she figured out what to do with it. The story started:

> "A Sharon housewife's ship has come in at last, and she'd give anything to get rid of it."

Sometimes leads come easily; they just seem to fall in place. More often than not, though, writing the lead will be the most difficult part of the story. Sometimes it's best to leave it till last, until you have the whole story written.

News and Features

What's the difference between a "straight" or "hard" news story and a feature story? Briefly, it's this: A straight news story deals mainly with facts, presented within an architectural structure that has remained traditional through the years. The purpose is to present information as clearly and concisely as possible, with the facts arranged in order of diminishing importance. Presenting the most important facts first allows the reader to grasp them quickly, in case he doesn't have time to finish the story; and when lack of printing space calls for a story to be shortened, it can be "cut" quickly from the end without losing important details. Reporters once were taught to cram all the major facts into one-sentence leads; today that has changed. Shorter sentences are the rule, and lead paragraphs may contain two or three sentences.

A feature story gets a different treatment. Usually newspaper features are in some way human-interest stories. These stories may be about people, animals, or funny occurrences. They may provide background for a major news story, or cover a unique angle of a news story. Whatever their purpose, the feature writer usually has more leeway to be creative and express himself than the straight news-story writer, whose work must fit into a certain pattern. Feature leads can be bright and imaginative. They need not tell the whole story at once; in fact, many feature stories are written with the climax at the end, rather than at the beginning.

If deletions are necessary, they are made carefully from the body of the story.

Magazine articles are, for the most part, written as features. Often they are longer than newspaper articles and, in a magazine feature, the writer can be creative with form and style.

Advertising

Some day you might be called upon to write an advertisement, whether it be for your school paper, company house organ or another type of publication. You will have to work with a limited amount of space—that is, you will have to find the most effective way to attract your reader's attention and influence him in the fewest number of words. Writing advertising copy—short, snappy headlines and concise text—will sharpen your ability to write simply and directly.

As with other forms of writing, organization comes first. You must decide what your most important point is, and how to say it to produce the result you want. You must also decide to whom you wish to appeal—who are the readers you want the advertisement to affect? Here's an advertisement with which to experiment.

Suppose you are publicity chairman of your school drama club, which is presenting Rodgers and Hammerstein's musical *Carousel* as the final production of the year. Your assignment is to write three advertisements: one for your school paper (100 words), one for the local paper, which has agreed to print it free (100 words) and a short radio spot (50 words) for the local station, which has agreed to broadcast an announcement as a public

service. Here is some information from which you must select the most important points.

1. The leads will be played by Arthur Coombs and Roberta Sanders, well known to the students as the best singers in the school.
2. Proceeds from the play will go to the school's scholarship fund.
3. The dates: June 21, 22, 23.
4. Performances will be Friday and Saturday at 8:30 p.m. and Sunday at 2 p.m.

5. The songs include "If I Loved You," "Carousel Waltz," "Mr. Snow," "Soliloquy," and "June is Bustin' Out All Over."
6. "Carousel Punch" will be served during inter-missions.
7. The school is located at Berry Street and Grand Ave.
8. The school orchestra will be conducted for the first time by Thomas King, director of the Municipal Symphony Orchestra.

Your imagination should be tempered only by your conciseness and accuracy!

Mechanics

You should learn how to submit manuscripts. They should be typewritten, of course, double-spaced or triple-spaced, with margins of about an inch and a half all around. This will leave room for editorial comments and marks. Always keep a copy of your work. It is also helpful to find out the name of the person or the exact department where your manuscript should be sent. That way, there will be less chance of its being lost.

Don't be discouraged if you receive a rejection slip for your efforts. Writing, in a sense, is like using your muscles. Exercising every day will keep your muscles in shape; similarly, the best way to strengthen and improve your writing is to *keep writing*.

5. Language: The Tools and How to Use Them

The usual classification of the parts of speech is by form: noun, pronoun, verb, adjective, adverb, preposition, conjunction. We can also group parts of speech by their use, or function. Once we have sorted out these tools and have learned how each is used, we can go on to construct clearer sentences.

A *noun* is a word that names a person, place, thing or quality:

Harry, Detroit, window, pen, happiness.

A *pronoun* is used in place of a noun:

Personal: I, we, he, she, him, it
Relative: who, which, that
Interrogative: who, which, what
Demonstrative: this, that, these, those
Indefinite: one, any, each, somebody
Reflexive: myself, yourself, himself

A *verb* is a word or group of words that expresses existence of a subject or action to or by the subject. The verb, together with any words that complete or modify its meaning, forms the *predicate* of the sentence.

An *adjective* is a word that describes or limits (modifies) the meaning of a noun or pronoun:

big house, *happy* birthday, *older* brother

An *adverb* is a word that modifies a verb, an adjective, or another adverb. It answers the questions *where, how* or *how much, when, why*:

good *enough*, walked *quickly*, smiled *happily*

A *preposition* is a word used to relate a noun or pronoun to some other word in the sentence:

at, in, by, from, toward

A *conjunction* is a word used to join words, phrases or clauses:

and, but, nor

A *clause* is a group of related words containing a subject and a predicate. It may be a short sentence, but not all clauses are sentences. There are two types of clauses.

An *independent* (or *main*) clause makes a complete statement and is not introduced by any subordinating word. It can stand alone, and, when it does, it is called a *simple* sentence.

He will make his report in June.

In this case, *He* is the subject; *will make his report in June* is the predicate. The verb—*will make*—is in the active voice (see page 250) and is in the future tense, indicating that the action will take place sometime in the future. The object of the verb, the words which answer the question, "What?", is *his report*. The words *in June* make up a prepositional phrase modifying the verb by answering the question, "When?"

A *dependent* (or *subordinate*) clause cannot stand alone as a complete sentence; it depends upon a word or words in the independent clause to complete its meaning. Dependent clauses may be used as:

ADJECTIVE: The man *who is accused of the murder* will be arraigned today.

ADVERB: *As soon as you are settled,* drop us a note.

NOUN: *Whoever wins the toss* will kick off.

Do not confuse a *phrase* with a clause. A phrase is a group of related words *without* a subject and predicate. Phrases are used as nouns, adjectives, adverbs or verbs and are classified as:

PREPOSITIONAL: The pencil is *in the drawer*.

PARTICIPIAL: The man *receiving the award* has worked long and hard.

GERUNDIAL: *Traveling* has become my hobby.

INFINITIVE: *To err* is human; *to forgive*, divine.

Sentence Classification

With these definitions of the basic parts of speech in mind, we can go on to describe the different types of sentence. Knowledge of sentence classification will help you to know which sentence is best for a particular job. A sentence is simply a thought expressed in words. To be a sentence, it must have at least two parts: subject and predicate. There are different kinds of sentences according to the number and type of clauses contained.

A *simple* sentence contains only one clause—an independent clause. This does not mean that it must be short. A single clause can include many phrases, a compound subject or predicate and a number of modifiers.

The reporter covered the story.

The reporter covered the news story and raced back to his desk, typing the copy quickly and efficiently and finishing it well in time to make the front page.

A *compound* sentence has two or more independent clauses, each of which may be written as a simple sentence. There are no dependent clauses in a compound sentence.

He discussed the symptoms with his doctor, and the doctor wrote a prescription.

A *complex* sentence contains one independent clause and one or more dependent clauses.

When we were ready to check out, we notified the desk to prepare our bill.

A *compound-complex* sentence contains at least two independent clauses and one or more dependent clauses.

Since the information you request is contained in the current issue of our magazine, I am enclosing a copy; I hope the article will answer all your questions.

6. Unsnarl Your Sentences

Once you have sorted out your ideas, you will set them down into sentences. Again, think first—don't just take a handful of ideas, fling them into a sentence and hope for the best. A clear sentence is a correct sentence. A touch of good grammar can untangle a sentence like magic.

Signposts

Co-ordinating conjunctions and *conjunctive adverbs* are "signpost" words that join principal clauses. There are words that stand for addition, contrast, choice or result. When you use the proper signpost, the relationship of the second clause to the first is clear.

SIGNPOST	EXAMPLE
Co-ordinating conjunctions:	
and : The next clause is equal in context and grammar.	We visited the Louvre, *and* we climbed the Eiffel Tower.
but : The following idea is opposite.	We visited the Louvre, *but* we did not climb the Eiffel Tower.
or : An alternate idea follows.	We may visit the Louvre, *or* we may climb the Eiffel Tower.

for: The next clause supports the first statement.	My feet hurt, *for* we walked around Paris all day.

Conjunctive adverbs:

furthermore, besides, moreover: These add ideas of equal strength.	The bowl I purchased in your store arrived broken; *furthermore,* the sweater I bought came with a moth hole in the left sleeve.
however, nevertheless: Contrasting idea is coming.	We are almost out of money; *however,* we are managing quite well.
accordingly, therefore: These express a result.	The last day of our excursion flight is next Wednesday; *therefore,* we will return on that day.

Correlative conjunctions are those familiar little words used in pairs to connect equal constructions. These include either-or, neither-nor, both-and, not only-but also. Remember: you must use the same construction after each member of the pair.

INCORRECT: *Either* take the exam now *or* you can make it up later.

(Both correlatives are followed by verbs, but one is imperative, the other indicative.)

BETTER: *Either* take the exam now *or* make it up later.

INCORRECT: In her four-room apartment she *not only* keeps four cats, *but also* three dogs. (The word "has" or "keeps" is omitted.)

BETTER: In her four-room apartment she *not only* has four cats, *but also* keeps three dogs.
She has taken in not only four cats, but also three dogs.

(In the first "better" example, the correlative is followed by two verbs; in the second, by number and nouns.)

More on Conjunctions

Since conjunctions are signposts, you should learn to use them in their most effective manner. Here's a list of some of the most troublesome conjunctions and what to do—or what *not* to do—about them.

1. *And* vs. *also*:
Also is a weak connective; it should not be used in place of *and* in sentences like this one:

He is strong, silent, also brave.

2. *And etc.*:
The abbreviation *etc.* stands for the Latin *et cetera*, meaning *and so forth*. An additional *and* is incorrect.

NOT: I will need shoes, gloves, a hat, a dress, and etc. for the wedding.

BUT: I will need shoes, gloves, a hat, a dress, etc., for the wedding.

288

3. *And which, and who, but which:*

Don't use *and which, and who, but which, but that,* etc., unless there is a preceding *who, which* or *that* in the sentence to complete the parallel construction.

NOT: I am looking for a course easy to pass and that will give me three credits.

BUT: I am looking for a course that will be easy to pass and that will give me three credits.

4. Too many *and*s:

Try not to string together a group of sentence elements all connected with *and.*

NOT: The pre-school schedule was researched and planned and tried out in experimental sessions at Teachers College.

BUT: The pre-school schedule was researched and planned at Teachers College; then it was tried out in experimental sessions there.

5. *But:*

Try not to use *but* to show contrast if the negative is already shown by another word in the sentence.

NOT: *In vain* we rushed through the airport to catch the 7:30 flight, *but* we missed it by five minutes.

INSTEAD: We rushed *in vain* to catch the 7:30 flight.

OR: We rushed through the airport to catch the 7:30 flight, *but* we missed it.

6. *And* or *but* to begin a sentence:

You may on occasion begin a sentence with *and* or *but*, or any other co-ordinating conjunction. A co-ordinate conjunction or a conjunctive adverb at the beginning of a sentence signals the reader that the thought is about to take a new direction.

7. *As, since, because:*

These are interchangeable when used to introduce clauses of cause or reason.

> *Because* I had read the book, I wanted to see the movie.

> *Since* I had read the book, I wanted to see the movie.

> *As* I had read the book, I wanted to see the movie.

Since and *as* have another function, however; *since* introduces clauses of sequence of time, and *as* introduces clauses of duration of time. The double functions of both these words may cause confusion unless they are used only in sentences in which they cannot be misunderstood.

> NOT: Since the course was developed to . . .
> (This could mean *since the time that* the course was developed . . .)

> BUT: Because the course was developed to . . .

> NOT: As I was coming in that morning, he decided to . . .

> (This could mean *during the time that* I was coming in . . .)

BUT: Because I was coming in that morning, he decided to . . .

Note: When an *as* or *since* clause comes last in the sentence, punctuation will clarify the meaning. If *as* or *since* is used as a time indicator, the clause it introduces is *not* set off from the sentence. If the clause is one of cause or reason, it *is* set off.

The gates have been closed since the students demonstrated against the through traffic.
(No punctuation; *since* means *since the time that.*)

The gates have been closed, since the students demonstrated against the through traffic.
(*Since* means *because* the students demonstrated.)

8. *If* vs. *whether:*
If introduces clauses of condition or supposition.

I can go *if* my parents allow it.
If you cannot attend, please notify us immediately.

Whether introduces clauses indicating an alternative.

Please let me know *whether* you received the package.

Whether or not he agrees, we must do it.

Some grammarians consider *if* and *whether* to be interchangeable in constructions such as:

Let me know *if* (*whether*) you received the package.

I wonder *if* (*whether*) he will be there.

I don't know *if* (*whether*) I can go.

Should there be any danger of misunderstanding, use *whether* in similar types of sentences.

Don't Forget to Signal

Grammarians tell us that in the early days of language, when life was a good deal simpler, there were no connectives. People spoke in short sentences that ran together, with no connectives at all to indicate relationships between phrases. As thought—and communication—grew more complex, man developed a system of modifiers and connectives in order to clarify meaning. Today our language abounds in connectives, and we are able to choose the one that will express the exact meaning we are after. By this choice, we can indicate to our readers the precise relationship between ideas. When we use connectives, we guide the reader through our writing, signaling when we add a thought, change to a different point of view, or shift to a different subject.

Just as punctuation marks act as traffic signals, telling the reader when to stop and start, when to speed up and when to slow down, connectives are verbal directional signals. When a driver signals for a left turn, the flashing light alerts the driver behind him. In the same way, when we use a connective, we signal the reader that we are going to change our approach. A driver who signals for a left and makes a right turn will certainly cause confusion—if not an accident. And a writer who uses the wrong connective will confuse his reader.

Four Flashing Lights

Four kinds of words can serve as connectives. You already know about conjunctions. The other three are:

292

prepositions, relative pronouns and relative adverbs. Each connects sentence elements and shows the relationship between them. Here we will discuss prepositions and explain how they are used.

Pick a Peck of Prepositions

A preposition connects the word, phrase, or clause that follows it (its object) with some other element in the sentence and shows the relationship between them. There are three types:

SIMPLE PREPOSITIONS: at, but, by, down, for, from, in, of, off, on, out, over, per, through, to, up, via, with . . .

COMPOUND PREPOSITIONS: about, above, across, after, against, along, among, around, before, behind, below, beneath, beside, besides, between, beyond, despite, except, inside, into, outside, toward(s), under, until, upon, within, without . . .

PHRASAL PREPOSITIONS: according to, because of, contrary to, inasmuch as . . .

Choosing the correct preposition can be either the simplest of matters or a frustrating puzzle. Some choices are easy because prepositions are so basic to our vocabularies that we choose them almost unconsciously. Sometimes a preposition seems exactly right; sometimes it just doesn't seem to fit at all. When the choice is difficult, it is because we lack the ability to sense the essential rightness or wrongness of the preposition. Hunting for a rule to defend our choice, we find none and, therefore, must fall back upon idiomatic usage. (See "Beware the Idiom," p. 313.) An idiom is an expression that defies grammar, but has become accepted through popular use. As anyone who has studied a foreign language knows, idioms simply have to be memorized, for they cannot be constructed through any logical rules. Idioms require us to say:

> able *to* sing   but   capable *of* singing
> the way *to* sew   but   the way *of* sewing (the method)
> try *to* win   but   aim *at* winning

As far as grammar is concerned, in each of the three illustrations, *to*, *of*, *for* and *at* are equally acceptable. But the idiom says that it doesn't make sense to say *aim to winning*; only *aim at winning* conveys the meaning.

Prepositional idioms outnumber most other idioms— one reference book lists more than 2,000. You may consult an unabridged dictionary, a dictionary of synonyms or a handbook of grammar.

294

A Shade of Meaning

The choice between prepositions is often based on the slight difference in meaning between them or on the preferences that grammarians have expressed. Here are just a few:

1. *at, in:*

These may often be used interchangeably. But when they are used in phrases concerning place or locality, writers should be aware of these distinctions:

(a) *In* is used when the reference to the interior of a building is stressed; *at* when the site itself is stressed.

> The charity ball was held *in* the Grand Ballroom of the Plaza.

> We met for lunch *at* the Plaza.

(b) *In* is usually used before the names of countries and sections; *at*, before the names of business firms, office buildings, etc.

> *In* Norway; *in* England; *in* the South.

> *At* the post office; *at* Blank and Co.

> He was educated *at* Harvard.

(c) *In* is used before the name of a city if the writer wants to leave an impression of permanence; *at* if he is indicating a temporary stay.

> I stopped *at* Chartres for a day and went on to spend a week *in* Paris.

> The group met *at* Richmond and, after a short visit, stayed *in* Williamsburg for the rest of the week.

(d) In local addresses, *in* is used before the name of the city; *at*, before the street number of the residence or office.

Mr. Smith lives at 564 West Main St. in Palmer.

2. *between, among:*

One of the knottiest of the preposition puzzles is the problem of when to use *between* and when to use *among*. Most of us know and use this familiar rule: Use *among* when referring to more than two persons or things or to more than two groups considered collectively; use *between* when referring to only two people or groups. But there are cases in which *between* should be used when more than two things are involved. Consider these alternatives and decide which you would use:

A treaty *among* (or *between*) three countries.
The contest is *among* (or *between*) five candidates.
We must choose *among* (or *between*) three alternatives.

Grammarians feel that neither *between* nor *among* expresses the relationship clearly. But no preposition exists that expresses the relation of a thing to several other things, not only with respect to the entire group, but also in relation to each of the members of that group. *Among* expresses the relation collectively and somewhat vaguely; some say it lumps together the objects too much. *Between*, though it is not exact, seems to indicate better that the relationship is to both the group *and* its individual members.

3. *below, beneath, down, under, underneath:*

Sometimes a subtle difference in the meanings of

296

prepositions can cause offense, if the wrong preposition is used. Sometimes these prepositions can be used interchangeably. When they cannot, the distinctions are usually natural, for using the wrong one would make an expression ridiculous. The sentence:

> His legs trembled *beneath* him.

would certainly sound odd if we said:

> His legs trembled *below* him.

You might say:

> He is *below* me.

meaning he lives downstairs, but to say:

> He is *beneath* me.

would mean something quite different. Used this way, *beneath* implies inferiority or contempt.

One Is a Crowd

Sometimes in talking we tend to use double prepositions, or a preposition where none is needed. These colloquialisms may sound all right in speech, but they look sloppy if you use them in your writing.

> NOT: We will divide *up* the money.

> BUT: We will divide the money.

> NOT: She is standing near *to* the exit.

> BUT: She is standing near the exit.

> NOT: I shall start *in to* write that paper.

> BUT: I shall start *to* write that paper.

Phrases Are Shrinkable

Phrasal prepositions tend to make writing wordy, heavy and often pompous. Most can be reduced to one word.

for the purpose of	*to*
prior to	*before*
inasmuch as	*since*

(These are discussed more fully in Chapter 7: Concise-ness Means Strength, page 301.)

A Rule You Need Not Put Up With

The old rule about never ending a sentence with a preposition has been relaxed in modern usage. Most writers agree that certain expressions sound much more natural—and less strained and awkward—when the preposition is left at the end of the sentence. For instance:

What did you want that *for*?

Here are the exams you passed *in*.

What do you have in common to talk *about*?

I don't see anything to object *to*.

Missing Prepositions

Always be careful, especially in formal writing, to include the second preposition before the second of two connected elements.

NOT: He spoke to us and our parents.
BUT: He spoke to us and *to* our parents.

NOT: He will argue with you and anyone else who dares to speak.
BUT: He will argue with you and *with* anyone else who dares to speak.

Watch carefully for split constructions, those in which two words are completed by two different prepositions. If both prepositions are not used, the sentence will not make sense.

NOT: He has a talent and an interest in drawing.
BUT: He has a talent *for* and an interest *in* drawing.

NOT: He had heard and was intrigued *by* the possibilities.
BUT: He had heard *about* and was intrigued *by* the possibilities.

Many good writers feel that these constructions are at best awkward. They recommend revising them:

He had heard about the possibilities and was intrigued by them.

The Prepositional Phrase

The prepositional phrase consists of the preposition plus its object, plus any modifiers of the object. The object of the preposition may be a word, a phrase or a clause; and the modifiers of the object may likewise be words, phrases or clauses.

The prepositional phrase functions most often as an adjective or an adverb; occasionally it may also serve as a noun. Writers should avoid overusing prepositional phrases—they make a sentence unwieldy and awkward. When he uses too many, the writer is faced with a puzzle. He must put the phrase as close as possible to the word or words it modifies—and sometimes this isn't easy. Using the active voice will simplify this problem considerably. (The verb is in the active voice when the subject does the acting. The verb is in the passive voice when the subject is acted upon. See page 250.) Compare these two examples:

PASSIVE: Please have the report prepared by your agency and the data furnished us on this matter at the earliest possible date.

ACTIVE: Please have your agency prepare the report and let us have the data as soon as possible.

7. Conciseness Means Strength

Some people, when they sit down to write, become afflicted with a strange disease. They forget that writing is often merely another form of talking. Short words suddenly inflate into long, pretentious words. Long, involved phrases sprout where two words would do. Trailing sentences twine together like jungle vines in a *Tarzan* movie. Suppose someone afflicted this way had written *Three Blind Mice*? It might go like this:

> A trio of decrepit rodents,
> A trio of decrepit rodents,
> Observe how they motivate,
> Observe how they motivate.
> They all perambulated after the agriculturist's
>   spouse,
> Who severed their appendages by means of a
>   culinary cleaver,
> Have you ever observed such a phenomenon in
>   your existence,
> As a trio of decrepit rodents?

One Little Word

Dignity, even scholarliness, *can* be achieved by using simple, direct language. Why, for example, are our most noted historians so famous? It may be for the originality of their contributions, to be sure, but it is also because they write so well; their books prove that history need not be a collection of dry facts and interminable footnotes. Here is a collection of "inflated" words and their simpler equivalents. A look at your own writing may provide you with others:

construct, fabricate	*make*
initiate, commence, inaugurate	*begin, start*
therefore	*so*
nevertheless	*but*
terminate	*end*
utilize	*use*
deem	*think*
assistance	*help*
reside	*live*
stated, declared	*said*
ascertain	*learn, find out*
procure	*get*
indicate	*show*

Sometimes, of course, a little word will not express precisely what you mean, and you will find a long word necessary. When you do, try to avoid purely technical terms and jargon and, to avoid looking ridiculous, be sure you know the exact meaning of the word you want to use.

Block That Phrase

Why use a whole mouthful of words, when often a single word will do? Here are some ways to knock the wind out of your phrases:

for the purpose of	*for*
in the nature of	*like*
along the lines of	*like*
prior to	*before*
subsequent to	*after*
with respect (reference, regard) to	*about*
in the amount of	*for*
on the basis of	*by, from,* etc.
in accordance with	*by*
by means of	*with, by*
in order to	*to*
on the occasion of	*when, on*
in the event that	*if*
in view of the fact that	*because*
for the reason that	*since*
with a view to	*to*
despite the fact that	*though*
in the time of	*during*

The phrase *the fact that* usually just takes up room in a sentence that might otherwise be much more direct. In most cases, try to eliminate it.

BAD: Judging by the fact that she did not attend, she did not consider the meeting important.

BETTER: Judging by her absence, she did not consider the meeting important.

Another word that is often used unnecessarily is *then*. *Then* has its place—when there might be, for example, an ambiguity in a time sequence—but normally this word can be discarded from your sentence.

BAD: I registered for the course, and then I went to the bookstore.

BETTER: I registered for the course and went to the bookstore.

Of should not be used with *all*:

NOT: The cat ate all of the food.
BUT: The cat ate all the food.

Sometimes one simple verb can do the work of a whole group of words:

give consideration to	*consider*
have need for	*need*
give encouragement to	*encourage*
come into conflict with	*conflict with*
give instruction to	*instruct*
make use of	*use*
is of the opinion that	*believes*
make an adjustment to	*adjust*

And sometimes an adverb or an adjective can replace a full-blown clause:

is due in large measure to	*is largely due to*
the lights, which were flickering on and off,	*the flickering lights*

Action, Please

Whether you are writing to a friend, doing a term paper on the Renaissance or writing a business letter, your writing will be livelier and more concise if you use the active voice, rather than the passive. (See page 250.)

Active verbs are more direct. They convey a more concrete picture than do passive verbs. For example:

PASSIVE: Four stores were destroyed this morning by a five-alarm fire which was brought under control by fire fighters at 6 a.m.

ACTIVE: A five-alarm fire destroyed four stores early this morning. Fire fighters brought the blaze under control at 6 a.m.

PASSIVE: A survey of all city hospitals was conducted by the Department of Public Health. It was found that standards were not being met by many hospitals.

ACTIVE: The Department of Public Health conducted a survey of all city hopsitals. The survey found that many hospitals were not meeting minimum standards.

Use the passive voice when you want to emphasize the object—by making it the subject of the sentence. For instance, in the sentence, *He will make his report in June*, if you want to emphasize the *report*, switch the sentence to read: *The report will be given in June.*

But remember that putting a verb into the passive voice does not necessarily make it more formal. Don't use the passive voice as a device to give importance to formal correspondence.

Say It Again . . .

But only if you must. Repetition is fine for emphasis, but be careful not to say unintentionally the same thing twice:

305

The house was ~~completely~~ destroyed.

Thomas Jefferson was born in 1743 ~~in the 18th century.~~

I have not finished my term paper ~~at the present time.~~

Useless Words

When you write a formal letter, such as an application for a job, a complaint, or an order, do you stall before you start?

~~It is my feeling that~~ I would be well qualified to handle the assignment ~~due to the fact that . . .~~

~~You are advised that~~ a new edition of the . . .

Attached ~~hereto~~ is . . .

Enclosed ~~herewith~~ is . . .

Rx for Long Sentences

According to current standards, the average length of a "readable" sentence should be about twenty words. But if every sentence conformed to that standard, reading would be a bore no matter what the content. Long sentences do have their place in the writer's repertoire. One of the most effective tools for making long sentences readable is "parallel construction." By putting logically parallel thoughts in grammatically parallel words, phrases or clauses, you help the reader to grasp the thought easily. It works like this: Express similar ideas in similar form. For example:

> INCORRECT: I like read*ing*, swimm*ing*, *to* skate and *to* ride.

CORRECT:	I like *to* read, *to* swim, *to* skate and *to* ride.
CONFUSING:	The hill was so icy that the car, its wheels spinning, *slid* slowly down the hill, *stopping* at the edge of the river bank.
BETTER:	The hill was so icy that the car, its wheels spinning, *slid* slowly down the hill and *stopped* at the edge of the river bank.

No Padding, Please

Your sentences may be clear and effective, but if you've tied them up in a bulky, awkward bundle of a paragraph, you'll confuse your reader anyway. Like sentences, paragraphs must be planned and organized. Each paragraph should be a step in the logical structure of the entire piece, whether it be a letter, an essay or an article for publication. Each paragraph should have a topic sentence—a sentence that tells the reader: now we will discuss *this* aspect of the subject. Just as a symphony movement has a major theme followed by development of that theme, a paragraph has its topic sentence, followed by sentences that relate to it. Sentences should be linked in logical order; remember, too, that the beginning and ending of a paragraph are its strongest points. You can learn to use these points effectively. Paragraphs should not be too long, especially in letters, where the sight of an endless paragraph can weary a reader before he starts. But vary paragraphs as you do sentences, for the sake of visual interest.

In order not to leap too abruptly from one subject to another, it's a good idea to use transitional sentences to link your paragraphs logically, especially when changing subjects. Transitions are usually built into the first sentence of the paragraph. This can be done simply by repeating a word or phrase from the preceding paragraph:

> However, *Socrates'* approach would never work today, when . . .

Tying in a thought from the preceding paragraph will lead the reader gently into the new thought. Sometimes entire paragraphs serve as transitions between ideas.

Try your hand at editing the following paragraph:

> I am of the opinion that a career in the field of oceanography would be an excellent career to give consideration to at this time. This is because the oceans have just begun to be explored by man in his current quest for new sources of minerals and food and ways by which to process these.

Due to the fact that world famine is a very real possibility in the future, oceanographers will be demanded in all parts of the world. There will be undersea vessels as common as planes, there will be a need for men to pilot them, too.

Wordiness never pays off. Most students who "pad" essays and themes find that teachers can see through verbiage like a bird watcher spotting a red-breasted grosbeak. Sometimes the best cure for wordiness is simply to know your subject well. This is true also for specialists, who must keep in mind their audience. Jargon is permissible when you are writing for someone in your field who understands it; but when you write to someone who doesn't, the best way is the simple, concise way.

8. Booby Traps

Unless you are purposely being funny, you don't want your readers to chuckle when they read your best efforts. If you are aware of some of the booby traps that can change a sentence from sublime to just plain ridiculous, this won't happen. Even when you write in a hurry, take time to check for these common errors.

Dangling Modifiers

When you misplace a modifier, you usually misplace the meaning along with it. Here are some examples:

PARTICIPIAL PHRASE: Imagine our thrill when, breaking through the clouds, Rome came into view.

Rome did not break through the clouds. *Rewrite*:

Imagine our thrill when the plane broke through the clouds and Rome came into view.

GERUNDIVE PHRASE: After standing in line three hours, the registrar announced the course was full.

The registrar did not stand in line for three hours. *Rewrite:*

After I had been standing in line for three hours, the registrar announced the course was full.

PREPOSITIONAL PHRASE: It was so cold we went to see the Tower of Pisa in our heaviest clothes.

The Tower did not wear heavy clothes. *Rewrite:*

It was so cold we went in our heaviest clothes to see the Tower of Pisa.

INFINITIVE PHRASE: To learn to swim properly, time is needed for practice.

To learn cannot modify *time. Rewrite:*

To learn to swim properly, you need time to practice.

Mysterious Modifiers

Sometimes a clause or phrase may be placed in a sentence so that the reader does not know which word the phrase modifies. Try to place modifiers close to the words to which they relate.

> I knew I would marry you on that evening when I saw you for the first time.

> *Does the writer mean?*

> When I saw you for the first time, I knew I would marry you that very evening.

> *Or:*

> On that evening when I first saw you, I knew I would marry you.

Better Than — What?

Incomplete comparisons will leave your readers puzzled. Which of two meanings did this writer have in mind?

> I like classical music better than the Beatles.

> *Does the writer mean?*

> I like classical music better than I like the Beatles.

> *Or:*

> I like classical music better than the Beatles do.

In another type of error, though you may have completed your comparison, the two things mentioned may not be logically compared. For example:

312

INCORRECT: Paris streets have a unique atmosphere; they are unlike any other city.

You cannot compare *streets* to *city*.

CORRECT: Paris streets have a unique atmosphere; they are unlike *those* of any other city.

INCORRECT: He told me my style was very like Picasso.

CORRECT: He told me my style was very like Picasso's.

Leave It to Poets

Alliteration may have its place in poetry, and even in some prose, but when it turns up in ordinary writing, it can make a sentence ridiculous. When you are caught up in the action of writing, you may not notice that many words start with the same letter; be sure to check for this "booby trap."

EXAMPLE: We have found, fortunately, that fifty fine furs of the type furnished by . . .

Beware the Idiom

Every language has its idioms—ways of saying things that defy grammar. If idioms were taken literally, they would either conjure up some strange pictures, or make no sense at all. Through common usage, these expressions have become part of the language. Be sure you use idioms correctly. The most common errors occur when writers use the wrong preposition with a noun, adjective or verb. The word *differ*, for example, may be used with four different prepositions:

> When it comes to politics, we differ *from* each other considerably.

> We differ considerably *in* our opinions on politics.

> We differ *on* the best course for the country to take.

> He differs *with* me on every aspect of politics.

If you are not sure which preposition to use, check an unabridged dictionary.

Some Grammatical Villains

Writers of run-on sentences have a habit of sprinkling commas about like salt. One of the most common villains responsible for garbled sentences is the *comma splice*, which occurs when two main clauses are linked by a comma without a co-ordinating conjunction. For example:

INCORRECT: In many countries soccer is the most popular sport, in the United States it is not.

BETTER: In many countries soccer is the most popular sport; in the United States it is not.

OR: In many countries soccer is the most popular sport, but in the United States it is not.

OR: In many countries soccer is the most
       popular sport. In the United States
       it is not.

Two other villains can also snarl sentences and puzzle
your readers. One is *split construction*; the other is *faulty
reference of pronouns*. Both can slip easily into a sentence;
both will leave your reader wondering what you meant.

Split Construction

When you split closely related parts of a sentence,
such as a subject and verb, or two parts of a parallel construction, you obscure the meaning. Sometimes constructions are split purposely to emphasize a particular
part of the structural unit. But generally speaking, it is
wise to avoid separating parts of a sentence that belong

315

together. For example, this sentence grinds to a halt because subject and verb wind up miles away from each other:

> The committee has announced that more than 1,000 *members* of the party, most of whom, according to recent polls conducted regionally and nationally, seem to be confused rather than enlightened by the pre-convention jockeying for position by the several potential candidates, *will attend* a dinner next Saturday night at the Grand Hotel.

Your Antecedents Are Showing

When you substitute a pronoun for a noun, make sure the reader knows the word for which the pronoun stands. There are three ways to clear up ambiguous references:

1. You can change an indirect to a direct statement:

UNCLEAR: Mrs. Jones told Mrs. Smith that her children were playing in the mud.

BETTER: Mrs. Jones told Mrs. Smith, "Your children are playing in the mud."

2. You can repeat the antecedent:

Separate whites from yolks and beat the yolks lightly.

3. You can put the pronoun closer to its antecedent.

UNCLEAR: The students invited teachers to attend because they wished to learn more about the project.

BETTER: The students, who wished to learn more about the project, invited the teachers to attend.

OR: The students invited the teachers who wished to learn more about the project to attend.

One other point: A pronoun should not refer to the entire preceding idea. Add a summarizing word, or revise the sentence to eliminate the pronoun:

INCORRECT: I have not yet received the material, which has kept me from completing the job.

BETTER: I have not yet received the material, and this has kept me from completing the job.

OR: Because I have not yet received the material, I have been unable to complete the job.

9. Punctuation: Traffic Signs of Language

Traffic signs are posted to insure a smooth, safe flow of traffic. In language, punctuation serves the same purpose: to insure a smooth, coherent flow of thought. Some people think punctuation is a nuisance and ignore it. Their writing is like a verbal traffic jam—uncoordinated thoughts piled on one another with hardly a comma or period to point the way.

Punctuation should come naturally, yet it is perhaps the most troublesome aspect of writing. When we talk, we punctuate with our tone of voice, with pauses, with inflections. Punctuation is the written equivalent of these verbal traffic signs. It shows the relationship of the parts of our sentences and, thus, of our thoughts.

No Stamps

Punctuation is an integral part of writing. You can't stick it on, like a stamp on an envelope, after a piece of writing is finished. You should punctuate naturally as you write, to separate and emphasize your thoughts the way you want them to sound. Because the trend today is toward simpler sentences, there is a tendency to use less punctuation—it's logical that the more involved the sentence, the more "traffic signs" you'll need to

give the reader direction. It is important that a writer maintain a degree of consistency, so that the reader will not be left floundering. Most of the punctuation we use can be grouped into three functions:

1. To separate one idea from another so that the reader may see them distinctly:

His birthday was Saturday, and we gave him a party.

2. To enclose incidental or parenthetic expressions:

The house, which stood close to the sea, was an early Victorian mansion.

3. To emphasize certain elements in a sentence by setting them apart from the rest of the sentence.

The painting, newly restored, hung like a jewel on the east wall.

(If the sentence read, "The newly restored painting hung . . ." there would be less emphasis on *newly restored*.)

The versatile comma is the mark that most often performs these functions; being the most widely used mark, it is also perhaps the most misused (see *comma splice*, p. 314). The following formula for the use of the comma may help you when you are puzzling over how to punctuate: *Use one comma to separate; two to enclose.*

A Glossary of "Traffic Signs"

Use the *comma*:

1. To separate main clauses joined by a co-ordinate conjunction.

The rain came, but the game continued.

The telephone rang, and she ran to answer it.

He has never been there, yet he feels at home.

Note: Two simple sentences joined by *and* or *but* do not always need a comma, but you must use a comma before the co-ordinate conjunction *for* to avoid confusing it with the preposition *for*:

He is studying late tonight, *for* the examination is tomorrow.

2. To separate and stress short, parallel main clauses not joined by a co-ordinate conjunction.

The bells rang, the organ played, the procession slowly began.

3. To separate the two independent clauses of an echo question.

You never wrote, did you?

4. To set off a nonrestrictive adjective modifier.

The program, *taped last week*, will be repeated tonight.

Fascinated, they listened to his story.

Mrs. Green, *who has three children*, is looking for a baby sitter.

5. To set off a nonrestrictive adverbial modifier at the end of a sentence, especially if it is long or requires special emphasis.

She will let you know later, *after she has returned from shopping*.

6. To set off a nonrestrictive appositive.

My sister, *Sue*, received a college scholarship.

Many birds and animals, *such as the whooping crane and the polar bear*, face extinction.

7. To set off an introductory adverbial modifier. (If the modifier is short and clear, no comma is needed.)

Because he has contributed much to his field, he will be honored at a special ceremony next week.

When you arrive in Rome, be sure to cable.

8. To separate an introductory prepositional phrase demanding emphasis.

In spite of the driving rain, we kept moving toward our destination.

9. To set off an introductory transitional expression that is not closely related to the meaning of the sentence.

However, we will discuss the pros and cons of the entire situation.

10. To set off an interrupting transitional expression.

If you are determined, *however,* you are welcome to try.

11. To set off an interrupting expression identifying speaker or source.

The speech, *he thought,* was an excellent one.

"Put your mittens on," *she said,* "before you go out."

The passage of the law is urgent, *the Governor said,* and should be acted upon at once.

12. To set off addresses, dates, titles.

His new job will take him to *Anchorage, Alaska.*

The article appears in the issue of *July 8, 1967.*

Send boxtops to: Cookbook, Box 2346, Stillwater, Wyoming.

13. To set off a nominative absolute phrase.

The apartment having been painted, they began to decorate it.

The story having been printed, there was nothing they could do.

14. To set off words in direct address.

"Tell me, *Doctor,* is it really twins?"

15. To separate words in a series. Note that a series with a connective joining the last two members may be punctuated in either of two ways:

EITHER: He bought *apples, pears, and oranges.*

OR: He bought *apples, pears and oranges.*

Note: The trend seems to be toward omitting the comma before the conjunction. However, if there is the possibility that the last two members of the series may be considered as one when they are two, use the comma to separate them.

16. To set off consecutive adjectives which are *co-ordinate.* Adjectives are co-ordinate if (a) they can be linked by *and,* and if (b) they independently modify the substantive (noun or noun substitute).

Co-ordinate (each adjective independently modifies the substantive):

A *long, peaceful* afternoon.

But, a long afternoon; a peaceful afternoon; a long and peaceful afternoon; a peaceful and long afternoon. (No commas.)

Not co-ordinate (each adjective modifies all that follows it):

Red flannel underwear

(Flannel underwear that is red.)

A *new jet* aircraft

A *male Irish* setter

Use the *semicolon:*

1. To separate main clauses not joined by a co-ordinate conjunction.

> *The sun seemed to hang in the sky; the air was ominously still.*

2. To separate main clauses joined by a conjunctive adverb.

> The fire seemed under control; *however*, in a few hours it had broken out again.

> The paper is not valid without a witness; someone, *therefore*, must be present to sign it.

3. To emphasize one of three main clauses in a sentence.

> The lights dimmed, and the overture began; *and the curtain slowly rose.*

4. To separate co-ordinate items in a series when the items contain internal commas.

> Attending the symposium were John Forest, sports editor; Robert Gaines, center, Northwest All-Stars; Terry Dunn, sportswriter, *Johnston Daily Press*, and Dan Spinelli, Johnston High School basketball coach.

Use the *colon:*

1. Between main clauses when the second clause completes or explains the first.

We have two alternatives: We can ignore the problem, or we can face it and solve it.

2. After an expression that introduces a list, an explanation or a quotation.

You will need the following supplies: canteen, cooking utensils, flashlight, matches, knapsack and jackknife.

In his closing remarks, the Senator said: "We are determined to have peace and will pursue all possible paths to obtain it."

Use the *dash:*

1. Between main clauses when the second clause explains the first.

Our plight was obvious—*we were becalmed with neither a motor nor paddle to help.*

His record is impeccable—*in 40 years he has never missed a day.*

2. To set off a nonrestrictive modifier or parenthetical element that is normally set off by commas.

I said to him—*and he paled at the question*—how do you expect to pay for that?

3. To emphasize a nonrestrictive appositive.

It is up to one man — *the President* — to decide such matters.

Use *parentheses:*

1. To enclose a nonrestrictive modifier or parenthetic element that is only loosely connected with the thought of the sentence.

Mrs. Johnes (*who has never been a fashion plate*) looked almost chic at the ball last night.

The play (*produced on Broadway in 1948*) will be presented at the Banks County Playhouse in August.

Note: When punctuation is needed at the same place where parentheses occur, place it after the closing parenthesis. However, if the punctuation pertains to the material within the parenthesis, it belongs inside the marks.

This year he will again exhibit at the Flower Show (to be held for the first time at the Arena); last year his roses won first prize.

The information is available from the National Safety Association. (Request pamphlet No. 234.)

Use the *period:*

1. To mark the end of a declarative sentence—one that is not a question or exclamation.

The course will be given next semester.

2. After a request, to distinguish it from a direct question.

Will you please send a copy of the report by Friday.

3. After words or phrases that stand as sentences. Sentence fragments should be followed by periods.

Will you change your mind? Never.

Midnight in London. The streets were quiet.

4. After abbreviations and initials.

The director of the aquarium is A. L. Smith.

5. To indicate an omission from a quotation, use three periods in addition to any other punctuation required.

> Mrs. Jones stated, "The time has come when we can no longer ignore the problem; the time has come for us to stand together."

> Mrs. Jones stated, "The time has come . . . for us to stand together."

Use the *question mark*:

1. After a sentence that asks a direct question.

Where is your brother going?

But:

He asked where my brother was going. (Indirect question.)

2. To show doubt about the correctness of a statement.

> He grew up in Boston (?) and moved to New York at the age of 27.

> The school was founded in 1914 (?) and has grown rapidly since then.

3. To replace commas in an interrogatory series in order to emphasize the individual members of the series.

Where are the suitcases? The money? The jewels?

Use the *exclamation point:*

1. After an exclamatory sentence or remark. Good writers show restraint in using exclamation points. Used too often, exclamation points lose their effect and make writing look amateurish and "gushy."

That was the toughest exam I ever had!

Good grief!

Use *quotation marks:*

1. To enclose direct quotations, whether a single word, a sentence or a long passage of several paragraphs. Do not include within quotation marks explanatory expressions which are not part of the quoted passage.

The President called the legislation *"vital to the nation"* and *"long overdue."*

2. To enclose an entire quotation—not individual sentences, when the quotation contains more than one sentence.

"You are absolutely right," he said. "I can see your point; however, you must take into consideration several factors. You are not sure when you will be returning. You are not sure how difficult the task will be. You are not even sure you can persuade him."

Note: Use quotation marks at the head of each *paragraph* of quoted material, but at the *end* of the final paragraph only.

"From the days of Homer through Athens' 'Golden' 5th century and continuing through modern times, Greece has had a rich and varied culture. Although little is known about Homer, the blind poet who gave Europe the *Iliad* and the *Odyssey*, his epics have never been surpassed for strength and heroic beauty.

"Less well-known than Homer, but also extremely important in the development of European poetry is Sappho . . ."

3. To enclose titles that are part of a larger work, such as articles from magazines, chapters from books, poems taken from anthologies. Titles of complete works are usually italicized in printed copy and underlined in typed copy.

"The Blue Whale," from the *National Geographic*, June, 1968.

4. Use single quotation marks to enclose a quotation within a quotation.

John shook his head. "I can't believe he really said, 'You needn't come to class' and really meant it," he said.

5. Do not use quotation marks for indirect quotations. These are usually introduced by *that*.

"I left after the first act," he said.

He said that he left after the first act.

6. Commas and periods are placed inside the quotation marks whether or not they are part of the quoted material. Semicolons, colons, question marks and exclamation points are placed outside quotation marks unless they are part of the quotation.

"Did he really say, 'You needn't come to class'?"

"I believe in equal justice"; and that was how he ruled his life.

7. Use only one terminal punctuation mark at the end of sentences.

"Have you read that book?"

"Would you describe the reaction as 'enthusiastic'?"

Conclusion

Using punctuation as traffic signals to guide your thoughts, and using the other principles of writing discussed in this book, you should now be able to express yourself more clearly, more concisely and more effectively than you ever have before. The ability to express yourself in writing will benefit you in every area of your life and bring you the satisfaction that comes with doing anything well.

Refer back to this book whenever you feel you are "stale" or "stumped" for the right slant or way of organizing your thoughts. Keep your writer's notebook and clippings, and refer to them for inspiration.

Index

SPELL IT RIGHT

By
Harry Shaw

For

> *Jane Bayard Wilson Shaw*
> *who, through love and knowledge,*
> *fostered the lifelong interest of*
> *her son in the subject of spelling*

CONTENTS

PREFACE

Correct spelling is essential for intelligent communication. It is taken for granted and expected at all times. Yet many people realize their writing sometimes contains spelling errors, and they are embarrassed by doubts and fears about the correct spelling of difficult words. Distraction, confusion, and misunderstanding result from errors in spelling. Therefore, no one should be satisfied with anything less than perfection.

Perhaps you are one of those people who feel disturbed by their spelling errors and have enough of a spelling conscience to do something about it. Or perhaps you are among those who doubt their ability to master this difficult subject. You may have tried many times and failed. If so, is there any hope for you?

The answer is that if you really have a desire to learn to spell perfectly you can, provided:

1. You can pronounce such words as *accept* and *except* so that they will not sound exactly alike.

2. You can look at such words as *sad* and *sand* and in a single glance, without moving your eyes, detect the difference between them.

3. You can sign your name without looking at the paper on which you are writing and without even consciously thinking about what you are doing.

4. You can tell your friend Bill from your friend Sam by a mere glance.

5. You can learn a simple rhyme, such as "Old King Cole was a merry old soul . . ."

6. You can remember that a compliment is "what *I* like to get."

7. You can learn the alphabet, if you do not know it already.

8. You can equip yourself with a reliable desk dictionary.

9. You can learn what a syllable is and proofread your writing syllable-by-syllable.

10. You have normal intelligence, here defined as the ability to

read and write simple English and keep out of the way of speeding automobiles.

If you can honestly meet these ten provisions, you can learn to spell *without ever making a mistake*. If you can pass Number 10 and only three or four of the others, you can still double your spelling efficiency. It's worth trying, isn't it?

The approaches and attacks are all included in the chapters which follow. If you just cannot wait to start, skip to Chapter 2 and begin there. If you lose heart, turn back to the first chapter. It can be very helpful, too.

Wherever you start, start NOW.

1—You and the Problem of Spelling

The one thing demanded of anyone who has had educational advantages is that he be able to spell. In your daily work or in social situations you may not need to be able to add a column of figures. Few people will care. Not often will you be thought stupid if you don't know the dates of historical events—say, the Battle of Waterloo. Your knowledge of economics can be nil. You may not know the difference between an oboe and an ibis, an atom and a molecule. But if you can't spell, you're in trouble. Rightly or wrongly, fairly or unfairly, misspelling is the most frequently accepted sign of illiteracy.

Why is this? You can argue that the ability to think clearly is far more important than spelling. So are clear expression of thoughts, an attractive personality, and demonstrated ability in one's job. The fact remains that incorrect spelling is heavily penalized in our society—so heavily that it keeps people from getting jobs they want or prevents them from moving up to better positions. Inability to spell gives people complexes just as much as unsureness about grammar or proper methods of dress and social behavior.

The main reason for this somewhat illogical reliance on spelling as an index of intelligence and literacy is that correct spelling is the one fixed and certain thing about our language. The overwhelming majority of English words are spelled in only one way; all other ways are wrong. The accepted system *is* accepted. It is the system in which our business communications, our magazines, our newspapers, and our books have been written for generations.

This uniformity applies to no other aspect of our language. You can vary your choice of words as much as you please. You can write sentences which are long or short and punctuate them in various ways. In most circles you can split an infinitive or use a double negative and not be penalized. But you can spell a word in only one correct way. In a rapidly changing world this substantial uniformity is understandably attractive to many people, particularly to those who are good spellers.

Even where alternative spellings are possible, only one will be thought correct for a given piece of writing. For example, both *telephone* and *phone* are commonly used, the latter a colloquial form of *telephone.* Your employer or the editor for whom you are writing may insist on *telephone,* and that full spelling will then be the right one. Both *theater* and *theatre* are correct spellings, but you would probably use the former in the United States and the latter in England.

One might argue logically that many wrong spellings are "better" than the right ones since they "show" the word more clearly. *Wensday* more clearly reveals the sound of the word than does *Wednesday.* But logic and common sense will not help; in Old English *Wōdnes dæg* was the day of the god *Woden,* and the *d* has remained. Spelling is frequently a matter of conforming not to logic but to custom and tradition.

If enough people make a "mistake" in punctuation, or grammar, or the meaning of a word, that "mistake" becomes acceptable usage. This is a scientific fact of language. Through the years our language has changed, and will change, in its idioms, its vocabulary, its pronunciation, and its structural form. Change is the essential, inevitable phenomenon of a living language, as it is of any living organism. But this observation, this law, does not yet apply to the spelling of English words.

For many generations, spelling practice has been supported by sentiment, convention, prejudice, and custom. This is strong support, since each of us can think of many other activities similarly reinforced. The world is largely ruled by sentiment. A hundred, a thousand, observances are based only upon convention. Think briefly of the clothes people wear, table manners, office etiquette, and you will see the point. If sentiment, convention, and custom were removed from our social order, our way of living would be altered beyond recognition.

If English spelling were much more illogical than it is, the problem might be solved. Then no one could spell correctly; all of us would be bad spellers together. But enough people have learned to spell correctly to make things difficult for those who can't. This is the situation today, and we must make the best of it.

At some time in the distant future, correct spelling may be thought unimportant. Until that time, we can take comfort in realizing that spelling, like every other activity of the human mind, *can* be learned. It will have to be if we are to free ourselves from the doubts and frustrations which diminish our self-confidence when we write. It will have to be if we wish to "get ahead," to be socially acceptable, to be considered educated and literate.

WHY SPELLING IS DIFFICULT

Correct spelling is so important for social and business reasons that we feel obligated to learn to spell as well as we can, perfectly if possible. The task is not simple. It would be easier if spelling were always logical and consistent. But from bitter experience we know that the spelling of English words is illogical and inconsistent. In fact, it is downright eccentric and, on occasion, idiotic—as writers through the years have gleefully, or wrathfully, pointed out. Thorstein Veblen, famed author of *The Theory of the Leisure Class*, once wrote that English spelling satisfies all the requirements "of conspicuous waste. It is archaic, cumbrous, and ineffective . . . failure to acquire it is easy of detection . . ." as many of us know to our sorrow. And former President Andrew Jackson once angrily commented that it is a poor mind which cannot think of more than one way to spell a word.

Why is spelling difficult? The primary reason is that the correct spelling of many words does not even approximate the sounds being represented. Our speech has steadily drifted away from traditional writing and the process is continuing. Because our language is constantly changing, it is likely that spelling will tend to differ more and more from pronunciation. Unless spelling undergoes reform (and strong opposition has always prevented this) our spelling may proceed to the point where many words become ideographic. This means that a written symbol (a spelled word) will represent something directly rather than stand for the actual sound of the word itself. This tendency—exemplified by the contrasting pronunciation and spelling of such words as *cough*, *Worcester*, and *knife*—has been evident for centuries. Some experts believe that this difference will become greater and greater.

Not only are numerous words not spelled as they sound, but

many which sound alike are spelled differently. Any system is suspect which tolerates *fine* and *sign*. We have identical pronunciations for *no* and *know*; *cite, sight,* and *site* sound alike. No one unfamiliar with English and English spelling would ever imagine that *kernel* and *colonel* have the same sound.

No adequate history of English spelling has ever been written, and certainly this small book is not the place to attempt one. But a brief review of known facts about our language will help to account for some of the admitted difficulties of English spelling.

For about one thousand years before the Christian era, our linguistic ancestors were semi-savages wandering through northern Europe. These tribes consisted of Angles, Saxons, and Jutes and spoke several dialects of what is known as Low German, or *Plattdeutsch*. They had some contact with the Roman Empire and promptly began a process which has continued unabated to the present day: they started borrowing words from Latin and placing them in their own vocabularies. We still use many everyday words borrowed by these tribes: *bishop, butter, cheap, cheese, church, plum, kettle, street,* etc.

When the Roman Empire began to weaken, it had to give up its occupancy of what we now know as England, and the Germanic tribes, commonly called Anglo-Saxons, began to move in. We know little about the arrival of the Anglo-Saxons in England in the fifth century A.D., but we do know that after the year 600 they were converted to Christianity and that borrowing from Latin became even more pronounced. To what was then Anglo-Saxon, or Old English, were added many words which are in use today, such as *alms, anthem, martyr, palm,* and *priest*.

England even then was considered an attractive place, and Norsemen from Denmark and the Scandinavian peninsula began a long series of hit-and-run raids. Forays of the Norsemen continued until the eleventh century, with the linguistic result that many Norse words were added to the language. Examples are *crawl, egg, law, race, scowl,* and *tree*. Even our pronouns *they, them,* and *their* are of Norse origin. So is our suffix *-by*, the Danish word for "farm" or "town," which appears in so many place names, such as *Derby*.

Another event of great importance to our language (and spelling) was the Norman Conquest. The Normans, originally from

Scandinavia, settled in northern France in the tenth century and adopted the French language. In 1066 they crossed the English Channel and became the masters of England. French became the language of the nobility, the court, and polite society, although the common people continued to use English. Our language was profoundly affected by the introduction of French; literally thousands of words were added to the English vocabulary between 1100 and 1500. A few examples will serve to show this borrowing: *bacon, baptism, biscuit, blanket, bucket, chess, curtain, fault, flower, government, grammar, incense, lamp, lemon, logic, parson, religion, scarlet, surprise, towel.*

Beginning about 1500, the discovery of new lands brought many thousands of other new words to the English language. Words from such remote regions as India, China, Africa, and North America enriched the language tremendously. Among familiar words borrowed, for example, from the North American Indians may be mentioned *Connecticut, Massachusetts, Monongahela, squaw, tomahawk,* and *wampum.*

In short, during the past thousand years our language has far more than doubled its size. Words have come pouring into the language from French, Latin, Greek, Hebrew, Arabic, and a score of other tongues. Many of these words are difficult to spell, at least in part because of their pronunciation.

This brief comment on English is grossly inadequate as linguistic history, but its purpose is to make clear one dominant reason why spelling and pronunciation are so far apart. When these many thousands of words first arrived in English they often appeared with the spellings, or phonetic (sound) approximations of the spellings, which they originally had and which did not always conform to the customs of English. Sometimes, the spellings of words were modified to conform to the English tongue; many times they were not. The English language is a linguistic grab bag with tremendous range and flexibility. Unfortunately, its very richness compounds our spelling problems.

English is indeed a polyglot language, but that is not all. Present-day spelling often reflects pronunciations of several centuries ago. Between the time of Chaucer (1340–1400) and Shakespeare (1564–1616) our language underwent changes in pronunciation which contributed to the chaos of modern spelling.

For example, in Chaucer's time *mouse* sounded like our *moose; moon* resembled our pronunciation of *moan.* These shifts in vowel sounds (as well as in others) were thorough. However, since we have retained some of the Chaucerian (Middle English) system of spelling, Modern and Chaucerian English seem closer than they really are. Genuine differences are hidden by our spelling system.

Another change during this period from Chaucer to Shakespeare was the complete elimination of a vowel sound in certain positions. Chaucer pronounced *name* and *dance* as two syllables. Shakespeare pronounced them as one, as do we. Similarly, Chaucer pronounced the word *laughed* as two syllables: laugh-ed, but of course we do not. This elimination of a vowel sound affected hundreds of quite common words and gave a different aspect to the language. The "silent" vowel in English is responsible for as many misspellings as any other one cause (it will be discussed in Chapter 4).

These two changes in pronunciation (but not in spelling) account for some of the basic differences between the English of Chaucer's time and that of today. Furthermore, a number of other sound changes have occurred since the time of Shakespeare and are still going on. People in the sixteenth and seventeenth centuries, for example, pronounced *reason* as we do *raisin.* They also sounded the *l* in a word like *palm.* Our pronunciation has changed, but our spelling has not—with consequent grief for all poor spellers.

Why is it that pronunciation is ever changing and spelling is not? Many reasons can be cited, but two are outstanding.

First, standardization of spelling is due more to the invention of printing than to any other single cause. Prior to the introduction of printing into England by William Caxton in 1475, most people were not concerned with spelling. Reading and writing were activities carried on only by monks and other learned men. So long as people communicated solely by speech, spelling was no problem. But when printing came in, some standards had to be set up; otherwise, chaos would have resulted because those who read would have been utterly confused by whimsically varied spelling. As larger and larger numbers of people began to read and write, they saw and used the standardized spellings employed by scholars, "editors," and printers. These standards were loose and flexible, to be sure, but they represented a forward step in communication.

This unification of the language, though partial and imperfect, had a profound effect on writing but not, of course, on speech.

Second, a major regulatory and controlling influence on the language came from early dictionary-makers. The first English dictionary in 1603 spelled and briefly defined a little more than two thousand words. Its compiler did what his predecessors had done when translating Latin words into English: he copied. Naturally, on numerous occasions he imitated the spellings of his predecessors and thus tended to freeze them.

This earliest dictionary was imitated, or expanded upon, by several other lexicographers. In 1755, Dr. Samuel Johnson published his famous dictionary, a serious, important work which has influenced all lexicographers ever since. His dictionary dominated —and tended to fix—English spelling and usage for more than a century.

In the United States the great pioneer in dictionary-making was Noah Webster. His first work, published in 1806, advocated spelling *head* as *hed* and *thumb* as *thum*, but his efforts at spelling reform were generally rejected by the public. In other respects, however, his work was widely accepted; and in 1828 his *An American Dictionary of the English Language* began to exert its lasting influence on English in this country. Lexicographers since Webster have been somewhat more reliable than he in reporting actual usage but they, too, have had to report spelling as it is found in printed sources. Thus, spelling has become fixed and largely unchangeable, although it frequently does not represent actual pronunciation and often departs from common sense.

SOME COMFORTING THOUGHTS ABOUT SPELLING

If you have read this far, you may have become discouraged about ever learning to spell correctly. You may say, and with reason, that such a weird and illogical system deserves not study but contempt. Nevertheless, you know from experience that powerful social and business considerations force you to master the subject. Actually, the problem is not so difficult to solve as it may seem.

In the first place, psychologists and experienced educators have proved over and over again that any person of normal intelligence can learn to spell. Like any other activity of the human mind, spelling can be approached, grasped, and mastered. It is easier for some people to spell correctly than it is for others. This is understandable; some people can master calculus or ice-skating or sewing or typing or reading more easily than others. Spelling correctly may not be simple for you, but it surely cannot be termed impossible. Hundreds of thousands of "bad" spellers have conquered their difficulties. So can you, if you really desire to and will apply yourself to the task. No special quality of mind, no rare set of mental or motor reflexes, is involved.

It is true, however, that minds work in different ways. The best and easiest way for John or Mary to learn to spell correctly may not be the most efficient for George or Abigail. But one or more of the six approaches discussed in this book will help John, Mary, George, Abigail—and you. What you need is the will, the desire, to learn. Having that, and normal intelligence, you are fully equipped. One commentator on spelling has flatly stated: "All the investigations indicate that any *child* of normal intelligence can learn to spell with very little difficulty in a reasonable length of time."

A second comforting thought about spelling is that probably only a few words cause most of the trouble. Learning to spell may seem a hopeless task because so many thousands of words must be mastered. But remember that no one is expected to be able to spell every word on demand. A physician might be able to spell *sphygmomanometer*, but nearly everyone else would have to look it up in a dictionary. And since physicians are no better spellers than any other group of educated people, they, like us, would properly consult a dictionary when writing such "demons" as *piccalilli*, *platyrrhine*, and *pseudepigrapha*. (These words may seem strange because many of us have never used them in our entire lives. Yet each appears in standard desk dictionaries.)

One authority on spelling has stated that 95 per cent of all spelling errors occur in only 1,000 words. Since each of us has his own special writing vocabulary, this statement may not be entirely accurate. But a reliable estimate, based on carefully controlled studies, is that 90 per cent of all writing consists of only 1,000 words. Learning to spell 1,000 words (most of them simple, everyday words) is hardly an insuperable task. Even the 2,000 words which make up 95 per cent of writing are not impossible to learn, since probably most of us can easily spell the great majority of them already. If you wish to write the word *Mississippi* and are not certain about its spelling, use a dictionary. Remember that you are far more likely to misspell (and not look up) such comparatively simple words as *all right, its, it's, there,* and *their;* you are much more likely to misspell such words as *argument, business,* and *definitely* than *anesthetize, duodenum,* or *sacrilegious.*

You can come to terms with the spelling problem if you will narrow your sights and concentrate on the few, but very real, troublemakers. When driving a car haven't you often noticed in the distance a hill which looked very steep, the road up it almost vertical? As you got closer, the road seemed to smooth out, didn't it? What seemed an impossibly sharp climb became a simple grade. Learning to spell involves climbing a grade, but not a very steep one, once you get close to the problem.

Another reassuring thought about learning to spell is that the task can become good fun and provide much pleasure. This statement may seem absurd, but it is an acknowledged fact of human behavior that the more proficient a person becomes in some activity, the greater his pleasure in it. Ever watch a figure skater? Two boys with a baseball? A woman knitting? A mother giving her child a bath? Two chess players? Someone lost in a book?

Learning to spell involves discipline, concentration, and some hard work. But so do figure-skating, baseball, knitting, and reading. Proficiency provides pleasure in these activities; often the more skill attained, the greater the pleasure. Further, most activities can best be learned by actually participating in them, not just memorizing rules or reading about them in books or magazines.

After you have attained greater proficiency in spelling by following the suggestions in this book, you will find word games enjoyable. Crossword puzzles and cryptograms are not recommended for the initial phases of spelling study. Yet they can, and do, provide pleasure for many people and unquestionably increase one's basic vocabulary and spelling proficiency. Many average spellers have become excellent ones through games like Scrabble and anagrams. Only a few decades ago, spelling bees were commonly held in almost every grade school in the country. They provided fun and excitement for those who participated, as some of my readers can testify. National spelling bees are still an annual occurrence. Perhaps some television program will revive the old-time spelling bee, with pleasure and profit for contestants and viewers.

Recently, my wife and I had dinner with another couple. After returning to the living room, our host suggested that instead of playing bridge or engaging in small talk, we try a spelling game. Each of us wrote down on paper three words which we thought would cause spelling difficulties for the others. We read out our lists in turn and the others wrote them down. When each of us had written the twelve words, we read out the spellings and settled arguments by using a dictionary. Result: we added some new words to our vocabularies, fixed their spellings in mind, and enjoyed ourselves immensely. You might like to know a few of the "demons" used that night. Here they are: *picnicking, phthisic, deciduous, gnat, medieval, ptomaine, dahlia, garrulous, tendency, picayune, ecstasy, liquefy, battalion, dilemma, obsession, amoeba, iridescent, supercilious.*

Several of these words are of little practical value. That's not the point. What is important is that four people of ordinary intelligence derived pleasure and profit from a "dull" spelling game.

Learning to spell well is not a matter of tricks and mirrors; it is not a dull and dreary chore; it is not an unending task which stretches out indefinitely. It is a subject which can be mastered with some effort and imagination—and a common-sense approach.

2—Tackling the Problem

Nearly every spelling authority who has written on the subject has presented some sure-fire approach to the problem of poor spelling. All other methods are wrong; his is the only true one. And his method *has* worked—for some people. For others it has been a flat failure. There was nothing especially wrong with his method except that it did not allow for the fact that people differ. They differ in sex, color, and personality—and they differ in ways of learning. The system by which A learns easily and quickly may work poorly for B or may not work at all. There is no one guaranteed method for everyone, but some plans for studying spelling are sounder than others. Actually, spelling is sometimes "taught" in such a fashion as to preclude any possibility of real success. Before explaining the six approaches recommended in this book, we should review a few facts about people and the learning process.

Our minds operate in accordance with certain principles. We may call them *laws* if we wish, although reputable experimental psychologists would hardly do so. For instance, you have probably long since found out that you can remember something which is important to you. You can remember it so well, so clearly, that you think you could never forget it. You also realize that you can conveniently fail to remember things you wish to forget—dental appointments, for example.

Incentive, then, or a strong motive to remember, will facilitate memory. And a good memory will aid the process of learning. Thus, the task of learning to spell will come easier to you if you bear in mind the practical value to be gained and discipline yourself to study and practice.

The mental process most important in word study is the ability to form mental pictures, or *mental images* as they may be called. These images are of several types. For example, each of us can form some sort of visual image when a suggested idea calls up in our minds a picture. When the word *church* is suggested to you, you

351

immediately "see in your mind" a picture of the object named. So do I, although your visual image and mine may differ. Almost any object—automobile, child, office manager, snow—will summon up for you, and for everyone, some sort of visual image.

This power of visualization is far stronger in some people than in others. You may know every detail about your bedroom and yet not be able to see it in your mind's eye. Many of us have lapses in our powers of visualization. Therefore, the suggestion set forth later, that you "mentally see" words, may or may not be helpful to you. If it isn't, some other approach will make more sense. It's no discredit not to have visual memory, although it is true that this mental process can be trained. You probably can close your eyes and, without difficulty, see your own signature. But you may not be able to "see" any of the words you persistently misspell. If so, try another approach.

When a suggested idea summons up a memory of what the object sounds like, we have an *auditory* (hearing) image. Some of us can, and some cannot, "mentally hear" the sounds named in "the bark of a gun," "the popping of hot fat," "the song of a lark," "the laughter of children." Being auditory-minded is not especially helpful in learning to spell, unless we are also visual-minded. If we are both, the sounds of a few words can be compared with their visual images. Some of the memory devices (*mnemonics*) suggested later (Chapter 13) depend upon this relationship.

Related to the visual image and the auditory image is the *motor* image. Motor images are connected with the use of different muscles in the body. If you are a swimmer and think of the last lap in a long race, you can summon up the feeling of weary arm and leg muscles.

How can a motor image apply to spelling? Have you ever said of the spelling of a word you have in mind: "That may not be correct. Wait until I write it"? If so, you have called upon a motor image (hand-motor memory) to aid your visual memory. Motor memory is, for some people, a powerful aid in spelling; they apparently can actually feel the motions called into play by writing. You can close your eyes and without conscious thought write your signature entirely from "feel": this is motor memory.

The more mental images you have of words, the better your spelling will become. Visual, auditory, and motor images can aid in recalling correct spellings. This fundamental principle of the human mental process has an enormously important bearing on learning to spell and explains why some methods are ineffective and wasteful. For one example, you may have tried to learn the spelling of some word by repeating its letters to yourself over and over. If you have an especially well developed "auditory memory," this method may work. But auditory images are difficult or impossible for many people to summon up. In fact, some psychologists maintain it is the least developed means of recall for most of us. Mouthing words over and over is a complete waste of time for a majority of people.

When you were in school and misspelled a word, your teacher may have required you to write it correctly ten, twenty, or a hundred times. Such drill was designed to fix the word so firmly in your motor memory that you would never misspell it again. Unfortunately, such drill can, and often does, become rote; you perform the exercise without conscious attention to what you're doing. You are expending muscular effort but not relating it to visual or auditory images. We all realize that we perform certain acts with little or no conscious attention so that we are hardly aware of the process involved: shifting automobile gears, sewing, walking, carrying food to our mouths with a fork, even reading. But learning to spell requires attention and concentration, not rote methods that have little or no relationship to forming important mental images.

Well, if these are poor methods of learning to spell, what is the most effective? First, there is no *one* best method. Learning to spell is an individual matter. What works for you may not work for your friend, and vice versa. (It's even possible, but not likely, that some people can learn to spell words by mouthing them or writing them down a hundred times.) But there are a half-dozen approaches which may be effective. One or more may work for you, depending upon your mental make-up. Almost surely, one method will be better than others for you.

My suggestion is that you select a small group of words whose spelling causes you difficulty. Try studying them in turn by the methods mentioned below and developed in succeeding chapters. It should be fairly simple to decide which approach works best for you—that is, which is quicker, surer, and has the longest lasting effects.

These six methods, discussed fully in chapters which follow, have worked for millions of people. Each is psychologically sound; each has individual merits. But not all of them will work for you. If you can't "visualize" words (the most helpful approach for the largest number of people) don't lose heart; one of the other methods may suit your individual mental processes far better. Here then, are the six methods:

1. Mentally see words as well as hear them.
2. Pronounce words correctly and carefully.
3. Use a dictionary.
4. Learn a few simple rules of spelling.
5. Use memory devices.
6. Spell carefully to avoid errors.

For a selected list of words upon which to try out these approaches, see Chapter 14, page 452, or Exercise 25, page 475.

3—Actually See Words As Well As Hear Them

As was pointed out in Chapter 2, visual memory is part of everyone's mental equipment. It is better developed in some people than in others, but each of us has at least a trace. Otherwise, we could hardly recognize a sight or a person previously noticed with only casual observation. You do not need to undertake a feature-by-feature examination to distinguish George from Sam: you know instantly, from visual memory, which friend is which. No matter how poorly developed, your visual memory is a storehouse of familiar images.

The ability to visualize words, to see them in the mind's eye, is the hallmark of the good speller. To mix some metaphors, it is his "ace in the hole," his "secret weapon." When a word is mentioned, a proficient speller can "see" the word in full detail, every letter standing out, as though it were written on paper, or the floor, the wall, the sky—against whatever background object he calls to mind. If you are a poor speller, you lack this ability to some degree. Why is this so?

Perhaps one reason is that you learned to read words as units and were not required to sound them out letter-by-letter and syllable-by-syllable. Such a method of teaching was partly a protest against the chaotic or nonexistent relationship between sound and symbol in many English words. This approach also recognized that we *do* read words as units, not as successions of letters. Possibly this "modern" method of teaching reading helped to create many poor spellers.

It is quite possible to learn the general appearance of words on flash cards and later to recognize them elsewhere. You have no difficulty in visualizing such words as *cat, hat, dog,* and *run.* But unless you have actually studied them, you may mistake *their* for *there,* or *its* for *it's,* to mention only two examples of oft-misspelled

355

words. (Fortunately, most teachers have long since modified this new approach and now teach not only by word units but also by sounds, letters, and syllables.)

Again, your difficulty in visualizing words may have to do with your perception span. Some people can form a remarkably definite and complete impression of an entire room at a single glance; others can look at the same room for minutes on end without really "seeing" it at all. Similarly, many words contain too many letters for some people to take in at a single glance; possibly three to five letters is all they can perceive at one time. (Please remember that we are here discussing not reading but accurate and detailed mental pictures.)

If your ability to "see words in your mind" is weak and faulty, begin by dividing the words you are studying into syllables. Then you can focus on one syllable at a time (usually two to five letters) and not stretch your perception (seeing) span beyond reasonable limits. After learning to "see" each syllable separately, you can more and more easily visualize the complete word made up of separately seen units. For example, if you cannot mentally see the word *compete*, focus first on *com* and then on *pete*. When you have learned to see each unit, you can readily see them combined. If you cannot "see" the word *competitively*, try focusing on each of the individual units and then combine them: *com-pet-i-tive-ly*. (See Chapter 12.)

A principle of photography may be of help in this problem. What we call a snapshot is an instantaneous photograph—a picture taken with a small amount of exposure time. Other pictures require longer exposure for varying reasons. Simple words like `cat, dog, boy,* and *am* may be called snapshots—they make an instantaneous clear image on the mind. But words like *cataclysm, dogged, boycott,* and *amphibious* require longer exposure. That is, you must look at them, probably by syllables, long enough to form clear and precise mental images of them.

When you have a strong, completely established mental picture of a word, you can spell it on any occasion without hesitation or difficulty. The greatest single mistake of the poor speller is not looking at a word with enough care and time to fix it in his mind firmly and forever. Don't say that you can't do this; you already have done so with many words. You can picture and spell without hesitation many simple and even some very complex words. You can do this for your own name, for your town or city, and for the street on which you live. That is, you have looked at these words and have actually *seen* what you looked at.

Here is a good method of learning to "see" words mentally:

1. With your eyes on the word being studied, pronounce it carefully. If you don't know the proper pronunciation, consult a dictionary.
2. Study each individual letter in the word; if the word has more than one syllable, separate the syllables and focus on each one in turn.
3. *Close your eyes* and pronounce and spell the word either letter-by-letter or syllable-by-syllable, depending upon its length.
4. Look at the word again to make certain that you have recalled it correctly.
5. Practice this alternate fixing of the image and its recall until you are certain that you can instantly "see" the word under any circumstances and at any time.

Such a procedure is especially valuable when dealing with tricky words which add or drop letters for no apparent reason; which contain silent letters; or which transpose or change letters without logical cause:

explain but *explanation*	*curious* but *curiosity*
proceed but *procedure*	*maintain* but *maintenance*
pronounce but *pronunciation*	*fire* but *fiery*

The most frequent error in visualizing words is mistaking one for another similar to it. A *homograph* is a word identical with another and therefore causes no spelling trouble, whatever difficulty it may provide in pronunciation and correct usage. The *bow* in *bow tie* is spelled the same as the word *bow*, meaning "to bend," but differs in pronunciation and meaning.

Homonyms, however, do cause spelling trouble. They are words identical in pronunciation but have different meanings and often have different spellings. If you spell *bore* when you mean *boar*, or *meet* when you mean *meat*, you have incurred homonym trouble. The only sure remedy for this type of blunder is to study such words until they and their meanings are fixed in your mind.

You should understand the meanings of each of the following words and not use one when you mean another. If you will concentrate on each individual word and its meaning as suggested in the five steps on page 357, you should be able to bring it to mind whenever you have occasion to use it. Each group of words in this list bears some resemblance, although many of them are neither homonyms nor homographs. Carefully "seeing" them will remove your spelling problems with this class of words. Pronunciation is still another matter; not all of the grouped words which follow are pronounced identically, but all those in one group do have some resemblance to each other.

This list is far from complete. Hundreds of additional words could have been included, but those given here are the ones most often confused. Also, please remember that some of the words which follow have more than one part of speech. Usually, only one part of speech is indicated, since we are concentrating on spelling rather than grammar. Again, not all meanings are provided for every word. Consult your dictionary if you need further information about variant meanings of the words and word groups which follow.

LOOK-ALIKES AND SOUND-ALIKES

1. **Abjure**—To renounce. He *abjured* all his property rights.
   Adjure—To entreat or appeal. The judge *adjured* the spectators to be silent.
2. **Accent**—Emphasis in speaking. Put more *accent* on the first syllable.
   Ascent—A rising, a going up. The path has a steep *ascent*.
   Assent—Consent, agreement. The proposal easily won our *assent*.
3. **Accept**—To receive. Joan would not *accept* the gift.
   Except—To omit or exempt. The soldier was *excepted* from guard duty that day.
4. **Access**—Admittance, way or approach. He has *access* to the vaults.

Excess—Surpassing limits. The meeting was marked by an *excess* of good feeling.

5. **Adapt**—To change, make suitable. He *adapted* himself to the new plan.
   Adept—Skilled, expert. Joan was *adept* in cooking.
   Adopt—To choose, select. I shall *adopt* your proposal.

6. **Adverse**—Hostile, opposed. George had an *adverse* opinion.
   Averse—Unwilling, reluctant. He was *averse* to joining us.

7. **Advice**—Counsel (a noun). Please accept my *advice*.
   Advise—To give counsel (a verb). I *advise* you to go.

8. **Affect**—To influence, produce change. Your plan *affects* my purpose.
   Effect—Result, change. What will be the *effect* of your decision?

9. **Air**—Mixture of gases. He likes to breathe fresh *air*.
   Heir—One who inherits. She was my daughter and only *heir*.

10. **Aisle**—Passageway, corridor. Mary walked slowly down the *aisle*.
    Isle—Land surrounded by water. He wants to live on a deserted *isle*.

11. **Alimentary**—Connected with food, nutrition. The surgeon removed an obstruction in Sue's *alimentary* canal.
    Elementary—Connected with rudiments, fundamentals. The little boy has just started *elementary* school.

12. **Allay**—To rest, to relieve. Medicine will *allay* your pain.
    Alley—Narrow passage. This *alley* leads nowhere.
    Alleys—Narrow passages (plural). The city has many blind *alleys*.
    Allies—Partners, comrades (plural). The *Allies* defeated Germany.
    Ally—To join with (verb), one who joins (noun). England has often been an *ally* of the United States. Please *ally* yourself with our campaign.

13. **All ready**—All are ready. We'll leave when we are *all ready*.
    Already—Earlier, previously. When we arrived, Bill had *already* left.

14. **All together**—All in company. The family was *all together* for the event.

Altogether—Wholly, completely. He was not *altogether* pleased by the outcome of the election.

15. **Allude**—To make reference to. The speaker *alluded* to the bad record of his opponents.

    Elude—To escape, to evade. Big money has always *eluded* my group of friends.

16. **Allusion**—A reference to (noun). He made an *allusion* to those not present.

    Illusion—Deception (noun). This is an optical *illusion*.

17. **Altar**—Place of worship (noun). Many knelt at the *altar*.

    Alter—To change (verb). Do not *alter* your scheme.

18. **Always**—Continually, forever. I shall *always* love Joy.

    All ways—Without exception. He is prepared in *all ways* to do the job.

19. **Amateur**—Nonprofessional. He is an *amateur* chef.

    Armature—Armorlike covering. The *armature* of this dynamo needs repair.

20. **An**—One, each. This is *an* excellent report.

    And—Also, plus. He ate a peach *and* a pear.

21. **Angel**—Celestial being. You are far from being an *angel*.

    Angle—Geometric figure. The *angle* of the street was sharp.

22. **Ante-** —Prefix meaning "before," "prior." She waited in the dentist's *anteroom*.

    Anti- —Prefix meaning "opposite," "against." Iodine is an effective *antiseptic*.

23. **Appraise**—To judge, to estimate. The diamond was *appraised* at one carat.

    Apprise—To inform, notify. We *apprised* him of his election.

24. **Are**—Form of the verb "to be." We *are* ready to eat.

    Or—Conjunction suggesting an alternative. Pay the price *or* walk out.

    Our—Form of the pronoun "we." This is *our* job.

25. **Assay**—A test or "to test." He began to *assay* the mineral.

    Essay—An attempt, or "to try." He *essayed* the difficult job.

26. **Assure**—To convince, to guarantee. I *assured* him of my good will.

    Insure—To secure. He *insured* his house against fire.

27. **Attendance**—An attending, meeting. The *attendance* was greater than expected.

Attendants—Persons present. The bride had nine *attendants*.

28. **Aught**—Any little part, any respect. For *aught* I know, you are correct.

    Ought—Indicating duty, obligation. Every citizen *ought* to vote.

    Naught—Nothing, zero. Our efforts availed *naught*.

29. **Bail**—Deposited credit. The accused was free on *bail*.

    Bale—Package or bundle. The stevedores hauled *bales* of cotton from the ship.

30. **Bald**—Lacking covering. This is an American *bald* eagle.

    Bawled—Yelled, shouted. The baby *bawled* for an hour.

31. **Ball**—Round object. Nan threw the *ball* to me.

    Bole—Tree trunk. The *bole* was twenty inches in diameter.

    Boll—Pod of a plant. This is a cotton *boll*.

    Bowl—A receptacle (noun) or "to roll" (verb). This is a china *bowl*. He likes to *bowl* every night.

32. **Baring**—Uncovering. There he stood, *baring* his head to the rain.

    Barring—Excepting. *Barring* the captain, everyone was in the lifeboat.

    Bearing—Carrying, enduring. He is *bearing* up under grave difficulties.

33. **Bazaar**—Market, shop. The church had a *bazaar* to raise money for the altar.

    Bizarre—Odd, queer. The clown's appearance was *bizarre*.

34. **Beach**—Sandy shore, strand. Atlantic City has a famous *beach*.

    Beech—Tree. Peel the bark from that *beech*.

35. **Bear**—To carry (verb) or mammal (noun). People must *bear* their burdens. There is a *bear* in the zoo.

    Bare—Uncovered, empty. This is a *bare* room.

36. **Beat**—To hit or to strike. He *beat* the rug to clean it.

    Beet—A plant. The *beet* is a source of sugar.

37. **Berry**—Fruit. This is a small, juicy *berry*.

    Bury—To preserve, conceal. Please *bury* the evidence.

38. **Berth**—Place to sleep. Henry slept in a lower *berth*.

    Birth—Act of being born. His *birth* occurred in 1930.

39. **Biding**—Waiting, expecting. The nominee was *biding* his time.

Bidding—Command, summons (noun). The *bidding* for property was brisk.

40. **Blew**—Past tense of "blow." The wind *blew* hard.

    Blue—Color. He wore a *blue* shirt.

41. **Bloc**—Group of people. They formed a solid *bloc* in the campaign.

    Block—A solid (noun) or to impede (verb). This is a heavy *block* of stone. Don't try to *block* this action.

42. **Boar**—Male hog. He shot a splendid wild *boar*.

    Bore—To drill or dig. He thinks we should *bore* for water at this place.

43. **Board**—Flat piece of wood. The *board* was heavy.

    Bored—Wearied. He was *bored* by the meeting.

44. **Boarder**—Lodger. Mr. Jones is a new *boarder* at this house.

    Border—Boundary or frontier. The river forms a *border* between the two states.

45. **Boer**—Dutch colonist. He is a *Boer* from South Africa.

    Boor—Ill-mannered person. He acted like a *boor*.

46. **Born**—Given birth to. Mamie was *born* in 1935.

    Borne—Form of "to bear." The casket was *borne* to the grave.

    Bourn (bourne)—Goal or limit. "The undiscovered country from whose *bourne* no traveler returns."

47. **Borough**—Governmental unit. She lives in the *borough* of Queens.

    Borrow—To receive with the intention of returning. He wants to *borrow* my coat.

    Burro—Donkey. I'll ride the horse; you ride the *burro*.

48. **Brake**—Device for stopping. The *brake* on this truck needs repair.

    Break—To separate, destroy. Be careful not to *break* the glasses.

49. **Bread**—Food. Give her a slice of *bread*.

    Bred—Hatched, born. This is a finely *bred* horse.

50. **Breadth**—Distance, width. The box is four inches in *breadth*.

    Breath—Exhalation. His *breath* froze in the cold air.

    Breathe—To inhale or exhale air. Please *breathe* slowly and deeply.

51. **Brewed**—Fermented, steeped. Jane *brewed* a cup of tea.
    Brood—Offspring. The hen had a large *brood* of chicks.
52. **Bridal**—Referring to a bride. You are invited to the *bridal* supper.
    Bridle—Headgear for an animal. The horse objects to his new *bridle*.
53. **Britain**—Short for *Great Britain*. London is the capital of *Britain*.
    Briton—An Englishman. He is proud to be a *Briton*.
54. **Broach**—To bring up (verb). Let's not *broach* that subject.
    Brooch—Pin with a clasp. She wore an expensive *brooch*.
55. **Build**—To make, establish. Let's *build* our home here.
    Billed—Form of "to bill." He was *billed* for the entire sum.
56. **Bullion**—Ingots. Much gold *bullion* is stored at Fort Knox.
    Bouillon—Broth. The patient ate a cup of chicken *bouillon*.
57. **Calendar**—Table, register. I have no appointments on my *calendar*.
    Calender—Machine with rollers. The *calender* gave the cloth a glossy finish.
    Colander—Pan with perforations. Use a *colander* for washing lettuce.
58. **Calvary**—Name of a hill outside Jerusalem. Jesus was crucified on *Calvary*.
    Cavalry—Troops on horseback. Stonewall Jackson was a *cavalry* leader.
59. **Cannon**—Large gun. Men pulled the *cannon* into position.
    Canon—Law or rule. He lives by the *canon* of good taste.
60. **Canvas**—Cloth. The *canvas* was stiff with mud.
    Canvass—To solicit, request. Please *canvass* the block for donations.
61. **Capital**—For all meanings other than "a building." He raised *capital* for the work.
    Capitol—A building. Many sightseers go to the state *capitol*.
62. **Carat**—Weight. The stone weighs two *carats*.
    Caret—Mark. Insert a *caret* to show the missing letter.
    Carrot—Vegetable. Scrape the *carrots* slowly.
63. **Casual**—Not planned, incidental. This is a *casual* visit.
    Causal—Relating to cause and effect. A *causal* factor in his decision was illness.

64. Ceiling—Overhanging expanse. Your room has a high *ceiling*.

Sealing—Fastening, closing. Try *sealing* the envelope more carefully.

65. Censer—Incense burner. There is a lovely ornamented *censer* in the church.

Censor—To examine. I do not wish you to *censor* my mail.

Censure—To condemn. The judge will strongly *censure* your action.

66. Cent—Coin. It's not worth a *cent*.

Scent—Odor. The *scent* of the skunk was powerful.

67. Charted—Mapped. The trapper *charted* the wilderness.

Chartered—Hired, engaged. We *chartered* a bus for the picnic.

68. Chased—Pursued, followed. Joe often *chased* after pretty girls.

Chaste—Pure, unsullied. A *chaste* reputation is considered priceless.

69. Choir—Group of singers. Joy sings in a church *choir* every week.

Quire—Measurement of paper. He used up a *quire* of paper.

70. Choose—To pick out, select. I do not *choose* to go today.

Chose—Past tense of "to choose." I *chose* not to go yesterday.

71. Chord—Combination of musical tones. The pianist played the opening *chords*.

Cord—String or rope. Tie this package with a strong *cord*.

72. Cite—To summon, quote. Please *cite* your authority.

Sight—View, vision. The valley was a beautiful *sight*.

Site—Location. This is a good *site* for our camp.

73. Claws—Talons, curved nails. This kitten has sharp *claws*.

Clause—Group of words. This sentence has no dependent *clause*.

74. Climactic—Pertaining to "climax." This was the *climactic* scene in the drama.

Climatic—Pertaining to "climate." He likes the *climatic* conditions in Florida.

75. Clothes—Body covering. Tom bought a suit of *clothes*.

Cloths—Pieces of cloth. Dirty dish *cloths* hung near the sink.

76. **Coarse**—Unrefined, common. The driver's *coarse* speech offended the passengers.
Course—Way or passage. He took the easy *course*.
77. **Coma**—Unconsciousness. Mr. Jones fell into a deep *coma*.
Comma—Mark of punctuation. This word should be followed by a *comma*.
78. **Complacent**—Smug, self-satisfied. Your attitude is annoyingly *complacent*.
Complaisant—Obliging. The patient was *complaisant* about hospital routine.
79. **Complement**—Something that completes. This necklace will *complement* your dress.
Compliment—Flattery. She enjoyed the *compliment* paid to her.
80. **Comprehensible**—Understandable. To be *comprehensible* use nontechnical language.
Comprehensive—Inclusive, including much. This was a *comprehensive* account of the battle.
81. **Confidant**—One trusted with secrets. Jill made David her *confidant*.
Confident—Assured, certain. Jack was *confident* of success.
82. **Conscience**—Sense of right and wrong. His *conscience* began to bother him.
Conscious—Awake, able to feel and think. The injured boy was still *conscious*.
83. **Conscientiousness**—Uprightness, honesty. The notary was rewarded for his *conscientiousness*.
Consciousness—Awareness. The victim died before regaining *consciousness*.
84. **Consul**—An official. He called the American *consul* at Naples.
Council—Assembly, group. This is a *council* of older citizens.
Counsel—Advice. The physician gave me sound *counsel*.
85. **Coral**—Skeletons of marine animals. The ship foundered on a *coral* reef.
Corral—Pen or enclosure. This ranch needs a better *corral* for horses.
86. **Core**—Center. The *core* of an apple is not edible.

Corps—Group of people. They were assigned to a *corps* of engineers.

Corpse—Dead body. The *corpse* was carried to the local cemetery.

87. **Corporal**—Concerning the body (adjective), or low-ranking officer (noun). The teacher does not approve of *corporal* punishment. He was promoted to the rank of *corporal*.

Corporeal—Material, tangible. He left no *corporeal* property.

88. **Costume**—Clothing. Your *costume* is too colorful.

Custom—Established practice. It was his *custom* to walk there every day.

89. **Creak**—To make a sound. He felt as though his very bones would *creak*.

Creek—Small stream. Bill waded in the *creek*.

90. **Crews**—Seamen or groups of persons. The *crews* of all vessels were discharged.

Cruise—Voyage. They left on a *cruise* around the world.

91. **Currant**—Small, seedless raisin. This recipe for fruit cake requires the use of *currants*.

Current—A stream (noun) or contemporary (adjective). This river has a swift *current*. I like to read about *current* events.

92. **Cymbal**—Musical instrument. Is the *cymbal* made of brass or bronze?

Symbol—Sign or token. The flag is a *symbol* of our country.

93. **Dairy**—Milk enterprise. He drove the cows from the field to the *dairy*.

Diary—Daily record. Eleanor kept a *diary* during her entire trip.

94. **Days**—Plural of "day." I was in the hospital for ten *days*.

Daze—To dazzle or stupefy. The policeman was *dazed* by a sharp blow.

95. **Dear**—Beloved, precious, expensive. Bill is my *dear* friend.

Deer—Animal. Usually only the male *deer* has antlers.

96. **Decease**—Death. He was buried two days after his *decease*.

Disease—Sickness. This *disease* must run its course.

97. **Decent**—Respectable, suitable. Please wear a *decent* hat.

Descent—Act of descending. The *descent* from the mountain top was slow.

Dissent—To differ, disagree. I *dissent* from your opinion.

98. **Definite**—Explicit, clear. The speaker made a *definite* proposal.

Definitive—Decisive, final, complete. This is the *definitive* biography of Mrs. Siddons.

99. **Dependence**—Condition of being supported. My *dependence* upon you is complete.

Dependents—Those supported by others. He claimed six *dependents* on his tax return.

100. **Deprecate**—To express disapproval. He *deprecated* his own efforts.

Depreciate—To lower in value. The property *depreciated* quickly.

101. **Des'ert**—Barren ground. The *desert* is two hundred miles wide.

De sert'—To leave behind. Don't *desert* your friends.

Dessert—Sweet food. Ice cream is my favorite *dessert*.

102. **Detract**—To lower the quality of, to reduce the value of. His loud voice *detracted* from his personality.

Distract—To divert. Don't *distract* me with radio music.

103. **Device**—Contrivance (noun). The inventor came up with a clever *device*.

Devise—To make, invent (verb). The coach will *devise* a plan for winning the game.

104. **Die**—To cease to live. Everyone must *die* some time.

Dye—To color. I wish to *dye* this dress.

105. **Dining**—Eating. This is a pretty *dining* room.

Dinning—Pertaining to noise, uproar. The sound of the wheels was *dinning* in my ears.

106. **Discomfit**—To frustrate, thwart. Your proposal will *discomfit* my hopes and plans.

Discomfort—Uneasiness, distress. His broken leg caused him *discomfort*.

107. **Discreet**—Judicious, thoughtful. You should be more *discreet* when talking to the boss.

Discrete—Separate, distinct. These two problems are *discrete*.

108. **Divers**—Several or sundry. She has *divers* means of support.

Diverse—Different, varied. Their personalities were powerful but *diverse*.

109. **Dual**—Twofold. The actress has a *dual* role in this play.
     Duel—Combat. Hamilton and Burr fought a *duel*.
110. **Due**—Payable. The money is *due* today.
     Do—To perform, act. Kindly *do* as your foreman suggests.
111. **Emigrate**—To leave a country. The foreman *emigrated* from Poland.
     Immigrate—To enter a country. Many people have tried to *immigrate* to this country.
112. **Eminent**—Noteworthy, outstanding. Mr. Hughes is an *eminent* lawyer.
     Imminent—Near at hand. Outbreak of war is *imminent*.
113. **Envel′ op**—To cover, wrap up. Fire caused smoke to *envelop* the block.
     En′ velope—A covering. This *envelope* has no postage stamp.
114. **Errand**—Trip or task. Please run this *errand* for me.
     Errant—Roving, wandering, mistaken. Please correct your *errant* behavior.
     Arrant—Notorious. The soldier proved himself an *arrant* coward.
115. **Ever**—Always. He is *ever* in a jovial mood.
     Every—Without exception. *Every* person present will please stand.
116. **Exalt**—To raise, praise. Shall we *exalt* God the Father?
     Exult—To rejoice. Don't *exult* over your victory.
117. **Exceptionable**—Objectionable. Your constant tardiness is *exceptionable*.
     Exceptional—Out of the ordinary. Joy's singing is *exceptional*.
118. **Extant**—Still existing. He is the greatest musician *extant*.
     Extent—Size, length. What is the *extent* of your farm?
     Extinct—No longer existing. The dinosaur is an *extinct* beast.
119. **Factitious**—Artificial. The greatest *factitious* need of today is money.
     Fictitious—Imaginary. His account of the journey was entirely *fictitious*.
120. **Fain**—Ready, eager (rarely used). She would *fain* go with you.
     Feign—To invent, fabricate. The sailor *feigned* illness.
121. **Faint**—To lose consciousness. I feel as if I am about to *faint*.

Feint—To pretend, deceive. The player *feinted* his opponent out of position.

122. **Fair**—All uses except those for "fare." The day was cold and *fair*.

Fare—To travel (verb); transportation money (noun). I shall soon *fare* forth. Please pay your *fare*.

123. **Find**—To discover. Try to *find* happiness where you can.

Fined—Punished. The motorist was *fined* fifty dollars.

124. **Fir**—Tree. This is a grove of beautiful *firs*.

Fur—Animal hair. This coat has a collar of *fur*.

125. **Flair**—Talent, ability. She has a certain *flair* for designing clothes.

Flare—To blaze up. The fire suddenly *flared* up.

126. **Flea**—Insect. The *flea* is a small, wingless creature.

Flee—To run away. We had to *flee* from the burning house.

127. **Flour**—Ground grain. This is enough *flour* to feed us.

Flower—A blossom. The rose is Gray's favorite *flower*.

128. **Flout**—To mock, to scoff. She was determined to *flout* all convention.

Flaunt—To make a gaudy display. He *flaunted* his new prosperity all over the city.

129. **Fondling**—Caressing, coddling. Will you stop *fondling* that cat?

Foundling—Abandoned child. This is a home for *foundlings*.

130. **Forbear**—To refrain. I cannot *forbear* telling you this.

Forebear—Ancestor. His *forebears* came from Greece.

131. **Foreword**—Preface, introduction. This book needs no *foreword*.

Forward—Movement onward. The troops marched *forward*.

132. **Formally**—Ceremoniously. The envoy greeted us *formally*.

Formerly—Earlier. He was *formerly* a champion.

133. **Fort**—Enclosed place, fortified building. The attackers burned the *fort*.

Forte—Special accomplishment. His *forte* is outdoor cooking.

134. **Forth**—Onward. I shall be with you from this day *forth*.

Fourth—Next after third. The *Fourth* of July is a holiday.

135. **Freeze**—To congeal with cold. He asked me to *freeze* the vegetables.

Frieze—Architectural term. The castle had several beautiful *friezes* on the walls.

136. Funeral—Ceremonies at burial. The *funeral* was attended by hundreds of friends.

Funereal—Sad, dismal. Molly wore a *funereal* look.

137. Gait—Manner of moving. This saddle horse has four excellent *gaits*.

Gate—Door or opening. Open the *gate* and come in.

138. Gamble—To wager, bet. He *gambled* on cards and dice.

Gambol—To skip about. The children *gamboled* on the village green.

139. Genius—Great ability. Beethoven was a man of *genius*.

Genus—Class, kind. What is the *genus* of this plant?

140. Gibe—To scorn or sneer at. I'm trying hard; don't *gibe* at me.

Jibe—Same meaning as "gibe" but also "to change direction." The boat *jibed* twice on the homeward run.

141. Gild—To overlay with gold. Please *gild* this vase.

Guild—Association, union. Sam belonged to a *guild* of craftsmen.

142. Gilt—Gold on surface. This glass has a layer of *gilt*.

Guilt—Wrongdoing, crime. He immediately announced his *guilt*.

143. Gorilla—Manlike ape. This *gorilla* is five feet tall.

Guerrilla—Irregular soldier. He belonged to a band of *guerrillas*.

144. Gourmand—Large eater. Diamond Jim Brady was a *gourmand*.

Gourmet—Fastidious eater, epicure. Many French people are notable *gourmets*.

145. Grip—Act of holding firmly. He took a firm *grip* on the tire.

Gripe—To pinch, to distress. What he ate had *griped* his digestive system.

146. Grisly—Horrible, ghastly. The execution was a *grisly* scene.

Gristly—Pertaining to tough, elastic tissue. This is a *gristly* cut of meat.

Grizzly—Grizzled, gray. There is only one *grizzly* bear in the zoo.

147. Hail—To greet. We *hailed* him as our leader

Hale—Healthy, vigorous. He wanted to be *hale* in mind and body.

148. **Hair**—Threadlike outgrowth. He had no *hair* on his head.
Hare—Rabbit. The dog chased the *hare* for an hour.

149. **Hart**—Male deer. The old *hart* was king of the forest.
Heart—Muscular organ. His *heart* was beating quickly.

150. **Heal**—To make sound, well. My hope is to *heal* you in mind and body.
Heel—Part of the foot. His *heel* was punctured by a nail.

151. **Hear**—To become aware of sounds. I can't *hear* you.
Here—In this place. Will you be *here* with me?

152. **Hoard**—Laid-up store. Here is where he had his *hoard* of money.
Horde—Crowd. A *horde* of riders clattered toward us.

153. **Hole**—Cavity. The boys dug a *hole* in the ground.
Whole—Intact, complete. I've told you the *whole* story.

154. **Holy**—Sacred, consecrated. A church is a *holy* place.
Wholly—Completely, entirely. I'm *wholly* on your side.

155. **Hoping**—Wanting, desiring. I'm *hoping* you will accept my invitation.
Hopping—Leaping, springing. I'm *hopping* a train tonight.

156. **Human**—A person. He was a real *human*, not a mere animal.
Humane—Tender, merciful, considerate. He was a *humane* ruler of his people.

157. **Idle**—Worthless, useless, pointless. We engaged in *idle* talk.
Idol—Image. Ben made an *idol* of prestige.

158. **Immunity**—Exemption from duty. Heart disease gave him *immunity* from military service.
Impunity—Exemption from punishment. He could eat with *impunity* whatever he pleased.

159. **Impassable**—Not passable. The road over the mountain was *impassable*.
Impossible—Incapable of being accomplished. The order was *impossible* to carry out.

160. **Incidence**—Range of occurrence, influence. The *incidence* of influenza was high that winter.
Incidents—Events, happenings. Which *incidents* of your trip did you enjoy the most?

161. **Indict**—To accuse, charge with crime. He was *indicted* for theft.

     Indite—To write, compose. He *indited* a beautiful letter to the sorrowing widow.

162. **Ingenious**—Clever, tricky. This is an *ingenious* computer.

     Ingenuous—Innocent, artless. She is an *ingenuous* young girl.

163. **Invade**—To enter, intrude. The soldiers were soon ordered to *invade* our country.

     Inveighed—Attacked in words, assailed. He *inveighed* against all his enemies.

164. **Its**—Possessive pronoun. This company should have *its* proper place in history.

     It's—"It is." *It's* a delightful day.

165. **Jealous**—Resentful, envious. Mary is *jealous* of Jane's beauty.

     Zealous—Diligent, devoted. The senator was *zealous* in committee work.

166. **Knave**—Unprincipled man or boy. The attorney called the gangster a *knave*.

     Nave—Part of a church. Chairs were placed in the *nave*.

167. **Knew**—To have fixed in mind or memory. The salesman *knew* all the buyer's objections.

     New—Of recent origin. This is a *new* model.

168. **Know**—To understand, perceive. Do you *know* how far it is to town?

     No—Word used to express denial, dissent. *No*, I shall not go with you.

169. **Later**—Referring to time. It's *later* than you think.

     Latter—Second of two. I prefer the *latter* course of action.

170. **Lead**—Conduct, guide. John will *lead* the choral group.

     Lead—A metal. This is a *lead* pipe.

     Led—Past tense of "to lead." Grant *led* his soldiers into Vicksburg.

171. **Leaf**—Outgrowth of a stem. This is a lovely oak *leaf*.

     Lief—Gladly, willingly. I'd as *lief* go as stay.

172. **Lean**—Scant of fat, flesh. This is a *lean* strip of bacon.

     Lien—Legal right. He procured a *lien* on the property.

173. **Least**—Smallest, slightest. This was the *least* of my worries.

     Lest—For fear that. Please keep writing *lest* we forget you.

174. **Lessen**—To become less, diminish. Now all your financial problems will *lessen.*
     Lesson—Something to be learned. May this be a *lesson* to you.
175. **Levee**—Embankment. The river overflowed the *levee.*
     Levy—To impose. The judge will *levy* a large fine.
176. **Lie**—Falsehood. He told me a *lie.*
     Lye—Alkaline substance. Keep this bottle of *lye* away from children.
177. **Lifelong**—For all one's life. His *lifelong* desire was to go to Europe.
     Livelong—Whole, entire. Birds sing the *livelong* day.
178. **Lightening**—Making less heavy. His kindness was *lightening* my weight of sorrow.
     Lightning—Discharge of electricity. The rain was preceded by thunder and *lightning.*
179. **Lineament**—Feature, characteristic. What is the most noticeable *lineament* on his face?
     Liniment—Medicated liquid. The trainer rubbed the boxer's legs with *liniment.*
180. **Liqueur**—Highly flavored alcoholic drink. Joe's favorite after-dinner *liqueur* was chartreuse.
     Liquor—Distilled or spirituous beverage. Scotch was Abe's favorite *liquor.*
181. **Loan**—Act of granting, lending. I secured a *loan* of fifty dollars.
     Lone—Solitary, standing apart. He was the *lone* rebel in the office.
182. **Loose**—Not fastened tightly. A *loose* wire caused all the trouble.
     Lose—To suffer the loss of. Don't *lose* what you have gained.
     Loss—A defeat. He felt keenly the *loss* of the money.
183. **Mail**—Letters, etc. The *mail* came at ten o'clock.
     Male—Masculine. This cat is *male.*
184. **Main**—Chief, principal. Is this the *main* highway?
     Mane—Long hair. The horse's *mane* was filled with cockleburs.
185. **Manner**—Way of doing. They treated us in a civilized *manner.*

Manor—Landed estate. Sir Charles is lord of the *manor*.

186. Mantel—Shelf. The *mantel* above the fireplace is of sturdy oak.

Mantle—Loose covering. Has the *mantle* of Moses descended upon this judge?

187. Marshal—Officer. The *marshal* arrested him.

Martial—Warlike. The governor placed the community under *martial* law.

188. Material—Crude or raw matter, substance. What is the *material* in your dress?

Matériel—Equipment in general. This military campaign required vast *matériel*.

189. Maybe—Perhaps. *Maybe* she doesn't like you.

May be—Verb form expressing possibility. It *may be* going to rain this afternoon.

190. Meat—Flesh. His favorite foods are *meat* and potatoes.

Meet—To come in contact. We plan to *meet* tomorrow.

191. Medal—Commemorative design. The major gave him a *medal* for bravery.

Meddle—To interfere. Please don't *meddle* in my business.

Metal—A hard substance obtained from ores. Gold, silver, and copper are *metals*.

Mettle—Disposition, temper. The battle revealed the soldier's *mettle*.

192. Miner—One who extracts minerals. He is a *miner* from Pennsylvania.

Minor—Person under legal age. A *minor* has no voting privileges.

193. Moat—Trench. The *moat* around the castle was filled with water.

Mote—Particle, speck. He had a *mote* of dust in each eye.

194. Moors—Mohammedans. Many *Moors* live in North Africa.

Moors—Open land. These flowers came from the Scottish *moors*.

Mores—Folkways, customs. *Mores* here differ from those in my country.

195. Moral—Good or proper. His *moral* code was high.

Morale—Condition of the spirit, state of being. The *morale* of the workers was excellent.

196. **Morning**—Early part of the day. We shall leave early tomorrow *morning*.

     Mourning—Sorrowing, grieving. The *mourning* family went to the cemetery.

197. **Motif**—Theme or subject. What is the *motif* of that composition?

     Motive—Spur or incentive. The *motive* of the murder was revenge.

198. **Naval**—Pertaining to ships. England is a great *naval* power.

     Navel—Pit or depression on the abdomen. He suffered a wound near his *navel*.

199. **Of**—Preposition with many meanings. He is a native *of* Ohio.

     Off—Away from. The car rolled *off* the highway.

200. **On**—Preposition with many meanings. Please put the bread *on* the table.

     One—Single unit or thing. He bought *one* orange for five cents.

201. **Oracle**—Place or medium for consulting gods. The senator visited the Delphic *oracle*.

     Auricle—Anatomical term. The *auricle* of her left ear was infected.

202. **Oral**—Spoken. The message was *oral*, not written.

     Aural—Pertaining to the sense of hearing. After the accident, his *aural* sense was below normal.

203. **Ordinance**—Rule, decree. There is a city *ordinance* against double parking.

     Ordnance—Military weapons. Captain Baker is an instructor of *ordnance* at West Point.

204. **Oscillate**—To swing, vibrate. The pendulum of the clock *oscillates* smoothly.

     Osculate—To kiss. Some explorers say Eskimos do not *osculate*.

205. **Pail**—Bucket or other container. Please fetch a *pail* of water.

     Pale—Of whitish appearance. My face turned *pale* in fear.

206. **Pain**—Suffering, distress. John had a *pain* in his back.

     Pane—Plate of glass. The baseball shattered the *pane*.

207. **Pair**—Two of a kind. This is a new *pair* of gloves.

     Pare—To peel. He *pared* a basket of apples.

208. **Palate**—Roof of the mouth. Peanut butter sticks to my *palate*.

    Palette—Board for painters. The artist mixed an array of autumn colors on his *palette*.

    Pallet—Small, makeshift bed. I was stiff and sore from a night spent on that *pallet*.

209. **Passed**—Moved by. The car *passed* us at a high speed.

    Past—Just gone by. The *past* year was a good one for me.

210. **Peace**—Freedom from disturbance. What this world needs is *peace*.

    Piece—Portion. Please give me a *piece* of pie.

211. **Pedal**—Lever. One *pedal* of the organ needed repair.

    Peddle—To hawk, sell at retail. He *peddled* fresh fruits in a residential section.

212. **Pendant**—An ornament. She wore a gold *pendant* around her neck.

    Pendent—Hanging or suspended. The *pendent* tapesty was Oriental.

213. **Persecute**—To oppress, harass. The Pilgrims were *persecuted* because of their religious beliefs.

    Prosecute—To bring legal proceedings. The district attorney *prosecuted* the case against me.

214. **Personal**—Private. This is your *personal* property.

    Personnel—Body of persons. This company has recruited interesting *personnel*.

215. **Petition**—A request. The manager read our *petition* for a coffee break.

    Partition—Division, separation. Only a thin *partition* separated the two rooms.

216. **Physic**—Medicine. The physician recommended a strong *physic*.

    Physique—Body structure. He has a robust *physique*.

    Psychic—Pertaining to the mind or soul. The gypsy claimed *psychic* powers.

217. **Pillar**—Upright shaft. The ceiling was supported by eight *pillars*.

    Pillow—Support for the head. He sleeps without a *pillow*.

218. **Pistil**—Seed-bearing organ. This is the *pistil* of a flowering plant.

Pistol—Small firearm. The sheriff carried his *pistol* in a holster.

219. **Plain**—Simple, or a level stretch of ground. He prefers *plain* foods. This *plain* contains hundreds of acres.

Plane—Carpenters' tool, or level of existence. Try smoothing it with a *plane*. Your families are on the same financial *plane*.

220. **Portion**—Part, quantity. This is a larger *portion* of the roast.

Potion—A drink. He drank the fiery *potion*.

221. **Pray**—To beseech, entreat. Please *pray* for my safety.

Prey—Plunder, booty. The eagle is a bird of *prey*.

222. **Precede**—To come or go before. Will you *precede* me into the room?

Proceed—To advance. He then *proceeded* to the next town.

223. **Prescribe**—To direct, order. The physician will *prescribe* a cure.

Proscribe—To banish, to outlaw. Caesar ordered that he be *proscribed*.

224. **Principal**—Chief, foremost. He had a *principal* part in the action.

Principle—Rule or truth. This is a sound *principle* to follow.

225. **Prophecy**—Prediction (noun). What is your *prophecy* about the future?

Prophesy—To foretell (verb). He could *prophesy* the results.

226. **Propose**—To put forth a plan. I *propose* that we take a vote.

Purpose—Intention, aim. What is your *purpose*?

227. **Quarts**—Measure. This bucket will hold eight *quarts*.

Quartz—Mineral. The geologist discovered *quartz* deposits near here.

228. **Quay**—Wharf. The ship was anchored a hundred yards from the *quay*.

Key—Instrument for locking, unlocking. Sue lost the *key* to her apartment.

229. **Quiet**—Still, calm. It was a *quiet* meeting.

Quit—To stop, desist. He *quit* his job on Friday.

Quite—Positive, entirely. I have not *quite* finished the book.

230. **Rabbit**—A rodent of the hare family. Mrs. MacGregor put him into a *rabbit* stew.

Rabid—Extreme, intense, or mad with rabies. He was known as a *rabid* partisan.

Rarebit—Welsh rabbit. The phrase should be "Welsh rabbit" not "Welsh *rarebit*."

231. **Rain**—Precipitation. We had four inches of *rain* last week.

Reign—Rule. Queen Elizabeth I had a long *reign*.

Rein—Check, curb. Lena could not *rein* in her mare going for the barn.

232. **Raise**—To lift, elevate. Please *raise* your eyes and look at me.

Raze—To tear down. The wreckers will *raze* the building.

Rise—To get up. When the president enters, everyone should *rise*.

233. **Rebound**—To spring back. His spirits *rebounded* at the good news.

Redound—To have a result or effect. Your excellent performance will *redound* to your credit.

234. **Reck**—To have care or concern. He *recks* not the costs involved.

Wreck—Destruction, damage. Hard living made him a *wreck* of a man.

235. **Reek**—Vapor, fume. There is a *reek* of turpentine in this room.

Wreak—To give vent to. He *wreaked* his anger on the secretarial pool.

236. **Respectably**—Properly, decently. The widow lived quietly and *respectably*.

Respectfully—With esteem, honor. He closed the letter "*Respectfully* yours."

Respectively—In order. He referred to Tom, Dick, and Harry *respectively*.

237. **Retch**—To try to vomit. He *retched* several times and then lay still.

Wretch—Miserable person. The poor *wretch* had threadbare clothing.

238. **Reverend**—Title for clergymen. The *Reverend* Stanley Smith is our pastor.

Reverent—Characterized by respect, sacredness. The audience was in a *reverent* mood.

239. Right—Correct, or direction. What is the *right* way to town? Turn *right*, not left.

Rite—Ceremony. The *rite* of burial was indeed solemn.

240. Sail—Material to catch wind. The *sails* were fluttering in the breeze.

Sale—Special offering of goods. He bought a suit which was on *sale*.

241. Satire—Work that expresses ridicule or contempt. He wrote a *satire* on office parties.

Satyr—Woodland deity, a lecherous man. John is more wolf than *satyr*.

242. Scarce—Not plentiful. The berries were *scarce* this year.

Scare—To startle, frighten. He was *scared* by news of the epidemic.

243. Serf—A slave. The manager treats me as though I were his *serf*.

Surf—Waves. The boat capsized in the heavy *surf*.

244. Serge—Fabric. This *serge* suit cost fifty dollars.

Surge—To swell, to increase suddenly. His anger *surged* at the insult.

245. Shear—To cut, clip. It is time to *shear* the sheep.

Sheer—Very thin. Her stockings were black and very *sheer*.

246. Shone—Glowed. Her face *shone* with happiness.

Shown—Appeared, made known. The salesmen have *shown* themselves to be capable.

247. Shudder—To shake or tremble. Reading about an accident makes me *shudder*.

Shutter—Screen or cover. The owner painted the *shutters* green.

248. Sleight—Deftness. He performed several *sleight* of hand tricks.

Slight—Slender, light. Jill is a very *slight* girl.

249. Sole—Single, one and only. Bernard was the *sole* survivor of the wreck.

Soul—Spiritual entity. The minister prayed for the dying man's *soul*.

250. Stair—A step. Mount the *stairs* carefully.

Stare—To gaze, glare. He stood there and *stared* at me.

251. **Stake**—Post, pole. Joan of Arc was burned at the *stake*.
     Steak—Slice of meat. We served a four-pound *steak*.
252. **Stationary**—Fixed in position. This statue is obviously *stationary*.
     Stationery—Paper for writing. I ordered a new box of *stationery*.
253. **Statue**—Sculptured likeness. His *statue* is in the museum.
     Stature—Height. He was six feet in *stature*.
     Statute—Law. This *statute* forbids gambling within city limits.
254. **Steal**—To take without permission. It is a sin to *steal* another's property.
     Steel—Metal. The sword was made of *steel*.
255. **Stile**—A step. Use the *stile*; don't vault the fence.
     Style—Manner of expression. This is furniture in the modern *style*.
256. **Stimulant**—Anything that stimulates. This drug is a heart *stimulant*.
     Stimulus—Something that rouses. His family's needs provided him a *stimulus* to work hard.
257. **Straight**—Uncurved. The road ran *straight* for five miles.
     Strait—Narrow passageway. We crossed the *Strait* of Magellan.
258. **Suit**—Clothing. This is an expensive new *suit*.
     Suite—Set of rooms, or furniture. They engaged a *suite* of rooms at the hotel.
259. **Tail**—Rear appendage. This is the *tail* of a donkey.
     Tale—Story. He told us a *tale* of his trip to the planetarium.
260. **Taught**—Trained, instructed. We were *taught* how to add and subtract.
     Taut—Tightly stretched, tense. She gave us a *taut* smile.
261. **Than**—Particle denoting comparison. I am taller *than* Alfred.
     Then—At that time. It was *then* that he left.
262. **Their**—Possessive pronoun. *Their* faces all look alike to me.
     There—In or at that place. He was *there* on time.
     They're—Shortened form of "they are." *They're* improving all the time.
263. **Therefor**—For this, for that. He selected a car and paid cash *therefor*.

Therefore—Consequently, hence. I have no money and *therefore* can't go.

264. **Thorough**—Complete. His examination was *thorough*.

Though—Notwithstanding, although. *Though* you may be right, I can't agree with you.

Threw—Tossed or hurled. They *threw* more wood on the fire.

Through—From one end or side to the other. Let's walk *through* this field.

265. **Timber**—Building material. He bought *timber* for a new doghouse.

Timbre—Quality of sound. I like the *timbre* of his voice.

266. **To**—Preposition with many meanings. Let's walk *to* town.

Too—More than enough, in addition. You have already said *too* much.

Two—Number after "one." There are *two* sides to this problem.

267. **Tortuous**—Winding, crooked. The path up the mountain is *tortuous*.

Torturous—Full of, or causing, torture or pain. The surgeon began a *torturous* examination of my spine.

268. **Treaties**—Agreements. Soviet Russia does not honor its *treaties*.

Treatise—Systematic discussion. The professor wrote a *treatise* on this subject.

269. **Troop**—An assembled company. The *troop* of Girl Scouts made camp.

Troupe—Traveling actors. He joined a *troupe* of Shakespearian actors.

270. **Urban**—Characteristic of a city. Do you prefer *urban* to rural life?

Urbane—Suave, smooth. His manner and speech were *urbane*.

271. **Vain**—Worthless, empty. He made a *vain* attempt to save money.

Vane—Direction pointer. This is a new weather *vane*.

Vein—Blood vessel. The knife severed a *vein*, not an artery.

272. **Venal**—Corruptible, mercenary. The *venal* judge was soon removed from office.

Venial—Excusable, pardonable. That was a *venial* sin, not a mortal one.

273. **Vial**—Small vessel. This is a *vial* of perfume.
Vile—Repulsive, offensive. His language was *vile*.
Viol—Musical instrument. The *viol* was often played in the sixteenth century.

274. **Vice**—Evil practice. The reformers are opposed to *vice* in every form.
Vise—Device for holding. The carpenter has many uses for a *vise*.

275. **Waist**—Middle section of a body. His *waist* is thirty-four inches.
Waste—To squander, to employ uselessly. Save your energy; don't *waste* it.

276. **Waive**—To relinquish, give up. Don't *waive* your right to a jury trial.
Wave—Ridge or swell of water. The *wave* tossed the small craft up.

277. **Want**—To wish or desire. I *want* to stay at home.
Wont—Accustomed, used. He was *wont* to take a nap every afternoon.
Won't—Contraction of "will not." I *won't* do what you ask.

278. **Weak**—Not strong. Your excuse is *weak*.
Week—Period of seven days. This has been an active *week* for me.

279. **Weather**—State of atmosphere. We had good *weather* for the trip.
Whether—Conjunction implying alternatives. We didn't know *whether* to stay or go.

280. **Were**—Form of verb "to be." *Were* you there yesterday?
We're—Contraction of "we are." *We're* going with you.
Where—In or at what place. *Where* did you put it?

281. **While**—During the time that. I was working *while* you ate.
Wile—Trick, stratagem. She practiced her feminine *wiles* on my roommate.

282. **Whose**—Possessive case of "who." *Whose* pencil is that?
Who's—Contraction of "who is." *Who's* going out for coffee today?

283. **Wrench**—To twist, pull, jerk. He *wrenched* his knee when he fell.
   Rinse—To wash. He *rinsed* the clothes several times.
284. **Wring**—To squeeze, press. *Wring* out your bathing suit.
   Ring—Band of metal. He paid little money for the wedding *ring*.
285. **Wry**—Twisted, distorted. He made a *wry* face.
   Rye—Cereal grass. This is *rye* flour.
286. **Yeller**—One who shrieks or screams. He is the *yeller* on this team.
   Yellow—A color. You are wearing a beautiful *yellow* dress.
287. **Yolk**—Part of an egg. The recipe calls for six *yolks*.
   Yoke—Frame or bar. The oxen were harnessed with *yokes*.
288. **Yore**—Time long past. Knights were bold in days of *yore*.
   Your—Belonging to or done by you. Is this *your* idea?
   You're—Contraction of "you are." *You're* going to make more money soon.
289. **Yowl**—Howl, wail. The dog's *yowl* woke him up.
   Yawl—Sailboat. We sailed the *yawl* across the bay.
290. **Yule**—Christmas. This is a wonderful *yule* log.
   You'll—Contraction of "you will" or "you shall." If *you'll* help me, I shall try.

4—Pronounce Words Carefully and Correctly

> Just compare heart, beard, and heard,
> Dies and diet, lord and word,
> Sword and sward, retain and Britain,
> (Mind the latter, how it's written)
> Made has not the sound of bade;
> Say, said, pay, paid, laid, but plaid.*

These lines of doggerel amusingly demonstrate that pronunciation is not a safe guide to spelling. A system which tolerates, for example, *cough* and *through* is quite imperfect. (A frequently cited illustration is that if you use the sound of *f* as the *gh* in *enough*, of *i* as the *o* in *women*, and of *sh* as the *ti* of *fiction*, you can spell *fish* as *ghoti*.) For another example of confusion confounded, consider the sound of *ain*, the sound we have in *pain*. It can be, and is, represented by these entirely different spellings: compl*ain*, p*ane*, r*eign*, v*ein*, camp*aign*, champ*agne*. In fact, pronunciation is so unreliable a guide to spelling that you can quite logically spell *coffee* as *kauphy*, with not a single corresponding letter in the two words.

Scholars agree that there are only about 50 speech sounds in the English language, nearly all of which are used in dictionaries to record pronunciation. To express these sounds we have only 26 letters in our alphabet and they appear in about 250 spelling combinations. This problem has already been illustrated by the sound of *ain*. For another example, consider the sound of long *e*, the sound we have in *equal*:

1. *e*ve	5. p*eo*ple	9. p*ie*ce
2. s*ee*d	6. k*ey*	10. amo*e*ba
3. r*ea*d	7. qu*ay*	11. C*ae*sar
4. rec*ei*ve	8. pol*i*ce	

* G. N. Trenité, *Drop Your Foreign Accent* (London: George Allen & Unwin, Ltd., 1932).

384

This is entirely illogical, isnt it? Of course. But for several reasons the situation is not hopeless.

First, not all sounds and spellings differ so much as those just cited. The examples given are designedly extreme. Actually, some relationship often exists between sound and spelling; a large number of words are spelled exactly as they sound, and many others have sounds and spellings almost alike. The words *bat, red,* and *top* are spelled as they sound to most people. Many longer words are also spelled as they sound, especially if you break them into syllables: *lone-li-ness, mem-o-ry; part-ner,* for example. The situation is not without hope.

Second, many of the words which differ most greatly in sound and spelling are those which you rarely need to use. Like almost everyone else, including good spellers, you would look up such words in a dictionary before attempting to write them; they do not have to be learned. Few people can spell, on demand, such a word as *phthisic.* They consult a dictionary, and so should you.

Third, actually *mispronouncing* words causes more trouble than does a difference between the spelling and sound of a correctly pronounced word. In other words, correct pronunciation is sometimes of little help in spelling, but *mispronouncing* often adds an additional hazard. You have noticed that this fact applies to some words in the list of "Look-Alikes, Sound-Alikes" beginning on page 358. It is probably improper pronunciation which would make you spell *Calvary* when you mean *cavalry. Affect* and *effect* look somewhat alike, but they do have different pronunciations as well as different meanings. A *dairy* is one thing; a *diary* is another and will be so indicated by correct pronunciation. There is some reason why, from sound, you might spell *crowd* as "croud" or *benign* as "benine." But there is no reason except poor pronunciation for spelling *shudder* as "shutter," *propose* as "porpose," or *marrying* as "marring."

Spelling consciousness, an *awareness* of words, depends in part on correct pronunciation. Properly pronouncing the following words will help some people to spell them correctly. Mispronouncing them will cause nearly everyone spelling trouble. Look at each word, as suggested on page 357, until you are fully aware of it. Pronounce each word correctly, consulting your dictionary often and carefully.

The list is merely suggestive; people mispronounce so many words in so many different ways that no list can be complete. But the author has encountered faulty spellings of the words listed here and suspects that they represent fairly general mispronunciations. For other examples, consult the list beginning on page 358. The first part of the following list deals with perfectly good words that have been confused. The second part reveals pronunciations resulting in nonexistent, incorrect words.

WORDS CONFUSED IN PRONUNCIATION

1. caliber
   caliper
2. carton
   cartoon
3. casualty
   causality
4. celery
   salary
5. cemetery
   symmetry
6. concur
   conquer
7. color
   collar
8. dinghy
   dingy

9. elicit
   illicit
10. errand
    errant
11. faucet
    forceps
12. finally
    finely
13. gesture
    jester
14. gig
    jig
15. impostor
    imposture
16. minister
    minster
17. pastor
    pasture

18. plaintiff
    plaintive
19. relic
    relict
20. sculptor
    sculpture
21. sink
    zinc
22. specie
    species
23. tenet
    tenant
24. veracity
    voracity
25. way
    whey

CORRECT	INCORRECT
corsage (small bouquet)	*corsarge* or *cosarge*
exercise (physical activity)	*excercise*
garage (storage place)	*gararge*
height (distance from bottom to top)	*heighth*
imagine (to form an idea)	*imangine*
irrelevant (unrelated)	*irrevelant*
poem (literary composition)	*pome*
radio (transmission of sound waves)	*raido* or *radeo*

CORRECT	INCORRECT
research (systematic inquiry)	*reaserch*
strategic (favorable or advantageous)	*stragetic*
temperature (degree of heat)	*tempreture*
third (Number 3 in a series)	*thrid* or *therd*
tragedy (serious drama or event)	*tradegy*

MISSPELLINGS DUE TO INCORRECT PREFIXES

You don't transpose or otherwise confuse letters as is done in the list above? Good. The misspellings do look senseless and are characteristic of poor spellers. But you may have difficulty pronouncing and spelling certain words which have prefixes. (A prefix is usually one syllable added to the beginning of a word to alter its meaning or create a new word. The syllable *pre* is itself a prefix meaning "before in time," "earlier than.") Many prefixes were borrowed from Latin and Greek and do cause some people trouble with pronunciation, and hence spelling. Here are a few examples of words beginning with *per*, *pre*, and *pro*, the only prefixes which cause real trouble in pronouncing and spelling English words:

CORRECT	INCORRECT
perform (to act, to do)	*preform*
perhaps (possibly, probably)	*prehaps*
perjury (breaking an oath)	*prejury*
perspiration (sweating)	*prespiration*
perversely (persisting in error)	*preversely*
precipitate (to cause action)	*percipitate*
professor (a teacher)	*perfessor* or *prefessor*
proposal (a plan, scheme)	*porposal* or *preprosal*

MISSPELLINGS DUE TO ADDED VOWELS

Some words are misspelled because in pronouncing them an extra vowel is added. A list of them would not be long, but since many of them are frequently used they merit careful study. Mispronouncing them may cause you not only to misspell but also to be looked on as careless in speech or uneducated, or both.

CORRECT	INCORRECT
athletics (sports, games)	*athaletics* or *atheletics*
disastrous (causing harm, grief)	*disasterous*
entrance (act or point of coming in)	*enterance*
explanation (interpretation)	*explaination*
grievous (serious, grave)	*grievious*
Henry (proper name)	*Henery*
hindrance (obstacle, impediment)	*hinderance*
hundred (the number)	*hundered*
laundry (washing of clothes)	*laundery* or *laundary*
mischievous (prankish)	*mischievious*
monstrous (huge, enormous)	*monsterous*
nervous (emotionally tense)	*nerveous*
partner (associate)	*partener*
remembrance (souvenir, keepsake)	*rememberance*
similar (alike)	*similiar*
Spanish (pertaining to Spain)	*Spainish*
umbrella (shade or screen)	*umberella*

MISSPELLINGS DUE TO DROPPED VOWELS

There are many different ways to misspell words: you can do so by dropping vowels as well as by adding them. Educated speakers often drop vowels in pronouncing some words in the following list; therefore you should study this list carefully since even acceptable pronunciation is not always a sure guide. However, a few of these words could not be pronounced correctly from the faulty spelling shown—whole syllables would drop out. Only in highly informal speech or television advertising would *caramel* be pronounced *carmel*.

1. John's truck *accidentally* (not *accidently*) hit the child.
2. This is an *auxiliary* (not *auxilary*) gasoline tank.
3. The physician prescribed *beneficial* (not *benefical*) drugs.
4. The pianist gave a *brilliant* (not *brillant*) recital.
5. This harsh *criticism* (not *critcism*) is merited.
6. He is a soldier, not a *civilian* (not *civilan*).
7. She is a *conscientious* (not *conscientous*) housewife.
8. This *convenient* (not *convenent*) room is for your use.
9. John is *deficient* (not *deficent*) in his accounts.

10. Mary is an *efficient* (not *efficent*) typist.
11. Your face is *familiar* (not *familar*).
12. I seek your *financial* (not *financal*) help.
13. King Cole was a merry, *genial* (not *genal*) soul.
14. Beethoven was a man of *genius* (not *genus*).
15. Your sentence is *grammatically* (not *grammaticly*) sound.
16. The money is only *incidentally* (not *incidently*) important.
17. The chemistry *laboratory* (not *labortory*) is large.
18. I like to read good *literature* (not *literture*).
19. *Mathematics* (not *mathmatics*) deals with numbers.
20. A child is a *miniature* (not *minature*) man.
21. Your *opinion* (not *opinon*) is valid.
22. This is an *original* (not *orignal*) idea.
23. Sir Henry is a member of *Parliament* (not *Parliment*).
24. He is *proficient* (not *proficent*) as a manager.
25. Sue has an even *temperament* (not *temperment*).

In addition to these twenty-five words illustrated in sentences, check your pronunciation of the following. Some people slur over the vowels which are shown in bold face; some omit them entirely; some pronounce them with considerable stress. Pronounce each word as you normally do. If the letters in bold face are silent, or lightly stressed in your speech, you are likely to omit them from your spelling.

accompaniment	delivery	misery
accuracy	family	Niagara
aspirin	frivolous	operate
bachelor	history	particular
boundary	ignorant	privilege
casualties	lengthening	regular
considerable	liable	scenery
criminal	luxury	similar
definite	magazine	temperature
different	memory	victory

MISSPELLINGS DUE TO DROPPED CONSONANTS

As we have noticed, spelling is definite, fixed, and unyielding. But not so with pronunciation, since that is constantly changing, differs from place to place, and is even varied on different occasions by the same speaker. The word *garden* is always spelled g-a-r-d-e-n, but it can be, and is, pronounced in half a dozen different ways. You can drop the *r* or retain it. You can use any of three different sounds for the two vowels in the word, with or without shadings of sound. Each of these pronunciations is correct and normally is completely understood when used.

Such variation in pronouncing words sometimes does cause spelling problems. If our visual memory of words is stronger than our auditory image, no harm is done. But when a letter is incorrectly omitted in pronouncing a word, we have to be on guard. The following representative list of words should be studied carefully. If you master this list, you will then be alert to still other words in which consonants are slurred over or remain silent. In each word the "offending" consonant is set in bold face; try to pronounce it fully, sounding it out as an aid to your auditory memory.

1. Mr. Avery is an old a**c**quaintance of mine.
2. The Ar**c**tic Circle is entirely imaginary.
3. This puts me in an awk**w**ard position.
4. He is a candi**d**ate for the office.
5. The driver was convicted of drunken**n**ess.
6. He stopped school in the eig**h**th grade.
7. Mac grew up in a poor enviro**n**ment.
8. Feb**r**uary is the shortest month in the year.
9. He is opposed to all forms of gover**n**ment.
10. He owns a luc**r**ative business.
11. Karen is now a proud kin**d**ergarten pupil.
12. There are thousands of books in her library.
13. The barn was struck by light**n**ing.
14. You are per**h**aps too hasty in judging me.
15. Sam is proba**b**ly the best salesman in the company.
16. He purchased a large quan**t**ity of food.
17. This is a qua**r**ter, not a dime.
18. Mae did not seem to re**c**ognize me.
19. He was a good representa**t**ive for the firm.
20. This statement su**r**prised me.

In addition to these twenty illustrated words, and as a start on your additional list, pronounce each of the following as you ordinarily do. Perhaps your pronunciation will offer a clue to the cause of some of your misspellings. In each word, the "offending" consonant appears in bold face. Some of these consonants are silent or are slurred over.

accep*t*	gran*d*father	recognize
ac*q*uire	han*d*le	r*h*eumatism
an*d*	han*d*ful	r*h*ythm
authen*t*ic	hus*t*le	slep*t*
colum*n*	iden*t*ical	sof*t*en
condem*n*	kep*t*	swep*t*
contemp*t*	lan*d*lord	temp*t*
consum*p*tion	lis*t*en	ten*t*ative
em*p*ty	nes*t*le	tres*t*le
excep*t*	of*t*en	use*d* to
fas*c*inate	prom*p*t	wres*t*le
fas*t*en	pum*p*kin	yello*w*

MISSPELLINGS DUE TO UNSTRESSED VOWELS

No words in English are more often misspelled than those which contain unstressed (or lightly stressed) vowels. An unstressed vowel, like the *a* in *dollar*, is uttered with little force; its sound is faint, indistinct, blurred.

A technical name, *schwa* (ə), is used to indicate this sound of unstressed vowels. It resembles a kind of "uh," a quiet sound much less vigorous than the stronger "uh" sound found in such words as *mud* and *rush*.

This unstressed vowel sound may be represented in spelling by any one of the letters: *a, e, i, o, u*.

a
gramm*a*r, sof*a*, *a*bove

o
profess*o*r, spons*o*r, *o*ccur

e
corn*e*r, mod*e*l, *e*stablish

u
murm*u*r, sulf*u*r, lux*u*ry

i
nad*i*r, per*i*l, or*i*gin

The letter *y* is sometimes a vowel also. Its unstressed sound is illustrated in the word *martyr*.

Although the schwa sound ("uh") is the most frequent unstressed vowel sound, it is not the only one. An unstressed *i* sound appears in such words as *solid* but is not always spelled as *i*. Note, for example, such words as priv*a*te, privilege. Still other unstressed vowel sounds occur in American speech, but isolating them is not helpful in learning to spell.

Unless both your auditory and visual memory are excellent, you must be suspicious of words containing lightly stressed syllables. It may help to exaggerate the "trouble spots" when you pronounce such words. Doing so may result in strained or even incorrect pronunciation, but you will increase your auditory image of words which, by sound alone, could be spelled in various ways. If the word *separate*, for example, causes you trouble, pronounce it "sep-A-rate" until you have its spelling firmly fixed in your visual, auditory, and motor images. Here is a representative list of sixty words often misspelled because of the unstressed vowels they contain:

academy	dollar	occur
accident	ecstasy	optimism
actor	excellent	origin
applicant	existence	peril
arithmetic	fakir	politics
benefit	grammar	possible
business	hangar	private
calendar	humorous	privilege
category	hunger	professor
clamor	hypocrisy	propaganda
comparative	loafer	repetition
competitive	luxury	respectable
corner	maintenance	ridiculous
democracy	martyr	separate
describe	mathematics	sofa
despair	medicine	solid
develop	model	sponsor
dilute	monastery	swindler
discipline	murmur	terror
distress	nadir	vulgar

MISSPELLINGS DUE TO SILENT LETTERS

Some spelling authorities believe that the single greatest cause of misspelling connected with pronunciation is the silent letter.

Sounds have been dropping out of our language for many centuries, but their disappearance has affected pronunciation much more than spelling. Actually, many letters no longer pronounced in certain words persist in our spelling, for no good reason: the *l* in such words as *could*, *would*, and *should* has been silent for hundreds of years, but it hangs on in spelling.

The problem is compounded when we realize that the majority of the letters in our alphabet appear as silent letters in one word or another:

de*a*d	*h*onest	famo*u*s
dou*b*t	wei*r*d	ras*p*berry
s*c*ene	*k*nife	of*t*en
hand*s*ome	sa*l*mon	g*u*ess
com*e*	*m*nemonics	ans*w*er
of*f*	colum*n*	ya*c*ht
si*g*n		bou*gh*

Some silent letters cause little difficulty in spelling. If you are "visual minded," you will automatically put a *k* in *knee* or a *g* in *gnat*. But other letters which are silent, or are so lightly sounded as to be almost unheard, do cause trouble. Here is a list of some common words which, in the pronunciation of most educated people, contain silent letters:

align	gnaw	pneumatic
benign	hymn	pneumonia
bomb	indebted	prompt
comb	knack	psalm
condemn	knave	psychology
crumb	knee	through
daughter	kneel	thumb
dough	knit	tomb
dumb	knob	womb
eight	knock	wrap
fourth	knot	wreck
ghastly	know	wrench
ghost	knuckle	wretch
gnash	plumber	wring
gnat		write

Once again, pronunciation is not a safe guide to spelling. But *faulty* pronunciation sometimes adds hazards. Pronouncing words correctly is at least a slight aid in correct spelling. Try to form clear and definite *auditory* and *visual* images of words whose pronunciation can compound spelling problems.

5—Use a Dictionary: Etymology

When you are suspicious of the spelling of any word you should check it immediately in your dictionary. "Doubt + dictionary = good spelling" is a reliable formula. However, it is a counsel of perfection, one that few of us is likely always to follow. Not only that, our sense of doubt may be so great that we spend half our writing time flipping dictionary pages rather than communicating and thus grow bored and frustrated.

Also, you may have tried to look up a word in the dictionary and been unable to find it. If your visual image of a word is weak, you can frustrate yourself even more: look for *agast* and you may give up before discovering that the word is *aghast*. You won't find *pharmacy* and *photograph* among words beginning with *f*. In fact, the confusion of sound and spelling has caused more than one reputable publishing firm seriously to consider preparing a dictionary for poor spellers. Such a dictionary would have been helpful to the man who was away on a trip and telephoned his secretary to send his gun to him at a hunting resort. The secretary could barely hear him (the connection was poor) and asked her boss to spell out what he wanted. "Gun," he shouted. " 'G' as in *Jerusalem*, 'u' as in *Europe*, 'n' as in *pneumonia*." Whether or not he received his *jep* is unknown; maybe she sent him a dictionary instead.

Even topnotch spellers consult a dictionary for the spelling of some words. You may not hesitate over *chiaroscuro* or *chimerical*, but you may need to look up *aficionado* or *solipsism* or *Yggdrasill*. Granting that few of us would use these words in the first place, most of us would check our doubts by consulting a dictionary each time. In addition, compound words frequently require hyphens for correct spelling; even superb spellers must look up many such words.

If you haven't done so yet, now would be a good time to get thoroughly acquainted with your dictionary. Better still, make it your friend; best of all, make it your constant companion. To paraphrase the words of Dr. Samuel Johnson, a great dictionary-maker, you would be well advised to "Give your days and nights to wise study of your dictionary."

CHOICE OF A DICTIONARY

But you should know that there are dictionaries and dictionaries. Some, such as a pocket dictionary, are so small as to be virtually worthless save as a limited guide to spelling and pronunciation. Others, of fair size, may have been so hastily and carelessly produced that they are unreliable. Even the name "Webster" in the title is no longer a guarantee of quality because as a label "Webster" is no longer copyrighted and appears alike in the titles of both reliable and unreliable dictionaries. You should have— and if you don't have, you should buy—a dictionary you can trust.

Here are some reliable dictionaries, comparable in size, price, and quality:

The American College Dictionary
Webster's New Collegiate Dictionary
Webster's New World Dictionary

Slightly smaller, slightly less expensive, but adequate for most needs is the *Thorndike-Barnhart Comprehensive Desk Dictionary*. Excellent large dictionaries provide more information than any of these, but they are expensive and difficult to carry around. Usually placed in libraries and offices are such volumes as *Webster's New International Dictionary*, *The Shorter Oxford Dictionary* (2 volumes), Funk and Wagnalls' *New Standard Dictionary*, and the 20-volume *New English* (*Oxford*) *Dictionary*.

My advice is that you secure for your own use one of the three desk-size dictionaries mentioned first above. You will find it a never-failing help in time of spelling trouble. Not only that: intelligent use of a dictionary can help to *prevent* trouble, too. That is, certain approaches to the vast amount of knowledge recorded in even a desk-size dictionary can fix certain principles and patterns in our minds so that we do not have to consult it for, *at most*, more than 5 per cent of the words we use. Certain facts about word derivations, prefixes, suffixes, plurals, apostrophes, hyphens, and capitalization can be learned easily. They will apply to large numbers and classes of words and help to improve our spelling in almost wholesale fashion. First, let's consider word derivations.

ETYMOLOGY (WORD DERIVATION)

Etymology, a word taken from Greek, means an account of the history of a given word. More particularly, etymology deals with the origin and derivation of words. Knowing what a word comes from will often help you to spell it correctly. For example, the word *preparation* is derived from the Latin prefix *prae* ("beforehand") plus *parare* (meaning "to make ready"). Knowing this, and accenting the first *a* in *parare*, may help you to spell the word correctly: prep*a*ration, not prep*e*ration.

Similarly, our word *dormitory* (a building containing sleeping rooms) is derived from the Latin word *dormitorium*. Noting the first *i* in this Latin word, and perhaps also knowing that the French word for sleep is "dorm*i*r," may help you to spell *dormitory* with an *i* and not an *a*.

A study of etymology primarily will aid one in building his vocabulary. But it also has its uses in learning to spell. Here are somewhat simplified etymological comments on a few other common words which may fix this principle in your mind and lead to further study:

1. **Calendar.** This word is descended from the Latin word for "account book," *calendarium*. Note the *a*; we frequently misspell the word as *calender* (a perfectly good word with an entirely different meaning).

2. **Consensus.** This word comes from the same Latin root as *consent* (*con* + *sentire*, to feel). Note the *s* in *sentire* and you will not spell the word *concensus*, as is frequently done.

3. **Equivalent.** This frequently misspelled word may be easier for you if you remember that it means "equal in value" and is derived from the prefix *equi* + *valere*. Accent the *val* sound in *valere* (value).

4. **Extravagance.** This word is composed of *extra* (beyond) plus the Latin word *vagans* (*vagari*, to wander). "Extravagance" is

wandering beyond limits. Accent the letters *v - a - g* in the root word to insure correct spelling.

5. Familiar. This common word, often misspelled with an *e* where the second *a* should appear, is related to the Latin word *familia* (servants in a household).

6. Finis. This synonym for "end" has the same origin as the words *definite* and *finite*. Accent the "i" sound and come up with two *i*'s in this word.

7. Medicine. Many people tend to spell the second syllable of this word with an *e*. Its origin goes back to Latin *medicina* (*medicus*). Accent the *i* as an aid to correct spelling.

8. Optimism. This word comes to us by way of the French word *optimisme* (from Latin *optimus*, meaning "best"). Focus on the two *i*'s in *optimism*.

9. Privilege. From *privus* (private) plus *lex, legis* (law), this word can be remembered as "privy" (private) with the "y" changing to "i" plus *legal*, which fixes *leg* in *privilege*.

10. Recommend. This word comes from Latin *recommendare*. Think of it as *re + commend* and avoid that all-too-present double "c."

11. Sandwich. This word owes its existence to the Earl of Sandwich (1718–1792) who was so fond of the gaming table that he refused to stop gambling for regular meals and instead ate bread with fillings of meat or fish. Remember that Sandwich was a gambler, not a *witch*, and thus avoid the misspelling *sandwitch*. (Or maybe you would like to be able to eat a sandwich in the tropical Sandwich Islands, the former name for the Hawaiian Islands?)

12. Sentiment. This word derives from Latin *sentire*, meaning "to feel," "to perceive." Note the *i* in *sentire* and thus spell the word *sentiment*.

13. Sophomore. This word comes from the Greek word *sophos*, meaning "wise," and *moros*, meaning "foolish." There seem to be enough *o*'s in the original words to help us to remember that we spell this word for "wise fool" as sophomore.

14. Thermostat. This word comes from a Greek word, *thermos*, meaning "hot," plus another Greek word meaning "stationary." Remember the *o* in *thermos* and spell the word "thermostat."

15. Unanimous. This word comes from Latin *unus*, meaning "one," plus *animus*, meaning "mind." Our word begins with the first syllable of *unus* and the first two syllables of *animus*: unani-. Now you will just have to remember to insert an *o* to come up with *unanimous*.

As a beginning for your list of words whose origin may help you with spelling, consult a good dictionary for the derivations of the following:

1. addict	8. dictaphone	14. kindergarten
2. amorphous	9. epilogue	15. monotone
3. assess	10. exhilarate	16. pantomime
4. astronomy	11. genesis	17. photograph
5. atheist	12. hypodermic	18. professor
6. auditorium	13. interdict	19. recognize
7. boycott		20. resemblance

A considerable number of the memory devices beginning on page 449 are based upon etymology. Study them now or, when you come to them, refer again to this chapter.

6—Use a Dictionary: Prefixes and Suffixes

Prefixes, as we have noted, are syllables added to the beginning of words to alter or modify their meanings or, occasionally, to form entirely new words. For example, we add the prefix *mis* to the word *spell* and form *misspell*.

Suffixes are syllables added at the end of words to alter their meanings, to form new words, or to show grammatical function (part of speech). Thus we add *ish* to *small* and form *smallish*.

The readiness with which prefixes and suffixes are tacked on to root words in the English language is an indication of the freedom in word formation which has characterized our language for many centuries. For example, consider the word *recession*. This is derived from a Latin word *cedere* (*cessus*) which has the general meaning of "go." To this base we add the prefix *re*, which has a generalized meaning of "back" or "again," and the suffix *ion*, an ending which shows that the word is a noun (name of something).

Related to *recession* are many words with still other prefixes and suffixes but all coming from a similar root, or base: *recede, recess, recessive,* etc. The same root appears in *concession, procession, secession,* etc. The prefix of *recession* occurs in such words as *reception* and *relation*. Examples like this could be extended indefinitely.

For one final example, you can select the root word *scribe* (derived from the Latin equivalent of "to write"). From this root, you can easily form well-known words by using prefixes and suffixes:

ascribe, ascription	prescribe, prescription
circumscribe, circumscription	proscribe, proscription
describe, description	subscribe, subscription
inscribe, inscription	transcribe, transcription

A knowledge of the ways in which prefixes and suffixes are added to words will not only increase your vocabulary but also improve your spelling. However, we shall discuss here only a few common prefixes and suffixes appearing in everyday words. Those interested in these additions to words can consult any of a number of lengthy studies available in almost any library.

PREFIXES

The following is a list of common prefixes, which will be of considerable aid in spelling:

a-, ab- (from, away) as in *avert, absent*
ad- (toward, to) as in *adhere, adverb*
ante- (before) as in *antecedent, antedate*
anti- (against, opposite) as in *antidote, antitoxin*
con-, com- (with) as in *confide, commit*
de- (away, down) as in *decline, depressed*
di-, dis- (separation, reversal, apart) as in *divert, disappoint*
e-, ex- (out of, former) as in *elect, exclude*
hyper- (over, above) as in *hyperacidity, hypercritical*
in- (in, into) as in *induce, invert*
in- (not) as in *inexact, invalid*
inter- (between) as in *intercede, intervene*
mis- (wrong, bad) as in *misconduct, mistake*
non- (not, not one) as in *non-American, nonresident*
ob- (against) as in *object, oppose*
poly- (many) as in *polygamy, polytechnic*
pre- (before) as in *predict, prenatal*
pro- (forward) as in *proceed, propel*
re- (again, back) as in *repay, restore*
sub- (under) as in *subscribe, submarine*
trans- (across) as in *transfer, transport*
ultra- (beyond) as in *ultramodern, ultraviolet*
un- (not) as in *unhappy, untruth*

This is a very brief list of prefixes, but they appear in a large number of misspelled words. Here are notes on the spelling of words containing a few of these prefixes:

Ad-

This prefix alters its form according to the root word to which it is attached. For example, before a root beginning *sc* or *sp*, the *d* is dropped, as in *ascent* and *aspire*. Before such letters as *c, f, g,*

l, n, p, and *t,* the *d* in *ad-* is assimilated (becomes the same as the following letter): *accommodate, affix, aggression, allegation, announce, appoint, attend.*

Ante-, anti-

The first of these prefixes is of Latin origin and means "before" or "prior." Anti- is from Greek and means "opposite" or "against." Note these different spellings:

> *ante-*bellum (before the war)
> *ante*meridian (before noon; A.M.)
> *ante* mortem (before death)
> *ante*room (room before)
> *ante*type (an earlier form)
> *anti*aircraft (defense against aircraft)
> *anti*biotic (defense against bacteria)
> *anti*climax (contrast to preceding rise in action)
> *anti*freeze (against freezing)
> *anti*septic (against infection)

De-, dis-

These prefixes will cause spelling problems when you don't distinguish clearly between root words beginning with *s* and the prefixes themselves. Note these spellings:

> describe (write down) *de* + *scribe*
> despoil (strip down) *de* + *spoil*
> dissemble (disguise) *dis* + *semble*
> dissimilar (unlike) *dis* + *similar*

Remember: only about thirty common words begin with *diss* but ten times as many begin with *dis.* Only three fairly common words (and their derivatives) begin with *dys: dysentery, dyspepsia, dystrophy* (as in "muscular dystrophy").

A simple rule: when the prefixes *dis* and *mis* are added to a root word beginning with *s,* neither *s* should be omitted: *dissatisfied, misstep.* When they are added to roots not beginning with an *s,* use only one *s: disappear, misfortune.*

Inter-

This prefix meaning "between" is frequently confused with *intra,* which means "inside," "within."

interfere (carry between)
intercollegiate (between colleges)
interstate (between, among states)
intramural (within the walls)
intrastate (within a state)
intravenous (within a vein, veins)

Un-

When this prefix is added to a root word beginning with *n*, neither *n* is omitted:

unnamed	unneeded	unnoticed
unnatural	unnegotiable	unnumbered
unnecessary	unnoted	unnurtured
	unnoticeable	

SUFFIXES

It would be possible to make a list of suffixes but doing so would not in itself be much of an aid to correct spelling. For one thing, the list would have to be very lengthy; for another, many suffixes have several different meanings, others have vague or general meanings.

There are only eight suffix groups which cause major spelling problems. Within each group are many words that give trouble, some of the most often misspelled words in the language. Here is a brief discussion of each of the eight groups.

-Able, -Ible

Even excellent spellers have occasional difficulties with these endings; they can unhesitatingly spell most words having one or the other of these suffixes but once in a while they, too, must seek out their dictionaries.

With this spelling problem the best advice is to "Stop and Look." (It won't do any good to "listen," for pronunciation is identical.) To an efficient speller a word which should end in "ible" doesn't "look right" when it ends in "able." He is relying entirely on his visual image of the correct spelling.

But for those whose visual recall is deficient, there *are* some guiding principles concerning *-able* and *-ible*. They are fairly easy

to learn and involve no more exceptions than most rules for spelling. There are five group forms for *-able*, the same number for *-ible*.

-Able

1. The ending should usually be *able* if the base (root) is a full word: *eat + able*.

Fortunately, many of our most familiar, most used words add *able* to form adjectives. Note that if you drop *able* from each of the following you are left with a *complete* word:

acceptable	dependable	peaceable
available	detectable	perishable
avoidable	detestable	predictable
breakable	discreditable	presentable
changeable	drinkable	profitable
comfortable	fashionable	readable
commendable	favorable	seasonable
companionable	laughable	taxable
considerable	noticeable	thinkable
creditable	passable	workable

2. The ending should usually be *able* if the base is a full word except for lacking a final *e*: *desire + able = desirable*.

Fortunately, this group of *-able* words is not nearly so large as the preceding one. The following words illustrate the basic principle:

believable	excitable	pleasurable
debatable	excusable	presumable
deplorable	likable	sizable
describable	lovable	usable
desirable		valuable

3. The ending should usually be *able* if the base ends in *i* (the original word may have ended in *y*): *enviable*.

This principle of spelling makes more sense than most spelling "rules." If it were not followed we would have a double *i* (*ii*), an unusual combination even in our weird spelling system.

appreciable	enviable	reliable
classifiable	justifiable	satisfiable
dutiable		sociable

4. The ending should usually be *able* if the base has other forms with the sound of long *a: demonstrate, demonstrable.*

This principle will be helpful only if you actually sound out another form (or forms) of the root word to see whether it has (or they have) the long *a* sound: *abominate, abominable; estimate, estimable,* etc.

delectable	inflammable	intolerable
durable	inimitable	inviolable
flammable	innumerable	irreparable
impenetrable	inseparable	irritable
impregnable		reparable

5. The ending should usually be *able* if the base ends in hard *c* or hard *g.*

Hard *c* is sounded like the *c* in *cat*; hard *g* has the sound of *g* in *get*. The following words illustrate this principle:

amicable	explicable	navigable
applicable	implacable	practicable
despicable	indefatigable	irrevocable
		revocable

These five principles cover most of the fairly common words which have endings in *able*. But there are a few exceptions. If you wish to be able to spell all words ending with *able*, then study the following by some other method suggested in this book; rules won't help much:

affable	ineffable	palpable
arable	inevitable	portable
culpable	inscrutable	potable
equitable	insuperable	probable
formidable	malleable	unconscionable
indomitable	memorable	vulnerable

-Ible

1. The ending should usually be *ible* if the base is *not* a full word.

Contrast this principle with Number 1 under -*Able* (above). If the base is a complete word, we then add *able: mail + able =* *mailable.* If the base is not a complete word, we add *ible: ris + ible* = *risible,* and *poss + ible = possible.*

audible	feasible	irascible
combustible	horrible	negligible
compatible	incorrigible	ostensible
credible	indelible	plausible
dirigible	infallible	tangible
divisible	intelligible	terrible
edible		visible

2. The ending should usually be *ible* if the base ends in *ns.* *respons + ible = responsible.*

These words illustrate this spelling principle:

comprehensible	indefensible	reprehensible
defensible	insensible	responsible
incomprehensible	irresponsible	sensible
	ostensible	

3. The ending should usually be *ible* if the base ends in *miss:* *admiss + ible = admissible.*

Comparatively few words belong in this category. Here are several examples:

dismissible	permissible	remissible
omissible		transmissible

With roots not ending in *miss,* but closely related, are such words with *ible* endings as *accessible, compressible, irrepressible,* and *possible* (which also fits under Group 1 above).

4. The ending should usually be *ible* if *ion* can be added to the base without intervening letters: *collect, collection, collectible.*

Quite a few words create such new forms by the immediate (nothing coming between) addition of *ion*. All such words form adjectives ending in *ible*; here are a few samples:

accessible	contractible	inexhaustible
affectible	convertible	perfectible
collectible	corruptible	reversible
connectible	digestible	suggestible

You should note that this rule is tricky: if *ion* cannot be added to the root immediately (without intervening letters), the *able* ending is more likely as in *present, presentation, presentable*.

5. The ending should usually be *ible* if the base ends in soft *c* or soft *g*.

This principle should be compared with Number 5 under *-Able*. A soft *c* sounds like an *s* (force); a soft *g* sounds like a *j* (tangent). The following words contain a soft *c* or a soft *g*. Also note that, with few exceptions, the roots are not complete words.

conducible	illegible	legible
convincible	incorrigible	negligible
deducible	intangible	producible
eligible	intelligible	reducible
forcible	invincible	seducible
	irascible	

Just as there are a few exceptions to the rules for *able* endings (see page 65) so are there for words ending in *ible*. The commonly used words which are exceptions are not numerous. Among those words which, by rule, should end in *able* but do not are the following:

collapsible	flexible	inflexible
contemptible	gullible	irresistible
discernible		resistible

The following words merit careful study because each is an exception to the principles discussed above:

correctable	dispensable	indispensable
detectable		predictable

-*Ally*, -*Ly*

These two suffixes are often confused by spellers with inadequate visual memories. Because these endings appear so often in commonly used words, they account for large numbers of misspellings. The same advice applies: when in doubt, consult your dictionary.

Perhaps these basic principles concerning -*ly* will also be helpful:

1. The suffix *ly* is used to form an adverb from an adjective: *poor* + *ly* = *poorly*. If the adjective ends in *l*, *ly* is tacked on to the complete root, thus producing an *lly* ending.

   Here is a list of frequently used, and occasionally misspelled, adverbs:

accidentally	fundamentally	personally
actually	generally	physically
annually	incidentally	practically
continually	individually	really
coolly	intentionally	skillfully
cruelly	literally	successfully
especially	logically	truthfully
exceptionally	morally	universally
finally	naturally	unusually
fully	occasionally	usually

2. The suffix *ly* is added to basic words ending in silent *e*, and the *e* is retained.

absolutely	immediately	scarcely
completely	infinitely	severely
entirely		sincerely

3. If an adjective ends in *ic*, its adverbial form ends in *ally*.

   This is a simple, clear rule with only one exception: *publicly*. This word you must simply fix in your visual memory. Here are examples of adverbs formed from adjectives with *ic* endings:

academically	basically	lyrically
artistically	emphatically	scholastically
automatically	fantastically	systematically
	grammatically	

The following adverbs do not completely follow the principles just enumerated. Fix them in your visual memory:

duly	only	truly
incredibly	possibly	wholly
	terribly	

-Ance, -Ence

The suffixes *ance* and *ence* are added to root words (verbs) to form nouns: *attend, attendance; prefer, preference.*

With one exception, to be noted below, there is no uniform guiding principle to your choice of *-ance* or *-ence*. Here again, correct pronunciation is of no help. True, if you know the conjugation of Latin verbs you can form a helpful rule, but so few of us do know Latin that it's useless to state the principle. Your only safe procedure is to consult your dictionary and try to form good visual images of *-ance* and *-ence* words.

One helpful principle, and one only, is this: if a verb ends in *r* preceded by a vowel and is accented on the last syllable, it forms its noun with *ence*:

abhorrence	deference	preference
coherence	inference	recurrence
concurrence	interference	reference
conference	occurrence	transference

Here are lists of often misspelled words ending in *ance* and *ence*. Study each until you have a total recall of its appearance.

Frequently Misspelled -Ance Words

abeyance	appearance	distance
abundance	arrogance	elegance
acceptance	assurance	endurance
acquaintance	attendance	entrance
admittance	balance	furtherance
allegiance	brilliance	grievance
alliance	continuance	guidance
allowance	contrivance	instance
ambulance	defiance	insurance
annoyance	deliverance	irrelevance

Frequently Misspelled *-Ance* Words (*Cont'd*)

maintenance	relevance	significance
nuisance	reliance	substance
observance	remembrance	sustenance
performance	remittance	temperance
perseverance	repentance	tolerance
radiance	resistance	vengeance

Frequently Misspelled *-Ence* Words

absence	difference	obedience
abstinence	eminence	patience
audience	essence	permanence
circumference	evidence	preference
coherence	excellence	presence
coincidence	existence	prominence
competence	experience	prudence
conference	impudence	reference
confidence	incidence	residence
conscience	inference	reverence
convenience	influence	sentence
correspondence	innocence	silence
deference	insistence	subsistence
dependence	interference	violence

-Ar, -Er, -Or

The suffixes *ar*, *er*, and *or* have various origins, functions, and meanings. Their most common shared meaning denotes an actor, a doer, "one who." Many thousands of English words end in *ar*, *er*, and *or*, but here again accurate pronunciation is little aid in spelling; furthermore, no rules or principles are applicable to their correct spelling. Consult your dictionary; try to form accurate visual images.

Following are lists of *-ar*, *-er*, and *-or* words often misspelled. In not every word is the ending a true suffix, but correct spelling is now your objective, not a study of word origins or of word-building.

Frequently Misspelled Words Ending in *Ar*

altar	familiar	pillar
angular	grammar	polar
beggar	hangar	popular
burglar	insular	regular
calendar	jugular	scholar
caterpillar	liar	similar
cedar	lunar	singular
cellar	molar	spectacular
circular	muscular	sugar
collar	nectar	vehicular
curricular	particular	vinegar
dollar	peculiar	vulgar

Frequently Misspelled Words Ending in *Er*

advertiser	debater	messenger
adviser	defender	minister
alter	diameter	murder
announcer	disaster	observer
baker	employer	officer
beginner	examiner	partner
believer	foreigner	passenger
boarder	haberdasher	prisoner
border	jeweler	provider
boulder	laborer	soldier
carrier	lawyer	teacher
commissioner	lecturer	traveler
consumer	manager	writer
	manufacturer	

Frequently Misspelled Words Ending in *Or*

accelerator	anchor	bachelor
actor	auditor	behavior
administrator	author	benefactor
aggressor	aviator	cantor

Frequently Misspelled Words Ending in *Or*

collector	emperor	neighbor
commentator	escalator	odor
competitor	executor	pastor
conqueror	factor	prior
contributor	governor	professor
councilor	harbor	protector
counselor	humor	radiator
creditor	inferior	sailor
debtor	inventor	sculptor
dictator	investigator	senator
director	janitor	suitor
distributor	legislator	supervisor
doctor	manor	tenor
editor	minor	traitor
educator	mortgagor	ventilator
elevator	motor	visitor

-Ary, -Ery

This suffix problem is simple. Hundreds and hundreds of English words end in *ary*. Only a half dozen fairly common words end in *ery*. Learn the -*ery* words by whatever device presented in this book works best for you. Spell all others with *ary*. It's as element*ary* as that.

Here are the words you might use which end in *ery*:

cemetery	distillery	monastery
confectionery	millinery	stationery

If you're a physician, you probably know how to spell *dysentery*. If you're not a physician, another word, more easily spelled, can and will suffice.

End all other words with *ary*. You'll be right every time unless you happen to use such a rare word as *philandery*. You will have no spelling problems with the endings of *auxiliary, boundary, dictionary, elementary, honorary, imaginary, library, secretary,* and *voluntary,* and hundreds of other such everyday words.

-Cede, -Ceed, -Sede

These suffixes cause a large number of misspellings because they appear in several common words. But the problem they present is quite simple because so few words are involved. Only twelve words in the language end in this pronunciation, "seed," and not all of these are in common use.

First, only one word in English ends in *sede: supersede*. It has this ending because of its origin; it comes from the Latin verb *sedeo*, meaning "to sit." As with many other "borrowed" words in English it maintains some connection with its source.

Second, only three of the twelve words ending with the "seed" pronunciation are spelled with *ceed: exceed, proceed*, and *succeed*.

Finally, the eight remaining words end in *cede*, and of these only three or four are in general, everyday use:

accede	concede	precede
. antecede	intercede	recede
cede		secede

It won't help with spelling the *ceed* and *cede* words to know their origin, but it will help in avoiding a *sede* ending: the eleven *ceed, cede* words derive not from *sedeo* (as *supersede* does) but from Latin *cedo*, meaning "to go." Thus, *pre + cede* means "to go or come before"; *inter + cede* means "to go or come between," etc.

-Efy, -Ify

These two suffixes cause much spelling trouble but here again the problem is simple when it is clearly looked at. Actually, only four words you are likely to use end in *efy* (and you probably won't use them every day, either). All the remainder, without exception, end in *ify*.

Therefore, learn these four words by whatever method seems best and spell all others with *ify*:

liquefy (to make liquid)	rarefy (to make or become
putrefy (to make or become	rare)
rotten)	stupefy (to make or become
	insensible)

Also, you should note that words built on these four tend to retain the *e* spelling:

liquefy, liquefies, liquefied, liquefying, liquefaction
putrefy, putrefies, putrefied, putrefying, putrefaction

rarefy, rarefies, rarefied, rarefying, rarefaction
stupefy, stupefies, stupefied, stupefying, stupefaction

-Ise, -Ize, -Yze

Some five hundred fairly common words in our language end in *ise, ize,* and *yze.* How can one master all these spellings, especially since correct pronunciation provides no help at all?

Consulting your dictionary will provide some help and so will training your visual memory until a word you've spelled with "ize" just "doesn't look right" if it should end in "ise." The best approach is to isolate the comparatively few words with *yze* and *ise* and to remember that *ize* is by far the most common suffix and that the chances of its being correct are mathematically excellent.

These are the only four fairly common words in English ending in *yze* and of them you will normally use only two:

analyze	electrolyze
catalyze	paralyze

Study these four words carefully, especially the first and last. Master them by whatever method seems best: four words (or two) are a small matter.

There are no clear rules for choosing between *-ise* and *-ize* endings. But although there are well over four hundred words ending in *ize* there are only some thirty or forty with an *-ise* suffix. (If you live in Great Britain, you will have to cope with a larger number; several words that the English spell with *ise* Americans spell with *ize.*)

The comparatively few words which end in *ise* can be grouped as follows:

1. Combinations with *-cise:*

exercise	exorcise	circumcise
excise		incise

These *cise* words are so spelled because they derive from a form, *incisus,* of a Latin word meaning "to cut."

2. Combinations with *-guise:*

guise	disguise

3. Combinations with -*mise:*

demise	premise
compromise	surmise

4. Combinations with -*prise:*

apprise	enterprise	reprise
comprise	emprise	surprise

5. Combinations with -*rise:*

arise	rise	sunrise
moonrise		uprise

6. Combinations with -*vise:*

advise	improvise	revise
devise		supervise

These *vise* words are derived from a form, *visus,* of a Latin word meaning "to see."

7. Combinations with -*wise:*

contrariwise	likewise	sidewise
lengthwise	otherwise	wise

8. Miscellaneous combinations with -*ise:*

advertise	despise	franchise
chastise		merchandise

This makes a total of less than forty common words ending in *yze* and *ise.* All others with this suffixal pronunciation end in *ize.* Here are a few of the hundreds of words with this ending:

agonize	colonize	harmonize
apologize	criticize	humanize
authorize	crystallize	jeopardize
baptize	demoralize	legalize
brutalize	economize	liberalize
cauterize	equalize	localize
characterize	familiarize	modernize
Christianize	fertilize	monopolize
civilize	generalize	moralize

nationalize	philosophize	solemnize
naturalize	plagiarize	specialize
neutralize	pulverize	subsidize
organize	realize	symbolize
ostracize	recognize	tantalize
particularize	reorganize	utilize
pasteurize	scandalize	vocalize
patronize	scrutinize	

7—Use a Dictionary: Plurals

You can consult your dictionary every time you are unsure about the spelling of a word but, as we have noted, if you do you'll be more a whirling dervish or page-flipper than a writer.

Many people find it fairly easy to spell the singular of a word (meaning "one") but have trouble forming and correctly spelling plurals (meaning "more than one"). This is quite understandable, since many English words form plurals in unusual ways. You can "look it up" in a dictionary when you are puzzled, but a few principles of plural-forming can easily be mastered.

1. The plural of most nouns is formed by adding *s* to the singular:

bed, beds	food, foods
book, books	hat, hats
chair, chairs	pot, pots
cracker, crackers	sheet, sheets
dog, dogs	table, tables

2. Nouns ending with a sibilant or *s* sound (*ch, sh, s, x, z*) form their plurals by adding *es*:

arch, arches	fox, foxes
box, boxes	loss, losses
bush, bushes	mass, masses
buzz, buzzes	tax, taxes
church, churches	watch, watches

3. Nouns ending in *y* preceded by a consonant usually change *y* to *i* before adding *es*:

activity, activities	forty, forties
category, categories	library, libraries
city, cities	quantity, quantities
community, communities	sky, skies
fly, flies	strawberry, strawberries

417

4. Nouns ending in *y* preceded by a vowel usually add *s* without changing the final *y*:

alley, alleys	money, moneys
attorney, attorneys	monkey, monkeys
chimney, chimneys	toy, toys
foray, forays	turkey, turkeys
key, keys	valley, valleys

5. Nouns ending in *o* preceded by a vowel add *s* to form their plurals:

cameo, cameos	radio, radios
folio, folios	rodeo, rodeos

6. Nouns ending in *o* preceded by a consonant often add *es* to form the plural:

buffalo, buffaloes	mosquito, mosquitoes
cargo, cargoes	Negro, Negroes
echo, echoes	potato, potatoes
embargo, embargoes	tomato, tomatoes
fresco, frescoes	tornado, tornadoes
hero, heroes	volcano, volcanoes

7. Some nouns ending in *o* preceded by a consonant, including many musical terms, add *s* to form their plurals:

alto, altos	gigolo, gigolos
banjo, banjos	memento, mementos
basso, bassos	piano, pianos
canto, cantos	quarto, quartos
concerto, concertos	silo, silos
contralto, contraltos	solo, solos
dynamo, dynamos	soprano, sopranos
Eskimo, Eskimos	zero, zeros

8. Nouns ending in *f* form their plurals in such variable ways that you should *always* consult your dictionary when in doubt. Nouns ending in *ff* usually add *s*. Most nouns ending in *fe* change *fe* to *ve* and add *s*. The following examples will be sufficient to make you remember the formula: doubt + dictionary = correct spelling:

belief, beliefs	roof, roofs
chief, chiefs	scarf, scarves
fife, fifes	self, selves
grief, griefs	sheaf, sheaves
half, halfs (or halves)	sheriff, sheriffs
handkerchief, handkerchiefs	staff, staves (or staffs)
leaf, leaves	tariff, tariffs
life, lives	thief, thieves
loaf, loaves	wife, wives
mischief, mischiefs	wolf, wolves

9. Certain nouns of foreign origin retain the plural of the language from which they were borrowed. Some borrowed words have gradually assumed plurals with the usual English *s* or *es* endings. Finally, some words have more than one plural form.

To reduce confusion, here is a list of fairly common nouns to fix in your mind by whatever device works best for you:

agendum, agenda	focus, foci, focuses
alumna, alumnae	formula, formulas, formulae
alumnus, alumni	genus, genera, genuses
analysis, analyses	hypothesis, hypotheses
appendix, appendixes,	index, indexes, indices
appendices	larva, larvae
axis, axes	memorandum, memorandums,
bacterium, bacteria	memoranda
basis, bases	parenthesis, parentheses
cherub, cherubs, cherubim	phenomenon, phenomena
crisis, crises	radius, radii, radiuses
criterion, criteria, criterions	stimulus, stimuli
datum, data	thesis, theses
erratum, errata	vertebra, vertebrae, vertebras

10. Compound nouns ordinarily form the plural by adding *s* or *es* to the important word in the compound.

Sometimes the element considered most important comes first in the compound, sometimes at the end. The end element is usually the one pluralized if it and other elements are so closely related as to be considered a single word· *handfuls, housefuls, basketfuls.* Just to confound the pluralizing of compound words, occasionally more than one element is pluralized in the same word. Here again, the best advice is: *Consult your dictionary.* The words listed below illustrate the erratic principles stated in this paragraph:

> attorney at law, attorneys at law
> attorney general, attorneys general, attorney generals
> brother-in-law, brothers-in-law
> bystander, bystanders
> commander in chief, commanders in chief
> consul general, consuls general
> father-in-law, fathers-in-law
> hanger-on, hangers-on
> major general, major generals
> master sergeant, master sergeants
> manservant, menservants
> pailful, pailfuls
> passer-by, passers-by
> son-in-law, sons-in-law

11. Some nouns have irregular plurals.

Surely you expected to read the statement above, sooner or later. Here is a representative list of words with plurals that are irregular or plain nonsensical or which follow none of the principles stated above. Try to master them by whatever device you have found most useful:

alkali, alkalies	moose, moose
bison, bison	mouse, mice
brother, brothers, brethren	ox, oxen
child, children	photo, photos
deer, deer	series, series
foot, feet	sheep, sheep
goose, geese	species, species
louse, lice	swine, swine
madam, mesdames	tooth, teeth
man, men	woman, women

12. Pronouns and verbs have plural forms just as do nouns. It is doubtful, however, that misspelling of pronouns is due to their

number. If you misspell *their*, a plural pronoun, you are probably confusing *their* and *there*, rather than having trouble with a plural. *We, they, our, us, them*, all plural pronouns, are easy to spell.

The plurals of verbs are quite simple. Main verbs have the same form for both singular and plural except in the third person singular, present tense: he *sees*, he *moves*, he *thinks*, he *does*, he *goes*. That is, most verbs add an *s* (*es*) in the third person to form a singular. It's easy to remember this: most nouns and verbs form their plurals in directly opposite ways.

8—Use a Dictionary: Apostrophes

An apostrophe is a mark of punctuation, not a letter, and yet when one is improperly added or omitted it causes you to misspell. The apostrophe has several uses, all with some influence on spelling: to indicate the possessive case, to mark omission of letters, to indicate the plurals of letters and numbers. The use of an apostrophe influences both punctuation *and* spelling. Since this book deals only with spelling, we will concentrate on uses of the apostrophe which result in misspelling.

1. Use an apostrophe and *s* to form the possessive case of a noun (singular or plural) not ending in *s*:

    children, children's   horse, horse's
    doctor, doctor's   town, town's

    Children's shoes are often expensive.

2. Use only an apostrophe to form the possessive case of a plural noun ending in *s*:

    boys, boys'   students, students'
    ladies, ladies'   weeks, weeks'

    The boys' coats are in the closet.

3. Use an apostrophe alone or an apostrophe with *s* to form the possessive of singular nouns ending in *s*:

Robert Burns, Robert Burns' (or Burns's)   Charles, Charles'

    She liked Robert Burns' (or Burns's) poetry.
    This is Charles' hat.

4. In compound nouns add the apostrophe and *s* to the last element of the expression, the one nearest the object possessed:

    my son-in-law's boat   King Henry IV's funeral
    somebody else's ticket   the city manager's salary

5. Use an apostrophe to show that letters or figures have been omitted.

aren't = are not	they're = they are
don't = do not	wasn't = was not
he's = he is	weren't = were not

The Civil War was fought 1861–'65. (1861 to 1865)
He left home in '59. (1959)

This use of the apostrophe is reflected in the most misspelled short and simple word in the English language. *It's* means "it is" and can never be correctly used for *its* in the possessive sense: "When a dog wags *its* tail, that is a sign *it's* happy." Never write the letters *i-t-s* without thinking whether or not you mean "it is."

6. Use an apostrophe and *s* to indicate the plurals of figures, letters, and words considered as words.

Small children cannot always make legible 5's.
Uncrossed *t*'s look like *l*'s.
He uses too many *and*'s and *but*'s in speaking.

7. Never use an apostrophe in forming the plural of nouns and the possessive case of personal relative pronouns.

The *Browns* (not *Brown's*) came to see us.

CORRECT	INCORRECT
ours	our's
ours	ours'
yours	your':
yours	yours'
his	his'
hers	her's
hers	hers'
its	it's
theirs	their's
theirs	theirs'
whose	who's

9--Use a Dictionary: Compound Words

The centuries-old tendency of the English language to combine words has created still another difficult problem for spellers. Even so, compound words have greatly increased the range and richness of the language and have provided many short cuts and timesavers.

Now look at the paragraph which you have just read. Note that *centuries-old* is a compound written with a hyphen; that *short cuts* is a compound written as two words; that *timesavers* is a compound written as one word (no hyphen, no separation). Any one of these words written otherwise would be misspelled.

And yet there are no rules or principles covering *all* combinations. Some few principles, easily learned, are discussed below, but for spelling the bulk of compound words you must use your dictionary whenever you are in doubt.

The general principle of word joining derives from actual usage. When two (or more) words first become associated with a single meaning, they are written separately. As they grow, through usage, to become more of a unit in thought and writing, they are usually hyphenated (spelled with a hyphen). Finally, they tend to be spelled as one word. This evolution may be seen in the following, the third word in each series now being the accepted form: *base ball, base-ball, baseball; rail road, rail-road, railroad*. This general principle, however, is not always in operation; many common expressions which one might think in the third stage are still in the first: *mother tongue, boy friend, girl scout, in fact, high school*.

Here is another way to demonstrate how seemingly illogical is the spelling of many compound words: look up in your dictionary some of the words which have *red* as the first part of the compound. Dictionaries differ among themselves, but the one the author consulted shows these distinctions: *red cedar, red cent, red clover, Red Cross, red deer, red light, red man, red oak, red pepper, red rose,* and *red tape; red-blooded, red-headed, red-hot,* and *red-letter; redbud, redcap, redcoat, redhead, redwing,* and *redwood*.

The hyphenated *red* words above offer a clue. The hyphen is a device to separate and also a mark to unify, to join. As a mark of spelling, it both joins and separates two or more words used *as an adjective*. And yet it may or may not be called for in forming compound adjectives because of position in a given sentence. For example, hyphens are generally used between the parts of an adjective preceding the substantive (noun) which it modifies but may properly be omitted if the compound adjective follows. You may write "He saw the *red-hot* coil" and just as correctly write "The coil was *red hot*." Since this is a book on spelling, not syntax, this illustration will have to serve as a warning and as a further plea for you to "look it up" whenever you are doubtful. But remember that dictionaries differ; they do not always indicate the distinction just made.

Finally, you should note that two or more words compounded may have a meaning quite different from that of the same two words not really joined:

Jim was a *battle-scarred* veteran.
The *battle scarred* the body and soul of Jim.
In this quarrel Sue served as a *go-between*.
The ball must *go between* the goal posts.

There is neither a short cut nor an all-inclusive rule for spelling compound words. But perhaps it will be of some help to remember that the present-day tendency is to avoid the use of hyphens whenever possible.

There are seven groups, or classes, of compound words with which the hyphen is used:

1. Two or more words modifying a substantive and used as a single adjective.

The hyphen is especially needed in combinations placed *before* the word modified. Examples of these combinations are

   a. adjective, noun, or adverb + participle (+ noun)
     Bob is a *sad-looking* boy.
     Bell-shaped hats are in fashion again.
     He jumped from a *fast-moving* train.
   b. adjective + adjective (+ noun)
     Mary has *bluish-gray* eyes.

c. adjective + noun (+ noun)
   He is a *first-rate* musician.
d. noun + adjective (+ noun)
   There will be a *city-wide* search for the criminal.
e. prefix + capitalized adjective (+ noun)
   We took a *trans-Andean* clipper to Chile.

The following are other instances of the combinations mentioned above:

able-bodied	loose-tongued
above-mentioned	midnight-black
absent-minded	ocean-blue
Anglo-Saxon	rose-red
best-known	six-room
far-fetched	soft-spoken
good-natured	stiff-necked
Latin-American	ten-foot
light-haired	un-American
long-needed	wild-eyed

2. Compound nouns.
Compound nouns consist of from two to as many as four parts. Practically every part of speech can become a component of a compound noun.

a. Two-part compound noun.
   Coke is a *by-product* of coal. (preposition + noun)
b. Three-part compound noun.
   My *brother-in-law* is a lawyer. (noun + preposition + noun)
c. Four-part compound noun.
   Harry is a *jack-of-all-trades*. (noun + preposition + adjective + noun)

Other examples of compound nouns are the following:

court-martial	leveling-off
ex-president	looker-on
fellow-citizen	mother-in-law
forget-me-not	secretary-treasurer
go-between	son-in-law
great-grandson	tête-à-tête

3. Compound words with *half, quarter,* or *self* as the first element.

half-and-half	self-conceit
half-asleep	self-control
half-truth	self-interest
quarter-final	self-made
quarter-hour	self-respect
quarter-share	self-sacrifice

4. Compound words made from a single capital letter and a noun or participle:

A-flat	S-curve
F-sharp	T-shirt

5. "Improvised" compounds:

holier-than-thou	make-believe
know-it-all	never-say-die
long-to-be-remembered	never-to-be-forgotten

6. Compound numerals from twenty-one through ninety-nine:

thirty-three	sixty-seven
forty-six	eighty-five

7. The numerator and denominator of fractions:

four-fifths	three-quarters
one-half	two-thirds

If the hyphen already appears in either numerator or denominator it is omitted in writing the fraction:

twenty-one thirds   three ten-thousandths

General Cautions in Using the Hyphen

a. All the examples cited above were checked in a good desk dictionary. If your dictionary differs, don't hesitate to take its word.
b. Do not use a hyphen when two adjectives preceding a noun are independent:

She wore a *faded yellow* hat.

c. Do not use a hyphen when an adverb modifies an adjective:

> She was a *highly trained* secretary.

d. Do not use a hyphen between double terms that denote a single office or rank:

> *Major General* Jones; *Executive Director* Adams.

e. Omit the hyphen in writing a fraction which is not an adjective:

> He ate up *one half* of the pie.

f. Do not use a hyphen with reflexive pronouns:

> *herself, himself, yourselves.*

g. Many compounds formerly spelled separately or with a hyphen are now written as single words:

> *almighty, hateful, inasmuch, namesake.*

Once again, but finally, the only way to be sure about every compound word is to consult your dictionary.

10—Use a Dictionary: Capitalization

Strictly speaking, a discussion of capital letters does not belong in a spelling book. One can argue with some reason that if a word contains all the right letters in the right places it is correctly spelled.

It is true that man has had to invent distinctions between capital letters and small letters and that these distinctions have varied from century to century and from author to author. At one time, for example, it was customary to capitalize all nouns, as it still is in writing German. Gradually, however, certain modern customs involving capital letters evolved. These customs aren't particularly logical. Perhaps because capitalization is as illogical as spelling and quite as much a matter of accident and convention it deserves discussion in this book.

To misspell is to violate a convention; to use capital letters wrongly is to violate a convention. And breaking conventions, as all of us know, can cause us embarrassment, anguish, money, or all three. Many people firmly believe that mistakes in using capital and small letters are as serious as misspelling. Indeed, they feel that such mistakes *are* misspellings. Probably they are right.

The applications of capitalization are so numerous, and so loaded with exceptions, that firm rules and principles cannot apply to every possible example. A few underlying principles may be helpful and are given below. The only sound principle for you to follow is *use a dictionary*.

1. Capitalize the first word of every sentence and the first word of every direct quotation.

> The engine needs repair.
> He asked, "Does the engine need repair?"

When only a part of a direct quotation is included within a sentence, it is usually not begun with a capital letter.

The reporter told me that the official said he felt "fine"
but thought that he should "take it easy" for a few weeks.

2. Capitalize proper nouns. Proper nouns include:

a. Names of people and titles used for specific persons:
George Washington, Theodore Roosevelt, the President,
the Senator, the Treasurer, the General, Mr. Chairman,
Father, Mother.

b. Names of countries, states, regions, localities, other geographic areas, and the like: United States, England, Illinois,
the Far East, the Dust Bowl, the Midwest, the Solid South,
the Rocky Mountains, the Sahara Desert, the Connecticut
River, Lake Michigan.

c. Names of streets: Michigan Boulevard, Fifth Avenue, Ross
Street, Old Mill Road.

d. Names of the Deity and personal pronouns referring to
Him: God, Heavenly Father, Son of God, Jesus Christ,
Saviour, His, Him, Thy, Thine.

e. Names for the Bible and other sacred writings: Bible, the
Scriptures, Book of Genesis, Revelations, Koran.

f. Names of religions and religious groups: Protestantism,
Roman Catholicism, Presbyterian, Jesuit, Unitarian,
Judaism, Shinto.

g. Names of the days and the months (but *not* the seasons):
Monday, Tuesday, etc.; January, February, etc.; summer,
winter, autumn, fall, spring.

h. Names of schools, colleges, universities: Woodberry Forest
School, Kentucky Military Institute, Davidson College,
Cornell University.

i. Names of historic events, eras, and holidays: Revolutionary
War, Christian Era, Middle Ages, Renaissance, the Fourth
of July, Labor Day, Thanksgiving.

j. Names of races, organizations, and members of each:
Indian, Negro, Malay, League of Women Voters, the
Junior League, American Academy of Science, National
League, San Francisco Giants, Big Ten Conference, an
Elk, a Shriner, a Socialist.

k. Vivid personifications: Fate, Star of Fortune, Destiny, the

power of Nature, the paths of Glory, the chronicles of
Time, Duty's call.
l. Trade names: Bon Ami, Mr. Clean, Ry-Krisp, Wheaties,
Anacin.

Note: If the reference is to any one of a class of persons or
things rather than to a specific person or thing, do not capitalize
the noun or adjective:

> He is not a captain.
> His name is Captain Draper.
> I am going to a theater.
> He is at the Bijou Theater.
> He attended high school.
> He attended Sumter High School.
> In college he took history and biology.
> In college he took History 12 and Biology 3.

3. Capitalize the first word of every line of poetry:

> I held it truth, with him who sings
> To one clear harp in divers tones,
> That men may rise on stepping-stones
> Of their dead selves to higher things.
> > TENNYSON

4. Capitalize each important word in the title of a book, play,
magazine, musical composition, etc.:

> *The Decline and Fall of the Roman Empire*
> *You Can't Go Home Again*
> *Romeo and Juliet*
> *Atlantic Monthly*
> *Madame Butterfly*

5. Avoid unnecessary and careless use of capitals.
   a. Do not carelessly make small (lower-case) letters so large
      that they resemble capitals (upper-case letters).
   b. Do not capitalize names of points of the compass unless
      they refer to a specific section.

> He lives in the West.
> He walked west along the street.

c. Capitalize nouns such as *father* and *mother* if they are not preceded by a possessive.

Your father is a tall man.
I love Father very much.
My sister thinks I am noisy, but Grandpa says I am not.

11—Learn a Few Simple Rules of Spelling

If you happen to study carefully a number of words which have similar characteristics you can make some generalizations about their spelling. In fact, observers have been doing just this for more than a century with the result that nearly fifty spelling rules have been formulated.

Generalizations about the groupings of letters which form classes of words will definitely help some people to spell more correctly. Those with good visual or motor memories will not need them. Other people apparently have a psychological block against rules. But experience has shown that rules—or at least a few of the more basic ones—do help some people to spell correctly certain classes of words. Applying spelling rules is only one approach to correct spelling; it may be more or less helpful to you than the other methods of attack presented in this book.

The rules which follow, with their corollaries, are simple and easily learned. Mastering them may help you to eliminate a large number of recurring errors in fairly common words. If this approach works for you, then consult other books on spelling or the section on orthography (spelling according to standard usage) in *Webster's New Collegiate Dictionary* for additional rules. The six rules stated and illustrated below are those which the author's experience has shown to be most useful and to apply to the largest number of commonly misspelled words.

Before studying the rules which follow, you should understand a few basic principles about them.

First, it is doubtful that anyone ever improved his spelling merely by saying a rule over and over to himself. Words come first, rules second; you should apply a rule, not merely memorize and mouth it.

Second, there are exceptions to every rule. And since there are so many exceptions you will need to use an additional approach: improve your visual or motor memory; use some remembering trick; consult your dictionary.

Third, the corollary and the reverse of every spelling rule are as important as the rule itself. For example, in the first rule given below, you are shown when not to use *i* before *e*, but the reverse of this pattern is fully as important and must be kept in mind and applied. Learning only part of a rule is about as silly and time-wasting as looking up a word in a dictionary and learning only one meaning of it, or only its spelling.

1. Words containing *ei* or *ie*.

One of the most frequent causes of misspelling is not knowing whether to write *ei* or *ie* in literally scores of everyday words. In fact, about one thousand fairly common words contain *ei* or *ie*. It helps to know that *ie* occurs in twice as many words as *ei*, but the problem is not thereby solved.

The basic rule may be stated in one of the best-known pieces of doggerel ever written:

> Write *i* before *e*
> Except after *c*
> Or when sounded like *a*
> As in *neighbor* and *weigh*.

This rule, or principle, applies only when the pronunciation of *ie* or *ei* is a long *e* (as in *he*) or the sound of the *a* in *fade*.

Here's another way to summarize the rule and its reverse:

When the sound is long *e* (as in *piece*) put *i* before *e* except after *c*.
When the sound is not long *e* (as it is not in *weigh*) put *e* before *i*.

Still another way to state this principle is this: When the *e* sound is long, *e* comes first after *c* but *i* comes first after all other consonants:

ceiling	conceive	perceive
conceit	deceit	receipt
conceited	deceitful	receive
	deceive	

achieve	belief	bier
aggrieve	believe	brief
apiece	besiege	cashier

chandelier	hygiene	retrieve
chief	mischief	shield
field	piece	shriek
fiend	pier	siege
frontier	pierce	thief
grief	priest	wield
grieve	relieve	wiener
handkerchief	reprieve	yield

This much of the rule is fairly simple: usually you write *ie* except after the letter *c* when you write *ei*—provided the sound is long *e*. The last two lines of the doggerel refer to words in which *ei* or *ie* sounds like *a*. Fortunately, only a few everyday words fall in this group, among them:

beige	heir	skein
chow mein	neigh	sleigh
deign	neighbor	surveillance
feint	obeisance	veil
freight	reign	vein
eight	rein	weigh
heinous		weight

A few words are either exceptions to this basic *ei-ie* rule or are not fully covered by the four lines of doggerel. The best advice is to learn the following words by some method other than trying to apply the rule, which doesn't work here:

caffeine	height	seize
codeine	hierarchy	seizure
either	leisure	sheik
Fahrenheit	neither	sleight
fiery	protein	stein
financier	Reid (proper name)	weird

Summary:

1. Use *ie* generally when sounded as long *e* (he).
2. Use *ei* after *c* when sounded as *e* (he).
3. Use *ei* when sounded as *a* (*eight*).
4. Watch out for exceptions.

2. Final *y*.

Forming the plural of nouns ending in *y* has already been

discussed on page 417. But the rule applies also to words other than nouns and their plurals. The basic principle is this:

a. Words ending in *y* preceded by a consonant usually change *y* to *i* before any suffix except one beginning with *i*:

> angry, angrily
> beauty, beautiful
> busy, busily, business
> carry, carries, carrying
> dignify, dignified, dignifying
> easy, easier, easily
> empty, emptier, emptiness
> happy, happier, happiness
> lovely, lovelier, loveliness
> lucky, luckier, luckily
> marry, married, marriage
> merry, merrier, merrily, merriment
> pity, pitiful, pitying
> pretty, prettier, prettiness
> study, studied, studious
> try, tried, trying

b. Words ending in *y* preceded by a vowel do not change *y* to *i* before suffixes or other endings:

> annoy, annoyed, annoyance   employ, employer
> betray, betrayal   stay, stayed, staying

To the two parts of this "final *y*" rule are so many exceptions that some experts feel the rule is not helpful. However, the exceptions among commonly used words are not numerous and can easily be mastered by some other approach suggested in this book. Here are some everyday words which follow neither part of the "final *y*" principle:

> baby, babyhood   say, said
> busy, busyness (state of being busy)
> day, daily
> lady, ladyship   shy, shyly, shyness
> lay, laid   slay, slain
> pay, paid   wry, wryly, wryness

3. Final *e*.

Hundreds of everyday English words end in *e*, and hundreds and hundreds more consist of such words plus suffixes: *hope, hoping; come, coming; safe, safety,* etc. In our pronunciation, nearly all *e*'s at the end of words are silent (not pronounced): *advice, give, live,* etc. Actually, the function of a final silent *e* is to make the vowel of the syllable long: *rate* but *rat; mete* but *met; bite* but *bit; note* but *not,* etc.

With those facts in mind we can now proceed to a rule which covers more words than any other spelling rule, many of them common words frequently misspelled. Here it is:

Final silent *e* is usually dropped before a suffix beginning with a vowel but is retained before a suffix beginning with a consonant.

advise, advising	hate, hateful
amuse, amusing, amusement	hope, hoping, hopeless
argue, arguing	ice, icy
arrive, arrival	judge, judging
awe, awesome	like, likable
bare, barely, bareness	live, livable
believe, believing, believable	love, lovable
bite, biting	move, movable, movement
care, careful, careless	owe, owing
come, coming	purchase, purchasing
desire, desirable	safe, safely, safety
dine, dining	sincere, sincerely
excite, exciting, excitement	sure, surely, surety
extreme, extremely	use, usable, useless

This basic rule is clear enough, but it does not cover all words ending in silent *e*. Here are some additions and exceptions to the general principle:

a. Silent *e* is retained when *ing* is added to certain words, largely to prevent them from being confused with other words:

dye, dyeing to contrast with *die, dying*
singe, singeing to contrast with *sing, singing*

> *swinge, swingeing* to contrast with *swing, swinging*
> *tinge, tingeing* to contrast with *ting, tinging*

b. Silent *e* is retained in still other words before a suffix beginning with a vowel. Sometimes this is done for the sake of pronunciation, sometimes for no logical reason at all:

acre, acreage	line, lineage
cage, cagey	mile, mileage
here, herein	shoe, shoeing
hoe, hoeing	there, therein

c. Silent *e* is dropped before a suffix beginning with a consonant in certain common words such as:

abridge, abridgment	nine, ninth
acknowledge, acknowledgment	nurse, nursling
argue, argument	possible, possibly
awe, awful	probable, probably
double, doubly	true, truly
due, duly	twelve, twelfth
incredible, incredibly	whole, wholly
judge, judgment	wise, wisdom

d. Silent *e* is retained in words ending in *ce* or *ge* even when suffixes beginning with vowels (*-able* and *-ous*) are added. This is done for the sake of pronunciation: to prevent giving a hard sound (*k* or hard *g*) to the *c* or *g*:

marriage, marriageable	advantage, advantageous
notice, noticeable	courage, courageous
service, serviceable	outrage, outrageous

e. A few words ending in *ie* in which the *e* is silent change *ie* to *y* before adding *ing*. Presumably this change occurs to prevent two *i*'s from coming together:

die, dying	tie, tying (or tieing)
lie, lying	vie, vying

4. Inserted *k*.

The letter *k* is usually added to words ending in *c* before a suffix beginning with *e, i,* or *y*. This is done in order to prevent mispronunciation: note the different pronunciations, for example, of *picnicking* and *icing*. Only a few common words are involved in this rule, but they are frequently misspelled:

colic, colicky

frolic, frolicked, frolicking

mimic, mimicked, mimicking

panic, panicky

picnic, picnicked, picnicker

politic, politicking

shellac, shellacked, shellacking

traffic, trafficked, trafficking

This rule must be applied carefully. Note, for examples, the words *frolicsome* and *mimicry*. Without adding a *k*, each *c* remains hard.

5. Doubling final consonant.

The rule for doubling final consonants is somewhat complicated, but mastering it and its parts will prevent many common misspellings. Despite its complexity, it is one of the most useful rules for spelling.

a. Words of one syllable and those of more than one accented on the last syllable, when ending in a single consonant (except *x*) preceded by a single vowel, double the consonant before a suffix beginning with a vowel.

This rule is fairly detailed, but it will repay careful study. It is especially helpful in forming the past tense, past participle, and present participle of many frequently used verbs. It is also helpful in forming the comparative and superlative degrees of adjectives. Here is a list of only a few of the thousands of words to which this principle applies:

> acquit, acquitted, acquitting, acquittal
> admit, admitted, admitting, admittance
> begin, beginning, beginner
> clan, clannish
> control, controlled, controller
> drop, dropped, dropping
> equip, equipped, equipping
> forget, forgetting, forgettable, unforgettable
> man, mannish
> occur, occurred, occurring, occurrence

overlap, overlapped, overlapping
plan, planned, planning
prefer, preferred, preferring
red, redder, reddest, redden
refer, referred, referring
run, running, runner
swim, swimming, swimmer
tax, taxes
tin, tinny
transfer, transferred, transferring

b. If the accent is shifted to an earlier syllable when the ending is added, do not double the final consonant:

confer, conferring, but conference
defer, deferring, but deference
infer, inferring, but inference
prefer, preferring, but preference

c. Cautions and exceptions:

1) Derivatives from basic words that change pronunciation from a long to short vowel follow the doubling rule:

write, writing, but written
bite, biting, but bitten
inflame, inflamed, but inflammable

2) Words ending in a final consonant preceded by *two* vowels do not double the final consonant:

appear, appeared, appearing, appearance
need, needed, needing, needy
train, trained, training, trainee

3) Words ending in *two* consonants do not double the final consonant:

bend, bending (not bendding)
turn, turned (not turnned)
insist, insisted (not insistted)

4) Words not accented on the final syllable do not ordinarily double the final consonant:

> happen, happened, happening
> murmur, murmured, murmuring
> benefit, benefited (but fit, fitted)

A helpful word in fixing this principle in your mind is *combat*. It may be pronounced with the accent on either syllable, but note the spelling:

combat′	combatted	combatting
com′bat	combated	combating

5) Like all spelling rules, this one for doubling has many exceptions or apparent exceptions. Rather than try to apply the rule slavishly you would gain by learning the following through some other approach suggested in this book:

cancellation	gaseous	overstepping
chagrined	handicapped	questionnaire
chancellor	humbugged	tranquillity
crystallize	legionnaire	transferable
excellence	metallurgy	transference
excellent	outfitter	zigzagged

6. The "one-plus-one" rule

When a prefix ends in the same letter with which the main part of the word begins, be sure that both letters are included.

When the main part of a word ends in the same letter with which a suffix begins, be sure that both letters are included.

When two words are combined, the first ending with the same letter with which the second begins, be sure that both letters are included.

Some spelling difficulties caused by prefixes and suffixes have been discussed in Chapter 6. The rule just stated in three parts is both supplementary and complementary to that discussion. It will take care of a larger number of often misspelled words such as:

accidentally	brownness	cruelly
bathhouse	cleanness	dissatisfied
bookkeeping	coolly	dissimilar

drunkenness	occasionally	suddenness
glowworm	overrated	transshipment
illiterate	override	underrate
interrelation	overrun	unnecessary
irresponsible	really	unneeded
meanness	roommate	unnoticed
misspelling	soulless	withholding

The only important exception to this rule is *eighteen* which, of course, is not spelled *eightteen*. Also, keep in mind that the same three consonants are never written solidly together: *cross-stitch*, not *crossstitch*; *still-life*, not *stilllife*. See the discussion of the hyphen (compound words) on page 424.

12—Spell Carefully

This is a short chapter, but its brevity bears no relationship to its importance in spelling correctly. Actually, this chapter discusses the cause of at least half of the spelling mistakes made; for this reason it is probably the most important chapter in this book.

When writing, you concentrate on what you are trying to say and not on such matters as grammar, punctuation, and spelling. This concentration is both proper and understandable. But in your absorption you are quite likely to make errors of various sorts, including some in spelling, which result from haste or carelessness, not ignorance. When you discover a mistake of this kind, or it is pointed out to you, you may reply "Oh, I know better. I just wasn't watching," or "thinking" or "being careful" or whatever excuse you choose to make.

Unfortunately, a mistake in spelling is a mistake until corrected. Your reader will not know, or care, what caused it. The office manager who received a letter from one of his staff recently inducted into the U.S. Army was delighted to hear from him but was more annoyed than puzzled to read: "It was the *frist* time we had to march ten miles and I nearly *collasped*." Certainly the young soldier knew better; he intended to write *first* and *collapsed* but, through haste, carelessness, or failure to proofread, the mistakes went through.

Isn't it fair to suggest that since so many English words really are difficult to spell, we should be careful with those we actually know? And yet it is the simple, easy words which nearly everyone *can* spell which cause over half the errors commonly made. Listed below are twenty words which the author has repeatedly found misspelled in letters, reports, and student papers. They are so easy that you are likely to look at them scornfully and say "I would never misspell any one of them." The fact is that you probably do misspell some of these words, on occasion, or other words just as simple:

443

a lot, *not* alot
all right, *not* alright
Britain, *not* Britian
curl, *not* crul
doesn't, *not* does'nt
forty, *not* fourty
high school, *not* highschool
in fact, *not* infact
in spite, *not* inspite
ninety, *not* ninty

piano, *not* panio
radio, *not* raido
research, *not* reaserch
religion, *not* regilion
surprise, *not* supprise
third, *not* thrid
thirty, *not* thrity
thoroughly, *not* throughly
whether, *not* wheather
wouldn't, *not* would'nt

Errors of this sort are easy to make. Our pen or pencil slips; a finger hits the wrong key; our minds wander. Even excellent spellers often repeatedly make such silly mistakes. What's the remedy?

Well, merely glancing over or even rereading what you've written is not likely to uncover all such errors. When we read we usually see only the outlines, or shells, of words. Only poor readers need to see individual letters as such; most of us comprehend words and even groups of words at a glance. As our eyes move along a line we neither see nor recognize individual letters and this, of course, is as it should be.

But have you ever noticed how much easier it is for you to detect spelling errors in someone else's writing than in your own? This may be due to the fact that we are looking for mistakes. Or it may be that we look more carefully at the writing of someone else than at our own because we are unfamiliar with it, are not previously aware of context, and have to pay closer attention in order to comprehend.

Whatever the reason for closer scrutiny, we narrow the range of our vision and thereby pick up mistakes hitherto unnoticed. In short, we detect careless errors in spelling not by reading but by *proofreading*.

It is indeed naïve for any of us to think that we can write rapidly without misspelling some words, even though we are good spellers. Only careful proofreading will uncover spelling errors in our own writing or, indeed, in anyone else's.

This kind of reading requires that we see words and phrases not as such but that we actually see every letter they contain. When each letter stands out distinctly, it is simple to detect errors in spelling.

This triangle will show you how wide your vision (your sight spread) is. Look at the top of the triangle and then down. How far down can you go and still identify each letter in each line with a *single* glance? Your central vision is as wide as the line above the one where you cannot identify each letter *without moving your eyes at all:*

<pre>
                a
              a r
            a r d
          a r d c
        a r d c f
      a r d c f g
    a r d c f g x
  a r d c f g x y
a r d c f g x y z
a r d c f g x y z p
a r d c f g x y z p w
</pre>

People differ in their range of vision as they do in nearly everything else. But most people have difficulty in identifying more than six letters at a single glance. Some have a span of vision embracing only three or four letters. Whatever your span, you should not try to exceed it when you are carefully checking for spelling errors. If you do, you are reading—perhaps with excellent understanding —but you are not *proofreading*. And only proofreading will enable you to eliminate spelling errors due not to ignorance or stupidity but to carelessness.

Here is a list of forty frequently misspelled words. Some are spelled correctly here; some are not. In which of them can you identify each letter at a single glance? Which require you to move your eyes even if only slightly?

1. acquaint
2. against
3. all right
4. amount
5. apear
6. arise
7. around
8. basas
9. begining
10. before

11. careless
12. clothes
13. comming
14. considerable
15. decide
16. extremely
17. field
18. finishing
19. likelyhood
20. lonely
21. mere
22. noblity
23. noticeable
24. occupying
25. opportunity
26. optomistic
27. pamplet
28. perseverance
29. preferable
30. primative
31. process
32. pursue
33. recomendation
34. representative
35. restaurant
36. sandwitch
37. siege
38. twelfth
39. unmanageable
40. yield

Eleven of these words are misspelled. Did your proofreading catch them all? Check your findings: the following contain errors— 5, 8, 9, 13, 19, 22, 26, 27, 30, 33, 36.

Keep in mind that at least 50 per cent of all errors come from omitting letters or transposing or adding them, writing two words as one or vice versa, and other similar acts of carelessness. Check and recheck, read, and reread your writing until you have eliminated at least all the careless mistakes which everyone makes. There will still be errors enough of other kinds to keep us humble or angry.

13—Use Memory Devices

Suppose that someone suddenly asks you, "How many days in March?" You may be able to answer instantly, but if you are like most of us you will come up with the answer, "31," only after you have run through your head the familiar lines beginning, "Thirty days hath September . . ." If so, what you have done is to use a device to aid memory.

One special kind of memory device has the rather imposing name of *mnemonics*. The word is pronounced *nee-MON-iks* and comes from a Greek word meaning "to remember." (Mnemosyne was the goddess of memory in Grecian mythology.) A mnemonic is a special aid to memory, a memory trick based on what psychologists refer to as "association of ideas," remembering something by associating it with something else. You may have been using mnemonics most of your life. The term applies to a very basic characteristic of the human mind.

For example, the author's physician used to confuse his home, office, and hospital telephone numbers. He could remember the exchanges all right, but frequently mixed up the three sets of four numbers which followed, sometimes with unfortunate results. Now he has no difficulty: his home number he associates with eating and the numbers 1-8-4-7 leap to mind as part of "Rogers 1847 Silverware." His office number represents the place where he *battles* the daily grind and he thinks of the date of the Battle of Hastings, "1066." The hospital is a place where many find peace and relief from pain; the doctor associates this idea with "1945," the end of World War II. His set of mnemonics has licked the problem for him. When the telephone company assigns different numbers he will probably invent other memory aids. In our own lives each of us quite likely uses many similar associations of ideas, however different they may be in details from those of the physician just mentioned.

Mnemonics *can* be used to improve spelling. The system will help some more than others and may not help some people at all. The entire system of association of ideas has been criticized because, of course, you can place a greater burden on your mind with elaborate mnemonics than is involved in the original item to be remembered. In addition, a memory aid that works for you may be useless to me, and vice versa. But a set of mental associations has proved useful to some people for spelling certain words, and a system of mnemonics is one legitimate approach to better spelling. The system is the main trade trick of memory experts for whom it works with astounding results.

As other chapters in this book try to show, the spelling of most words can be learned by improving visual or motor images and by spelling rules. But for each of us there probably is a small number of words the spelling of which is always troublesome. They fit no pattern; their spelling makes little or no sense. Learning them is a matter of sheer memory. For such words, an association of ideas may help. At least it will be more profitable than mouthing the hard words repeatedly or writing them over and over until they seem formless or grotesque.

Any mnemonic is a sort of crutch, something we use until we can automatically spell a given word without even thinking. But so is a rule a crutch, and, in a different sense, a dictionary is, too. In time, we can throw away our spelling crutches except on rare occasions; until then we can use them to avoid staggering and falling.

A mnemonic will be most helpful when you contrive it from some happening, or base it upon some person, meaningful in your life. That is, you must invent, or use, only mnemonics that have a *personal* association of ideas. Some of the mnemonics suggested below will help you; others will seem meaningless or downright silly. Some words which trouble you will not even be covered. You can then try devising mnemonics of your own for your particular spelling demons.

As was suggested in Chapter 5, a clue about the etymology or origin of a word will sometimes provide a mnemonic. Sometimes exaggerated pronunciation will form the association, the bond of relationship between word and spelling. Occasionally, breaking the word into parts will help. Sometimes a play on words will give a useful memory device. As you read the mnemonics below, you will note these and various other methods used in **manufacturing** them. On occasion you will see that more than one method is used to phrase a mnemonic for the same word. Adapt for your use the most helpful one.

If none of these mnemonics proves helpful, you will at least have suggestions for "rolling your own." If another approach to correct spelling better suits your learning abilities, then skip what follows. At any rate, these memory clues have helped some people to spell correctly the words listed:

all right—Two words. Associate with *all correct* or *all wrong.*

anoint—Use *an oil* to *anoint* him (each *n* appears alone).

argument—I lost an *e* in that *argument.*

balloon—Remember the *ball* in *ball*oon.

battalion—This comes from *battle*; it has the same double *t* and single *l.*

believe—You can't bel*ieve* a *lie.*

business—Busi*ness* is no *sin.*

calendar—The *D.A.R.* will meet soon.

capitol—A capit*ol* has a d*ome* (assoc. ate *o*).

cemetery—1. There is *ease* (*e*'s) in the c*e*met*e*ry.
　　　　　2. A place we get to with *ease* (*e*'s).

compliment—A compliment is what *I* like to get.

conscience—con + science.

corps—Don't kill a live body of men with an *e* (corpse).

definite—Def*inite* comes from *finite.*

dependable—An *able* worker is depend*able.*

descendant—A descend*ant* has an *an*cestor.

desert—The Sahara (one *s*).

dessert—Strawberry *s*undae (two *s*'s).

dilemma—In a dil*emma* was *Emma.*

disappoint—dis + appoint.

dormitory—The French word for sleep is *dormir.*

ecstasy—There is **no** "*x*" in ecstasy.

embarrassed—1. Double *r*, double *s*, double trouble.
　　　　　　　2. *R*obert and *R*ose were *s*hop *s*tewards.

February—**Feb*r*uary** makes one say "*Br!*"

genealogy—*Al* is interested in gene*al*ogy.

grammar—1. Accent the trouble spot: gramm*A*r.
　　　　　2. Don't *mar* your writing with bad gram*mar.*
　　　　　3. Write g—r—a—m: then start back: m—a—r.

hear—I *hear* with my *ear*.

indispensable—1. *Able* people are indispens*able*.

          2. This word refers to a thing one is not *able* to *dispense* with.

          3. *Sable* is indispens*able* to some women.

infinite—In*finite* comes from *finite*.

inoculate—*Inoculate* means to *in*ject.

irresistible—1. *I* am *i*rresist*i*ble to the opposite sex.

        2. Lipstick is *i*rresist*i*ble.

laboratory—People *labor* in a *labor*atory.

literature—It was an *era* of good lit*era*ture.

medicine—Associated with *medicinal*.

occasion—1. An *oc*casion *oc*curs.

        2. Don't be an *ass* on this occa*s*ion (one *s*).

occurrence—An occu*rr*ence may be a cu*rr*ent event.

outrageous—The out*rage*ous idea put me in a *rage*.

parallel—*All* lines are par*all*el.

piece—Have a *pie*ce of *pie*.

potatoes—Pota*toes* have eyes and *toes*.

preparation—1. From the base word prep*Are*.

         2. This comes from *prae* + *parare* (to make ready).

principal—A princip*al* rule is a m*a*in rule.

principle—A princip*le* is just a ru*le*.

privilege—Some special pri*vile*ges are *vile*.

professor—The abbreviation is *prof* (one *f*).

pronunciation—The *nun* knew pro*nun*ciation.

pursuit—A pickpocket took my *purs*e.

recommend—re + commend.

relative—*Relate*ive comes from *relate*.

repetition—Associate with "repeat."

resistance—Increase resis*tan*ce with *tan*.

ridiculous—Associate with "*ridicule*."

seize—Seize him by the *ear*. (*e* before *i*).

separate—1. Sep*ar*ate means "*a*part."

        2. Accent the trouble spot: sep*A*rate.

        3. There is a *rat* in sepa*rat*e.

sergeant—Think of serge + ant.

siege—An army *si*ts before a city (*i* before *e*).

significant—"Sign if I cant" (can't).

stationary—This word means "standing."

stationery—This is used for writing letters.

superintendent—A superintendent collects r*ent*.

supersede—1. Both first and last syllables begin with *s*.

        2. The word comes from Latin *sedeo*, "to sit."

surprise—That was *surely* a *surprise*.

temperature—She lost her *temper at* the heat.

together—to + get + her.

tragedy—1. Every *age* has its tr*age*dy.

      2. Old *age* may be a tr*age*dy.

tranquillity—Associate with *quill* (pens used in olden days).

vaccine—Vaccine is measured in cubic centimeters (*cc's*).

villain—The villain likes his *villa in* the country.

Wednesday—This word means "Woden's day."

14—Listing Misspelled Words

This chapter, the one with which many books on spelling begin, discusses an important phase of spelling study. It has been placed later for several reasons.

One reason is that learning to spell is an individual, highly personal matter. As we have discovered, a single approach to correct spelling will work for one person and not for another. Also, the words whose spelling gives you trouble may not be the words which bother me or any of your friends and acquaintances. Perhaps it would be more precise to say that, altnough certain words cause trouble for a majority of people, any list of commonly misspelled words will contain some that give you no difficulty and omit others that do. The very best list of words for you to study is the one you prepare yourself to meet your own needs and shortcomings.

There's a lot of waste in any spelling list, including the list of 860 words which follows. It is simple to prepare a list of "spelling demons" and assert that these are the "most frequently misspelled" words in the language. In a sense, this statement would be correct, but it fails to recognize that, although these words are likely to be misspelled when used, they aren't used very often. Learning to spell a long list of difficult words is about as silly as trying to swallow a dictionary or an encyclopedia. You use a dictionary when you need to tap its resources, just as you turn a faucet to get water from a reservoir. You consult a list of misspelled words only when you have a definite need.

Another reason for deferring this chapter to the end is that by now you should have a sound basis for considering its contents. It doesn't help to try to memorize a list of miscellaneous words. But with what you have learned about various attacks on the spelling problem you can now *study* words in a list and *apply* to them principles you have learned.

Furthermore, you will be able to ignore words which you can already spell "without thinking" and will be alert to add words which give you trouble but which don't appear.

Once again, this chapter should serve primarily to start you on a list of your personal spelling demons. These words will be ones you need to learn to spell because you use them. And they may be simple or difficult; short or long; everyday words or ones which, although rare to others, are a part of your working vocabulary. The only sound basis for any list of misspelled words is its *use* value.

Regardless of whether we are housewives, businessmen, clerks, truckdrivers, or physicians, we all use certain basic words many scores of times more often than any others in the language. Any spelling list should start with them, but, fortunately, they are never (or hardly ever) misspelled by anyone who can write at all. The most frequently used words in the English language are *and, the, to, you, your, in, for, of, we, is, I,* and *its.* These give no trouble except for some occasional confusion between *your* and *you're* and *its* and *it's.*

Once past this basic list, however, selecting frequently used words becomes more difficult. *Table* is an everyday word, but a baker might use *bread* and a physician might use *temperature* more often. It is reassuring to know, however, that it is neither the most simple and common words nor the ones primarily used in a trade, profession, or industry that provide major spelling difficulty. The words in between are the troublemakers. And here we do have some authoritative studies of frequency word use and frequency misspellings. The short list which follows is based upon one of these major studies.

Of the five hundred words occurring most frequently in our speech and writing only twenty ever cause anyone except very poor spellers any trouble whatever. Probably few, if any, of them bother you. Here is the list:

across	dollar	possible	suppose
almost	don't	quite	their
believe	friend	receive	through
brought	government	should	whether
business	laugh	supply	your

Keep in mind that these twenty words, along with 480 even more easily spelled ones, are certain to appear in your speech and writing many times as often as all other words in the language. The best approach of all to correct spelling is to *master* the simple, everyday words that you use over and over. Doing so will solve the greater part of your spelling problem.

According to another authoritative estimate, previously quoted, a basic list of only one thousand words appears in 90 per cent of all writing. All of the thousand which involve spelling problems are included in the long list which follows. About 75 per cent of the words which follow are among the words most often misspelled regardless of frequency use. The other 25 per cent consists of words which the author has found repeatedly misspelled in business offices, in manuscripts submitted for magazine or book publication, and in college classrooms.

As suggested, many of the words you will have already mastered; you must supplement the list in accordance with your own needs. But remember to go slowly. Don't try to memorize the list. Thoroughly mastering five words a day is more productive than superficially learning one hundred.

And as you start studying the list of words, apply one or more of the varied approaches suggested in previous chapters. Examining these words without following one or several of the planned attacks discussed in this book will merely waste your time and result in further and prolonged frustration.

Consult your dictionary frequently. You must know the meaning of each of the words you are studying; otherwise, in your own writing you may correctly spell a perfectly good word but one which does not have the meaning you intended. Also, to keep this list within reasonable limits, not all forms of every word are shown; therefore, use your dictionary or one of the other approaches developed in previous chapters as a guide to word-building.

List of 860 Words Often Misspelled *

1. absence
2. absolutely
3. academic
4. accept
5. access

6. accessible
7. accident (accidentally)
8. accommodate (accommodations)
9. accompanying
10. accomplishment

11. according
12. accumulation
13. accurate
14. accuse
15. accustomed

16. ache
17. achievement
18. acknowledge (acknowledgment)
19. acquaint (acquaintance)
20. across

21. activities
22. actual (actually)
23. address
24. adequate
25. adjacent

26. admiration
27. adolescent
28. advantage
29. advantageous
30. advertisement

31. advice
32. advisable
33. advise
34. adviser
35. affect

36. afraid
37. aggravate
38. aggressive
39. aisle
40. allot (allotting)

* The list given has been checked against some of the major studies of frequency word use and frequency misspelling of the last forty years, as follows:

William Niclaus Andersen, "Determination of a Spelling Vocabulary Based upon Written Correspondence," *University of Iowa Studies in Education*, II, No. 1 (1917).

Alfred Farrell, "Spelling as a College Subject," *Journal of Education*, CXXII (January, 1939), 20, 21.

Arthur I. Gates, *Spelling Difficulties in 3876 Words* (New York: Bureau of Publications, Teachers College, Columbia University, 1937).

John G. Gilmartin, *Gilmartin's Word Study*, rev. ed. (New York: Prentice-Hall, 1936).

Harry V. Masters, "A Study of Spelling Errors," *University of Iowa Studies in Education*, IV, No. 4 (1927–1929).

Thomas Clark Pollock, "Spelling Report," *College English*, XVI (November, 1954), 102–109.

Edward L. Thorndike and Irving Lorge, *The Teacher's Word Book of 30,000 Words* (New York: Bureau of Publications, Teachers College, Columbia University, 1944).

41. allotment
42. allowance
43. all right
44. almost
45. alphabet

46. already
47. altar
48. alter
49. although
50. all together

51. altogether
52. amateur
53. ambitious
54. American
55. among

56. amount
57. analysis
58. analyze
59. announcement
60. annual

61. answer
62. antecedent
63. anticipation
64. antidote
65. antiseptic

66. anxiety
67. apartment
68. apology
69. apparatus
70. apparently

71. appearance
72. appendicitis
73. applied
74. appointment
75. appreciation

76. approach
77. appropriate
78. approval
79. approximately
80. arctic

81. argue (arguing)
82. argument
83. aroused
84. arrangement
85. article

86. ascend
87. assistance
88. association
89. athletic
90. attack

91. attendance
92. attitude
93. attractiveness
94. audience
95. author

96. authority
97. autobiography
98. autumn
99. auxiliary
100. available

101. awkward
102. bachelor
103. balloon
104. bargain
105. basically

106. basis
107. beautiful
108. beauty
109. becoming
110. beggar

111. beginning
112. behavior
113. believing
114. beneficial
115. benefit (benefited)

116. boundary
117. breath
118. breathe
119. Britain
120. business

121. cafeteria
122. calendar
123. campaign
124. candidate
125. capital

126. career
127. careless
128. carrying
129. category
130. celebrate

131. cemetery
132. century
133. certain
134. challenge
135. changeable

136. characteristic
137. chauffeur
138. cheerfulness
139. chiefly
140. chocolate

141. choose
142. chose
143. chosen
144. circumstance
145. clothes

146. coincidence
147. column
148. comfortably
149. commercial
150. commission

151. committee
152. communication
153. community
154. companies
155. comparatively

156. comparison
157. compatible
158. compel (compelled)
159. competence
160. competition

161. completely
162. complexion
163. compliment
164. composition
165. comprehension

166. concede
167. conceivable
168. conceive
169. concentrated
170. concern

171. condemn
172. confidence
173. congratulations
174. connoisseur
175. conscience

176. conscientious
177. conscious
178. consensus
179. consequently
180. considerable

181. consistent
182. consolation
183. contemporary
184. contempt (contemptuous)
185. continually

186. continuous
187. contribution
188. controlled
189. controversy
190. convenience

191. correspondence
192. councilor
193. counselor
194. countries
195. courageous

196. courtesy
197. criticism
198. criticize
199. cruel
200. curiosity

201. curriculum
202. customary
203. customer
204. cylinder
205. dangerous

206. dealt
207. deceive
208. decidedly
209. decision
210. defenseless

211. deficiency
212. deficient
213. definite (definitely)
214. definition
215. delinquent

216. democracy
217. demonstrated
218. dependent
219. depression
220. descendant

221. descent
222. describe (description)
223. desert
224. despair
225. desperate

226. desperation
227. dessert
228. destruction
229. determination
230. detriment

231. devices
232. difference
233. difficulty
234. dilemma
235. diminish

236. dining room
237. diphtheria
238. disappear
239. disappoint
240. disastrous

241. disciple
242. discipline
243. discoveries
244. discrimination
245. discuss

246. disease
247. dissatisfied
248. dissipate
249. distinguished
250. divide

251. divine
252. doctor
253. doesn't
254. dominant
255. dormitories

256. drunkenness
257. ecstasy
258. edition
259. education
260. effect

261. efficiency
262. efficient
263. eighth
264. eighty
265. either

266. elementary
267. eligible
268. eliminate
269. eloquently
270. embarrass

271. emergency
272. emigrate
273. eminent
274. emperor
275. emphasize

276. emptiness
277. encouragement
278. enemies
279. English
280. enormous

281. enough
282. enterprise
283. entertainment
284. enthusiasm
285. entirely

286. entrance
287. environment
288. equally
289. equipment
290. equipped

291. equivalent
292. escape
293. especially
294. essential
295. eventually

296. everybody
297. evidently
298. exaggerating
299. exceed
300. excellent

301. except
302. exceptionally
303. excess
304. excitable
305. exercise

306. exhausted
307. exhibit
308. exhilarate
309. existence
310. expectation

311. expenses
312. experience
313. experiment
314. explanation
315. extravagant

316. facilities
317. faithfulness
318. fallacy
319. familiar
320. families

321. fantasy
322. fascinating
323. favorite
324. feasible
325. February

326. fictitious
327. finally
328. financially
329. financier
330. foreign

331. foreword
332. formally
333. formerly
334. forty
335. forward

336. foundation
337. fourteen
338. fourth
339. fraternity
340. friendliness

341. fulfill
342. fundamental
343. funeral
344. furniture
345. further

346. gaiety
347. gauge
348. genius
349. gentleman
350. genuine

351. glorious
352. goggles
353. gorgeous
354. government
355. governor

356. grammar
357. grandeur
358. grievous
359. guarantee
360. guidance

361. handicapped
362. handkerchief
363. happening
364. happiness
365. harass

366. haughtiness
367. healthy
368. hear
369. heartily
370. heavier

371. height
372. helpful
373. here
374. heroes
375. heroines

376. hindrance
377. hopelessness
378. hoping
379. hospitality
380. huge

381. humiliate
382. humorous
383. hungry
384. hurriedly
385. hygiene

386. hypocrisy
387. hypocrite
388. ignorance
389. imaginary
390. imagine

391. immediately
392. immense
393. immigrant
394. impassable
395. important

396. impossible
397. inadequate
398. inauguration
399. incidentally
400. increase

401. incredible
402. indefinitely
403. independent
404. indictment
405. indispensable

406. individual
407. industrial
408. influence
409. influential
410. ingenious

411. initiative
412. innocence
413. insistence
414. installation
415. instructor

416. instrument
417. intellectual
418. intelligent
419. interest (interesting)
420. interference

421. interpretation
422. interruption
423. intolerance
424. introductory
425. invariable

426. involved
427. irrelevant
428. irresistible
429. irritable
430. island

431. its
432. it's
433. January
434. jealousy
435. jewelry

436. kindergarten
437. knowledge
438. labeled
439. laboratory
440. laboriously

441. language
442. leisurely
443. lengthening
444. libraries
445. license

446. lieutenant
447. lightening
448. lightning
449. likelihood
450. literature

451. liveliest
452. livelihood
453. liveliness
454. loneliness
455. lose (losing)

456. lovable
457. loyalty
458. luxuries
459. magazine
460. magnificent

461. maintenance
462. management
463. managing
464. maneuver
465. manufacturing

466. marriage
467. marriageable
468. material
469. mathematics
470. meanness

471. meant
472. mechanics
473. medicine
474. mentality
475. merchandise

476. metropolitan
477. millionaire
478. miniature
479. miscellaneous
480. mischief

481. mischievous
482. misspelled
483. modified
484. monotonous
485. month

486. moral
487. morale
488. mosquitoes
489. multiplication
490. muscle

491. musician
492. mysterious
493. narrative
494. nationalities
495. naturally

496. necessary
497. negative
498. Negro
499. Negroes
500. neighbor

501. neither
502. Niagara
503. niece
504. nineteen
505. ninety

506. ninth
507. noticeable
508. noticing
509. numerous
510. obstacle

511. occasion (occasionally)
512. occupying
513. occur (occurred)
514. occurrence
515. occurring

516. o'clock
517. omission
518. omit
519. omitted
520. operate

521. operation
522. opinion
523. opponent
524. opportunities
525. oppose

526. optimism
527. optimistic
528. organization
529. origin
530. originally

531. overwhelming
532. paid
533. pamphlet
534. pandemonium
535. pantomime

536. parallel
537. paralyze
538. participated
539. particularly
540. partner

541. passed
542. past
543. pastime
544. peace
545. peaceable

546. peculiarities
547. penniless
548. perceive
549. performance
550. permanent

551. permissible
552. permit
553. perseverance
554. persistent
555. personal

556. personnel
557. perspiration
558. persuade
559. pertain
560. phase

561. phenomenon
562. Philippines
563. philosophy
564. physical
565. physician

566. picnicking
567. piece
568. planned
569. planning
570. plausible

571. playwright
572. pleasant
573. politician
574. portrayed
575. possessions

576. possibility
577. possible
578. poverty
579. practically
580. prairie

581. precedent
582. preceding
583. predominant
584. prefer
585. preferable

586. preference
587. preferred
588. prejudice
589. preparation
590. prepare

591. prescription
592. presence
593. prevalence
594. previous
595. primitive

596. principal
597. principle
598. privilege
599. probably
600. procedure

601. proceed
602. process
603. professor
604. prominent
605. pronounce

606. pronunciation
607. propaganda
608. proprietor
609. provisions
610. psychology

611. punctuation
612. pursue
613. qualities
614. quantity
615. quarter

616. questionnaire
617. quiet
618. realize
619. really
620. receipt

621. receivable
622. receive
623. recognition
624. recognize
625. recollection

626. recommend
   (recommendation)
627. reference
628. referred
629. regard
630. refrigerator

631. regrettable
632. relative
633. relevant
634. relieve
635. religion

636. religious
637. remember
638. remembrance
639. reminisce
640. renowned

641. repentance
642. repetition
643. representative
644. requirements
645. research

646. resources
647. response
648. responsibility
649. restaurant
650. reverend

651. reverent
652. reviewing
653. rhythm
654. ridicule
655. ridiculous

656. righteous
657. rivalry
658. roommate
659. sacrifice
660. safety

661. sandwich
662. satirical
663. satisfaction
664. satisfied
665. Saturday

666. saucer
667. sausage
668. scarcity
669. scene
670. scenery

671. schedule
672. scheme
673. scholarship
674. scientific
675. secretary

676. seize
677. selection
678. semester
679. sentence
680. separate

681. seriousness
682. several
683. severely
684. shepherd
685. shining

686. shoulder
687. shriek
688. siege
689. significance
690. similar

691. sincerely
692. situation
693. solution
694. sophomore
695. sorrowful

696. source
697. sovereignty
698. specialization
699. specifically
700. specimen

701. spectacle
702. speech
703. sponsor
704. statement
705. stationary

706. stationery
707. stenographer
708. stopping
709. straighten
710. strength

711. strenuous
712. stubborn
713. studied
714. studying
715. subscription

716. substantiate
717. substitute
718. subtle
719. succeeding
720. successful

721. suddenness
722. sufficient
723. summarize
724. summary
725. superintendent

726. supersede
727. superstitious
728. supervisor
729. suppose
730. suppress

731. surprise
732. surrounded
733. susceptible
734. suspense
735. suspicious

736. swimming
737. syllable
738. symbol
739. symmetrical
740. synonymous

741. system
742. tactfulness
743. technical
744. technique
745. temperament

746. temperate
747. temperature
748. temporarily
749. tenant
750. tendency

751. tenement
752. territory
753. than
754. their
755. then

756. theories
757. therefore
758. they're
759. thirtieth
760. thirty

761. thoroughly
762. thought
763. thousand
764. to
765. together

766. tomorrow
767. too
768. tradition
769. tragedy
770. transferred

771. transportation
772. tremendous
773. trespass
774. try (tried)
775. truly

776. Tuesday
777. twelfth
778. twentieth
779. two
780. typical

781. tyranny
782. unanimous
783. unbelievable
784. uncivilized
785. unconscious

786. uncontrollable
787. undesirable
788. undoubtedly
789. uneasiness
790. unforgettable

791. universities
792. unmanageable
793. unnecessary
794. until
795. unusual

796. usage
797. useful
798. usual
799. usually
800. vacuum

801. valleys
802. valuable
803. varieties
804. various
805. vaudeville

806. vegetable
807. vengeance
808. ventilate
809. verbatim
810. vernacular

811. versatile
812. veteran
813. vicinity
814. victim
815. view

816. village
817. villain
818. villainous
819. vinegar
820. virtuous

821. visible
822. vitamin
823. volume
824. waive
825. wander

826. warranted
827. wave
828. wealthiest
829. weather
830. Wednesday

831. weird
832. whenever
833. where
834. wherever
835. whether

836. whole
837. wholesale
838. wholly
839. whose
840. wintry

841. withal
842. withholding
843. witnessed
844. wonder
845. wonderful

846. wrench
847. writing
848. written
849. yacht
850. Yankee

851. Yiddish
852. yield
853. your
854. you're
855. yourself

856. zealot
857. zenith
858. zero
859. zigzag
860. zinc

1 Insert *ei* or *ie* in the following:

ach_____ve	n_____ther
bel_____f	p_____ce
br_____f	perc_____ve
c_____ling	rec_____pt
conc_____t	rel_____ve
dec_____ve	rev_____w
for_____gn	sh_____ld
financ_____r	shr_____k
misch_____vous	v_____l
n_____ghbor	y_____ld

2. Insert *ei* or *ie* in the following:

cash_____r	rec_____ve
ch_____f	retr_____ve
f_____ld	s_____zure
fr_____ght	sh_____k
h_____nous	st_____n
h_____r	surv_____llance
h_____ght	th_____f
l_____sure	v_____n
p_____r	w_____ght
pr_____st	w_____rd

3. Add *-ed* and *-ing* to the following:

array	deny	marry
copy	destroy	pay
dally	empty	pity
delay	imply	pray

Adding -*ed* and -*ing* (*Cont'd*)

pry	reply	toy
rally	say	try
rely	stay	typify

4. Add -*ness* to each of the following:

bare	happy	pretty
busy	icy	shy
empty	lively	wry
	lovely	

5. *Study—studies—studied—studying.* Supply the same verb forms for each of the following:

bury	dignify	pity
carry	enjoy	pray
cry	envy	stay
	marry	

6. Add -*ing* and -*ment* to each of the following:

abridge	amuse	judge
acknowledge	atone	move
advise	argue	settle
	excite	

7. Add -*ed* and -*ing* to each of the following:

acquit	infer	tax
admit	occur	transfer
control	prefer	transmit
	refer	

8. The prefix *mis-* means "bad" or "wrong." It is found in many

words such as *mistake, misnomer, misadvise, misinformation, mis-pronunciation, misrepresent, misgauge, misadventure, misbelief,* etc. First, write as many words as you can recall beginning with each of the following prefixes. Then expand your lists by reference to a good dictionary:

ad-	inter-	pro-
de-	non-	sub-
hyper-	ob-	ultra-
	poly-	

9. By means of a suffix (*-ible* or *-able, -ly* or *-ally, -ence* or *-ance, -ion,* etc.) form an adjective, adverb, or noun from each of the following words. Example: *admire: admirable, admirably, admiration.* Not all these parts of speech can be formed from each word, but one or more can be:

accept	deduce	love
advertise	describe	notice
allow	detect	remark
	discern	

10. Add *-ed* and either *-able* or *-ible* to the following:

avail	dismiss	reverse
comprehend	excite	suggest
depend	like	value
	presume	

11. Add *-ally* or *-ly* to each of the following:

accident	incident	occasion
complete	incredible	physic
entire	intention	true
	lyric	

12. From many verbs nouns may be formed which end in *-ance,*

-ence; -ar, -er, -or; -ary, -ery. Example: *contribute, contributor.* Form a noun from each of the following words:

act	defer	prefer
adhere	defy	protect
beg	distill (distil)	provide
carry	lecture	repent
collect	lie	station
confer	occur	subsist
counsel		visit

13. Form plurals of each of the following:

apparatus	dwarf	poet laureate
area	dynamo	quota
billiards	elf	synopsis
bureau	hoof	tactics
bus	measles	thief
cross-examination	metropolis	torpedo

14. Some compounds are spelled as one word (*football*), some as hyphenated words (*four-dimensional*), some as two words (*reading desk*). Indicate the correct spelling of:

airtight	helterskelter	quietspoken
boobytrap	highschool	runin
campfire	inspite	schoolboy
chickenhearted	laborsaving	selfstarter
downstairs	offstage	sodawater
drawbridge	pitchdark	sunrise
hangeron		twentyfour

15. Supply the missing letter in each of the following:

ab_____ence	caf_____teria
absor_____tion	calend_____r
apol_____gy	cem_____tery
Ba_____tist	compar_____tive

Supplying missing letter (*Cont'd*)

disinfect_____nt	min_____ature
dorm_____tory	opt_____mistic
excell_____nt	sacr_____legious
exigen_____y	sep_____rate
han_____kerchief	sim_____lar
iden_____ity	temper_____ment

16. Supply the missing letter in each of the following:

appar_____nt	nes_____le
cors_____ge	priv_____lege
crim_____nal	p_____rsue
def_____nite	r_____diculous
friv_____lous	sacr_____fice
gramm_____r	su_____prise
ignor_____nt	tra_____edy
instruct_____r	tres_____le
irresist_____ble	vulg_____r
livel_____hood	We_____nesday

17. Some of the following words are correctly spelled, some incorrectly. Indicate which ones are which.

atheletic	height	perseverance
competition	mischieveous	reccomend
desireable	naturally	safty
discipline	obstacal	sulphur
dissappointed	occassion	suppress
embarassed	outragous	vengeance
environment	villain	

18. Which of the following are correctly spelled, which incorrectly?

alright	appelation	commited
analogous	changable	conscientious

Continue to indicate which of the following are correctly spelled, which incorrectly.

developement	paralel	scurrulous
ecstasy	pidgeon	symetrical
innoculate	questionaire	temperature
occasionally	renege	tendency
pantomime	rythmical	

19. Which of the following proper names are correctly spelled, which incorrectly?

Americian	Hawaian	Rockerfeller
Britian	Kruschev	Saturday
Brughel	Louisiana	Tennesee
Burma	Massachusetts	Tripali
Conneticut	Oragon	Uraguay
Edinburg	Phillipines	Wisconson
February		Worcestershire

20. Consult your dictionary for the preferred or variant spellings of:

analyze	esthetic	savior
armor	fulfil	sextet
canyon	instalment	sulphur
catalogue	judgment	theatre
center	medieval	tranquillity
defense	monologue	traveler
dialogue		vigor

21. The combining form *graph* appears in many English words. It comes from the Greek *graphos* (*graphein*, to write). Two examples are *telegraph*, "writing from a distance," and *monograph*, "writing on a single subject." Make a list of as many words as you can think of, or find in your dictionary, containing *graph* as a combining form.

22. The following is a list of everyday words with pronunciations as shown in reliable dictionaries. Spell each of them correctly:

Webster's New Collegiate Dictionary	The American College Dictionary	Webster's New World Dictionary
ă·pēl′	ə pēl′	ə-pēl′
bĭz′nĕs	bĭz′nĭs	biz′nis
drī	drī	drī
ĕk·sĕl′	ĭk sĕl′	ik-sel′
kăl′ĕn·dēr	kăl′ən dər	kal′ən-dēr
kōld	kōld	kōld
nĕs′ĕ·sĕr′ĭ	nĕs′ə sĕr′i	nes′ə-ser′i
ôr′ĕnj	ôr′ĭnj	ôr′ənj
prŏ·pōz′	prə pōz′	prə-pōz′
thûr′ȯ	thûr′ȯ	thûr′ō

23. Whether a good or bad speller, you will need to consult your dictionary frequently. You will lose time by not knowing the alphabet so thoroughly that you do not have to hesitate. Arrange the following words in the order in which they appear in a dictionary.

jump	radio
jean	read
jilt	refine
jerk	running
jiffy	risk
jeer	race
juvenile	round
jelly	rainfall
jeep	remain
join	red

24. Determine whether a study of the derivations of the following words will aid you in spelling them correctly:

absence	catercorner
assign	criticism
bilious	descend

emerald	pasteurize
foreign	possess
halitosis	research
instrument	ridiculous
judicial	shoulder
language	typical
mathematical	Wednesday

25. Using directions given in Exercise 21, list as many words as you can containing each of these combining forms:

electro-	phon-
forma-	-phone
para-	-ward

26. Correctly place apostrophes (only where needed) in the following:

> My mother-in-laws room
> My 5s are legible; yours look like ss.
> Hasnt he forgotten the troops uniforms?
> "Its theirs, not ours," Jack replied.
> He prefers Sophocles plays to Marxs tracts.
> King Edward VIIIs operation
> Thats somebody elses work, not hers.
> World War II (1939–45)
> Whos going to whose party tonight?
> You use too many *could bes* and *maybes*.

27. Which word in each of the following pairs of words is spelled correctly? Find on pages 433-442 the spelling rule which applies.

achieve *or* acheive	carries *or* carrys
unnamed *or* unamed	fortieth *or* fortyeth
replacable *or* replaceable	thief *or* theif
amusement *or* amusment	mimicking *or* mimicing
photostatted *or* photostated	guideance *or* guidance

28. Using suggestions given on pages 447-451, devise a mnemonic for each of the *ten* words which give you the greatest spelling difficulty. Don't strain, but also don't worry if a mnemonic is quite bizarre: it's for your use only.

29. As pointed out several times in this book, studying lists of words difficult to spell is not really helpful. First, the only useful lists are of words which trouble you yourself. Second, most lists of "demons" contain words which are rarely used and which would stop even excellent spellers.

Here is a list of seventy-five troublesome words, most or all of which you might use. Choose the correct (or preferred) spelling from the two columns. A score of sixty or more qualifies you as a superior speller.

1.	absence	abscence
2.	accidently	accidentally
3.	accomodate	accommodate
4.	acheive	achieve
5.	acknowledgment	acknowledgement
6.	acquaintance	aquaintance
7.	allotted	alloted
8.	analize	analyze
9.	anoint	annoint
10.	arguement	argument
11.	assistant	assisstant
12.	bankruptcy	bankrupcy
13.	basically	basicly
14.	benefited	benefitted
15.	changable	changeable
16.	commission	commision
17.	commitee	committee
18.	connoiseur	connoisseur
19.	conscientious	conscientous
20.	defenseless	defenceless
21.	dilettante	dilletante
22.	disappoint	disapoint
23.	disasterous	disastrous
24.	dissatisfied	disatisfied
25.	dissipate	disippate
26.	drunkenness	drunkeness
27.	embarrassment	embarassment
28.	encouragment	encouragement
29.	exhiliration	exhilaration
30.	familiar	familar

31. fascinating	facinating
32. Febuary	February
33. genealogy	geneology
34. goverment	government
35. harrass	harass
36. hypocrisy	hypocricy
37. incidently	incidentally
38. innoculate	inoculate
39. iridescent	irridescent
40. labortory	laboratory
41. leisurely	liesurely
42. loneliness	lonliness
43. neice	niece
44. nineth	ninth
45. noticeable	noticable
46. occurence	occurrence
47. optomistic	optimistic
48. pamphlet	pamplet
49. permissable	permissible
50. picnicking	picnicing
51. practicly	practically
52. preparation	preperation
53. pronunciation	pronounciation
54. puntuation	punctuation
55. recommend	reccommend
56. restaurant	restarant
57. scarsity	scarcity
58. seize	sieze
59. siege	seige
60. superstiton	superstition
61. supprised	surprised
62. temperament	temperment
63. tradegy	tragedy
64. truly	truely
65. tyrany	tyranny
66. ukelele	ukulele
67. unforgetable	unforgettable
68. unnecessary	unecessary
69. vacilate	vacillate
70. villianous	villainous

71. Wednesday   Wensday
72. weight   wieght
73. weird   wierd
74. wield   weild
75. yeild   yield

30. You are an above-average speller if you can score 75 or more on the following list of 100 words which range from "trouble makers" to outright "demons." Master them. Then try them on your friends—and your enemies.

1. academy
2. accessory
3. accumulate
4. acoustics
5. alimentary
6. aloha
7. anonymity
8. apparatus
9. attendant
10. avoirdupois
11. baccalaureate
12. bullion
13. buoy
14. bureaucracy
15. cantankerous
16. catechism
17. collaborate
18. consensus
19. corollary
20. dahlia
21. defendant
22. desiccated
23. dilapidated
24. disastrous
25. eleemosynary
26. emphatically
27. eulogy
28. exaggerate
29. exercise
30. facile
31. fascinate
32. frantically
33. fulfilled
34. garage
35. *Gesundheit*
36. gnome
37. haughty
38. hearse
39. homogeneous
40. impromptu
41. innuendo
42. irreducible
43. irrelevant
44. jeopardize
45. knapsack
46. labyrinth
47. larynx
48. licorice
49. liqueur
50. mediocre
51. millennium
52. moratorium
53. naphtha
54. negotiable
55. notarize
56. octogenarian
57. orchid
58. overrun

59. paralysis
60. perennial
61. pharmaceutical
62. phosphorus
63. phrenology
64. phylactery
65. poinsettia
66. precinct
67. pseudo
68. psychiatry
69. queue
70. quinine
71. rarefied
72. rehearsal
73. rendezvous
74. reservoir
75. rheumatic
76. saxophone
77. schedule
78. seismograph
79. separation

80. sieve
81. silhouette
82. spontaneity
83. surveillance
84. thermometer
85. tonsillitis
86. tranquil
87. turgid
88. ultimatum
89. umbrella
90. uterus
91. vice versa
92. vitamin
93. vulnerable
94. wharf
95. wiener
96. wrestle
97. xylophone
98. yeast
99. zinnia
100. zoological

Glossary: Terms Used in This Book

Any book on spelling must use expressions which may be unfamiliar to you, but which are closely tied up with the spelling problem. Below you will find brief definitions or explanations of several linguistic terms. Some of these are fully defined in the book itself; others are used or implied. When studying the book itself, refer to this glossary if you come across an expression which you do not fully understand. An effort has been made to include all terms likely to need clarification. If you are still in doubt, consult your dictionary.

Accent: Accent is the emphasis given to a letter or syllable or word when speaking it. This increased force results from stress, or pitch, or both. In dictionaries, marks are used to show the placing and kind of emphasis required. For example, in the word *envelop* the second syllable is accented: en vel'op. In *envelope*, the first syllable has primary stress, or accent: en' vel ope. See *Stress*, below.

Adjective: A not entirely satisfactory definition of this term is that it is a part of speech modifying a noun, pronoun, or other substantive. It modifies by describing, limiting, or in some other closely related way making meaning more nearly exact. An adjective may indicate quality or quantity, may identify or set limits. Therefore, adjectives are of three general kinds: descriptive (a *yellow* coat, a *hard* rock, a *smashed* fender); limiting (the *fifth* payment, her *latest* sweetheart, *many* dollars); proper (an *English* tweed, a *Carolina* peach). Most adjectives have endings which mark them as such: *-y* (hilly); *-ful* (hateful); *-al* (cordial); etc.

Adverb: An adverb modifies a verb, adjective, or other adverb by describing or limiting in order to make meaning clearer or more exact. An adverb usually indicates *how, when, where, why, how much, how often*. Adverbs are commonly, but not always, distinguished from adjectives by the suffix *-ly*: bad, badly, sure, surely. Some adverbs are distinguished from corresponding nouns by the suffixes -*wise* and -*ways*: sidewise, endways. An adverb sometimes may modify an entire statement: He was, *however,* not feeling well that day.

Base word: Any word, or part of a word which is a combining form, to which may be added prefixes, suffixes, etc. Thus we refer to *mortal* as the base word, or element, of *mortality* and *cede* as the base element of the word *accede.* See *Root word,* below.

Capitals: Any letters written or printed in a form larger than, and often different from, that of corresponding small letters: A,B,C; a,b,c. The use of capital letters (sometimes called upper-case letters as contrasted with small, or lower-case, letters) is discussed in Chapter 10.

Clause: A group of words which forms a sentence or a part of a sentence. A clause contains a subject (substantive) and a predicate (verb). "*John studied* and *I played the radio*" illustrates two separate and independent clauses. In the following sentence, the first group of italicized words is an independent clause, the second is dependent upon the first: "*I shall telephone you/when I arrive.*"

Compounds: Compound words are combinations of two or more words: *doorkeeper, inasmuch as.* The use of hyphens (which see) with compound words is discussed in Chapter 9.

Conjunction: A part of speech which serves as a linking or joining word to connect words or groups of words such as phrases and clauses: *and, but, for, because, since,* etc.

Consonant: A consonant is a speech sound produced by restricting or stopping the breath. Consonants may be contrasted with *vowels* (which see) since the latter involve sounds made with less friction and fuller resonance. The consonants *b, d, g, k, p,* and *t* are produced by stopping and releasing the air stream. The consonants *l, m, n,* and *r* are produced by stopping the air stream at one point while it escapes at another. In sounding the consonants *f, s, v,* and *z,* the air stream is forced through a loosely closed or narrow passage. In short, consonants are those letters (sounds) of the alphabet which are not vowels: *a, e, i, o, u.*

Diacritical mark: A mark added to a letter to indicate pronunciation by giving it a particular sound (phonetic) value or stress which distinguishes it from an unmarked letter of similar form.

Thus the sound we utter in starting the alphabet may be indicated as ā, as in the words *date* and *able*. The sound of *a* in *art* and *father* is represented by ä. Every dictionary worthy of the name devotes considerable space to its own system of diacritical marks, usually running a condensed list of them on the bottom of each righthand page and a detailed explanation inside the front or back cover or in pages at the front of the dictionary. Diacritical marks are essential to correct pronunciation and thus are important in learning to spell correctly. You should become thoroughly familiar with the marks used by your dictionary.

Etymology: The branch of linguistic study which deals with the origin and development of words. For further discussion see Chapter 5.

Grammar: The science which deals with words and their relationships to each other. Grammar is a descriptive statement of the way language works and includes a discussion of words, their use in phrases, clauses, and sentences, their tenses, cases, and other changes in form according to their relationship to each other.

Homograph: A word with the same spelling as another but with a different origin and meaning: a *bow* tie, to bend a *bow; row,* meaning a noisy dispute and a straight line; *fair,* meaning "beautiful" and also "a market"; *lead,* the metal and a word meaning "to conduct"; *air,* "atmosphere" and "a melody"; *pale,* an enclosure and "faintly colored." See Chapter 3 for further discussion.

Homonym: A word with the same pronunciation as another but with a different origin, meaning, and sometimes spelling: *hear, here; steal, steel; meat, meet; pale, pail.* For further discussion, see Chapter 3.

Hyphen: A mark used between the syllables of a divided word or the parts of a compound word. It is more a mark of spelling than of punctuation. See Chapter 9.

Long sound: A pronounced vowel or consonant which is held or sounded for a relatively long time. For example, the *a* in *ape* is long; it may be held for as long as your breath lasts. In dictionaries it is marked ā. Similarly, the *e* in *easy* is long; the *i* in *mile,* etc.

Morpheme: This is a rather learned word which applies to any word or part of a word which cannot be divided into smaller elements and which conveys meaning. It is the *smallest* word unit which conveys meaning: *a, anti,* etc.

Noun: A part of speech naming a person, place, thing, quality, idea, or action: *Gregson, field, paper, duty, patriotism, dancing.* Nouns may be identified by the following characteristics: (1) they are usually preceded by such "determiners" as *my, a, the, some;* (2) most nouns express the idea of "more than one" by various devices, the most common of which is the addition of *s;* (3) certain groups of nouns have typical endings like *-tion, -ness, -ment;* (4) some nouns are distinguished from verbs by stress in pronunciation: n. *ob'ject,* v. *ob ject'.*

Orthography: This is a ten-dollar word to indicate what this book is all about. It means, simply, correct spelling, or spelling as a science.

Particle: This is an omnibus word, a convenient catchall which includes short and indeclinable parts of speech such as articles, prepositions, conjunctions, and interjections, as well as prefixes and suffixes. These are particles: *but, oh, in, ad-, -ion.*

Parts of speech: The classifications to which every word must belong: noun, pronoun, adjective, adverb, verb, preposition, conjunction, interjection. The same word may belong to several parts of speech depending upon how it is used in a sentence.

Person: The change in the form of a pronoun or verb—sometimes, merely a change in use as with verbs—to indicate whether the "person" used is the person speaking (first person), the person spoken to (second person), or the person or thing spoken about (third person): *I* read, *you* read, *he* reads.

Phoneme: The smallest meaningful unit of *sound* in a language. The letters in our alphabet comprise about forty phonemes. For example, the word *wean* consists of three phonemes: *w, ē,* and *n.* Compare with *Morpheme,* above.

Phonetics: The branch of language study dealing with speech sounds, their production and combination, and their representation by symbols.

Phrase: A group of related words not containing a subject (substantive) and predicate (verb). It may contain from two to twenty words but is always a part of a sentence and is never independent: *was running, having finished my typing, my work done, out into the cold night,* etc.

Plural number: A classification of nouns, pronouns, etc., to indicate two or more units or members. *Singular* number is the classification to indicate one. For further discussion, see Chapter 7.

Prefix: A syllable, group of syllables, or word united with or joined to the beginning of another word to alter its meaning or to create a new word. *Pre* itself is a prefix in *preheat* (to heat beforehand). For further discussion, see Chapter 6.

Preposition: A part of speech showing the relationship of a noun or pronoun to some other word: *at* the office, *across* the street. The word literally means "placed before": "pre-position."

Pronoun: A part of speech which is used instead of a noun, primarily to avoid repetition and prevent overuse of the noun. The word *pronoun* consists of *pro*, meaning "for" or "instead of," plus *noun*.

Pronunciation: The art or manner of uttering words with reference to the production of sounds, accent, etc. Pronunciation is complex and many-faceted; it involves, among other things, levels of pronunciation, dialect, provincialisms, and, most importantly, spelling. For further discussion, see Chapter 4.

Root word: A base, a morpheme, to which prefixes, suffixes, etc., may be added. See *Base word* and *Morpheme*, above.

Short sound: Sounds which are relatively brief in duration. See, above, *Consonant* and *Long sound*. Many letters of the alphabet are sounded with short duration or stress and in varying degrees. Contrast the long *a* in *hate* with the short *a* in *hat*, for only one of many examples of short sounds.

Sibilants: A hissing sound or the symbol for it. *S, sh, z, zh, ch,* and *j* are sibilants: *pressure, shirt, zero,* etc.

Singular number: See *Plural number*, above.

Stress: The relative force with which a syllable is uttered. In English there are primary (strong) stress; secondary (light) stress; zero (silent) stress. See *Accent*, above, and Chapter 4.

Substantive: An inclusive term for a noun, pronoun, phrase or clause used as a noun, and for a verbal noun. The only practical value of the word *substantive* is that its use avoids repeating all the words used in this definition. Like most catchalls, it is a somewhat loose term.

Suffix: A sound, syllable, or syllables added at the end of a word or word base to change its meaning, alter its grammatical function, or form a new word: *dark,* dark*ness.* See *Prefix,* above.

Syllable: A word or part of a word, usually the latter, pronounced with a single, uninterrupted sounding of the voice. Note the syllables in these words: *sec re tar y* (4 syllables); *fun ny* (2 syllables); *fa mil iar i za tion* (6 syllables).

Syntax: The arrangement of words in a sentence to show their relationship. Briefly, it may be identified as *sentence structure* and is not an especially helpful term.

Tense: The time of the action or of the state being expressed by the verb. The three simple, or primary, tenses are *present, past,* and *future.* The three compound, or secondary, tenses are *present perfect, past perfect, future perfect.*

Verb: A part of speech expressing action or a state of being: The river *flows,* I *am* here.

Vowel: A speech sound articulated so that there is a clear channel for the voice through the middle of the mouth. Grammatically, the vowels in English are *a, e, i, o, u* and, in some instances, *w* and *y.* See *Consonant,* above.

Index

My Personal Spelling Demons